Rights Guide to Non-Means-Tested B

16th edition

Richard Poynter
and Clive Martin

Child Poverty Action Group

Published by CPAG Ltd
1-5 Bath Street, London EC1V 9PY

© CPAG Ltd 1993

A CIP record for this book is available from the British Library

ISBN 0-946744-48-3

Designed by Devious Designs, 0742 755634
Cover design by Liz Redgate, 081 677 5469
Typeset by Boldface Typesetters, London EC1
Printed by Bath Press, Avon

The authors

Richard Poynter is a solicitor. For the last seven years he has worked for Sinclair Taylor & Martin in North Kensington where he has specialised in helping advice workers and representing claimants in disputes with the DSS and local authorities. He has been involved in many test cases and lectures and writes extensively on social security and administrative law.

Clive Martin has worked as a rights adviser for Disability Alliance and as a hospital-based welfare rights officer in Manchester. Clive has been employed as a consultant with Ferret Information Systems Ltd in the development of benefits-related software and is currently a team manager with Manchester welfare rights services.

Acknowledgements

As always, this year's *Guide* has benefited from readers' comments on previous editions and from new points which other advice workers have come across in practice, and shared with us. We are grateful to all those who have taken the trouble to write to us or make suggestions for improvements. In particular, the comments of Vera Baxter, Paul Lewis, Richard Roxburgh and David Williams, and Pauline Thompson's contribution to the disability living allowance chapter, are acknowledged with thanks. If you have any comments on this edition please write to us c/o the Citizens' Rights Office at 4th Floor, 1-5 Bath Street, London EC1V 9PX.

We would also like to thank CPAG's solicitor, Penny Wood, who despite having to shoulder an even higher workload than normal because of staff changes in the Citizens' Rights Office, nevertheless made herself available day and night to answer our questions; and Barbara Zolynski, European Communities Librarian at the Law Society, who not only did the initial research on a large number of obscure points, but also put up with one of the authors while the book was being written. This thankless task was shared by Caroline Freedman and the partners and staff at Sinclair Taylor & Martin. We would like to reassure them that their support and understanding is appreciated!

Many thanks to Mary Shirley for her meticulous work on the production of the text and to Richard Kennecy for getting the book to press in the face of extremely tight deadlines. As ever, our thanks to Virman Man and June Taylor at Boldface Typesetters for the high quality of their work and to Kay Hart for her accurate proofreading and splendid index.

Finally, we are once again extremely grateful to Nick Warren who, as in previous years, not only gave up his time to read the whole of the *Guide* in draft and place his knowledge and experience at our disposal, but met the tight schedule imposed on him by unavoidable delays elsewhere. In preparing this edition we have benefited more than anything else from his perceptive comments and advice.

Contents

STANDARD RATES OF BENEFIT FROM 12 APRIL 1993

Earnings replacement benefits	Claimant £pw	Adult dependant £pw	Child dependant £pw
Unemployment benefit			
under pensionable age	44.65	27.55	
of or over pensionable age	56.10	33.70	10.95*
Sickness benefit			
under pensionable age	42.70	26.40	
of or over pensionable age	53.80	32.30	10.95*
Invalidity pension	56.10	33.70	10.95*
Invalidity allowance			
higher rate	11.95		
middle rate	7.50		
lower rate	3.75		
Statutory sick pay			
higher rate	52.50		
lower rate	46.95		
Severe disablement allowance	33.70	20.15	10.95*
Age-related addition – higher rate	11.95		
middle rate	7.50		
lower rate	3.75		
Statutory maternity pay (lower rate)	47.95		
Maternity allowance	43.75	26.40	
Invalid care allowance	33.70	20.15	10.95*
Widowed mother's allowance	56.10		10.95*
Widow's pension	56.10		
Non-contributory widow's benefit	33.70		10.95*
Retirement pension			
Category A	56.10	33.70	10.95*
Category B for a married woman	33.70		10.95*
Category B for a widow	56.10		10.95*
Category B for a widower	56.10		10.95*
Category C for a person not a married woman	33.70	20.15	10.95*
Category C for a married woman	20.15		10.95*
Category D	33.70		

Benefits for the severely disabled   £pw

Attendance allowance
  higher rate   44.90
  lower rate   30.00
Disability living allowance

		£pw
care component	higher rate	44.90
	middle rate	30.00
	lower rate	11.95
mobility component	higher rate	31.40
	lower rate	11.95

Industrial injuries benefits

Assessment of disablement	*lower rate*	*higher rate*
Disablement benefit		
100 per cent	56.10	91.60
90 per cent	50.49	82.44
80 per cent	44.88	73.28
70 per cent	39.27	64.12
60 per cent	33.66	54.96
50 per cent	28.05	45.80
40 per cent	22.44	36.64
30 per cent	16.83	27.48
20 per cent	11.22	18.32

£pw above lower rate/higher rate columns.

Constant attendance allowance
  higher maximum   73.40
  lower maximum   36.70
Exceptionally severe disablement allowance   36.70
Reduced earnings allowance (maximum)   36.64
Retirement allowance (maximum)   9.16

Industrial death benefit   £pw

Widow
  higher permanent rate   56.10
  lower permanent rate   16.83
Widower   56.10
Child   10.95*

Benefits for children   £pw

Child benefit
  for the only, elder or eldest child for whom benefit is being claimed   10.00
  for other children   8.10

One parent benefit   6.05
Guardian's allowance   10.95*
Child's special allowance   10.95*

* These are reduced by £1.15 for any child for whom you receive the higher rate of child benefit

Foreword

It goes without saying that, for anyone who wants to find their way round the British social security system, this volume and its companion, the *National Welfare Benefits Handbook*, are indispensable. It also goes without saying that, for up-to-date information, last year's edition won't do. Not a year goes by without major changes in the rules. As a result, the 16 editions of this book that have appeared since 1977 provide a unique guide to the changes in social security policy over that period.

Looking back to Richard Drabble's first edition, there are some obvious contrasts. Richard managed in 1977 to cram the whole system of non-means-tested benefits into 62 pages – less than a quarter of the size of this edition. The price was 60p, less than a tenth of the present price. Bearing in mind, however, that prices in general are now seven times as high, and taking into account the increased length of the guide, the 1993 equivalent price would be about £17 – nearly three times the price of this edition. So CPAG must be congratulated on an important contribution in the fight against inflation.

The changes in the benefit system itself have been no less dramatic. In 1977, child benefit, replacing family allowances and tax allowances for children, was just starting: benefit for the first child (previously excluded from family allowances) began the month after the guide was published. Largely as a result of CPAG's campaigning, child benefit has survived, but a heavy price has been paid for the failure to tie it to average earnings. With the completion of the phasing-in of child benefit in April 1979, it was worth £4 per child, equivalent to about £14 at 1993 earnings levels; yet today's child benefit rates are only £10 for the first child and £8.10 for others – a much smaller contribution to the reduction of inequalities due to family size. Even taking account of only price rises since 1979, child benefit is now worth less – and for families with two or more children, a lot less.

Child benefit was never intended to cover in full even the minimum cost of a child. National insurance benefits, therefore, were increased where there were dependent children. In 1977, the combined value of these 'child dependency additions' and the basic child benefit was £4.05 per child for a family receiving short-term sickness or unemployment benefit and £7.45 per child for those on long-term benefits (mainly widows and invalidity pensioners). Even if these rates had been raised only in line with prices rather than earnings (the uprating policy to which the present government is theoretically committed) they would now be £14 per child for people on short-term benefits and nearly £26 for those on long-term benefits. Instead, the short-term child additions have been abolished altogether and the value of the long-term additions reduced. Instead of

£14 per child, short-term sick and unemployed claimants get only child benefit of £10/£8.10, while widowed mothers and the long-term sick get, instead of £26 per child, a total of £19.80 for the first child and £19.05 for others.

Benefits for children are only a small part of the story. None of the benefits Richard Drabble wrote about in 1977 has emerged unscathed. Some no longer exist; others have, at best, been uprated in line with prices, so that the gap between benefits and other incomes has steadily widened; and changes in the rules of entitlement have excluded many people who would have qualified for benefits in 1977. Little of this made headlines. The benefits abolished in the 1980s were, in varying degrees, inadequate and ripe for reform, and the parliamentary debates often took place in committee rooms where the press seldom intrude. For those who have lost entitlement, however, the cumulative effects have been severe.

Unemployment benefit has been a favourite target for cuts. In a recent CPAG fact sheet, I compared the benefits a man on average earnings, with a non-earning wife and two children, would have received during the first six months of unemployment in 1979 and in 1992. The 1979 benefits totalled £47.20 a week, including a £12 earnings-related supplement. Uprated in line with prices, the 1992 equivalent would have been £127.70; in line with average earnings, £166.55. But the 1992 benefits amounted to only £87.15; and that is without taking into account the fact that, since 1982, unemployment benefit has been taxable.

Of the various cuts which produced this result, the biggest was the abolition in 1981-82 of the earnings-related supplement (ERS) which, since 1966, had been added to short-term benefits for the first six months. Egalitarians were never very keen on ERS, and its neglect by successive governments had reduced it to a somewhat unedifying muddle. So there was certainly a case for reform and perhaps even abolition. With all its faults, however, ERS made a significant contribution to many unemployed people's income. To abolish it without putting something more effective in its place was cruel and indefensible.

Many of the innovations of the 1980s, such as statutory sick pay, statutory maternity pay and the arrangements for clawing back social security benefits out of compensation payments for personal injury, were products of the Thatcher government's zeal for privatisation. The results have been chaotic: a recent National Audit Office report reveals an error rate of 25-30% in statutory sick pay and maternity pay cases examined by DSS inspectors. The biggest privatisation of benefits was the introduction of so-called 'personal pension schemes' in 1988 to encourage more people to opt out of the state earnings-related pension scheme. Pensioners are, reasonably enough, not CPAG's main concern. The immediate effects of pension privatisation, however, are felt by people of working age. Personal pensions are sold, by methods as bizarre as the offer of free cinema tickets, often to people on low earnings with little or no understanding of the choices and risks involved, who then become a target for salesmen offering a variety of other financial 'products' which they do not need and cannot afford.

For CPAG, benefits are primarily a means of preventing poverty. At first sight this seems consistent with the 'safety net' view of social security: that only the poor need help from the state. But there is no surer way of perpetuating poverty than a system of minimum incomes, leaving those who can to make better provision for themselves. A healthy social security system will provide benefits that are valued – and will therefore be defended – by the haves as well as the have-nots. Over most of the 16-year life-span of this guide, the trend has been in the opposite direction. The extent and depth of poverty in the twenty-first century will be strongly influenced by whether that trend can be reversed before it is too late.

TONY LYNES
Social security analyst
Former Director, CPAG

PART ONE

Introduction

CHAPTER ONE

Introduction to the social security system in Great Britain

This chapter covers:

1 Means-tested and non-means-tested benefits
2 Contributory and non-contributory benefits
3 Earnings replacement and other non-means-tested benefits
4 Short-term and long-term benefits

The social security system is notoriously complex. This chapter provides a brief introduction to it and to this *Guide* by describing the various types of benefit which are available.

This *Guide* covers only benefits under the legislation of **Great Britain**, which consists of England, Wales and Scotland, but *not* Northern Ireland, the Isle of Man or the Channel Islands (see p199).

With one exception, the rules for each non-means-tested benefit are set out in Part Two. The exception relates to war pensions which are administered under a separate system within the Department of Social Security (DSS). A brief description of them is contained in Appendix One, together with other forms of compensation and assistance not generally regarded as part of the social security system.

Some rules are common to all or many of the benefits and to save space these have been set out once in Part Three rather than repeated for each of the benefits to which they apply. As well as the contribution and residence conditions and the overlapping benefits rules (see p4), Part Three deals with the special rules for people in hospital or in prison, what happens to your benefit if you go abroad, how earnings are calculated and what a 'period of interruption of employment' is.

Part Four deals with the rules about the administration of the social security system – ie, how and when to claim, what happens to your claim when you have made it and what to do if you are unhappy with the outcome.

The *Guide* tries to give answers to most of the problems which claimants meet in practice. But to answer a particular question, you may sometimes also have to look at the Acts of Parliament, regulations and decisions of the courts and Social Security Commissioners which govern the social security system. The footnotes in each section are designed to tell you where to find the relevant legislation and cases, and a list of all the most important Acts and regulations is contained in Appendix Six. Appendix Five has a list of books and periodicals to which you can refer for help and the section on 'Checking the law' in Chapter 16 may give you tips for further research even if your problem has not yet reached the stage where you are preparing an appeal.

1 Means-tested and non-means-tested benefits

Some benefits are paid only if you have limited income and capital. These benefits are known as **means-tested benefits** because there is an investigation into your means before you can be paid them. The most important are:

- income support if you *are not* in full-time work;
- family credit if you *are* in full-time work;
- disability working allowance if you *are* in full-time work; *and*
- housing benefit and council tax benefit whether or not you are in full-time work.

These benefits are *not* covered in this *Guide*. Instead, you should look at CPAG's *National Welfare Benefits Handbook* (23rd edn, 1993 £6.95 post-free from CPAG Ltd).

This *Guide* is concerned with *non-means-tested benefits*, which do not involve a detailed investigation of your finances. You will be entitled if you satisfy certain basic conditions (called 'conditions of entitlement') such as being available for work, disabled or widowed. It may still be relevant to ask whether you have any earnings or an occupational pension, because many of the benefits are designed to compensate for your loss of earnings, but other types of income will not affect your entitlement. Similarly, you may be entitled to non-means-tested benefits even if you have savings or other capital.

2 Contributory and non-contributory benefits

The most important division of non-means-tested benefits is between those which are contributory and those which are not.

Contributory benefits	Non-contributory benefits
Unemployment benefit	Severe disablement allowance
Sickness benefit	Invalid care allowance
Invalidity benefit	Non-contributory widows' benefits
Maternity allowance	Category C & D retirement
Widow's payment	pension
Widowed mother's allowance	Disability living allowance
Widow's pension	Attendance allowance
Category A & B retirement	Industrial injuries benefits
pensions	Child benefit
Graduated Retirement Benefit	One parent benefit
	Guardian's allowance
	Child's special allowance

Contributory benefits are paid out of the National Insurance Fund. This is funded by social security contributions and one of the conditions of entitlement to contributory benefits is that you should, in the past, have made sufficient contributions to the Fund. These are known as 'contribution conditions' and are discussed in Chapter 12. However, unlike non-contributory benefits, there are no residence conditions (see below) for contributory benefits.

Non-contributory benefits are paid out of general taxation (except guardian's allowance which is paid out of the National Insurance Fund). It is a condition of entitlement to all of them that you must have lived in Great Britain (or, in some cases, in a member state of the European Community) for a period in the past. These are known as 'residence conditions'. Residence conditions are explained in detail in Chapter 13.

3   Earnings replacement and other non-means-tested benefits

Many benefits exist to compensate you for your inability to work through unemployment, sickness, pregnancy or old age. Others exist to meet particular needs because you are disabled or have children, irrespective of your ability to work.

Earnings replacement	Other benefits
Unemployment benefit	Disability living allowance
Sickness benefit	Attendance allowance
Invalidity benefit	Industrial injuries benefits
Severe disablement allowance	Child benefit
Maternity allowance	One parent benefit
Invalid care allowance	Guardian's allowance
Retirement pensions	Child's special allowance

The basic rule is that you may only receive one 'earnings replacement benefit' at a time. However, you may receive any number of the other benefits whether or not you also receive an earnings replacement benefit. These are known as the '**overlapping benefits**' rules (see Chapter 14).

Most earnings replacement benefits have '**earnings rules**' which limit the amount of earnings you may receive while remaining entitled to the benefit. Retirement pensions are an exception. The reason for this is that you (or your spouse) have earned your pension and ought not to lose out if you continue in employment. The decision to work or not is up to you.

Widows' benefits have not been included in the list above. They exist to replace the earnings of the widow's late husband and therefore her own earnings are ignored. The decision whether or not she should work is left to her, since her benefit was earned by her husband. Widows' benefits are not paid in addition to any other earnings replacement benefits which the widow may be entitled to in her own right. Special benefits are not usually paid to widowers – not even to those who were wholly financially dependent on their late wives. Widows' benefits are one of the few exceptions to the general rule of European Community law that social security benefits must not discriminate against men or women because of their sex (see p202).

Reduced earnings allowance and **retirement allowance** (both industrial injuries benefits and now being phased out) are payable on top of earnings replacement benefits.

4 Short-term and long-term benefits

This division only applies to earnings replacement benefits (including widows' benefits). As their names suggest, short-term benefits are paid for a limited period only whereas long-term benefits are paid for as long as the conditions of entitlement remain satisfied.

Short-term benefits	Long-term benefits
Unemployment benefit	Invalidity benefit
Sickness benefit	Severe disablement allowance
Maternity allowance	Invalid care allowance
Widows' payment	Widows' benefits (other than widow's payment)
	Retirement pensions (including graduated retirement benefit)

There are no non-contributory short-term benefits and, with the exception of widow's payment, the contributory short-term benefits all depend upon your having satisfied a contribution condition in the fairly recent past (unless you are over pensionable age). For widow's payment, the single contribution can have been satisfied in any year of the deceased husband's working life.

Short-term benefits are paid at a lower rate than contributory long-term benefits and, unlike long-term benefits, no increases are paid for dependent children.

If you are receiving a contributory long-term benefit, you may also be entitled to an additional pension under the State Earnings Related Pension Scheme (SERPS).

PART TWO

The benefits

CHAPTER TWO

Unemployment benefit

This chapter covers:

1   Conditions of entitlement[1]

- You claim within the time limit (see p224).
- You satisfy the contribution conditions (see p186) – these differ according to whether you are over or under pensionable age (see p38).
- For each day you receive benefit you are:
  - unemployed (but see p23); *and*
  - capable of, and available for, work (see p12).
- You are actively seeking employment (see p19).
- Each day for which you claim benefit falls within a 'period of interruption of employment' (see p203).

2   Payment

Amount of payment[1]

	Claimant under pensionable age £pw	Claimant of, or over, pensionable age £pw
Claimant	44.65	56.10
Adult dependant	27.55	33.70
Child dependant	–	10.95

The daily rate is one sixth of the weekly rate.[2] Payment is usually made fortnightly in arrears by Girocheque.[3]

Pensionable age is 60 for a woman and 65 for a man (see p89).

Unemployment benefit is paid at a reduced rate if you are over pensionable age and only partially fulfil the contribution conditions for a Category A or, (if you are a widow or widower) Category B retirement pension (see pp96 and 98). For other special rules for pensioners, see p38.

Duration

Unemployment benefit is not paid for the first three days of any 'period of interruption of employment'.[4] In practice this means that when you first claim unemployment benefit you will not normally be paid for the first three days you are out of work. These are known as *'waiting days'*.

However, you do not have to wait a further three days if you become unemployed within eight weeks from when you last received unemployment benefit, sickness benefit or invalidity benefit.

Examples
You lose your job and are unemployed for two weeks. You then obtain temporary employment for a fortnight before becoming unemployed again. You will not receive unemployment benefit for the first three days of the first spell of unemployment. However, you will be paid benefit from the very first day of your second claim.

You were employed on a temporary contract, but after you are injured in a car accident, your employer refuses to keep your job open for you. You receive sickness benefit while you are recovering, but when you become well enough to work again, you claim unemployment benefit as you no longer have a job to go to. You will be paid benefit from the first day of your claim.

This is the 'linking rule'. In some circumstances, two periods of unemployment or illness are treated as part of the same 'period of interruption of employment'. For more details, see p203.

Unemployment benefit is a short-term benefit (see p5) and, once you have served the 'waiting days' (see above) it is paid for a maximum of a year (or, more precisely, 312 days – 52 six day weeks[5]) within any single period of interruption of employment (see p203). Once this period has expired you can only become entitled to unemployment benefit again in one of two ways. *Either*:

- you *requalify* for benefit (see below); *or*
- you *break your claim* for benefit for at least eight *consecutive* weeks so that your old period of interruption of employment ends and, when you reclaim, a new one begins (see p10).

Requalifying for benefit[6]

To requalify for unemployment benefit you must work for at least 16 hours a week for 13 weeks after the end of the last week during which you were entitled to unemployment benefit. For this purpose a 'week' begins on a Sunday and ends the following Saturday.[7]

The 13 weeks need not be consecutive (indeed if you work for more than eight consecutive weeks, you no longer need to requalify – see below) but they must normally be within the 26 weeks before the date of your claim or, if that would be more favourable to you, your first day of unemployment since you last worked.[8]

However, this rule will not apply to you if during any week of the 26-week period:[9]

- you did not work or worked for less than 16 hours; *and*
- for at least one day in that week
  - you were entitled to statutory sick pay (see p50), sickness benefit (see p57), invalidity benefit (see p60), statutory maternity pay (see p70), maternity allowance (see p75), invalid care allowance (see p125) or severe disablement allowance (see p64);[10] *or*
  - you were undergoing Training for Work and entitled to a 'training allowance'.[11]

If any of these exceptions applies to you, then any such weeks are ignored when calculating the 26-week period as long as the 13 weeks' work is still done within the 78 weeks before you claim or the first day on which you are unemployed since you last worked.[12]

When you requalify you will have to serve a further three waiting days.[13]

Breaking your claim

If you do not claim unemployment benefit for eight consecutive weeks a new 'period of interruption of employment' (see p203) will begin when you reclaim benefit. After you have served a further three waiting days, unemployment benefit will be paid for up to a further 312 days, provided you satisfy the contribution conditions at the date of your new claim (see p186). So, if you have been off work for a long time, but have not yet used up the 312 days, it may be in your interest to break your claim.

But before you decide to sign off for eight weeks, you should consider your position very carefully. Firstly, for this purpose you cannot end your period of interruption of employment simply by not claiming. Unless you were working or genuinely unavailable for work – for example because you were abroad or on a long touring holiday in the United Kingdom[14] – you must be able to prove to the Benefits Agency that when you failed to claim, you did not intend to avoid the need to requalify. If you cannot, you will be treated as if you had been entitled to unemployment benefit during the time that you did not claim.[15]

You should also remember that if you make yourself unavailable for work, you are likely to lose any entitlement to income support and to be credited with Class 1 contributions (see p181) for that period.

3 How to claim

Unemployment benefit is administered on behalf of the DSS by the Employment Service, an 'executive agency' of the Department of Employment. Unless you live in a rural area (see p12), you claim by attending in person at an unemployment benefit office – not necessarily in the same place as the Jobcentre. This, and the subsequent claims which you will normally have to make each fortnight, is known as 'signing on'.

It is usual to sign on at the unemployment benefit office which is nearest to your home. But if a different office is more convenient for you – perhaps because it is easier to reach by public transport, you are entitled to sign on there. If you claim at an unemployment benefit office which is not near your home and you have not given a good reason, you may be suspected of fraud.

If at all possible, you should take your P45 tax form from your previous job with you when you go to sign on for the first time. Your employer is obliged to give you this immediately after paying you your last wages or salary. If s/he has not done so, or if you have mislaid it, do not delay your claim but take the P45 to the unemployment benefit office as soon as you receive or find it. In this case, the Employment Service will want to know your national insurance number (although again you should not delay your claim if you cannot remember it).

When you go to the unemployment benefit office for the first time, you will be seen by a member of staff called a 'new client receptionist'. His/her job is to provide you with a claim form and, unless this is inappropriate – for example if you are re-claiming after a short spell of temporary work – to arrange an appointment with a 'new client adviser' (see below). Unfortunately, there have been instances where new client receptionists (and sometimes other members of staff) have wrongly discouraged people from claiming and given incorrect advice about entitlement to unemployment benefit.

If this happens to you it can amount to 'good cause' for making a late claim (see p224) and/or give you grounds for suing the Employment Service for compensation for damages for negligent misrepresentation. But this is a cumbersome process and the best way to avoid being caught up in it is not to be put off at this early stage. Although an adjudication officer (see p226) may refuse you benefit (subject to your rights of appeal – see p244) no one, from the new client receptionist and the new client adviser to the Secretary of State him/herself, can stop you from making a claim for benefit and you should insist on doing so.

At your interview with the new client adviser your availability for work will be discussed (see p12) and you will be given a 'Back to Work Plan' containing details of some steps which you are advised to take to find work. For more details of the requirement that you should 'actively seek work' see p19.

Although the basic rule is that unemployment benefit is a 'daily benefit' and there is a reserve power to require you to sign on on each individual day for which you wish to be paid,[1] you will usually be allowed to make fortnightly claims and, at the end of your interview with the new client adviser, will be given a regular day and time to sign on.[2] It is important that you keep these appointments – failure to attend without good cause can lose you benefit.

You must attend in person at the unemployment benefit office if you are required to do so.[3] But, as a matter of administrative practice, the Employment Service allows claimants who live more than ten miles from the unemployment benefit office to claim by post. Those who live more than six miles but less than ten miles away have to claim in person at the beginning but can sign on by post afterwards. You can also claim by post if the journey to the unemployment benefit office would cause you hardship, either because you are disabled or the journey is very difficult.

If you are required to sign on every day, it is probably because you are suspected of working while claiming. This decision is taken by the Secretary of State rather than an adjudication officer and therefore you cannot appeal against it (see p229). However, you can try to persuade the Employment Service that their suspicions are unfounded, and that you should be allowed to sign on less frequently.

It will occasionally be in your interest to delay making a claim (see p186) but normally you should claim unemployment benefit on the very first day that you are out of work. If you do not do so, you are likely to lose money unless you have 'good cause' for a late claim (see p224).

4 Availability for work

Capable of work

If you are unable to work because you are ill or disabled then, obviously, you cannot be available for work. For this reason, it is a condition of entitlement to unemployment benefit that you should be 'capable of work'.[1] This is simply the opposite of being 'incapable of work' (see p43).

Similarly you cannot be available for work if you are not capable of working *legally*. So, if your immigration status prohibits you from taking employment or if you could not take a job without first applying for a work-permit, you are not entitled to unemployment benefit.[2]

Availability for work

As well as being capable of work, you must also be available to work as an 'employed earner' (see p139) in any job which you can reasonably be expected to do.[3] The reference to employment 'as an employed earner' means that refusal of an offer of self-employment will not be regarded as affecting your availability.

To be available, you must be willing and able to accept any suitable job offer *at once* (for exceptions see 'Deemed availability' – p14).

An adjudication officer can contest your availability for work without having to show that you have actually turned down a job offer.[4]

Restricting your availability

You are treated as not being available for work if you place restrictions on the sort of job you are prepared to accept[5] unless you can prove that you still have a reasonable chance of getting a job despite those restrictions.[6] This includes restrictions on:

- the type of work you are prepared to do; *or*
- the hours you are willing to work; *or*
- the conditions of employment you will accept; *or*
- the location of the job; *or*
- the rate of pay.

If you have a usual occupation this rule does not apply during your *permitted period*.[7] This is a short period of *up to* 13 weeks from the time you first claim unemployment benefit during which you are allowed to concentrate your search for work on vacancies in your normal line of work and to refuse to take or look for jobs that are not what you would normally do. But any restrictions you place on your availability during this period must be *consistent* with the conditions of work that are normal in your occupation. So, for example, if you are a professional footballer you will be allowed to refuse a job in a shop during your permitted period because that is not your usual occupation – but if you refuse a particular job playing football on the grounds that you prefer not to work Saturdays, you are likely to be refused benefit.

The length of your permitted period is in practice decided by the new client adviser at your interview when you first sign on. It can be, and often is, less than the maximum 13 weeks. In making the decision, s/he must take into account what your 'usual occupation' is, your skills and qualifications, the time you have spent training for and working in that occupation, how long it is since you last worked in that occupation and the availability of jobs in that area of work.[8]

You can also place restrictions on your availability if these are reasonable in view of your physical or mental condition.[9] So, if you suffer from angina you can refuse to undertake strenuous physical work and if you are agoraphobic you do not have to take a job as a gardener. If the restrictions you impose are reasonable ones for you, then it does not matter that they mean you have no reasonable prospects of obtaining employment. But if you have no prospects at all you should consider whether you are really capable of work. If not, it may be in your interest to claim one of the benefits in Chapter 3 instead of unemployment benefit. In particular, once you qualify for invalidity benefit, it is paid at a higher rate than unemployment benefit, lasts indefinitely and entitles you to a disability premium when your entitlement to income support and some other income related benefits is assessed (see CPAG's *National Welfare Benefits Handbook* for further details).

Even if you impose unreasonable restrictions on the work you will do, you will still be regarded as available for work if the *only* reason they stop you from having reasonable prospects of getting a job is because of *temporary* adverse industrial conditions in your area.[10]

'Deemed' availability

The requirement that you should be available for employment immediately could, if strictly applied, prevent you from doing any work – paid or unpaid – while you are claiming unemployment benefit. There are therefore a few limited exceptions to this rule. You will be treated ('deemed') as if you were available for immediate employment if:

- you are engaged in providing a service; *and*
  - you can be available on 24 hours' notice to start a job or attend an interview; *and*
  - it would not be reasonable to require you to be available at less than 24 hours notice.[11]

  This exception is mostly used to allow people to do voluntary work while claiming unemployment benefit but it applies whether or not you are being paid for the service you are providing. For more on part-time work while claiming unemployment benefit see pp23-27;
- you are
  - engaged in crewing or launching a lifeboat;[12] *or*
  - carrying out duties as a part-time firefighter;[13] *or*
  - working for the benefit of others by helping to save life, prevent injury or protect property in an emergency following a fire, flood, explosion, accident, national catastrophe or in an organised search for a missing person;[14]
- (for a maximum of 14 days – excluding Sundays – in any calendar year) you are attending a residential work camp organised by a charity or local authority providing a service of benefit to the community.[15]

There are also rules which may deem you to be available for work while a decision is being made on whether you are actually available for work (see p17).

Checking your availability

First interview

One of the forms which you will be given when you first visit the unemployment benefit office is an ES461 (which used to be known as a UB671). This form asks for a lot of information including:

- details of your last three jobs;
- your qualifications;
- the kind of job you are looking for;
- what other jobs you will accept;
- the minimum wage or salary you are seeking;
- the areas in which you are looking for, or would be prepared to accept, a job;
- when you can start;
- what hours you are prepared to work;
- whether your health imposes any limits on the work you can do; *and*

- whether you have children or dependent adults for whom you have to care during working hours.

Your answers to these questions will form the basis for your interview with the new client adviser (see above) and subsequently for the decision on whether you are available for work. It is very important that you fill it in properly.

If possible you should not fill in the form at the unemployment benefit office but take it home and complete it in your own time. As everyone's circumstances are different there are no 'right' answers but there are a number of general rules to bear in mind:

- Take your time, think carefully and read the notes that come with the form before answering the questions. Write out your answers in draft on a separate piece of paper if you are not sure. If English is not your first language or if you have difficulties with reading and writing, ask someone (preferably not an employee of the Employment Service) to help you.
- Be truthful. The other parts of this chapter explain what you have to do to qualify for unemployment benefit. If you have doubts about whether you come within the rules, it is far better to face up to any difficulty from the beginning and see if you can rearrange things so that you can make yourself eligible. For example, if you look after children and at present are not available to start work or attend a job interview at a moment's notice, you could try to change your childcare arrangements so that you have more flexibility. Above all, it is unwise simply to write out the standard answers you may have read in advice leaflets – your new client adviser has read them too and will use the interview to explore what they actually mean in your case. As a result you will still have to answer the questions but will not have the time you would otherwise have had to consider your replies.
- Keep a copy of your answers. You will certainly be asked the same questions again if you are unemployed for more than six months and it may be sooner than that. If your answers differ, there may well be a good reason but you should be prepared to explain what it is.
- Be realistic. When you fill in the form you should describe the sort of job you would be prepared to accept and not the sort of job you would ideally like. In particular, except during your 'permitted period' (see p13), you are not entitled to insist that you will only accept a job that pays as much as your last one – rather, it is *vital* that the minimum wage or salary you say you will accept should not be higher than the going rate for the jobs you have said you would be prepared to take. If it is, the Employment Service is likely to say that you are imposing unreasonable restrictions and have no reasonable prospects of obtaining employment (see p13). If you are not sure what figure to give, you can write 'the going rate for the job' and say that you will see what is on offer. Similarly, whilst it is always a good idea to emphasize that you are being flexible in your search for work, if there are good reasons why you cannot take certain types of job or jobs in certain areas, you should say so – if you do not, it may prove very difficult to justify turning down such a job if it is offered to you later.

Certain questions on the form present particular difficulties. For example:

- The questions about dependent children or adults need careful thought. If you have children and either your partner is working or you have no partner, the new client adviser will want to know what plans you have for their care if you get a job. Because you have to be available for work at short notice, you must be able to show that you have a plan worked out or the adjudication officer is likely to refuse your claim for benefit. You may have a particular childminder lined up. If not, are you intending to find one and to make use of a relative or friend as an emergency measure if a job suddenly comes up? If so, make sure they are not claiming unemployment benefit themselves before you tell the new client adviser!
- When answering the question about what hours and on which days you are prepared to work, remember that Saturday is an ordinary working day for unemployment benefit purposes. If you refuse to work on it you run the risk of losing a sixth of your benefit each week. And if you are looking for jobs in areas where Saturday working is customary, a refusal to work Saturday may lead to your being refused benefit altogether on the basis that because of this restriction on your availability, you do not have reasonable prospects of obtaining employment (see p13).
- Remember that you are normally expected to be prepared to travel for up to an hour both to and from work, unless you have a good reason why not. If you are too restrictive about the areas in which you say you are prepared to look for, or accept, work the adjudication officer may say that you are unavailable. The important thing is to be able to give a good reason for your answers. For example, if you do not drive and there is little public transport in your area, it may be reasonable to refuse to look for jobs beyond a distance which you could be expected to walk.

If, at the end of the interview, the new client adviser has doubts about your availability s/he will send your papers to an adjudication officer for a decision on this point, or perhaps you might be asked to see another adviser.

Restart interview

If you are still unemployed after about six months, you will be invited to a 'Restart' interview. This is an invitation you cannot refuse. You will be disqualified from benefit if:[16]

- you fail to attend the interview following a written request; *and*
- within 14 days of that interview, a further written notice is issued calling you to another interview; *and*
- without good cause, you fail to attend the second interview.

Benefit will be stopped from the date of your second missed interview until either you do attend an interview or the notice is revoked. If you had good reasons for not attending the interviews (for example, you did not receive the appointment, or there was a sudden emergency which you had to deal with, or you did try to attend but unexpected transport difficulties prevented you from doing so). You should put in an appeal *and* write directly to the person sending the notices. The latter may lead to your benefit being reinstated long before an appeal can be heard.

The form used as the basis for the Restart interview – form UB671R – is very similar to form ES461 (see p14) but goes on to ask you what you have been doing to find work and whether you need help to get back to work. You should bring the records you have kept of your attempts to find work (see p19) with you.

At the interview you may be given details of a job interview. Alternatively, you may be offered one or more of a number of options, including the opportunity to join a Jobclub, a Restart course, a Training for Work scheme, the Enterprise Allowance scheme or to do voluntary work. In some inner city areas, there are also job interview guarantee schemes. Full details of these schemes are beyond the scope of this *Guide* but can be obtained from the *Unemployment and Training Rights Handbook* and the other booklets published by the Unemployment Unit and Youthaid (see Appendix 5).

If you decline all offers of assistance, your case will be referred to an adjudication officer who may decide either that you are not really available for work or, if you have refused an offer of employment or training (see p35), that you should be disqualified from benefit for a specific period. You will be deemed to be available during the time that the adjudication officer takes to make up his or her mind.[17]

If you are asked to provide further evidence that you are available for work, you will also be deemed to be available for a month (or a longer period if the Employment Service agree) to give you time to comply with the request.[18] For more on 'deemed' availability see p14.

There may be a follow up Restart interview a few weeks after the main interview when further offers may be made.

Looking for a job can be a difficult, depressing and frustrating experience and many claimants find Restart interviews – and in particular having to justify their attempts to find work to a person in authority under the threat that their benefit may be stopped – very intimidating. If you feel this way, consider whether any of the following might help:

- take a friend or relative with you to act as a witness, provide moral support and take notes. This has a number of advantages:
  - misunderstandings by the Employment Service over your answers at the Restart Interview can lead to disputes about whether you are available for and/or actively seeking employment. You are much more likely to win an appeal if someone else heard what was said and agrees with your recollection of what happened – particularly if that is backed up by contemporaneous written notes. If you have difficulties with English, it is *vital* that someone else – preferably an interpreter – should be present;

- Employment service staff are told to treat claimants with courtesy but, as in any walk of life, a minority do not. Simply having someone else in he room is likely to inhibit discourteous or intimidating behaviour.
- If there is no one you can ask to come to the interview with you, make sure you take notes yourself.
- If you feel you have an irreconcilable personality clash with your adviser, ask for him or her to be changed.

Holidays while you are unemployed

While you are on unemployment benefit, you may be allowed to take up to two weeks holiday in a year.[19] A 'year' in this context means 'any period of 12 months' *not* a calendar year.

Example

You are unemployed and take two weeks holiday from 9-22 August 1993. You return to work in October 1993 and requalify for benefit but lose your job again in April 1994. While you were working, you booked a holiday from 20 June-3 July 1994.

Although the two holidays are in separate calendar years, they are in the same period of 12 months. You will not get benefit if you decide not to cancel the second.

The holiday rules excuse you from actively seeking employment while you are away but you still have to be available for work and the holiday must not 'materially' reduce your chances of finding a job. This means that holidays abroad will not be accepted and that you will be disqualified if the nature of the work you are looking for means that you must be personally present when recruitment takes place (eg, casual labouring on building sites)[20] – this is because your absence will be treated as materially reducing your chances of employment.

You must tell the Employment Service before you go on holiday and you will be asked to complete a 'holiday form'. This does not guarantee payment – the important question is whether you are still available for employment. You will be asked to provide an address or addresses where you can be contacted (remember that you can pick up mail at a post office) and if you can provide a telephone number for any calls this will also be helpful. If you cannot do this, offer to phone the local office or some other number regularly to see if there are any messages. You will also be expected to give an assurance that you will be willing and able to cut short your holiday if notified of a job.

When you return from your holiday you must sign on on the very next day your unemployment benefit office is open *even if that is not your usual signing-on day*. If you do not, you may lose benefit for the whole of the period you were away unless you can show that you had 'good cause' (see p224) for failing to do so. This is because of the technical rule that you are only excused from signing on every day if you sign on when you are directed to do so.[21] The holiday form tells you to sign on as soon as possible after your return and if you fail to do so, you have also failed to claim for every day in the intervening period.

Adjudication officers sometimes refuse benefit on the ground that you have not shown you were available for work if you have not signed on on the first possible day after you return. This is wrong: signing on is a method of *claiming* and a failure to do so does not mean that you were not available for work.

5   Actively seeking employment

You are only entitled to unemployment benefit for any particular day if that day is part of a week (see p21) in which you are (or are treated as if you were – see p20) actively seeking employment.[1]

In order to be treated as actively seeking employment, you must take reasonable 'steps' to find a job.[2] Taking one 'step' on a single occasion during a week will not be enough unless taking that step on that occasion was all that it was reasonable for you to do[3] – the implication is that taking two steps a week will generally be enough.

In order to check that you are actively seeking employment, the Employment Service will ask you from time to time to give details of the 'steps' you have taken (see below). It is therefore extremely important that you should keep records of your attempts to get a job. Apart from keeping copies of all the letters you send – and any replies you receive – the best way of doing this is to keep a diary and make a note every time you make a phone call or visit to a Jobcentre, a potential employer or an agency or do anything else which might count as a 'step' towards seeking employment. Ideally, these notes should be as detailed as possible and include the dates and times of the conversations, who you spoke to and what was said. If at all possible, it is also a good idea to keep copies of any advertisements which you reply to.

A person who cannot read or write should tell his/her claimant adviser of this. It may be possible for such a person to find a friend or relative to help compile a record (and to help to look for jobs). The Employment Service may be prepared to accept an oral report but the problem is that checks on whether or not you are actively seeking work are not carried out every single week (see p22) and without anything in writing to refresh them, memories fade over time. A written record is also much more convincing and will inevitably be more detailed.

Difficulties with English can present similar problems and a claimant adviser may be able to suggest organisations who can help maintain a record of the evidence a claimant will need to show that s/he is actively seeking work.

What counts as a 'step'?

The regulations say[4] that 'steps' include:

- making written or oral applications for employment to people who have advertised jobs or who appear to be in a position to offer employment;[5]
- seeking information from advertisements, advertisers, agencies or employers;[6]
- registering with an agency;[7] *or*
- appointing someone else to help you find employment.[8]

But this list is not exhaustive and other actions not mentioned above may count as 'steps' if they might lead to your being offered employment.

The 'steps' you take must be the ones which can reasonably be seen as the most likely to produce offers of employment in your case.[9] So, for example, if you are a hairdresser, replying to job advertisements in *The Nursing Times* probably will not count!

When the adjudication officer considers whether the steps you have taken are reasonable, s/he has to look at all the circumstances in your individual case including:[10]

- your skills, qualifications, abilities and physical and mental limitations;
- how long you have been unemployed;
- the 'steps' you have taken in previous weeks;
- the availability and location of jobs;
- any time you have spent launching or crewing a lifeboat or acting as a fire-fighter, helping in an emergency, undertaking voluntary work, attending an Outward Bound course or participating in training or study;
- whether you have applied for, or accepted a place on, or participated in a course or programme supported by public (including EC) funds for the purpose of selecting, training for, obtaining or retaining employment;
- if you are homeless, the fact that you have no accommodation and the steps which you have to take to find a home.

Again the list is not exhaustive and any other factors which are relevant must be taken into account.

When are you 'deemed' to be actively seeking employment?

Even if you are not actively seeking employment you will be treated as if you were during any week (see p21):

- which is the first week for which you have claimed unemployment benefit since *either*
  - you were in employment; *or*
  - you were on an employment or training programme for which a training allowance was payable for at least six consecutive days (excluding Sunday);[11] *or*
- which includes the last day of unemployment of any spell of unemployment[12] – a 'spell' of unemployment is any one or more days of unemployment (except that two or more such periods are treated as a single

'spell' unless they are separated by more than three consecutive days on which you are not entitled to unemployment benefit);[13] *or*
- for which you have given written notice that you will be away from home.[14] This rule allows you a total of two weeks (consecutive or not) away from home in any period of 12 months;[15] *unless*
  - you are blind, in which case you are allowed a maximum of six weeks (again consecutive or not) provided you are on a training course in the use of guide dogs for at least three days in each week;[16] *or*
  - you are on an Outward Bound course in which case you are allowed three weeks (again consecutive or not) provided you attend the course for at least three days in each such week;[17] *or*
- during which you are engaged in launching or crewing a lifeboat or acting as a fire-fighter or carrying out emergency duties for at least three days;[18] *or*
- (for a maximum of five consecutive weeks) during which you are on an employment or training course for which a training allowance is not payable;[19] *or*
- during which you are taking active steps to establish yourself in self-employment under the Enterprise Allowance Scheme. This only applies during a single period lasting no more than eight weeks and starting with the week during which you attend the meeting necessary before you can apply to participate in the Scheme.[20]

What counts as a 'week'?

Because the rules tell adjudication officers to look at the steps you have taken to seek employment during a particular week, the definition of 'week' is important.

Usually you are required to sign on fortnightly and the two weeks will be the two periods of seven days for which you sign on. There are special rules which apply at the beginning and end of your claim, if you do not sign on fortnightly or if your signing on day changes.

The basic rule is that a week is a period which begins immediately after one 'relevant day' and ends with the next.[21] 'Relevant days' are:[22]

- the day immediately before the first day of a period of interruption of employment (see p203) for which unemployment benefit is claimed; *and*
- every day on which you have to sign on during your claim; *and*
- if you do not have to sign on every seven days, the day in each week which corresponds to your last relevant day; *and*
- the last day of your claim.

Since you will normally be deemed to be actively seeking employment during the first and last weeks of your claim (see p20) these rules only really affect those who are required by the Secretary of State to sign on more frequently than once every seven days – probably because they are suspected of fraud. If this applies to you, then each of the periods of seven days ending with each of the days you sign on counts as a separate 'week'

– even if they overlap.[23] In practice this will mean that a 'step' taken on one day will count towards entitlement to unemployment benefit on that day and each of the following five days (excluding Sundays) but no longer.

In all other circumstances, if there would be more than one 'relevant day' in any period of seven days all but the last are ignored.[24] The effect of this is that if your signing on day is changed a 'week' may last for more than seven days.

Example

You sign on fortnightly on Tuesdays. The days you sign on are 'relevant days' and so are the Tuesdays in the intervening weeks because they correspond to your previous 'relevant day'. In Week 1 you sign on on the Tuesday but are told to sign on on Friday in Week 3. Tuesday in Week 3 would normally be a 'relevant day' as it corresponds to your last such day but, as it is in the same period of seven days as Friday of Week 3, it is disregarded and the 'week' lasts ten days – from Wednesday in Week 2 to Friday in Week 3.

Checking whether you are actively seeking employment

You are not normally expected to prove that you are actively seeking employment every time you sign on (although you will have to sign a formal declaration to this effect). However, the steps you have taken will be checked at Restart interviews (see p16) and by random checks on other occasions.

The claimant adviser will want to know what jobs you have applied for and why you have not applied for others. S/he may also make other suggestions about steps which might be helpful. You should be given the opportunity to explain the steps you have taken and to say whether you agree with the suggestions which have been made and, if not, why not.

If the claimant adviser thinks you are not trying hard enough to get work, you will be given a warning letter setting out up to five steps you should take, and you will be asked to go back to an 'Actively Seeking Review'. At the Review, your efforts will be discussed further and you may be offered a vacancy or a place on a work or training scheme.

If the claimant adviser is still not happy with the efforts you are making, s/he will refer your case to an adjudication officer. If this happens, you will be told why. The adjudication officer then has to decide whether the steps you took in the relevant week or weeks were sufficient to count as actively seeking work and if you are unhappy with the decision, you can appeal.

If your claim is referred in this way, your benefit will be suspended[25] and, if you are claiming income support, it will be paid at a reduced rate.[26] Arrears will be paid if the adjudication officer decides that you have been actively seeking work. It is important that you should continue to sign on, make yourself available for work and actively seek employment in the meantime as otherwise you may lose benefit even if the adjudication officer's decision ultimately goes in your favour.

6 Special rules if you work part-time

In a few cases you can get unemployment benefit even though you have a job of some sort. This section deals with entitlement to unemployment benefit in three different situations:

• you lose your job and take another for fewer days or hours each week;
• you are put on short-time working;
• your job is one where there are compulsory unpaid holidays.

The most important thing to remember is that if you do work and claim unemployment benefit during the same week, you must report the work you have done and any money you have earned to the Employment Service when you next sign on. If you do not you may have to repay any benefit which has been overpaid (see p237) and you may also be prosecuted (see p216).

Remember also that if you are claiming income support as well as unemployment benefit:

• any earnings over £5.00 per week (£15 in some cases) will reduce that benefit pound for pound;[1] *and*
• if you work for more than 16 hours a week, you will lose entitlement to income support altogether.[2] This in turn will mean that
  – if your mortgage interest is being paid by the Benefits Agency this will cease;
  – any entitlement to housing benefit and council tax benefit may also be reduced; *and*
  – you will lose the automatic right to 'passport' benefits such as free prescriptions.

For further details about income support, see CPAG's *National Welfare Benefits Handbook*.

Part-time workers must also show that they are available for work on the days for which they claim. You can do this if:

• there is a reasonable prospect of obtaining part-time employment for those days of the week on which you are not already working; *or*
• the part-time work you are doing would not interfere with a potential full-time job, perhaps because it is in the evenings; *or*
• you are prepared to give up your part-time job if you are offered a full-time one.

DSS leaflet FB26 contains useful information for part-time workers.

Unemployment benefit is a 'daily benefit' – that is, entitlement to it is theoretically assessed on a daily basis. In principle therefore, any work you do on one day should not affect your entitlement on another day. In practice, however, this would leave the system open to abuse – to take a slightly far-fetched example, it would be possible for employers and employees to agree that for a limited period they would work a full 36-hour week in three 12-hour days so that the employees could take home a normal week's wage and claim three days' unemployment benefit as well.

To prevent claimants from compressing their working hours into fewer days, and other more sophisticated schemes, a number of exceptions have been introduced to the principle of daily assessment – exceptions which can cause unfair and anomalous results.

The earnings rule

The most important exception is the earnings rule. This says that if you earn more than the lower earnings limit (currently £56.00 per week – see p173) in a week, you are not entitled to unemployment benefit on any day during that week. For the purposes of this rule, a week is a period of seven days (including Sunday) ending with the day of the week you sign on.[3]

The £2.00 rule

If you earn less than £56.00 in any particular week, then unless you are caught by the 'normal idle day rule' (see p25) or by the 'full extent normal' rule (see p26), you will be entitled to unemployment benefit for any day (except Sunday – see p205) on which:

- you do not work (so long as you satisfy all the other conditions of entitlement – see p8); *or*
- you do work as long as you continue actively to seek employment (see p19) and *all* the following conditions are satisfied:[4]
  - you earn £2.00 a day or less; *and*
  - you are not working as an employee in your usual main occupation, unless you are working either for a charity or for a local authority or health authority providing a charitable service; *and*
  - you are available for full-time work.

Earnings over a period of work are averaged out at a daily rate. For further details of what counts as earnings and how they are calculated see p212 but note that in this context certain payments to Members of Reserve Forces are ignored.[5]

Work which you do on a Sunday (or any day substituted for Sunday in your particular case – see p205) does not count for the purposes of the £2.00 rule. But any money you earn will count for the purposes of the earnings rule (see above) and Sunday work will almost certainly affect your entitlement to income support if you are claiming it.

If you work during the night and your shift begins before midnight and ends afterwards, there are special rules to determine which of the two days you are treated as working on (see p204).

With these two exceptions any work you do during the 24 hours following midnight counts as work on that day.

The 'normal idle day' rule

The effect of the earnings rule and the £2.00 rule is that part-time workers who earn less than £56 per week in total may be able to claim unemployment benefit for any day on which they earn less than £2.00. However, this position is complicated by two further rules, which apply if the claimant earns more than £12.00 per week and which are designed to deny benefit to those who do not 'normally' work a full working week. These are the 'normal idle day' rule[6] and the 'full extent normal' rule.[7]

The 'normal idle day' rule says that in certain circumstances you cannot get unemployment benefit for a day on which 'in the normal course' you would not work anyway. It is rarely applied in practice, but when it is, its most usual – although not its only – application is in relation to short-time working:

Example
You normally work a five-day week (Monday – Friday). You are put on two days a week short-time working (Tuesday and Wednesday). Provided you earn less than £56 on those two days, you will get unemployment benefit for three days (Monday, Thursday and Friday), but not for four as Saturday is a 'normal idle day'.

Inevitably it is not as simple as that. There is a long list of exceptions and occasions on which the rule does not apply. In particular, the rule does not apply:

- unless the claimant has a contract of employment with at least one employer which has not been terminated[8] – so if you normally work less than six days a week but lose your job altogether, you can get unemployment benefit for six days a week as long as you are available for employment on those days (see p12);
- in any week during which the claimant does not earn more than £12.00[9];
- if the claimant is only employed in 'casual' work;[10]
- if the claimant does not 'in the normal course' work for the employer for whom s/he is working;[11]
- if the claimant is unemployed or incapable of work (see p43) on every day of the week on which s/he would normally work except Sunday[12] (or any day substituted for Sunday – see p205);
- if the claimant's employment is suspended for at least six consecutive days (excluding Sunday or its substitute);[13]
- unless *either*
  - there is a recognised or customary working week for the work the claimant is doing; *or*
  - the claimant regularly works for the same number of days in a week for the same employer or employers.[14]

In contrast to the earnings rule, 'week' for these purposes means from Sunday to Saturday – not seven days ending with the day you sign on.[15]

The test for what your 'normal' days of work are is the same as for the 'full extent normal' rule (see below) and, as a result there is a considerable overlap between the rules.

The 'full extent normal' rule

As its name suggests, this rule prevents unemployment benefit from being paid during any 'week' (Sunday to Saturday) in which the claimant is employed to the 'full extent normal in his/her case'.[16]

The rule differs from the normal idle day rule, in that it applies even if a claimant's contract has been terminated altogether and that it is not restricted by reference to a 'day'.

Example
You normally work 18 hours a week – nine hours a day on Monday and Tuesday. One week your employer asks you to work six hours a day on Wednesday, Thursday and Friday and you claim unemployment benefit for Monday and Tuesday. Under the 'normal idle day' rule you would qualify for benefit as Monday and Tuesday are not normally idle days for you. But under the 'full extent normal' rule you will not – you have worked for 18 hours and that is the full extent normal in your case.

What is 'normal'?

If you have been working full-time and become unemployed, adjudication officers will generally accept at first that part-time work is not your 'normal' employment if you have taken it while looking for a full-time job.[17] But there comes a time when that part-time work does become your 'normal' employment even if you do not want it to. There is no hard and fast rule but traditionally your past full-time employment has been regarded as still being your 'normal' employment for at least a year.[18]

Adjudication officers sometimes argue that a job has become your 'normal' employment once you have worked for the same days every week for half of the year – with the effect that if you usually work the same days each week, you lose unemployment benefit after only six months. However, the commissioners' decisions[19] relied on by adjudication officers for this '50 per cent test' were concerned with people with irregular work patterns and ought not to be applied to you if you are usually employed for the same days each week.

A period of short-time working due to temporary adverse industrial conditions is disregarded when deciding what is 'normal' in your case.[20] The current recession is not regarded as temporary but, in any event, this rule is seldom relevant because the commissioners have not regarded people doing short-time working as working to their normal extent until they have been on short-time for a year.

Compulsory holidays

You are not entitled to unemployment benefit on any customary or recognised holiday while you are employed.[21]

The most common problem in this area is experienced by the employees of education authorities during school holidays when no work is done. Clearly **full-time staff** who are paid throughout the year are genuinely 'on holiday' for the whole of the school holidays. On the other hand some **ancillary staff** are only paid for two or three weeks of the holidays and it has been held that an employee in this position is entitled to unemployment benefit for the remaining weeks. Temporary teachers who are not paid during holiday periods are in a difficult position – they are usually treated as being on holiday unless they do not intend to teach again when term resumes (although it is important to investigate the precise terms of the contract with the education authority in each individual case).[22] The justification for this is that unemployment benefit is meant to insure against the *risk* of unemployment, not the *certainty* of it. In other words, a person taking work as a temporary teacher is considered to have accepted long unpaid holidays as part of the job. But, if you can show that in the past you have worked during holiday periods (and so do not accept the 'certainty' of unemployment), you may be entitled to benefit. Thus a teacher who was also a professional musician was held to have two jobs and awarded benefit during those parts of the school holidays when he was unable to obtain work playing music.[23]

If a person is employed under a series of renewable contracts, it can sometimes be difficult to tell whether a job has ended or not. This may be important as the holiday disqualification only applies if you are still employed. A good rule of thumb is that if, even if you did not give notice, you would not be in breach of your contract of employment if you did not return to work then your job has come to an end and you are entitled to benefit. However, if you think you may be in this position, you should seek advice (see p261).

7 Payments from your previous job

This section covers a variety of different payments which you may receive when you leave a job. It is important to consider how these will affect your unemployment benefit if you, or your union, are negotiating an agreement with your employers. The payments concerned are:

- compensation for unfair dismissal;
- payment in lieu of notice and other compensation for the loss of your job;
- occupational and personal pensions.

Compensation for unfair dismissal

If you take your former employers to an industrial tribunal, the money you recover may affect your entitlement to unemployment benefit in two ways:

- If the industrial tribunal orders your former employers to compensate you for loss of the money which you would have earned but for your unfair dismissal or a refusal to reinstate you, you are not entitled to unemployment benefit for any day in the *future* which is covered by that award or for a year, whichever is shorter[1]
- If you have already been paid unemployment benefit for a period in the

past covered by such an award, your former employers must pay it back under the 'recoupment provisions'[2] and the amount of compensation they have to pay you will be reduced by the same amount.

These rules only apply to payments made by your former employers as a result of an *order* of an industrial tribunal (or, on appeal, the Employment Appeal Tribunal[3]). So if you *settle* your case without an order of the tribunal, neither you nor your former employers will have to repay anything. There is therefore a financial advantage to both sides in settling cases. Even partway through a hearing, you can always withdraw your case or ask the tribunal to record the private settlement you have reached. Neither of these counts as an *order*.

If your former employers have gone into liquidation and you would therefore have to get court consent to enforce the tribunal's award, it will not affect your unemployment benefit[4] (because the award is not 'payable'[5]). But if they are not formally in liquidation but have just stopped trading, it is up to you to force them into liquidation. You will need legal advice in order to do this and may be entitled to legal aid (see p262).

You will be refused benefit for any period covered by a tribunal award, even if the tribunal reduces your compensation, for example, because it decides you were partly to blame for your own dismissal or that you have lost earnings because you have failed to look hard enough for other work. It is the *fact* of the award rather than the *amount* which leads to the disqualification.[6] Generally speaking, you should claim income support without delay if your award is reduced for any reason.

A reduced award also has consequences for the repayment of unemployment benefit which you received before the tribunal decision. If the tribunal decides that, for example, you were one third to blame for your dismissal and your employers two thirds, they will only have to repay two thirds of the benefit. In that case you will have to repay the other third if the adjudication officer can prove that you have failed to disclose a material fact (see p238). To avoid this it is very important that you should tell the Employment Service that you are considering going to an industrial tribunal at the earliest possible opportunity.[7] If you tell them later, you should not have to repay any benefit after that date.

Payment in lieu of notice and other compensation for the loss of your job

If you receive any compensation from your former employer for the termination of your employment, it is assumed that part of that payment is in lieu of any notice you were entitled to but not given. Accordingly, you are not entitled to unemployment benefit for any day which would have been covered by that notice and that can be treated as covered by the compensation.[8] This is known as the *'ineligible period'* (see p29).

What counts as 'compensation'?

Any payment made to you when you leave is treated as compensation except:[9]

- any pay for the period before your employment ended; *and*
- any holiday pay; *and*
- any redundancy payment; *and*
- any refund of contributions under an occupational pension scheme.

Although any of the above payments will affect you if you are claiming income support, your unemployment benefit will only be affected if you receive other compensation as well.

How long is the 'ineligible period'?

The 'ineligible period' always begins the day after your employment ended, but when it ends depends on what your former employers say about the payment.

   If your former employers say either that the payment is in lieu of notice or is in compensation for the early termination of a fixed-term contract, the 'ineligible period' ends either 52 weeks after it begins or (if it is sooner) on the 'due date'.[10] The 'due date' is *either*:

- the day when any notice to which you were entitled – either by contract or Act of Parliament, whichever is longer – (or to which you would have been entitled had you not waived it) would have expired; *or*
- if you had a fixed-term contract, the date when the contract was due to expire.[11]

If you are made redundant at the same time as at least nine other employees, your employers are obliged to consult any recognised trade union at least 30 days before making the redundancies (90 days where 100 or more employees are threatened with redundancy).[12] If your employers say that the payment is in lieu of these rights the 'ineligible period' ends either when the consultation period would have ended or (if the payment also includes compensation in lieu of notice) on the 'due date' (see above) or on the 'standard date' (see below), whichever is later.[13]

   In any other case – including if your employers do not say anything about the payment – the 'ineligible period' ends on the 'standard date'. This is *either*

- the 'due date' (see above); *or*
- the last day of the period (calculated in weeks by dividing the amount of the payment by £206 and rounding down to the nearest whole number.[14] This figure will be increased in the near future but details are not available at the time of going to press).[15]

Occupational and personal pensions

If you are 55 or over, and are receiving an occupational or personal pension of more than £35.00 per week gross, your unemployment benefit (including any increase for a dependent adult or child[16]) will be reduced by the amount of the excess.[17]

In this context, 'occupational or personal pension' means *periodical payments* which are made to you because your employment has ended:[18]

- from money provided wholly or partly by your former employer; *or*
- from money provided under legislation; *or*
- from most types of person pension schemes.

This is a wide definition and will catch periodical payments made under early retirement schemes and pensions paid to those who have retired on health grounds.[19] But lump-sum payments are not included (because they are not 'periodical payments') and neither are payments made *solely* because you have been made redundant (unless they are made under the rules of your pension scheme).[20]

If you are receiving an increase for an adult dependant, a separate earnings rule may mean that it will be affected by any pension paid to her/him. For further details see p166.

8   Disqualifications

Even if you would otherwise be entitled to unemployment benefit, you may be *disqualified* from receiving it if:

- you are dismissed from your job (or lose your place on an approved training scheme) for misconduct (see below); *or*
- you leave your job or give up your place on an approved training scheme voluntarily (see p33); *or*
- you do not take steps to obtain work or a place on an approved training scheme which have been recommended to you by the Employment Service or if you turn down the offer of a job or training place (see p35); *or*
- you are unemployed because of a strike or trade dispute at your place of work (see p37).

You will also be disqualified if you fail to attend a Restart interview without good cause (see p16).

Misconduct

If you are dismissed from your job[1] or lose your place on an approved training scheme[2] for misconduct you will be disqualified from unemployment benefit for up to 26 weeks and any income support to which you may be entitled will also be paid at a reduced rate.

What is misconduct?

Not every breach of your contract of employment or employers' rules or instructions amounts to misconduct – everyone makes mistakes or is inefficient from time to time. Even if you were sacked or forced to resign because of inadequate work, you are only guilty of misconduct if you have done – or failed to do – something which is *blameworthy*.

In one decision a former Chief Commissioner defined misconduct as being:

'conduct which is causally but not necessarily directly connected with the employment and having regard to the relationship of employer and employee and the rights and duties of both, can fairly be described as blameworthy, reprehensible and wrong'.[3]

So, for example, a naturally slow worker who, despite making every effort, cannot produce the output required by his/her employers will not be guilty of misconduct.

That having been said, you may be guilty of misconduct without being dishonest – serious carelessness or negligence may be enough although

'it is necessary to discriminate between that type and degree of carelessness which may have to be put up with in human affairs, and the more deliberate or serious type of carelessness which justifies withholding unemployment benefit because the employee has lost his employment through his own avoidable fault'.[4]

Negligence is more likely to be treated as misconduct if it occurs while you are exercising a special skill for which you are employed – for example as a driver. On the other hand, a bus driver who had a clean driving record for 21 years, and was dismissed for an accident which only caused slight damage, was not disqualified. It was held that an isolated error of judgment was not misconduct.[5]

Some behaviour is clearly misconduct. This includes:

- **Dishonesty** – theft, either from an employer or from fellow employees will always lead to a disqualification. Indeed a conviction for any offence of dishonesty – whether or not connected with your work – may lead to a disqualification if it causes your employers to dismiss you because they no longer trust you.[6] On the other hand, dishonesty which took place before your employment began cannot justify disqualification. For example, in one case an accountant who was dismissed when his employers found out about a previous conviction for fraud was not disqualified.[7]
- **Arson** and other forms of deliberate damage to the property of your employers or fellow employees.
- **Assaults** on your employers, fellow employees or customers.
- **Drunkenness** at work or working under the influence of illegal drugs – at least if it is repeated or endangers the safety of your fellow workers.
- **Bad timekeeping** and failing to report in time that you are sick.

The misconduct does not have to take place during working hours in order to justify disqualification. But it does have to be 'causally . . . connected with the employment' so as to give a reason for your employers to dismiss you. Convictions for dishonesty outside work have already been mentioned in this context. Another example would be of someone who needs to drive for his/her job and who loses his/her driving licence following a traffic offence. People in this position will usually be disqualified from unemployment benefit as well as from driving – particularly if drinking was involved – even if the offence took place outside work.

Deciding whether you are guilty of misconduct

When you claim benefit, your former employers will be sent a form asking whether you were dismissed and, if so, why. If their answer suggests there may have been misconduct, you will be sent a copy and asked to comment on it. Your remarks will, in turn be passed to your former employers for further comments.

Make sure you put on record the details of your case and why you contest the allegation of misconduct. If you are going to an industrial tribunal, say so. In this case you may want to discuss your reply with whoever is advising you on your claim for unfair dismissal as you may be asked questions at the industrial tribunal hearing about what you have said.

It is important to make your replies to the enquiries as full as possible as the adjudication officer has to decide from the information which s/he has gathered whether or not your loss of employment was due to misconduct on your part.

If the adjudication officer decides against you, you should consider whether to appeal (see p244).

Very often, the facts will be disputed. If so, it is usually a good idea to appeal the disqualification – particularly if it was for the full 26 weeks (see below) – so that the SSAT can see you in person and hear your point of view. Sometimes your former employers are asked to attend and you can ask your former workmates to give evidence. Although it is generally for the claimant to prove entitlement to benefit, the onus of proving misconduct is on the adjudication officer (who will normally have to rely upon evidence from your former employers).

Often a SSAT will recognise both sides' points of view by upholding the disqualification but reducing the length of it (see below).

Sometimes the same facts will have to be considered by other bodies – for example, industrial tribunals, the criminal courts, the Civil Service Board and other disciplinary and appeal bodies – as well as by the SSAT. The important thing to remember in such cases is that the questions which these other bodies have to inquire into may not be the same as the ones which the SSAT must ask itself. Industrial tribunals, for example, have to consider whether a dismissal is 'fair' and, while it may be fair to dismiss a slow employee, s/he is probably not guilty of misconduct. So a finding by an industrial tribunal that a dismissal was fair does not prevent an adjudication officer or SSAT from concluding that there has been no misconduct. Similarly, although SSATs will normally accept a criminal conviction as proof that a claimant has done what is alleged, it must still go on to consider whether this was connected with your employment and whether it amounts to misconduct.

While the question of possible misconduct is being investigated, your unemployment benefit will be suspended and income support will be paid at a reduced rate. You will receive arrears if it is later decided not to disqualify you.

The period of disqualification

The period of disqualification can be any length from one day to 26 weeks. The decision on how long it will be in your case is taken by the adjudication officer who decides your claim (see p226). S/he should consider your case on its individual merits.

If you feel that the period of disqualification in your case is harsh or unfair, it is worth appealing because SSATs (see p243) often reduce periods of disqualification. An appeal will give you a much better chance to put your side of the case – and to challenge your former employer's version of events – than any written comments which you may have made before the adjudication officer made his/her decision.

You will also be able to argue that 26 weeks is a maximum for really serious misconduct and that a lesser period is more fitting in your case. For example:

- a claimant was dismissed for stealing an item worth seven pence and which he believed to be valueless. A commissioner reduced the period of disqualification to two weeks;[8]
- an assault on a fellow employee which had been provoked would deserve a shorter period of disqualification than on which was premeditated and without provocation.

At present, the period of disqualification 'defers' your entitlement to unemployment benefit – ie, once the period has expired, you can receive your full entitlement up to a maximum of 312 days (see p9). However, the DSS now has the power to change this so that the period of disqualification reduces your entitlement. For example, if you were disqualified for six weeks (36 days) your maximum entitlement to unemployment benefit would be 276 days (312 days-36 days) rather than a year. This change has not yet been brought into effect.[9]

Leaving your job or training scheme voluntarily

You will also be disqualified if:

- you leave your job voluntarily without *just cause*;[10] or
- you give up your place on a training scheme voluntarily and without *good cause*.[11]

As with misconduct the maximum period of disqualification is 26 weeks and the length of the period in any individual case should be decided upon the merits of that case. If you are also claiming income support, it will be paid at a reduced rate during the period of disqualification.[12]

Although it is normally clear whether a person has left employment or training voluntarily, that is not always the case. If you are told to resign or put in a position where you have no practical choice but to do so you have not left voluntarily.[13]

Volunteering for *redundancy* does not count as leaving your job voluntarily[14] (but see below for the position if you volunteer for *early retirement*).

Just cause

Once it is established that you left of your own free will, it is up to you to show that you had *just cause* (or, if you left a place on a training scheme rather than a job, *good cause*). For the meaning of 'good cause' see p36 – '*just cause*' is a harder test to satisfy as it involves the adjudicating authorities (see p224) balancing your interests against those of all the other contributors to the national insurance fund. You must show not only that you acted reasonably in leaving but also that the circumstances of your case make it proper that the community should support you.[15]

So, for example:

- **If your job does not suit you,** you are expected to find, or at least seriously look for, another one before giving it up.[16]
- **If you volunteer for early retirement,** you probably will not have just cause.[17] However the circumstances in which you volunteer will be relevant to the length of the disqualification imposed particularly if you can say that it was in the public interest for you to have taken early retirement.[18]

  This rule only applies in cases where you have genuinely volunteered to leave. 'Early retirement' is often a euphemism for being sacked or made redundant (see above and p29) in which case you have not left your job voluntarily. Remember also, that in early retirement cases, the adjudication officer will want to be satisfied that you have not actually retired and that you are still available for and actively seeking work before awarding you unemployment benefit.
- **If you leave your job for personal or domestic reasons,** you may have just cause. For example, accommodation difficulties may justify you in giving up your job to take up an offer of proper housing in another district[19] (though a 21-year-old woman who left work to move with her parents was disqualified because it was reasonable for her to live alone[20]). Health reasons may also be sufficient, but it would be important to show that you had mentioned these to your employers when you left.[21] Married women who have left jobs to live with their husbands who have been posted elsewhere by their employers have not usually been disqualified[22] (although there can be other problems with unemployment benefit if the posting is abroad – even to another EC country[23]). Men who leave jobs to live with their wives should also receive the same treatment.[24]
- **If you give up work to look after a sick relative,** you probably have good cause,[25] but you may still be refused benefit because you are not available for work. Consider claiming invalid care allowance (see p125) and income support instead.
- **If you give up your job because of a change in your terms and conditions of employment,** you may have just cause (although you will be

expected to use any grievance procedure first). For example, a piece-worker who left because of a substantial, unilaterally-imposed, reduction in earnings was not disqualified.[26] Neither was an apprentice who was instructed to do work clearly outside the terms of his apprentice-ship.[27] If you do not feel *capable* of the new work – but your employers are satisfied that you are – you will need medical evidence to establish just cause.[28] If you give notice hastily when your terms of work are changed and then try to revoke it but are not allowed to by your employers, you should argue that the *period* of disqualification should be reduced.[29]

Trial periods

If you have not worked (or been in training or full-time education) for at least 26 weeks, there is an exception to the rules on giving up your job voluntarily which allows you to take a job for a trial period. This means that if you give up the job voluntarily after the end of the sixth week, but before the end of the twelfth week, you will not be disqualified.[30] For this purpose, it is assumed that you started work on the Sunday at the beginning of the week in which your job started, but any week during which you did not work for at least 16 hours is ignored.[31]

If you decide to accept a job on a trial basis you must also remember that if you do not claim unemployment benefit for at least eight consecutive weeks, a new period of interruption of employment (see p203) will begin when you next claim. This may be to your benefit as it will mean that a fresh period of 312 days' entitlement also begins. On the other hand you will have to serve a further three waiting days (see p9) and, more seriously, the question of whether you satisfy the contribution conditions (see p186) will be looked at again – probably by reference to later years than before. Because of this it is very important to work out whether, if you give up your job after a trial period of more than eight weeks, you will still meet the contribution conditions (see p186) when you re-claim benefit. If not, then you should make a final decision on whether you are suited to the new job before the eight weeks have expired.

Failing to take up a job or a place on a training scheme

If you repeatedly fail to take jobs that are offered to you, the adjudication officer may decide that you are not really available for or actively seeking work and refuse you benefit altogether.

You will be disqualified from benefit if:

• You are notified of a job vacancy or a place on a training scheme and *either*
  – you do not apply for it; *or*
  – you refuse to accept it if it is offered to you.[32]

A job or training place counts as having been 'notified' to you if you are

told about it by or on behalf of an employer, by the Employment Service or a local education authority or by certain agencies.[33]
- You fail to take a reasonable opportunity of getting a job or a place on a training scheme.[34]
- You do not carry out reasonable written recommendations given to you by the Employment Service to help you find a job.[35]

Again the period of disqualification is decided by the adjudication officer and should reflect the merits of the case. The minimum period is one day and the maximum 26 weeks. You can appeal against the decision to disqualify you, or the length of the disqualification or both.

Good cause

These disqualifications do not apply if you have 'good cause' for acting as you did. When reaching a decision on whether there was 'good cause', the adjudication officer must take all your relevant personal circumstances into account. The regulations say that these include:

- any personal circumstances suggesting that a particular job, course of training or official recommendation might cause you serious harm or subject you to excessive physical or mental stress;[36]
- any sincerely held religious or conscientious objection;[37]
- any responsibility for the care of another member of your household;[38]
- the travelling time involved.[39] Normally you are expected to be prepared to travel for up to an hour 'by a route and means appropriate to your circumstances' (see p16) each way to and from your job or training scheme. But less might be reasonable if your health would suffer or if you are responsible for the care of another member of your household;[40]
- any expenses which would be incurred in doing the job or attending the training scheme if they would have amounted to an unreasonably high proportion of your income.[41]

On the other hand, the adjudication officer is not allowed to take into account your family income except in relation to your work or training expenses.[42] This means that you cannot usually refuse a job because the wage or salary is too low.
But there are some limits on what you are expected to accept:

- You do not have to accept a job involving less than 24 hours' work a week.[43]
- You do not have to accept a job which is vacant because of a trade dispute – ie, you do not have to be a strike-breaker.
- During your 'permitted period' (see p13), you do not have to take a job except in your usual occupation and for at least your usual rate of pay.
- If you have trained for a job for at least two months, you do not have to accept work in any other kind of employment for four weeks after your training ends.[44]

- You do not have to take a job which you find out about by yourself[45] unless *either:*
  - you have also been notified of the job by the Employment Service;[46] *or*
  - you have worked for the employer within the past year *and* have a right to return (eg, after maternity leave) *and* your pay and conditions will be at least as good as before.[47]

  Remember, however, that if you do not take a job you have been offered, the adjudication officer may decide that you are not available for work (see p12).

Strikes and trade disputes

You will be disqualified from unemployment benefit if the reason you are not working is because:

- you have withdrawn your labour as part of a trade dispute;[48] *or*
- there is a stoppage of work due to a trade dispute at your place of employment (unless you are not 'directly interested' in the outcome of the dispute).[49]

Even if you are disqualified from unemployment benefit during a trade dispute, you may still be entitled to *income support* if you have a family – for further details see CPAG's *National Welfare Benefits Handbook.*

What counts as your 'place of employment'?

Often the answer to this question will be obvious. But if you work for a large business, you may be able to argue that a stoppage of work in another department is not taking place at *your* place of employment.

This is because there is a rule that says that if there are different kinds of work, which are commonly run as separate businesses, being carried on in the same factory but in different departments, each department is treated as a separate place of employment.[50]

'Department' refers to administrative as well as physical divisions. So, for example, electricians in a steel works and lorry drivers employed by a firm of ship repairers, have been successful in claiming unemployment benefit when the whole organisation has been shut down by a strike because both types of work are commonly carried out as businesses separate from the 'department' where the dispute was in progress.[51]

Who is 'directly interested' in a trade dispute?

Even if the stoppage is at your place of employment, you will not be disqualified if you can show that you are not directly interested in the dispute. This is very difficult. In effect you have to show that you have nothing to gain, either financially or in connection with your conditions of work, by the terms on which the dispute might be settled. It makes no difference that you are not a member of the union or group of workers in dispute if the outcome of the dispute will affect you because by a collective agreement or established custom, all workers have the same terms and conditions of employment irrespective of union membership.[52]

Period of disqualification

The disqualification continues for as long as the stoppage of work, whatever your personal circumstances, unless:

- having lost your job as a result of the trade dispute, you become employed elsewhere and lose your *second* job. In this case you will qualify for benefit, providing you can prove that the second job was genuine, and not a ploy aimed at requalifying for unemployment benefit;[53] *or*
- you have been made redundant during the course of the dispute. In this case you will become entitled to unemployment benefit from the date of the redundancy even though the stoppage of work is still continuing;[54] *or*
- you return to work during the dispute but become unemployed again before the stoppage of work ends. In this case you will not be disqualified if your reason for leaving was unconnected with the dispute itself.[55]

9   Special rules for people over pensionable age

You cannot receive unemployment benefit if you are over 65 if you are a woman or 70 if you are a man. If you are over pensionable age (60 for a woman, 65 for a man), unemployment benefit will only be paid if:[1]

- you would be entitled to a Category A retirement pension (see p93) or, if you are a widow or widower, a Category B retirement pension (see pp96 and 98); *and*
- you have deferred your retirement pension by not claiming it (see p90) or by electing to de-retire (see p92).

If your pension would have been paid at a reduced rate because you do not have a full contribution record (see p188), then the rate at which unemployment benefit (and any increase for a dependent adult)[2] is paid will be similarly reduced.

An increase is paid for dependent children if you receive unemployment benefit and are over pensionable age. This is not reduced if your contribution record is incomplete.

The difference in the pensionable age for men and women means that men aged between 60 and 65 are treated differently from women of the same age. The difference depends on your contribution record (and on whether you have dependent children).

Example
You are a woman aged 63. You have worked and paid full contributions for the past five years but, taken over your working life as a whole, your contribution record is incomplete and would only entitle you to 50% of the full rate of a Category A retirement pension. Unemployment benefit is paid at £28.05 per week (£56.10 ÷ 2). If you were male, unemployment benefit would be paid at the full 'under pensionable age' rate of £44.65 per week – you would be better off if you were a man.

You are a man aged 63 and have worked and paid contributions continuously since you were 16. Although you cannot claim it until you are 65, you have already paid sufficient contributions to entitle you to a full Category A retirement pension. You live with your 15 year-old daughter. Unemployment benefit will be paid at £44.65 per week. If you were female, it would be paid at the full 'over pensionable age' rate of £56.10 and you would receive a dependant's increase for your daughter worth £9.80 per week (after the operation of the overlapping benefit rules – see p212), a total of £65.90 – you would be better off if you were a woman.

If you would be better off being treated as a member of the opposite sex, you should argue that this discrimination between the sexes is against EC law (see p202). The general principle of EC law is that there must be no discrimination whatsoever in the rules for non-means-tested benefits. There is an exception which allows different pensionable ages for men and women[3] but it is not permissible to use this as a basis for rules governing entitlement to unemployment benefit.[4] You will probably have to appeal (see p244) – ask a local advice agency to contact CPAG's solicitor for further advice.

10 Special rules for students

Students are not entitled to unemployment benefit while they are on any *full-time* course of study. It makes no difference whether you receive a grant or whether you claim during term-time or during the vacation.[1]

The regulations do not define full-time education by reference to particular courses or hours of study, so whether or not your course is full-time is judged on the particular circumstances of your case. If you disagree with the adjudication officer's decision, you can appeal (see p244). Ask your union, student welfare officer or the college authorities to help you.

Your unemployment benefit will not be affected if you fill in time while unemployed by doing some limited studying, eg, evening classes, correspondence courses (such as the Open University) or a part-time course of education. However, you *must* remain **available for work**. An adjudication officer will take into account all your circumstances (including the length of the course, any fee paid and the level of commitment required) when deciding whether you are still genuinely available for work and free to take up any reasonable job offer immediately.

11 **Other benefits**

The other principal benefit for people who are out of work is income support. This is a means-tested benefit which you can claim if your weekly income (including unemployment benefit) is low enough to qualify and your savings and other capital are below the current limit.

Unlike unemployment benefit, income support is paid from the first day of your claim (ie, there are no waiting days), can include a payment to cover mortgage interest payments and 'passports' claimants onto other benefits such as housing and council tax benefits and free prescriptions and legal aid. So unless you are absolutely sure that you are not entitled (perhaps because you are living with someone who is in full-time work), you should claim income support as well as unemployment benefit.

The amount of income support is normally reduced if you are disqualified from unemployment benefit because you lost your job through misconduct or left it voluntarily or because you have refused an offer of employment or training (see p30).[1] There are also special rules for those involved in trade disputes.[2]

For further details on income support see CPAG's *National Welfare Benefits Handbook*.

While you are unemployed, you are entitled to Class 1 national insurance credits (see p181).

Unemployment benefit is an earnings replacement benefit (see p4) and 'overlaps' with widows benefits (except the lump-sum widow's payment). It is counted as income when calculating means-tested benefits. For the relationship between unemployment benefit and retirement pensions see p38. Adult dependency increases to unemployment benefit overlap with personal benefits (see p209) paid to the dependant in her/his own right (see p211).

12 **Tax**

Unemployment benefit is taxable except for increases in respect of dependent children.[1]

The tax is not deducted while benefit is being paid but reduces the refund you would otherwise receive through pay-as-you-earn (PAYE) when you return to work. As unemployment benefit is low, very few people will owe more tax at the end of a period of unemployment than at the beginning.

Any tax refunds of PAYE payments will be paid to you at the end (5 April) of the tax year to which they relate. Any other tax refund will be paid only when unemployment benefit ceases to be paid and the amount of refund will be affected by the amount of benefit you have received.[2]

In rare cases, you may end up owing tax. If so, your tax code will be adjusted when you return to work so that the tax deducted from your earnings will be increased until the money you owe from your period of unemployment has been collected.

CHAPTER THREE

Benefits for people incapable of work

This chapter covers:

1 Incapacity for work
2 Statutory sick pay
3 Sickness benefit
4 Invalidity benefit
5 Severe disablement allowance

Most people who are away from work due to sickness receive statutory sick pay (SSP) from their employers for the first 28 weeks. Those not entitled to SSP but who are unable to work receive sickness benefit from the Benefits Agency for the first 28 weeks provided they satisfy the contribution conditions or have suffered an industrial injury. Most of those who have been entitled to SSP or sickness benefit then become entitled to invalidity benefit until they retire or are able to work again.

If you do not qualify for SSP or sickness benefit you do not get benefit for the first 28 weeks unless you are entitled to income support (IS). IS cannot normally be paid for any day before you claim, so if you are not sure you will get SSP or sickness benefit, you should claim IS at the same time (see CPAG's *National Welfare Benefits Handbook*).

Even if you are not entitled to invalidity benefit, because, for example, you have not paid enough contributions, you may be entitled to severe disablement allowance instead after 28 weeks.

It is important to remember the difference between SSP and 'occupational sick pay'. Many employees are covered for sick pay by their contract of employment, which frequently gives a better level of payment, and a longer period of entitlement, than SSP. This is known as occupational sick pay. SSP is the minimum employers must pay. The amount of SSP is laid down by Act of Parliament and employers are partially reimbursed by the Secretary of State.

If you are disabled you may also be entitled to one of the benefits described in Chapter 8 or to disability working allowance (see CPAG's *National Welfare Benefits Handbook*). If you are ill or injured because of your work you should also read Chapter 9.

Incapacity for work

A 'day of incapacity'

All the benefits covered in this chapter are theoretically 'daily benefits'. This means that you have to satisfy the Benefits Agency (or in the case of statutory sick pay (SSP), your employers) that you are unable to work on *each day* for which you want to receive benefit. In practice, the Benefits Agency will usually allow you to claim less frequently than this and most medical certificates will also cover periods of more than one day. But the fact that entitlement is decided on a daily basis still has some practical effects. You may, for example, find that Benefits Agency decisions say that periods for which you have claimed were not 'days of incapacity' when what they mean is that the adjudication officer (see p226) does not accept that you were unable to work.

If you are claiming sickness benefit, invalidity benefit or severe disablement allowance, your days of incapacity must also form part of a 'period of interruption of employment' (see p203). To qualify for SSP, your days of incapacity must form part of a 'period of incapacity for work'. This is not the same as a 'period of interruption of employment' and the differences are discussed later in this chapter (see p52).

'Incapable of work'

To qualify as incapable of work you must prove *either*:

- that you are suffering from a disease; *or*
- that you are physically or mentally disabled; *and*
- that, as a result, you are unable to do any work which it is reasonable to expect you to do (but see below for exceptions).[1]

Even if you are able to work, the Benefits Agency will sometimes treat you as if you are not. This is known as 'deemed' incapacity. You will be treated as incapable of work if either:[2]

- you are under medical observation as the possible carrier of an infectious disease or have been in contact with a carrier. A Medical Officer of Environmental Health can give you a certificate 'deeming' you incapable of work; *or*
- you have a certificate from your GP stating that, for convalescent or precautionary reasons, you should not work *and* you are under medical care *and* you do not in fact work.

If you can do some work but not your normal job

Whether or not you can get benefit if you can do some work depends on whether it is *reasonable* to expect you to do other jobs. At the beginning of your claim, only your normal job will be considered. Once you show you are incapable of that, your claim would be allowed. However, as time goes on you will be expected to consider other work.[3] Usually the adjudication officer does not look at this question until you have been off work for about six months. At this stage you may have some idea whether you can return to your old job and, if so, when. If you are likely to return soon, it would not be reasonable to expect you to look at other jobs. But if you are likely to be unable to do your own job for a long time, you will be expected to consider other work. When looking at what it is reasonable for you to do, your age, education, state of health and skills are taken into account.[4] The adjudication officer must also look at you as you are and not how you could be if you retrained or were more highly skilled.

If you are only able to do a limited amount of light or 'therapeutic' work this will not, on its own, affect your rights to sickness benefit, invalidity benefit or severe disablement allowance (provided you meet the conditions set out below). You are not expected simply to sit at home and do nothing. However, (apart from any work you may do as a local councillor[5]) the Benefits Agency may take into account *any* work you do, including therapeutic work, as evidence that you are not 'incapable of work'.

Work you may do while claiming

If you are claiming sickness benefit, invalidity benefit or severe disablement allowance the Benefits Agency may (but does not have to) allow you to receive benefit (but not SSP) even though you are working if:[6]

- you do not earn more than £42.00 a week; *and either*
- you only work under medical supervision as part of your hospital treatment, either in hospital or as an outpatient; *or*
- you only do work which you have 'good cause' to do.

Such work is sometimes known as 'therapeutic' work.

For the rules on how earnings are calculated see p212. You cannot avoid the earnings rule by not claiming earnings which are due to you.[7]

If you are a local councillor and your net allowance (after deducting expenses) is more than £42.00 in any week your benefit will be reduced by the amount of the excess.[8]

Members of Disability Appeal Tribunals (see p249) are deemed to be incapable of work for up to one day a week when they are hearing appeals.[9]

It is difficult to say generally when you will have 'good cause' for doing any particular work. There will certainly be good cause if, on your doctor's recommendation, you do a small amount of light work (either as exercise or to take your mind off your disability) even though that work is not actually carried out under medical supervision. It is also clear that non-medical reasons can sometimes be good cause (eg, work done in an emergency), but it cannot be predicted in advance when non-medical good cause will exist and such situations will be exceptional. In particular, commissioners have held more than once that if your reason for working is to get more money, either generally or for a particular purpose, you will not have good cause.[10] This has not always been followed by other commissioners – eg, a woman who worked to pay for contact lenses which she needed to avoid going blind and could not get on the NHS was held to have good cause.[11] But it does indicate that the commissioners are anxious to prevent the 'good cause' rule from being used to undermine the principle that the people who get incapacity benefits must be unable to work.

If your purpose in working is to earn money, it does not make any difference if you do not actually succeed. So, claimants who have worked to develop small businesses do not have good cause even if the businesses did not make any profit.[12] This is because the claimants hoped to make money, albeit in the future, when they did the work.

Because it is much easier to show good cause if you have a doctor's recommendation, it is a good idea to speak to your GP before you do any work to see whether s/he agrees that it would be beneficial for you to do it. It is better still if your doctor is prepared to put that recommendation in writing as you will then be able to show it to the Benefits Agency.

Remember that the Benefits Agency does not have to allow you to do these kinds of work. It has a choice. If you are in any doubt you should contact your local office before taking a job, to see if it is acceptable. If you disagree with a Benefits Agency decision to refuse you benefit on this ground, you should appeal (see p244).

Training for work and incapacity for work

You cannot receive any of the benefits covered in this chapter while on a training course and receiving a training allowance.[13] However, your income will not be reduced because the training allowance is fixed at your previous benefit level, and you will also receive an extra training premium of £10 a week.

At the end of the course, your benefit is usually reinstated provided you reclaim within eight weeks of the course ending so that your periods of interruptions of employment can be linked (see p203). However, this is not automatic. If you have shown yourself to be able to work by attending the course or have acquired new skills which mean that there is now other work which you might reasonably be expected to do, an adjudication officer may decide that you are no longer incapable of work. If this happens you should claim unemployment benefit and/or income support instead and consider whether to appeal (see p46).

Proving you are unable to work

If you claim SSP or occupational sick pay, your employers will have requirements about how you prove you are too ill to work. These will be in your employment contract. But, for SSP, there are limits to what your employers can ask for (see p54).

For the DSS benefits, the general rule is that you must provide medical certificates.[14] The rules also allow you to prove that you are unable to work by using other evidence provided that it is 'sufficient in the circumstances', but this is to cover unusual cases and you should not rely on it unless it is absolutely necessary.

Normally your first certificate is the self-certification form (SC1) in which you state that you are too ill to work.[15] After seven days of self-certificated sickness, you will usually be expected to supply certificates from your GP. Doctors cannot charge for these if provided for social security purposes.[16] The certificate states that the doctor advises you to refrain from work. It is either a 'closed certificate', stating a date within the next two weeks on which you can return to work, or an 'open certificate' stating that you will be unfit to work for a specified period (up to six months) without stating that you will then be fit to return.

You can submit a medical certificate from other medical sources, such as an osteopath or chiropractor, or a certificate from your own GP which is not the standard national insurance one, or your evidence can be in the form of a letter rather than a certificate.

Disputes about incapacity for work

The adjudication officer will generally accept your doctor's certificate without question, particularly in the first few months of your illness or injury. However, at some stage your case may be referred to the DSS regional medical service. This will not normally happen until after six months, but may occur before then.

You should attend the appointment that the regional medical service arranges, otherwise you can be disqualified from receiving benefit (see p59). A regional medical officer assesses whether, overall, you are fit to work, taking account of your degree of capacity in specific functions, eg, climbing ladders, bending, and the capacity of certain parts of your body, eg, fingers, arms and legs. If the regional medical officer considers you are fit to do some work, s/he will inform your own doctor.

Sometimes this leads your doctor to stop giving medical certificates, which means you do not get the relevant benefit. Although in theory it is possible to receive benefit on the basis of your own evidence without any doctor supporting you, in practice it is very difficult to persuade anyone you are unable to work if your own doctor does not support you. But it is most important that your doctor makes up her/his own mind, rather than simply accepting the regional medical officer's opinion. Your doctor has known you a lot longer than the DSS doctor, and has a far better idea of your disabilities. The regional medical officer will probably have examined you for about 15 minutes during which period your arm may be assessed as at 'full function' if, for instance, you can raise it. But this is not the same as lifting it repeatedly to perform a job, and is a misleading assessment. So, using this example, you would need to explain fully to your doctor the nature of your job, and the extent of arm-raising in it and how it is likely to affect you.

If your doctor does disagree with the Regional Medical Officer and continues to give you certificates, the adjudication officer will have to weigh the conflicting evidence and decide who s/he agrees with.

At this stage it becomes important to look at the most recent decision to award you benefit. Like most other benefits, incapacity benefits are usually awarded for an indefinite period (subject to a maximum of six months in the case of sickness benefit) unless there is a good reason for the adjudication officer to make an award for a fixed period.[17] And unless you have been awarded benefit for a fixed period *and* that period has come to an end, the adjudication officer can only stop your benefit by carrying out a review[18] (see p230). In practice this means that, in these circumstances, it is for the adjudication officer to prove that you are capable of work rather than for you to prove that you are not.

If the adjudication officer does refuse you benefit, you should consider an appeal since invalidity benefit is paid at a higher rate than unemployment benefit, lasts indefinitely, is not taxable, and entitles you to disability premiums for means-tested benefits.

Sickness benefit, invalidity benefit and SDA are not paid while your appeal is waiting to be heard. For this reason, you should sign on for unemployment benefit and income support *immediately* benefit is refused. You may have difficulty convincing the Employment Service that you are available for work because you will be saying in your appeal that you are not. Tell the new client adviser that you will accept any reasonable work within your limitations.

It is important to send in medical certificates while you wait for your appeal to be heard because then you will not be required to sign on as available for work in order to qualify for income support. If your appeal is successful, you will receive arrears of benefit to make up for the reduction. Certificates are also important because otherwise you might win at the tribunal but have broken the period for which you have provided certificates. Remember that even if you have little immediate financial advantage from appealing, you may benefit in the future because of, for instance, automatic national insurance credits (see p181), or entitlement to invalidity pension or a higher rate of income support.

When deciding whether to appeal and how to prepare your case, bear in mind that the tribunal has to consider four distinct questions.

(a) What is the extent of your disability?

This is the major medical question, and has to be decided by the members of the social security appeal tribunal, who are not doctors, assessing the reports in front of them, and your own evidence.

If the only written evidence is your GP's certificate, against the report from the regional medical officer, you may well lose. You should strengthen your case by asking your GP or other doctor to write as detailed a letter as possible to the tribunal explaining why you are unable to work. A report from a consultant will carry more weight and your GP may be able to arrange this through the National Health Service. You can send the report to the tribunal yourself, or ask your GP to do so as part of her/his evidence. If your injury arises from an accident for which you are claiming compensation, your solicitor will probably have a consultant's report, or will be getting one. Your union may finance a report for a tribunal if the injury is work-related, or you could ask for a solicitor to obtain a consultant's report through the 'green form' scheme ('pink' in Scotland) for legal assistance. You can ask the tribunal to obtain a free medical report for you[19] (through the adjudication officer), but it will not normally do so unless the issue is reasonably arguable. Tribunals have been reminded by the commissioners of their power to obtain reports where claimants cannot afford them.[20]

It is often useful for a person who lives with you or knows you well to describe to the tribunal the day-to-day problems you suffer. You should also take with you a list of any medication you are taking.

Doctors cannot always see your symptoms and have to rely upon your description. For example, you must describe the pain, timing and duration of migraines; or the effect of cold damp weather on joints; or the aches in your legs or back after a day's work. Your own doctor's evidence would be very useful here. If the disability is painful but invisible, a tribunal has to decide the case, partially at least, on its assessment of you. Your appearance will be important, as well as your record in claiming benefit – a lengthy history of claims may count against you.

Watch out for the term 'functional overlay' in medical reports. This means incapacity for which there is no evident physical cause. It is often taken to be a euphemism for malingering or imaginary symptoms, although it does not actually mean the same thing. Genuine symptoms should be taken into account, even if there is a psychological element partly causing them.[21]

(b) **What work does your disability allow you to do?**

Unless your appeal follows a review by an adjudication officer (see p47), it is up to you to prove you are incapable of work, and if taken literally this would involve showing you could not do *any* work, so a more practical approach is taken.[22] If it is clear that you can manage a range of jobs, the tribunal will find against you. When you dispute whether or not you can manage a job, it is up to the adjudication officer to suggest to the tribunal the type of work that the Benefits Agency thinks you can do.[23] (The regional medical officer and disablement resettlement officer may make suggestions.) This requires considering what working at a particular job really involves. The adjudication officer will be expected to provide a job description of any job suggested, so the tribunal can decide if it is feasible given your disabilities.

> *Example*
> A building labourer in his 40s suffers from asbestosis, so the job of attendant in a car park is suggested – there is no heavy work in giving out tickets and checking to see they have not expired. However, car exhaust fumes accumulate even though the car park is in the open air, and this would aggravate his breathing problems. The work is not suitable.

You must examine each job described and find out what difficulties there may be. Thus if you have a bad back and a job as a messenger is suggested, you can point out that a messenger often has to carry parcels, which involves bending and lifting. In this sort of case a letter, or oral evidence, from someone who knows the type of work is more useful than medical evidence.

Another way to help your case is to ask your doctor to comment specifically on your ability to work at that particular job. If you have tried to go back to work but were unable to do so, or were forced to give up, this is useful evidence both of your motivation and of your disability.

An important point to bear in mind is that the job being considered must be one that some employer would pay you to do. [24] You can argue that, as a matter of common sense, no one will pay you if you can do certain tasks only for a short time or occasionally.

Example
You have a bad back strain. You cannot sit or stand for long, must alternate between the two every 30 minutes, and cannot bend or do heavy lifting. The adjudication officer suggests a job as an assembly worker in light engineering or component manufacture. You can tell the tribunal why it is unlikely that you would be given a job. For instance most jobs like this do not allow a worker to change position at her/his convenience. Products have to be lifted up and down and a seven- or eight-hour working day is the norm. You could also write to a local firm of this type, describing your limitations, and asking them to comment on the prospects of your being employed there. Alternatively your union representative may have wide experience and can comment.

This is not the same as saying that, as there is a lot of unemployment, you cannot get a job in your area. You are arguing that as you have got the disabilities described, no employer is likely to employ you.

(c)   Is it work that it is reasonable to expect you to do?

Because this question is not addressed properly claimants often lose appeals unnecessarily. The tribunal may accept that you can do some jobs but do not then go on to ask whether it is *reasonable* to expect you to do them. [25] This is an error of law and you should consider a further appeal (see p251). However, appeals take time to process and you will not get your benefit in the meantime. So, if there are reasons why you do not want to do the jobs which the adjudication officer says you are fit for you should tell the tribunal and back them up with evidence if possible. The reasons do not have to be related to your health (see p44).

(d)   What period is to be considered?

In practice the tribunal will make a decision on whether you are capable of work for the whole of the period from the adjudication officer's decision up to the date of the tribunal hearing. It is therefore important that you should, if you can, continue to submit medical certificates showing that you are still unfit for work while you are waiting for the appeal to be heard.

2 **Statutory sick pay**

SSP is administered and paid by your employers, *not* the Benefits Agency (although there are rights of appeal to an adjudication officer if you and your employers cannot agree). Your contract of employment may mean that your employers must also pay you occupational sick pay. But SSP is a legal minimum and, if you qualify for it, your employers are not allowed to pay you less.

Conditions of entitlement[1]

For every day you receive benefit:

* You must be an employee;
* You must be incapable of work (see p43);
* You must have begun a 'period of incapacity for work' (see p52) by being incapable of work for at least four consecutive days;
* The day must be a 'qualifying day' (see p53);
* Your 'period of entitlement' (see p52) must not have ended; *and*
* You must have notified your employer (see p54).

Who can get SSP?

You are entitled to SSP if you are an employee.[2] This does not mean you must have a written agreement, or even the statement of terms and conditions of employment which employers are required to give within 13 weeks of your starting work and which is popularly, but inaccurately, known as 'the contract'. It is the fact that you are employed which matters rather than the documents (though documents are useful for evidence in case of a dispute). Your right to SSP cannot be taken away by any document whether you sign it or not[3] and, if your employer sacks you to avoid paying SSP, then s/he is still liable to pay it after your contract has ended.[4] The question of whether you are an employee for SSP purposes is similar to the question of whether you are an 'employed earner' under the Industrial Injuries Scheme (see p139).

Even if you are an employee, your employers do not have to pay your SSP if they are neither resident nor present in Great Britain or exempt from the social security legislation because of an international treaty.[5]

Below are some other employees who will not get SSP.[6]

(a) **People over pensionable age**

If you are over pensionable age (65 for a man, 60 for a woman) you will not get SSP unless your 'period of entitlement' (see p52) began before your 65th/60th birthday and has not yet ended. This unequal treatment of men and women is almost certainly contrary to EC law.[7] If you are a woman aged between 60 and 65 and are refused SSP on this ground, then provided you are not also claiming a retirement pension, you should claim sickness benefit instead (see p57). If you would be better off having

SSP, apply for a decision from an adjudication officer and be prepared to appeal if necessary (see p244). If you need further advice, ask a local advice agency to contact CPAG's solicitors.

(b) People with short-term contracts

If your contract of employment lasts for less than three months, you cannot get SSP unless your period of entitlement began when you were working under a different contract and has not ended. This will be rare (see p53).

(c) People with low earnings

You cannot get SSP if you normally earn less than the lower earnings limit, currently £56.00 (see p173). It is your gross earnings (before tax and national insurance contributions are deducted) that are relevant here.

(d) Pregnant women

If you are entitled to statutory maternity pay (see p70) you cannot get SSP during the 'maternity pay period'.

If you are entitled to maternity allowance (see p75) you cannot get SSP during the 'maternity allowance period'.

If you are not entitled to statutory maternity pay or to maternity allowance you cannot get SSP for the six weeks before the week in which your baby is expected, for the expected week of confinement itself or for the 11 weeks after it.

(e) Prisoners[8]

You cannot get SSP for any day that you are in prison. If you become incapable of work while in prison you cannot get SSP for any of the subsequent days of the same period of incapacity for work, even if you are released in the meantime. This will apply even if you have been held on remand awaiting trial and are eventually acquitted.

(f) People involved in trade disputes

You cannot get SSP if there is a stoppage of work due to a trade dispute at your place of employment unless *either*:

• you can show that you did not have a 'direct interest' in it (see p37); *or*
• your period of entitlement began before the stoppage of work and has not yet ended.

This rule will prevent you from getting SSP during the whole period of your sickness even if the strike ends the day after you fall ill and even if you do not take part in the stoppage. You can claim sickness benefit instead if you have paid enough contributions or if you became ill as a result of an industrial injury or disease. You will not lose SSP if there is any industrial action short of a stoppage of work – eg, a ban on overtime or 'working to grade'.[9]

(g)   **People outside the European Community**[10]

You cannot get SSP if you are not in an EC country unless you are an airman or woman, a mariner or a continental shelf worker. If you spend any time outside an EC country on the first day of your period of incapacity for work you cannot get SSP for the remainder of that period.

(h)   **People who have not yet started work**

If you have agreed to go and work for an employer but have not yet started work and you fall ill you will not get SSP for any day during the same period of incapacity.

'Period of incapacity for work'

A period of incapacity is four or more consecutive 'days of incapacity' (see p43).[11] Every day of the week (including Sundays[12]) counts for this purpose even if they are not days on which you would normally work. Any two periods separated by not more than eight weeks are treated as a single period.[13]

For sickness benefit, odd days can be linked to form a period of interruption of employment if you are incapable of work on any two or more days in a week because you are receiving certain types of regular treatment such as dialysis (see p203). For SSP, that rule does not apply. If this prevents you getting SSP and you are receiving one of those forms of treatment, you should claim sickness benefit instead (see p57).

'Period of entitlement'

Your 'period of entitlement' begins with the commencement of a 'period of incapacity for work' (see above) and ends with whichever of the following first occurs:[14]

- the end of that 'period of incapacity for work';
- the day on which your contract of employment ends;
- the day before you are disqualified on the ground of pregnancy (see p51);
- the day on which you reach your maximum entitlement to SSP as against that particular employer;
- the third anniversary of the beginning of the 'period of entitlement';
- a day when you are not in an EC country (see p200). It is sometimes suggested that this means your period of entitlement ends when you are in international waters on your way from, say, Great Britain to France. If your SSP is stopped on that ground, you should ask for an adjudication officer's decision and be prepared to appeal (see p47). You should argue that the regulations clearly intend that you should be able to

travel freely within the EC and that, otherwise, they would be contrary to EC law. [15]

If your period of entitlement ends before your period of incapacity, you will not be entitled to SSP until your current period of incapacity ends and a new one arises. In practice this means that at least eight weeks must pass between when you recover and when you fall ill again.

If you have received sickness, invalidity or maternity benefits or severe disablement allowance, you must also wait at least eight weeks from the end of your period of interruption of employment (see p203) before you can get SSP again.

Periods of entitlement with the same employer separated by eight weeks or less are linked and treated as a single period. [16] This is why it is possible not to have exhausted your 28 weeks' entitlement to SSP before the third anniversary of the beginning of your period of entitlement.

Periods of entitlement with different employers cannot usually be linked. However, on leaving a job you should be given a leaver's statement on form SSP1(L). Provided that you give this to your new employers within a week of your first qualifying day, the two periods *can* be linked. [17] This affects your maximum entitlement and, therefore, when you can transfer to invalidity benefit, which for most claimants is preferable to SSP.

'Qualifying days'

Qualifying days are usually those days of the week on which you would normally work if you were not sick. However, other days may be selected as qualifying days by agreement between you and your employer if that would provide a better reflection of your contract of employment (eg, you work a complicated shift pattern). There must be a minimum of one qualifying day in each week, which begins on a Sunday. [18] You and your employers can agree that the qualifying days be those normally worked, so there may be a different number in each week depending on your shift arrangements. Or you can average these out to give a constant pattern, say five days a week for two weeks, and four days a week for another two weeks. If there is no agreement as to which days are qualifying days, they are presumed to be:

- the days on which it is agreed that you are required to work; *or*
- Wednesday, if it is agreed that you are required to work no days in that week – eg, offshore oil-workers, who may work two weeks 'on' and then two weeks 'off'; *or*
- every day in the week except days where you and your employers agree that no employee works (if you can agree at least to that extent). [19]

'Required to work' means required by the terms of your contract of employment. [20] Days when you can choose whether to work or not do not count – eg, voluntary overtime shifts.

Informing your employer that you are sick

The form in which employers require you to notify them that you are sick is for them to decide, or for negotiation with you or your union. Most employers have their own rules for notification, which must be set out in the notice of terms and conditions of employment you should receive when you start work. They must take reasonable care to tell you what these are.[21] Notification should be in writing unless there is an agreement to the contrary.[22] As far as SSP is concerned the employers *cannot* insist on notification by you:

- personally;
- in the form of medical evidence (as opposed to a simple medical certificate);
- more than weekly;
- on a document provided only by the employers;
- on a printed form.[23]

You can also negotiate how quickly you have to notify the employers of your absence. For their own purposes many employers insist that they should be notified within the first hour, or in the morning, or some such other rule. For SSP purposes, however, employers cannot insist on notification before the end of the first qualifying day.[24] If there is no agreement, notification must be within seven days.[25]

Notice given in a properly addressed prepaid letter is deemed to have been given on the day the letter was sent.[26] A late claim must be accepted if there is 'good cause' for the delay, but not later than 91 days after the first day of absence. The effect of a late claim is to delay your entitlement – you will still get a total of 28 weeks' payment of SSP if you are off that long after your first valid day of absence.[27]

The DSS relies on employers to administer SSP, but if the employers are suspicious of a long period of illness they can ask the DSS's regional medical centre to arrange an examination (see below).

For occupational sick pay schemes most employers adopt the requirements for the sickness benefit scheme and accept self-certification for the first seven days, with medical certificates thereafter.

Amount of payment[28]

SSP is payable at two weekly rates, depending on your earnings.

Earnings £pw	SSP £pw
195 or more	52.50
56.00 to 194.99	46.95

Both rates of SSP are below the lower earnings limit (see p172), so you will not have to pay national insurance contributions. These will be credited to you (see p181) but you must claim them from the Benefits Agency by sending medical certificates to your local office as well as to your employer.

For the purpose of calculating SSP, earnings are normal gross weekly earnings averaged out over the eight weeks before the beginning of the period of entitlement.[29] Only payments *actually made* during the eight weeks are counted.[30] If you receive less than the relevant amount (£195 or £56) your SSP is calculated accordingly even if, in theory, you should have been paid more.

Example
You are paid £60 for 25 hours a week. You go on two weeks' annual leave (weeks 2 and 3). Your employers pay you two weeks' holiday pay in advance which you receive during week 1. You fall ill in week 10. Your SSP is based on the average wages *received* in weeks 2 to 9, so the total is £360, not £480. This is divided by 8 to give £45, not £60. So you get no SSP.

Previous payments of SSP count as earnings when working out your average.[31]

The daily rate[32] depends on your weekly earnings and the number of qualifying days you have in a week. Therefore if you are a shift worker and have perhaps six or seven qualifying days in a week you will qualify more quickly, but you will get less money for each day. This is irrelevant if you are off a full week after qualifying, as the weekly rate of SSP is the same.

If you cannot work, you are entitled to SSP from any employment where you fulfil the qualifications. So you could get payments of SSP for each of two contracts with the *same* employer (you might be both a day-time teacher and an evening tutor with an education authority), or payments from two separate employers. It is possible, at the same time, to be unable to work on one contract and be entitled to SSP, but be able to work on a different contract – if, for example, you perform quite different tasks, such as manual and clerical work.

SSP is usually paid in the same way as your normal wages or salary. If you have some form of sick pay arrangement with your employers, SSP forms part of your weekly pay.

It is not paid for the first three qualifying days in a period of incapacity (see p52). These are known as 'waiting days'.[33]

Your maximum entitlement to SSP in one period of entitlement is 28 times the weekly rate in any period of incapacity for work.[34]

Other benefits

You can claim income support from the Benefits Agency (and/or housing benefit and council tax benefit from your local authority) as well as SSP. Your net SSP payment is counted in full as a resource for these purposes.

A day which falls within a period of entitlement, even if you do not receive payment because it is not a qualifying day, cannot count as a period of interruption of employment for benefit purposes.[35] However, when SSP has run out, the next three days are automatically treated as part of a period of interruption of employment if you are unemployed or unfit to work. So you get unemployment, sickness or invalidity benefit immediately.[36] The time you are on SSP may count towards the 168 days you need to qualify for invalidity benefit (see p60).

Tax

SSP is treated like any other earnings and you pay tax and national insurance contributions by PAYE in the normal way.[37]

Disputes, references and appeals

You have the right to request the following information from your employers within a reasonable time:[38]

- the days which they regard as qualifying days – ie, the days you are entitled to SSP;
- the reason that SSP is not payable for other days;
- the daily rate of SSP.

Your employers can require you to provide 'such information as may reasonably be required' for the determination of your claim for SSP.[39]

The intention is that your employer should administer SSP without any involvement by the DSS, but you are not left entirely at your employer's mercy because you can ask for a decision by an adjudication officer if your employer decides you are not entitled.

Employers are given detailed guidance by the DSS in leaflet NI 270 *Employer's Manual on SSP* (see Appendix 5). If your employer is not satisfied that you are really incapable of work, s/he can ask you to attend a medical examination to help her/him decide whether you can work, but you are quite entitled to refuse and the examining doctor is unlikely to be wholly independent. Alternatively, an employer can ask for DSS help in deciding whether you are capable of work. Again, this can only be done with your consent but, since your employer could simply refuse payment, you are unlikely to gain much by not consenting. The DSS will only help your employer in this way if you have been off work for two or three months, if your doctor has written 'NAD' (no abnormality detected) on your medical certificates *or* if you have been off sick for less than a week (and so have not submitted a doctor's certificate) four times within the last 12 months. If the DSS does help, a doctor from the regional medical service of the Department of Health speaks to your doctor and you may be asked to attend an examination (see p46). Your employer is then simply given the regional medical officer's view as to whether you are capable of work but is not given any medical report or other explanation. It is still for your employer to decide whether to pay SSP.

If you are dissatisfied with your employer's decision, you should write to your local Benefits Agency office asking them to make a decision. Any question whether you are an employee is dealt with by the Secretary of State (see pp139 and 229).[40] Most other matters are referred to an adjudication officer either by employees or by the Secretary of State, who meets most of the cost of SSP and might, in a rare case, want to object to an employer's decision to pay you. [41] Your employer has no right to refer a case because s/he can simply refuse to make any payment. The time limit for referring a matter to an adjudication officer is six months for an employee but only three months for the Secretary of State. [42] You (or your employer or the Secretary of State) can appeal against the adjudication officer's decision to a social security appeal tribunal (see p243). [43]

If your employer does not pay you after an adjudication officer has decided that s/he is liable to do so, you can obtain payment from the Secretary of State instead. [44] The liability is also a debt enforceable in the county courts (sheriffs' courts in Scotland) and, in criminal proceedings, employers can be fined up to £400 for non-payment. [45]

3 Sickness benefit

Sickness benefit is important for those in jobs where SSP is not payable, or where you satisfy the contribution conditions but are not currently in employment.

Conditions of entitlement [1]

For every day you receive benefit:

* you must claim within the time limit (see p223); *and*
* you must be incapable of work (see p43); *and either*
* you have paid (or been credited with) enough contributions; *or*
* you became incapable of work because of an industrial injury or prescribed disease (see p130); *and*
* you are not entitled to SSP; *and*
* the day must be part of a 'period of interruption of employment' (see p203).

Amount of payment [2]

	Claimant under pensionable age £pw	Claimant of, or over, pensionable age £pw
Claimant	42.70	53.80
Adult dependant	26.40	32.30
Child dependant	–	10.95

The daily rate is one-sixth of the weekly rate.

There is an 'earnings rule' for the dependant's increase (see pp166-68). People over pensionable age may receive less than the standard amount if the contribution conditions are only partially satisfied (see p58). So does a local councillor whose net allowances exceed £42.00 a week (see p44). You receive national insurance credits while in receipt of sickness benefit (see p181).

Tax and other benefits

Sickness benefit is not taxable but is counted as an income resource for income support purposes. Sickness benefit overlaps with other personal benefits (see p209) payable to the claimant. Any dependant's addition overlaps with other personal benefits payable to the dependant.

Payment

Payment is by Girocheque, usually sent to your home address. Sickness benefit is usually paid weekly in arrears.[3] The first payment is made about ten days after your first claim or your first becoming entitled. Payment is continued until six months after your claim, after which you will receive invalidity benefit (see p60).

How to claim

The claim procedure differs slightly, depending on whether or not you are employed.

If you are not employed

You do not have to go to a doctor for a medical certificate for the first week of incapacity for work.[4] You fill in a self-certification form (SC1) which you can obtain from the Benefits Agency local office, your doctor's surgery or a hospital. You should send the completed certificate within the time limits to the Benefits Agency (see p223).

If you are employed

You should normally be paid SSP, and any payments you are entitled to from your occupational sick pay scheme, if there is one. If your employers think that you are excluded from receiving SSP for one of the reasons listed on pages 50-52 or if your entitlement to SSP has run out, they must give you form SSP1 which includes a claim form for sickness benefit. Send this to your local Benefits Agency office. If you disagree with your employers' decision you can refer the matter to the adjudication officer (see p56) but do not delay claiming sickness benefit while you do so.

People over pensionable age

You may still claim sickness benefit if you are over pensionable age but only if:

• you have deferred entitlement to a retirement pension (see p90); *and*
• you would have been entitled to a Category A (or, in the case of a widow or widower, a Category B) retirement pension if you had not done so.[5]

The standard amounts (see p57) will be reduced if the contribution conditions for the retirement pension are not satisfied in full (see p188).

The unequal treatment of men and women aged between 60 and 65 is unlawful under European Community law for the same reasons as in the case of unemployment benefit (see p38). If you would be better off being treated as a member of the opposite sex, appeal to a tribunal. Ask a local advice agency to contact CPAG's solicitors for further help.

Sickness benefit and statutory sick pay

You cannot receive sickness benefit *and* SSP at the same time. When your SSP ends, normally after 28 weeks, you will usually go on to invalidity benefit. If SSP is not payable, you will get sickness benefit, which is not affected by any payments from an occupational sick pay scheme. Your employers should give you a transfer form SSP1(T) if you are claiming sickness benefit after your SSP entitlement has run out. Send the form with medical certificates or similar evidence to the local office of the Benefits Agency. You may need to get your last medical certificate back from your employer if it covers a period after your SSP entitlement has ended. *Do not delay your claim while you do this.* It is better to claim sickness benefit immediately and tell the Benefits Agency that you are trying to get the certificate.

At the end of your claim for sickness benefit, you will be given a form by the Benefits Agency. Keep it (if you are not employed), or give it to your employers, because the 'linking rule' means that you will have to claim sickness benefit and not SSP if you are ill again within the next eight weeks.

Disqualification

You may be disqualified for up to six weeks for one of the reasons given below.[6] Normally an adjudication officer disqualifies you for the full period. The fact of disqualification or the period or both can be appealed against.

The reasons are:

- **You are incapable of work because of your own misconduct.** This is conduct which is blameworthy or wrong, and does not include playing dangerous sports and accidents. Involuntary alcoholism is not 'misconduct', but drunkenness is.[7]
- **You fail to attend a medical examination,** having had at least three days' notice in writing, unless you have good cause. In practice the Benefits Agency will not disqualify you if you tell them that you have a good reason for not attending. You may have good cause if the refusal to attend is based on a firm religious conviction.[8]
- **You do not take suitable treatment.** You are not required to subject yourself to 'invasive' treatment – eg, innoculation, vaccination or surgery (unless it is very minor). The Benefits Agency recognises that many people, perhaps irrationally, fear or mistrust such treatment and it has risks. You can refuse any other treatment if you can show that you have a genuine, albeit irrational, fear of it, or that you are allergic to a drug or an anaesthetic.

- **Without good cause you behave in a way which will slow down your recovery.**
- **Without good cause you go away from home** (eg, to stay at a friend's or relative's house) **without leaving word** with the Benefits Agency as to where you may be found. This is so you can be called to a medical examination if needed. Write to the Benefits Agency giving the period you will be away, and where you are going.
- **You work** (except in the circumstances described on page 44).

4 Invalidity benefit

Invalidity benefit is the general term used to describe invalidity pension and invalidity allowance. The basic benefit is invalidity pension and, if you meet the relevant conditions, you may qualify for invalidity allowance as well.

Conditions of entitlement[1]

For each day you receive benefit:

- you must be incapable of work (see p43); *and*
- the day must be part of a 'period of interruption of employment' (see p203); *and either*
- you must have been entitled to sickness benefit, or maternity allowance for 168 days within the period of the interruption of employment; *or*
- you are deemed to have done so because you have received statutory sick pay (SSP) instead and satisfy the other conditions (see p56); *or*
- you qualify as a widow or widower (see p63).

If you are receiving sickness benefit you will be transferred automatically to invalidity benefit.

Amount of payment[2]

Invalidity pension

	£pw
Claimant	56.10
Adult dependant	33.70
Child dependant	10.95

In addition to invalidity pension, you may also receive an additional sum based on your earnings under the state earnings related pension scheme (SERPS) (see p189).

A reduced rate may be payable if you are over pensionable age (see p173) or you are a local councillor and your net allowances exceed £42.00 a week (see p44).

A Christmas bonus is paid to those on invalidity pension (see p213). You will also be entitled to national insurance credits (see p181).

The earnings rule in respect of a spouse is more generous than for sickness benefit (see p166). This means that if your spouse was earning too much to entitle you to an increase of sickness benefit, you may nevertheless be entitled to an increase of invalidity pension. You must make a separate claim for the increase. If you do not claim it within a month, you will find that only a month's arrears are paid unless you had 'good cause' for the late claim (see p224).

Invalidity allowance

This is payable on top of your invalidity pension if you are under 60 (men) or 55 (women) on the first day of incapacity for work in your period of interruption of employment (see p10). The amount is dependent on how young you were on that date.[3]

Men	Women	£pw
Under 40	Under 40	11.95
40-49 inclusive	40-49 inclusive	7.50
50-59 inclusive	50-54 inclusive	3.75

A commissioner has decided that the discrimination against women aged between 55 and 60 is unlawful under European Community law.[4] For advice on what to do if you are a woman who became incapable of work between the ages of 55 and 59 (inclusive) see page 64.

The amount of invalidity allowance is reduced by the amount of any pension you receive under SERPS, or its equivalent if you are 'contracted-out' of SERPS.

Tax and other benefits

Invalidity benefit is not taxable. It counts in full for income support purposes, though you will qualify for a disability premium or higher pensioner premium.

For five years, between 65 and 70 for a man or 60 and 65 for a woman, you can defer entitlement to retirement pension (see p90) and thus keep invalidity benefit. The advantage of this is that invalidity benefit is not taxable while retirement pension is. You should carefully consider the relative merits of each course of action if you are in this position. Note that you will *not* gain an increased retirement pension by deferring entitlement (see p91) if you are receiving invalidity benefit.

If you were receiving invalidity allowance in the eight weeks before reaching pensionable age, it will be added to your retirement pension.[5]

If you stop claiming invalidity benefit and try to go back to work but are unsuccessful, your period of interruption of employment will not end as long as you claim invalidity benefit again within two years and you have been continuously entitled to disability working allowance (see CPAG's *National Welfare Benefits Handbook*) in the meantime.[6] This means that you will not have to wait another 168 days before getting invalidity benefit again.

Invalidity benefit and statutory sick pay

A day for which you receive SSP cannot usually count as part of a period of interruption of employment.[7] However, for the purposes of satisfying the 168-day qualifying period for invalidity benefit, any week when you received a whole week's SSP counts as six days of entitlement to sickness benefit.[8] Odd days can also count depending on the number of days a week you usually worked. These rules only apply if you are no longer entitled to SSP and the first day of a period of interruption of employment was within 57 days of your last day of entitlement to SSP.[9]

Note also that a day when you received SSP cannot be treated as a day of entitlement to sickness benefit if it was before the first day on which you would have satisfied the contribution conditions for sickness benefit (see p186).[10]

Entitlement to invalidity allowance depends on your age on the first day of entitlement to SSP that can be treated as a day of entitlement to sickness benefit.[11]

Payment

Invalidity benefit continues to be payable for any days of incapacity within the same period of interruption of employment until you reach pensionable age (65 for a man, 60 for a woman).[12] See below for circumstances in which it may be paid to people over pensionable age. You will be paid by an order book or, if your doctor is giving you medical certificates for periods of less than eight weeks, by weekly Girocheques. Invalidity benefit cannot be paid by credit transfer into a bank account.

People over pensionable age

If you are over pensionable age, you are entitled to invalidity benefit only if you have deferred entitlement to retirement pension (see p90) and would have been entitled to a Category A (or, in the case of a widow or widower, a Category B) retirement pension if you had not deferred entitlement.[13] The amount of your benefit will be reduced if the amount of your retirement pension would have been reduced due to an inadequate contribution record (see p189). However, if you are incapable of work due to an industrial injury or disease, the minimum payment (including any additional pension) will be £56.00 a week.[14]

A commissioner has decided that the unequal treatment of men and women aged between 60 and 65 is unlawful under European Community law.[15] The DSS is appealing against this decision, but women claiming invalidity benefit who would be better off if they were male (including also women aged between 55 and 59 who are refused invalidity allowance – see p61) should ask for the decision in their cases to be reviewed immediately. If you are entitled to a higher rate of benefit as a result of the commissioner's decision, the DSS is likely to continue to pay you at the old rate until the result of its appeal is known but there is a discretion to pay you at the higher rate in the meantime if to continue to pay at the old rate would cause you exceptional hardship.[16] If you think this applies to you, you should write to your local Benefits Agency office and explain why.

Special rules for widows and widowers

Widows and widowers may be paid invalidity pension even if they were not entitled to sickness benefit first.

A widow is entitled if:[17]

- she was not entitled to widowed mother's allowance when her husband died, or her widowed mother's allowance has run out; *and*
- the period of interruption of employment (see p203) began before her husband died or her widowed mother's allowance ran out; *and*
- her husband died or her widowed mother's allowance ran out after 5 April 1979; *and*
- she receives no widow's pension or she receives a reduced widow's pension because of her age at the relevant time.

The invalidity pension paid to a widow will be either (a) the standard rate, or (b) an amount sufficient to take the total of invalidity pension and widow's pension (if any) up to the rate of widow's pension which the claimant would have received had her husband died when she was over the age of 55, whichever is higher.

A widower is entitled if his wife died after 5 April 1979 and either he was then incapable of work or he became incapacitated within 13 weeks of her death.[18]

There is no entitlement to invalidity pension until the claimant has been incapable of work for 168 days, although all or some of that period may be before the death of the spouse. Days in receipt of SSP count towards this period (see p56).

The invalidity pension paid to a widower will be either (a) the standard rate, or (b) an amount calculated in the way a widow's pension would have been calculated but on his wife's contribution record, whichever is the higher.

In either case, an additional pension may be payable under SERPS (see p189).

A widow or widower will not receive an invalidity pension under these provisions if already over pensionable age. But if you receive an invalidity pension and reach pensionable age while you are still incapable of work, you will get a Category A retirement pension at the same rate as your invalidity pension, unless you are entitled to a higher retirement pension on your contribution record.[19]

The rule allowing a widow to claim more than 12 months arrears if she did not know of her husband's death applies to invalidity pension and Category A retirement pension claimed under these provisions in the same way as it applies to widows' benefits (see p83). So does the forfeiture rule (see p81).

Disqualification

The rules are the same as for sickness benefit (see p59).

At the end of your claim

You will be given a form by the Benefits Agency when you recover and go back to work, or sign on for unemployment benefit (if relevant), or for income support. Keep it (if you are unemployed), or give it to your employers, because if you fall sick again within eight weeks of the end of a previous period of interruption of employment (see p203) you claim invalidity benefit and not SSP. For most people it is better to have invalidity benefit as it has additions for dependants and is not taxable.

If you do go off work again within eight weeks your employers should give you form SSP1(E). This, with any medical certificates, should be sent to the local Benefits Agency.

5   Severe disablement allowance

Conditions of entitlement[1]

- You satisfy the residence conditions (see p194).
- You are incapable of work (see p43).
- You have been incapable of work for 196 consecutive days (see p65).
- Either the 196-day period began before your 20th birthday (see p66); *or* you are disabled to the extent of 80 per cent (see p67) and have been so disabled for 196 consecutive days; *or* you have previously been entitled to non-contributory invalidity pension (see p67).
- You are not under 16 (nor under 19 if you are in ordinary full-time education at a university, college, school or comparable institution – see p66).
- You are not over pensionable age (but see p66 for exceptions).

Amount of payment[2]

	£pw
Claimant	33.75
Adult dependant	20.15
Child dependant	10.95

An age-related addition is also payable if you are young enough. The amount depends on your age on the first day of the 196-day qualifying period.

Age	£pw
under 40	11.95
40-49 inclusive	7.50
50-59 inclusive	3.75

You will also be entitled to a Christmas bonus (see p213). If you are a local councillor, the amount of your benefit is reduced by the amount by which your net councillor's allowances exceed £42.00 in any week (see p44).

A common problem is that older married women are not getting the correct age addition. A woman may have been incapable of work for many years but unable to claim a non-contributory invalidity pension (the benefit which was replaced by severe disablement allowance) because of the discriminatory 'normal household duties' test (see p67). The Benefits Agency often treats the 196-day period as beginning immediately before a woman's claim for severe disablement allowance. This is wrong. If you can prove that you have been continuously incapable of work before your 40th or 50th birthday, whether or not you claimed benefit then, you may be entitled to a higher age addition than the one you are getting. You should apply for leave to appeal late (see p244) and, if you are unsuccessful, seek a review (see p230). If you claimed a non-contributory invalidity pension, but were turned down because of the 'normal household duties' test, the Benefits Agency may have documents on file which will prove when you became incapable of work. If not, you may need to rely on the evidence of your doctor and of family or friends.

Tax and other benefits

Severe disablement allowance is not taxable. It counts as an income resource in full for income support purposes but will qualify you for a disability premium or higher pensioner premium. There are special rules for 16- and 17-year-olds[3] who receive severe disablement allowance and who also claim income support, which mean your income support will be paid at the higher 18- to 24-year-old rate. Together with the disability premium this means that your income support may exceed your severe disablement allowance and you will be paid the difference as income support. The Benefits Agency often overlooks this point. If you are refused income support, appeal and seek advice.

If you stop claiming severe disablement allowance and try to go back to work but are unsuccessful, your period of interruption of employment will not end as long as you claim it again within two years and you have been continuously entitled to disability working allowance (see CPAG's *National Welfare Benefits Handbook*) in the meantime.[4] This means that you will not have to wait another 196 days before getting severe disablement allowance again.

You are not entitled to severe disablement allowance for any day which falls within a period of entitlement to SSP (see p52).[5]

Calculating the 196 days

The 196 days must be consecutive, and for this purpose Sundays count, so that 196 days is 28 weeks. Days spent in prison or other detention in legal custody cannot count towards these 196 days.[6]

People over pensionable age

Under British legislation you are excluded from severe disablement allowance if you are over pensionable age, unless you were entitled to it or to non-contributory invalidity pension immediately before reaching that age (or you would have been but for the rules about 'overlapping'[7] (see p209)). However, this has been held to be contrary to European Community law because it involves sex discrimination (although the Secretary of State is challenging this decision in the European Court). [8]

Therefore both men and women can claim severe disablement allowance up to the age of 65 simply by satisfying the usual conditions. If you are over 65, the position is more complicated but see page 64 for a suggestion as to how the law works, as the rules for invalid care allowance are exactly the same.

When you reach pensionable age, you might become entitled to sickness benefit and then invalidity benefit instead of severe disablement allowance. That is because your contribution record may not have been good enough for you to qualify for sickness benefit when you were under pensionable age but it may be good enough when you are over that age because the contribution conditions are different (see p186).

Full-time education[9]

The exclusion of those in full-time education applies only to those aged *under* 19. Full-time education means 21 or more hours a week. In calculating the 21 hours, any special education or tuition designed for those with a physical or mental disability is ignored. [10] Temporary interruptions of education are disregarded. Periods of private study are also not included in the 21-hour limit.

Routes to qualifying

Severe disablement allowance is paid only if you are both incapable of work (having been incapable for 196 days) *and.*you satisfy one of three further qualifying conditions:

- you were under 20 when your 196 days of incapacity started;
- you have a disablement which is assessed at 80 per cent or above;
- you were previously entitled to non-contributory invalidity pension.

You were under 20 when incapacity started

If your 196 days of incapacity started before your 20th birthday and you are still incapable of work, you can qualify without satisfying further conditions about your disablement. You can still qualify by this route if you broke your period of incapacity (eg, by trying a job) in your late teens or early twenties. You will be allowed the benefit of this provision if: [11]

- you were incapable of work for one complete period of 196 days which started before your 20th birthday; *and*

- you have now been incapable of work for 196 days again; *and*
- the gap between these two periods is less than 182 days in aggregate; *and*
- the gap started when you were older than 15 years and 24 weeks.

Disablement assessed at 80 per cent

Appendix Two sets out the rates of disablement that have been adopted in the industrial injuries scheme. They apply to severe disablement allowance as well.[12] For instance, 80 per cent disablement is the equivalent of the amputation of a leg close to the hip or an arm close to the shoulder. The difficulty is that many claimants are likely to have less defined disabilities. The guidance given on pages 136-38 about the assessment of disablement for disablement benefit purposes applies equally to severe disablement allowance. You should apply if you think that your illness or disability is severe. The 'disablement questions' (ie, the extent of your disablement and the period to be covered by your assessment) are decided by the adjudicating medical authorities (see p229). You can appeal to a medical appeal tribunal (see p247).

In a wide variety of circumstances you are 'deemed' to satisfy the 80 per cent rule. You are automatically regarded as 80 per cent disabled for the purposes of the allowance if:

- you receive the higher or middle rate of disability living allowance care component (see p108), the higher rate of disability living allowance mobility component (see p101), attendance allowance or war pensioner's mobility supplement;
- you have previously been assessed for industrial injuries purposes or a war disablement pension as 80 per cent disabled;
- you are receiving a vaccine damage payment;
- you are registered blind or partially sighted, or have an invalid tricycle or car allowance from the DSS.[13]

Previous entitlement to non-contributory invalidity pension

Non-contributory invalidity pension was a benefit replaced by severe disablement allowance in November 1984. Entitlement to it did not depend on your being 80 per cent disabled *provided* you were incapable of work.[14] Nor did entitlement depend upon a claim having been made.[15] However, at the time, married women and women living with men as husband and wife were obliged by British legislation to show that they were not only incapable of work but were also incapable of performing normal household duties. That discrimination has been held to have been unlawful under the law of the European Community.[16]

You are entitled to severe disablement allowance now if you were entitled to non-contributory invalidity pension immediately before both 10 September 1984 and 29 November 1984, and your present claim falls within the same period of interruption of employment.[17] It is not necessary for you to show that you were receiving benefit at the time but you will not obtain more than a year's arrears of benefit if you make a claim now.

Married or cohabiting women who were refused, or did not claim, [18] non-contributory invalidity pension or severe disablement allowance because of the old (discriminatory) rules may establish entitlement to severe disablement allowance now if:

- you were incapable of work for 196 days before both 10 September 1984 and 29 November 1984; *and*
- you have been incapable of work ever since then except for gaps of less than eight weeks.

If these apply to you but you did not claim non-contributory invalidity pension, you should still get benefit for the future and at least 12 months' arrears. It is possible that you will also be entitled to arrears going back to November 1984 but these will not be paid until after a case now going to the European Court of Justice[19] has been decided. Details of developments on this case will be published in the *Welfare Rights Bulletin* as soon as they are available. Ask your adviser to contact CPAG's Citizens' Rights Office for further details.

If you did make a claim before then you can either seek leave to appeal out of time (see p244) against the old refusal of benefit or, alternatively, apply for a review (see p230) of that decision. On a review only 12 months' arrears of severe disablement allowance will be paid pending the European Court's decision, whereas on a late appeal arrears will be paid back to the date of claim, and possibly 12 months before that if you had good cause for a late claim (see p224). However, a chair of a tribunal does not have to give you leave to appeal out of time.

Claims

A claim for the allowance should be made in writing to the local office as soon as you think the conditions are fulfilled. On your first claim, backdating of up to one month can be allowed,[20] or up to a year if you had good cause for the delay (see p224). DSS leaflet NI252 incorporates a claim form. Mentally handicapped people aged 16 and over are a large category of claimants of this benefit. The benefit can be claimed on their behalf by another adult where they are not able to make the claim themselves (see p222). When a claim is submitted late, the question is whether the claimant, ie, the mentally handicapped person, had good cause for being late and not whether the person acting for her/him had good cause for being late unless someone had been *formally* appointed to act for her/him (see p226). The 80 per cent disablement test is referred to the adjudicating medical authorities (see p229).

If you have at one stage been receiving severe disablement allowance, you can make a further claim during the same period of interruption of employment. Provided you have become incapable of work again, you do not have to satisfy the principal conditions of a further 196 days of incapacity or 80 per cent disablement. [21]

Disqualification

The rules are the same as for sickness benefit (see p59). [22]

CHAPTER FOUR

Maternity pay and benefits

This chapter covers:

1 Statutory maternity pay
2 Maternity allowance

In April 1987 statutory maternity pay (SMP) was introduced on the same lines as statutory sick pay, and maternity allowance has faded in importance. Maternity grants were abolished, but those receiving income support or family credit may be entitled to a £100 payment per child from the social fund (see CPAG's *National Welfare Benefits Handbook*).

If you do not qualify for SMP and maternity allowance, perhaps because you have a difficult pregnancy and are away from work for more than 18 weeks, you may be entitled to one of the benefits described in Chapter 3.

1 Statutory maternity pay

Conditions of entitlement[1]

To receive statutory maternity pay (SMP) for any day, you must:

- be an employee, who is not excluded from the scheme (see p72);
- be employed for at least one day in the 'qualifying week' (see below) and have been continuously employed by the same employers for at least 26 weeks ending with that week;[2]
- have given your employers the appropriate notice and information (see p73);
- satisfy the earnings condition (see p74);
- not do any work for the employers paying you SMP;
- not work for other employers after the birth;
- be expecting a child within 11 weeks, or have recently given birth.

SMP is the minimum amount of wages that the law requires employers to pay during maternity leave. Many groups of employees have negotiated better rates of pay, or periods of entitlement. Your trade union representative should be able to tell you your rights, or the personnel department should give you the basic information. Your written particulars of employment might contain notes of your entitlement. *You do not have to return to work with the same employers in order to qualify for SMP.*

'One week' is defined as the period of seven days beginning at midnight between Saturday and Sunday.[3]

The 'qualifying week' is the 15th week before the week in which your child is expected.

Amount of payment

SMP is paid by your employer, not the Benefits Agency. There are two rates of SMP depending on how long you have been in paid employment.[4]

The higher rate is nine-tenths of your average weekly earnings and is paid for the first six weeks of SMP for which you qualify.[5] After this, you will receive the lower rate.[6] These earnings are calculated over the eight weeks immediately before the qualifying week (see above).[7] The problem is that if your earnings are low for any reason, such as short-time working, sickness or lay-off, you may fail to qualify. You are entitled to this higher rate if you have been working for your employers *either*:

- full-time (16 or more hours a week for at least two years) ending with the qualifying week (see p70); *or*
- part-time (at least eight but under 16 hours for at least five years) ending with the qualifying week (see p70).[8]

After the first six weeks on the higher rate (or for the full period if you are not entitled to the higher rate) you will receive the lower rate, currently £47.95 a week.[9]

As with statutory sick pay (SSP), if you satisfy the conditions with more than one employer, you can get SMP from each of them. You do not have to give up both jobs at the same time if you feel fit enough to carry on with one of them, because, for instance, it is less physically demanding than the other.

Tax and other benefits

SMP is treated as earnings and you pay tax and national insurance contributions as appropriate.[10] The lower rate is below the lower earnings limit so, unless your employers add to it, you do not pay national insurance contributions on it and, if you claim, you will be credited with a contribution for each week of your maternity pay period (see p180). If you have insufficient income after SMP is paid to you, you may claim income support. Alternatively, claim family credit, if you have a partner working over 16 hours a week and have at least one child already. SMP is counted in full as income for calculating income support and family credit.

You cannot get SMP for the same day as either SSP, unemployment benefit, sickness benefit or maternity allowance. SSP is not payable for any day in a maternity pay period. This period is not part of a period of interruption of employment (see p202),[11] but the maternity pay period can count towards the qualifying period for invalidity benefit if:

- you are suffering from a disease of disablement which would have made you incapable of work (see p43) even if you had not also been pregnant; *and*
- immediately before your maternity pay period began you were entitled to SSP or sickness benefit (or would have been entitled to sickness benefit if you had claimed it).

If you become entitled to invalidity benefit during the maternity pay period as a result of these rules, your invalidity benefit will be reduced by the amount of your SMP. [12]

Payment and periods of entitlement

SMP is usually paid in the same way as your normal wage or salary. [13] It cannot be paid in kind or by way of services or the provision of lodgings. You should not have to collect it in person and it is not paid in a lump sum but according to your normal wage payment periods – weekly, monthly etc. The maximum period of payment of SMP is 18 weeks, known as the 'maternity pay period'. [14]

Rules specifying when the maternity pay period starts and ends are complex. There is a core period of 13 weeks which starts with the sixth week before the week in which the baby is due. The other five weeks can be taken before or after the core period, or partly before and partly after, depending on when you finish work. So, the earliest at which you can take maternity leave to obtain your full SMP is 11 weeks before the expected week of confinement, and the latest is six weeks. [15]

Therefore if you intend to claim the maximum entitlement to SMP, your last working week should be at least six weeks before the expected week of confinement. If you work for a week or part of a week after this you will lose SMP for that time. It is entirely up to you when you give up work and start to draw SMP.

The maternity pay period starts with the week after you stop work or the sixth week before expected confinement, whichever is earlier. Therefore the earliest time you can give up work and then claim SMP is the last day of the twelfth week before the baby is due. Your SMP will start the next week, that is the eleventh. [16]

If you prolong your work to the last possible date before the SMP period starts, you will be entitled to SMP till 11 weeks after the expected week of confinement (ie, six weeks before *plus* the week of confinement *plus* 11 weeks after = 18 weeks). [17]

If you work for another employer before your confinement, your entitlement to SMP is unaffected. However, if you work for another employer after your confinement you will usually lose your entitlement to SMP for the rest of your maternity pay period, even if you stop working again. [18] The only exception to this rule arises if the other employer is one for whom you were working immediately before the 'qualifying week' (see p70) but who is not liable to pay you SMP. Working for such an employer does not affect your entitlement to SMP at all. [19]

Employers, employees and excluded employees

An employee is a person who either pays, or should pay, Class 1 national insurance contributions [20] (see p176). Employers are the persons or firm paying national insurance contributions for you. [21]

Employers cannot restrict your right to SMP by their own rules or 'contract' with you – it is a right established by statute. Nor can employers require you to contribute towards the cost of SMP.[22] They cannot avoid liability by dismissing you once you have qualified for SMP. They are also liable if they dismiss you before you qualify and dismissal was 'solely or mainly' to avoid paying SMP. Provided you were employed for eight weeks or more by that employer, you are deemed to be entitled to SMP.[23]

The only employees excluded from entitlement are those who:

• have normal gross earnings below the lower earnings limit (currently £56 a week);
• go abroad, outside the EC;
• are in legal custody, eg, prison.[24]

If your employers think that you are in an excluded group they will give you a completed form SMP1 and return your maternity certificate. This allows you to claim the benefit known as maternity allowance (see p60). You can challenge the employers' decision (see p74).

If you are not entitled to either SMP or maternity allowance, you will be regarded as incapable of work and may be entitled to sickness benefit for at least the period beginning six weeks before the baby is expected until two weeks after the date of birth.[25]

Notification and information

You must give your employers details of the expected date of birth and notice of when you intend to stop work.[26] The details of the expected date of birth are on form MAT B1 which you will be given by your GP, clinic or midwife. Your employers need to see this certificate, or a copy, to work out your SMP, and you have to provide this within three weeks of the start of the maternity pay period. To ensure that you are eligible to return to work you should also tell the employers, in writing, that you do intend to return. You have a statutory right to return to work if you have been employed until the start of the eleventh week before the expected date of confinement and have, at that time, been continuously employed by your employer for at least two years. You may also have more favourable terms about returning to work under your contract than the statutory rules allow.

If you do not have form MAT B1 the employers can require, or accept, other medical evidence. The time limit for presenting this is extended to the end of the thirteenth week if you have good cause for the delay.[27]

You must give your employers your notice of leaving at least 21 days before you mean to stop work, or as soon as practicable after that.[28] It is up to your employers to say what form such notice should take – most require it in writing. If you are late handing it in the employers must decide whether your reason for delay is acceptable. If they do not accept your reason you can challenge that decision (see p74).

You have to keep your employers informed of any change of circumstance (eg, going abroad) which may affect your entitlement and you *must* tell your employers if you start working for someone else.[29]

If you are requested to supply information by the local office of the

Benefits Agency, in the name of the Secretary of State, you must do so within ten days or risk prosecution. [30]

Notification to employers or the Benefits Agency counts once it is put in the post. [31]

Disputes and appeals

If you consider that you are owed SMP by an employer or you are paid an amount you consider wrong, you can ask them for a written statement showing:

- if SMP has been refused, the reason why;
- if SMP is being paid, how many weeks they consider it should be paid for, and the amount they will pay. [32]

If you disagree with either part of the statement you should ask the adjudication officer at the local Benefits Agency office to give you a ruling on the question. Employers cannot seek a ruling, although they can ask an adjudication officer for advice. The adjudication officer will ask both sides to put their case in writing. Take care to deal with the main points logically and clearly. When the adjudication officer gives a decision both sides have a right to appeal to a social security appeal tribunal (see p241). If the tribunal finds in your favour and the employers do not pay, or become insolvent, the Secretary of State may make the payments in default. [33]

Before applying to the adjudication officer you should consult your trade union representative, and try to resolve the problem using the grievance procedure if there is one, but you must not leave it for more than six months from the first day which is in dispute or you will lose your right to have the adjudication officer make the decision.

The earnings condition [34]

To qualify for SMP your average weekly earnings for the period of eight weeks (up to the last pay day before the end of the qualifying week – see p70) must be at least the lower earnings limit for national insurance contributions (currently £56). In calculating your average weekly gross earnings, your employers must take into account bonuses, overtime, SSP and any other earnings. [35] Gratuities (tips) and money paid from a holiday fund, or from a trust scheme, or through a profit-sharing scheme are excluded. [36]

Continuous employment rule [37]

You must have worked for your employers for a continuous period of 26 weeks including at least one day in the qualifying week (see p70). Periods when you were previously on maternity leave, sickness benefit or SSP, away from work, or on short-time working all count. [38] A strike does not break your continuity of employment, but nor does it count towards the 26 weeks. [39] If your employment is transferred from one employer to another as a result of a commercial deal, or you are transferred from one local authority or health service employer to another (and in certain other circumstances), your employment is unbroken.[40] The rules are broadly the same as those for calculating continuous employment when looking at redundancy pay and unfair dismissal.

What happens if your baby is born early?[41]

If your baby is born before your expected date of confinement your SMP rights may change.

- If you have your baby after you have started your maternity pay period, SMP is not affected even if the birth is earlier than you expected.
- If your baby is born more than 11 weeks before the week in which it was expected, your maternity pay period will begin the following week. You must give your employers notification of the date of confinement within 21 days or as soon as practicable. The eight weeks for satisfying the earnings condition are the last eight weeks before the week of the birth. You satisfy the continuous employment rule if you would have done so had the baby been born on the expected date.
- If your baby is born less than 11 weeks before the week in which it was expected, but before your maternity pay period was due to start (because you had not given notice to your employers, or had told them that you would not be giving up work till later), the normal rules apply. However, you must give your employer notice of your confinement within 21 days.

If the birth takes place earlier than expected, it does not entitle you to more than the 18 weeks' maximum period of SMP – the maternity pay period simply starts, and ends, sooner (see p72). You can go on to SSP or sickness benefit, if you are still off for medical reasons at the end of the period.

Multiple or stillbirths

No additional SMP is payable if you are expecting or giving birth to more than one baby.

If a stillbirth occurs after 24 weeks of pregnancy, SMP is payable in the same way as for a live birth.[42] If earlier, SMP is not payable but SSP or sickness benefit may be while you are incapable of work.

2 Maternity allowance

You cannot get SMP if you have recently given up or changed your job, or have been self-employed, but you may get maternity allowance.

Conditions of entitlement[1]

- You satisfy the contribution condition (see p186).

- You are either expecting a child within the next 11 weeks, or else have recently given birth (see p75).
- You are not working. [2]
- You have been employed for at least 26 weeks in the year (52 weeks) ending at the end of the 'qualifying week' (see below).

The 'qualifying week' is the same as for SMP. But, unlike SMP, the period of 26 weeks need not be continuous and you do not have to have worked for the same employer for the whole of that period.

Amount of payment [3]

	£pw
Claimant	43.75
Adult dependant	26.40

Tax and other benefits

Maternity allowance is non-taxable but is taken into account when calculating income support. Once you are within the maternity allowance period (see below) in your pregnancy, you can receive income support without having to be available for work.

You are not entitled to SSP during the maternity allowance period. If you are already claiming SSP when you reach this period, your employers should give you form SSP1(T) explaining that you are no longer entitled. If you continue to work into the maternity allowance period and fall sick, your employers should give you form SSP1(E) explaining that you are excluded from entitlement to SSP (see p51).

You cannot receive maternity allowance for any week when you are entitled to SMP. [4]

Any day within the maternity allowance period (see below) counts as a day of incapacity for work for the purposes of making a period of interruption of employment [5] (see p202). This may help you later when claiming sickness or unemployment benefit.

Period of payment

The allowance is payable for 18 weeks. The earliest it can start is from the beginning of the eleventh week before the week of the expected birth. The period of 18 weeks is known as the 'maternity allowance period'. The rules for the calculation of the period, and late or early confinement, are the same as those for SMP [6] (see pp72 and 75).

How to claim

If you are working you may be entitled to SMP. You should claim from your employers. If your employers do not consider that you are entitled, they must give you form SMP1 with which you can claim maternity allowance.

You must normally provide a certificate from your doctor or midwife giving the expected date of birth of your child. [7]

If you have already stopped working by the beginning of the maternity allowance period, you should claim the allowance in the three weeks preceding the eleventh week before the expected date of birth. If you continue working after the beginning of the eleventh week before, you should claim as soon as you stop working. [8]

Widows' benefits

This chapter covers:

I Introduction

Entitlement to the three main widows' benefits depends on your late husband having satisfied the contribution conditions.

These contributory benefits are:

- **Widow's payment** – a lump-sum payment of £1,000.
- **Widowed mother's allowance** – a weekly benefit paid to widows who have children or who are pregnant.
- **Widow's pension** – a weekly benefit paid to widows who are aged at least 45 (formerly 40) when their husband dies or their widowed mother's allowance ceases.

Non-contributory benefits are paid only to the widows of men who were already aged 65 on 5 July 1948 – ie, you can only get them if your husband would now be 109 years old, were he still alive.

If your husband died as the result of an industrial accident or disease, you are treated as though he had satisfied the contribution conditions for the above benefits. This provision has replaced **industrial death benefit** for widows where husbands died after 10 April 1988, but industrial death benefit is still paid to the widows of those who died before 11 April 1988.

Widowhood

A widow is a woman who was married to a man at the date of his death.

If you were divorced, you are not a widow. It does not matter if you were living apart when your husband died as long as you were not divorced. A divorce becomes effective only when the decree absolute is pronounced. So, if you were in the process of obtaining a divorce and had obtained a decree nisi, you are still entitled to widows' benefits if your husband died before the decree was made absolute.

If your husband has disappeared and a court has decided that he has probably died, the adjudication officer will normally accept that you are a widow. Even without such a decision from a court, an adjudication officer may presume your husband to be dead if he has not been seen or heard of for seven years by those who would be expected to have seen or heard of him.[1]

A marriage which is 'void' (eg, a bigamous one) is treated as no marriage at all and so cannot give rise to any entitlement to widows' benefits even if it has not been annulled.[2]

A marriage which is 'voidable' (eg, one that has not been consummated) is treated as a marriage until a decree absolute of annulment is pronounced.[3] So, if your husband dies before your marriage is finally annulled, you may claim as his widow.

A marriage which is polygamous is treated as a marriage for the purposes of widows' benefits only if, at the time of the husband's death, neither party had any other spouse.[4]

Remarriage

If you remarry, you lose all entitlement to widows' benefits based on your first husband's contribution record. This is less favourable than the rule for cohabitation (see below) when widows' benefits are only suspended, not stopped altogether. If your second husband has also died, your entitlement to widows' benefits depends on your second husband's contribution record. If your second marriage was 'void' you are entitled to widows' benefits based on your first husband's contribution record once you have ceased cohabiting with your second husband. If your second marriage was voidable, you are entitled to widows' benefits on your second husband's contribution record if he died before decree absolute was pronounced. However, if a voidable second marriage is annulled, no widows' benefits are payable in respect of either husband's death.

If you remarried after 4 April 1971, you can still claim a Category B retirement pension based on your first husband's contributions, even though you cannot claim widows' benefits on them (see p97).

Cohabitation

You are not entitled to widows' benefits while you and a man to whom you are not married are living together as husband and wife. The benefits stop only during the period of cohabitation and are payable again if the cohabitation stops.[5]

Defining 'cohabitation' or 'living together as husband and wife' is complicated. The extreme positions are clear. The widow who lives with Mr Jones and calls herself Mrs Jones is likely to be cohabiting. So also are the man and woman who share their money, eat together, sleep together and spend most of their leisure time together. On the other hand, a widow who has a 'boyfriend' who stays with her two or three nights a week, but who has a separate address and does not eat with her regularly or contribute to the household fund, is unlikely to be cohabiting. A widow with a male lodger should not lose her benefit unless there is substantially more to the relationship than the provision of board and lodging for payment. Each case depends on its own circumstances.

'Living together as husband and wife'

Your benefit can be stopped only if you and the man with whom you are alleged to be cohabiting are 'living together as husband and wife'. The burden of proof lies on the adjudication officer. [6]

If the man has a different address which he regards as 'home', that is very strong evidence that you are not 'living together'. But living under the same roof does not necessarily involve 'living together' because 'living together' implies a common household. [7] So, if you keep separate stocks of food, do your cooking and washing separately, have separate televisions and so on, you are unlikely to be regarded as 'living together'. Sharing some facilities does not necessarily mean that you are 'living together'. It is a matter of degree.

Even if you are 'living together', it does not necessarily mean that you are 'living together as husband and wife'. It is still necessary for the adjudication officer to consider any sexual relationship, any financial relationship and your general relationship. [8]

The relevance of any sexual relationship

A sexual relationship is an important part of any marriage. So, if there has never been any sexual relationship between two people then that is strong evidence that they are not living together 'as husband and wife'. [9] If you are in this situation, it is important that you should tell the adjudication officer that you have never slept together because s/he will probably not ask you unless you bring the subject up first. Even though this may cause you some embarrassment, you may lose benefit which you ought to get if you do not let the adjudication officer know the true situation. If there is, or has been, a sexual relationship, that is evidence of the affection and trust between the parties. However, an occasional sexual relationship does not imply cohabitation if the rest of the relationship is casual and unlike a marriage.

The relevance of any financial relationship

It is not necessary for the adjudication officer to show that one party is supporting the other. For cohabitation the relationship should usually be such that one party would support the other *if necessary*. For that reason, you should borrow from someone other than your alleged cohabitee if you need money after your benefit is stopped, or at least make it quite clear that the money is a loan. Money lent out of friendship should not lead to a finding of cohabitation, but it can be misinterpreted.

The financial relationship between lodger and landlady often comes in for scrutiny. Adjudication officers sometimes say the payments are too high or too low and so indicate that the relationship is not purely financial. There are a number of things which can be said in reply. First, an adjudication officer seldom, if ever, produces any evidence of other charges made in private arrangements, so that an adjudication officer's idea of too high or too low is just one opinion. Second, many widows have no idea of what other landladies charge and merely charge enough to cover their expenses and provide something towards the mortgage repayments. They often do not increase charges to keep up with inflation. It is important to explain how the charge came to be as it is. However silly the charge may look in retrospect, it is the reasoning which led to it at the time which is important. Third, a widow may have many motives for having a lodger apart from purely commercial ones or cohabitation. She may well want another adult in the house to do occasional babysitting or simply to talk to. Friendship between lodger and landlady does not mean cohabitation.

Your general relationship
It is always most important to explain your general relationship because it provides the context for any sexual or financial relationship. You have to explain how you see each other. The extent to which you lead separate lives should be emphasised, with particular reference to other men friends and women friends. The way you organise the household is also relevant, and the reasons for doing it that way are even more important. If you have moved home together in the past, that will also have to be explained.

In one case, a disabled widow and a disabled widower who had been friends for years moved in together at the suggestion of a social worker who pointed out that they would have one rent to pay. They had never had a sexual relationship and did not share a bedroom but shared other accommodation. Household chores were managed jointly and meals and leisure were usually taken together. The widower paid the bills. These circumstances taken together were not sufficient to establish that the couple were living together as husband and wife. [10]

Died 'as a result of' an industrial accident or disease

For the meaning of industrial accident or disease, see pages 130-135.

The industrial accident or disease must have been a cause of death, but it need have been only one of several causes and need not have been a direct cause. [11]

If your husband died when entitled to constant attendance allowance at at least the lower weekly rate (see p141), he is deemed to have died as a result of the relevant injury or disease. This also applies if constant attendance allowance had been stopped solely because he was in hospital. [12]

Death is also deemed to have been due to the relevant disease if your husband was, at the time of his death, assessed as at least 50 per cent disabled due to pneumoconiosis or byssinosis and he died from a lung disease. [13]

The forfeiture rule

The forfeiture rule is a general rule of law which prevents people gaining anything from their own crimes. It prevents you from obtaining widow's benefit (or any other benefit based on your late husband's constributions) if you unlawfully killed your husband unless it is decided that it should not apply in your particular case.

Any question concerning the forfeiture rule is decided by a social security commissioner rather than an adjudication officer or tribunal (see p251). [14]

If you have been convicted of **murder**, the forfeiture rule *must* be applied and no widow's benefit is payable. [15] If you have been convicted of **manslaughter** or of some other offence or you have not been convicted at all, the commissioner *may* decide that the forfeiture rule may be modified so that you should lose only some benefit. S/he could decide that you should receive only part of your benefit or that benefit should be reduced or withheld for a limited period of time. [16]

The rule can be applied even if you have not been convicted of any offence but, if you have been charged with manslaughter and acquitted, you are unlikely to lose any benefit unless the acquittal was on a technicality or the jury did not hear all the evidence. [17]

A commissioner may direct that her/his decision should affect any future claim by you. [18] However, a decision on the forfeiture rule may be reviewed by a commissioner on the ground that there has been a change of circumstances. [19] A decision may also be reviewed on the ground that it was made in ignorance of, or was based on a mistake as to, a relevant fact. To apply for a review, write to one of the commissioners' offices (see p280).

Earnings

There is no limit to the amount you may earn while remaining entitled to widows' benefits.

Tax and other benefits

The lump-sum widow's payment is not taxable. Other widows' benefits are taxable apart from any increase in respect of children. [20]

There are special rules to help widows claim invalidity benefit (see p63) and retirement pensions (see p95). Widows are also entitled to credited contributions for some other purposes (see p183).

If you are entitled to a widow's benefit and invalidity benefit you may receive both basic benefits subject to a maximum of £56.10 a week. You are also entitled to both additional pensions under SERPS, subject to a maximum (equal to the amount one person could theoretically receive as an addition to one benefit). Usually, the widow's benefit is paid in full, with any additional benefit being paid as invalidity benefit. [21] However, as invalidity benefit is not taxable, it may be advantageous to apply for the full invalidity benefit, with widow's benefit merely topping it up. This also has the advantages that you will be entitled to a disability premium for the purposes of means-tested benefits – eg, income support, housing benefit and council tax benefit; and that you will be credited with Class 1 contributions (see p181).

Widows' benefits are counted in full as income for income support purposes.[22] If you are over 50 *and* have not worked for the last ten years *and* would not have been required to be available for work during that period (eg, because you were bringing up children), you are not required to be available for work as a condition of entitlement to income support, unless you have a real prospect of future employment.[23] As a single parent, a widowed mother receives an extra £4.90 a week income support, but one parent benefit is not payable if you receive widowed mother's allowance.[24]

If you receive income support, family credit, housing benefit or council tax benefit, you may be entitled to a grant for funeral expenses from the social fund. Your widow's payment is not treated as capital for this purpose.[25] Any such grant will be recovered from your husband's estate if there is enough money in it. For general practical advice about preparing funerals and registering deaths, obtain DSS leaflet D49, *What to Do After a Death*.

Claims and payments

You will usually have to provide the adjudication officer with your husband's death certificate and your marriage certificate. You get an extra copy of the death certificate for social security purposes when you register the death and, if you complete the form on the back, you will be sent the claim form for widows' benefits. Arrears will be paid up to a maximum of 12 months. Do not delay just because you do not have a certificate. Make sure you get your claim in within the 12-month period.

The 12-month limit on arrears will only be waived if:[26]

- you did not make a claim for widow's benefit before 13 July 1990; *and either*
- your husband's body has not been discovered or identified, *and*
  - an adjudication officer (or tribunal etc) has determined that he has died or is presumed to have died, *and*
  - you claimed widow's benefit within 12 months of that determination; *or*
- you did not know that your husband's body had been discovered or identified but you found out within 12 months of it having been identified *and*
  - you claimed widow's benefit within 12 months of your finding out about the identification.

Widow's benefit is then payable from the date of death or presumed death. This is useful where a marriage has broken down and a woman has lost touch with her husband, provided that either she finds out about his death within a year of his body being identified or the DSS has also lost track of him and it has to be presumed that he has died.

The benefits are normally paid weekly in advance, but widowed mother's allowance and widow's pension may be paid into your bank account four-weekly or quarterly in arrears if you prefer (see DSS leaflet NI105).

2 Widow's payment

Conditions of entitlement[1]

- Your husband satisfied the contribution condition (see p186); or
- your husband died as the result of an industrial injury or disease (see p81); and either
- you were under 60 when your husband died; or
- if you were 60 or over, he was not entitled to a Category A retirement pension when he died (eg, because he was under 65, or had deferred entitlement, or he had an inadequate contribution record); and
- you claimed within 12 months of his death.

Amount of payment

A lump sum of £1,000.[2] Widow's payment is not the same as a funeral grant from the social fund and if you are not receiving a means-tested benefit, you may be entitled to both. See CPAG's *National Welfare Benefits Handbook* for more about the social fund.

Disqualification

No payment is made if at the time of your husband's death you were living with another man as his wife (see p79).[3]

3 Widowed mother's allowance

Conditions of entitlement[1]

- *Either* your husband satisfied the contribution conditions (see p187); or
- your husband died as the result of an industrial injury or disease (see p81); and either
- you are expecting a child by your husband; or
- you are entitled to child benefit in respect of a qualifying child (see below); or
- you have residing with you a person under the age of 19 who would be a qualifying child for whom you would have been in receipt of child benefit if s/he had not been abroad at the relevant time. It may be sufficient that the person lives with you at weekends only, and a temporary absence does not matter even if it lasts several months.

Amount of payment[2]

	£pw
Claimant	56.10
Child dependant	10.95

An additional pension may be paid on top of the basic figure if your husband died after 5 April 1979 (see p188).

Increases in respect of child dependants are payable only if the children are qualifying children (see below) and the usual conditions are also met (see p169).

These are the standard weekly rates. You may receive less if your husband's contribution record was incomplete (see p188).

You are also entitled to a Christmas bonus (see p212).

The allowance is paid as long as your children qualify you for it. It ceases if you remarry, and is suspended during any period in which you are cohabiting (see p72).[3] You may become entitled to widow's pension after widowed mother's allowance ceases (see below).

'Qualifying children'

The following count as qualifying children:[4]

- a child of yourself and your late husband;
- a child for whom your husband was entitled to child benefit immediately before his death;
- if you were residing with your husband immediately before his death, a child for whom you were then entitled to child benefit.

If you have been twice widowed, your second husband is treated as having been entitled to child benefit in respect of a child if:[5]

- your first husband was entitled to child benefit for the child immediately before his death. (If you were living with him or being maintained by him and you were receiving child benefit, he is treated as having been entitled to it.); and
- you were entitled to child benefit for the child immediately before the death of your second husband.

4 Widow's pension

Conditions of entitlement[1]

- *Either* your husband satisfied the contribution conditions (see p187); *or*
- your husband died as the result of an industrial injury or disease (see p81); *and*
- you are not entitled to widowed mother's allowance; *and either*
- your husband died before 11 April 1988 and you were over 40 but under 65 either at the date of his death or when you ceased to be entitled to widowed mother's allowance (eg, because your children had grown up); *or*
- your husband died on or after 11 April 1988 and you were over 45 but under 65 either at the date of his death or when you ceased to be entitled to widowed mother's allowance; *and*
- you are still under 65.

Amount of payment

The basic rate is £56.10 a week. [2]

You may receive an additional pension based on your husband's earnings if you were widowed after 5 April 1979 (see p188).

The basic amount may be reduced if your husband had an incomplete contribution record (see p188).

If you were widowed after 10 April 1988, your pension is reduced if you were under the age of 55 when you first qualified for your pension. The amount of widow's pension you would otherwise receive is reduced by seven per cent for every year that you were under the age of 55 on the relevant date. [3] That proportion remains the same for as long as you continue to receive widow's pension.

Example

You would be entitled to £60 a week by way of basic and additional pension, and you were 49 when you ceased to be entitled to widowed mother's allowance. Your pension is reduced by

6 years $(55 - 49) \times 7\%$ of £60 pw $= 42\%$ of £60 pw $= £25.20$ pw

You receive £34.80 pw.

If you were widowed before 11 April 1988, the pension is reduced by seven per cent for every year that you were under 50 (instead of 55) at the relevant date. [4]

You will be entitled to a Christmas bonus (see p212).

The pension is paid for as long as the conditions are satisfied, but ceases if you remarry. It is suspended while you are living with a man as his wife (see p72). [5] When you reach pensionable age, you become entitled to a Category B retirement pension payable at the same rate as your widow's pension (see p96).

5   Non-contributory widows' benefits

Conditions of entitlement [1]

- Your husband was over 65 on 5 July 1948, ie, he would now be at least 109 years old; *and either*
- your husband was at some time entitled to a Category C non-contributory retirement pension (see p89); *or*
- he died before 2 November 1970 and you and he satisfied the residence conditions for such a pension (see p194).

Benefit corresponding to widowed mother's allowance [2]

Provided you satisfy the conditions set out above, this is payable if you would have been entitled to widowed mother's allowance but for your husband's failure to satisfy the contribution conditions. The rate of benefit is £33.70 a week plus £10.95 for each child dependant who is a qualifying child.

A Christmas bonus is payable (see p212).

Benefit corresponding to widow's pension[3]

Provided you satisfy the principal conditions set out above, this is payable if you are under 65 and were under 40 (45 if you were widowed after 10 April 1988) when your husband died or, if you were subsequently entitled to a non-contributory benefit corresponding to widowed mother's allowance, when you ceased to be so entitled.

The standard rate of pension is £33.70 a week but it is reduced by seven per cent for every year that you were under 50 (55 if you were widowed after 10 April 1988[4]) at the relevant date.

A Christmas bonus is payable (see p212).

6 Industrial death benefit for widows

If your husband died after 10 April 1988, you will not be eligible for industrial death benefit. However, if his death was due to an industrial accident or disease, he will be deemed to have satisfied the contribution conditions for widow's payment, widowed mother's allowance and widow's pension.

Conditions of entitlement[1]

- Your husband died before 11 April 1988; *and*
- your husband died as a result of an industrial accident or disease (see p81); *and either*
- you were 'residing with' (see p166) your husband when he died; *or*
- you were receiving periodical payments for your maintenance at the rate of at least 25 pence a week (or would have been but for the accident or onset of the disease); *or*
- although you were not actually receiving such payments, you were entitled to receive them because of a court order, trust or agreement which you had taken reasonable steps to enforce. [2]

Amount of payment

Benefit is paid at two different rates. The **higher permanent rate**[3] is £56.10 a week and is payable if:

- you are entitled to industrial death benefit in respect of a child (see p159); *or*
- you are residing with a person under 19; *and either*
  - your husband was, at the time of his death, entitled to child benefit for that person; *or*

- he would have been entitled to child benefit if that person had been under 16 or not been abroad; *or*
- you were over 50 when your husband died; *or*
- you were over 40 when you ceased to be entitled to industrial death benefit for a child, or you ceased to reside with a person under 19 as above; *or*
- you were permanently incapable of self-support when your husband died.

The **lower permanent rate**[4] is £16.83 a week and is payable if you do not qualify for the higher permanent rate.

You will be entitled to a Christmas bonus (see p212).

Disqualification

You cease to be entitled if you remarry and the benefit is suspended if you are living with a man as husband and wife (see p72).[5]

If you have children residing with you, cohabitation does not affect your right to receive industrial death benefit in respect of them (see p153). Remarriage, however, does.

CHAPTER SIX

Retirement pensions

This chapter covers:

1 Introduction
2 Category A retirement pension
3 Category B retirement pension for a married woman
4 Category B retirement pension for a widow
5 Category B retirement pension for a widower
6 Category D retirement pension
7 Graduated retirement benefit

I Introduction

There are three main categories of retirement pension.

* **Category A** retirement pension is payable on *your* contribution record.
* **Category B** retirement pension is payable on your *spouse's* contribution record. There are different conditions depending on whether you are a married woman, a widow or a widower.
* **Category D** retirement pension is a non-contributory pension payable to those over 80.

The vast majority of male pensioners receive Category A retirement pensions. Women usually receive either Category A or Category B retirement pensions or both.

Category C retirement pensions are non-contributory pensions which are paid to:[1]

* men who are at least 109 years old; *and*
* women who are at least 104 years old *or* who are married to (or in some cases divorced from) a man who is at least 109 years old *or* who are widows and whose husbands would now be at least 109 years old if they had lived.

Given these rules (and the fact that there is also a residence test) not many people now qualify. If you think you might be one of them, please see the 15th edition of this guide. The current rates for the pension are set out in the table at the beginning of this book.

Pensionable age and retirement

To get a retirement pension:

* you must have reached 'pensionable age'. Pensionable age is 65 for a

man and 60 for a woman.[2] This rule discriminates on grounds of sex but is not contrary to EC law (see p201);
- you must claim (see below). You do not automatically become entitled to your retirement pension just by reaching pensionable age. If you do not claim you will be treated as having 'deferred' your retirement (see below). If you are getting invalidity benefit or severe disablement allowance you should take advice before claiming (see p61) but do not wait for more than a year after reaching pensionable age before making a decision or you may lose out (see below);
- you do *not* have to retire. You can choose whether or not to give up work. If you decide to go on working your earnings will not reduce the pension you receive (although if your spouse is still working you may not be able to get an increase in your pension for her/him (see p167)).

Claiming your retirement pension

A claim should be made within 12 months of your becoming entitled to the pension. If you claim later, only 12 months' arrears will be paid.[3]

Claims for retirement pensions may be made up to, but no more than four months in advance.[4] You should take full advantage of this provision as it takes a long time to sort out your contribution position. Normally the Benefits Agency will send you an application form about four months before you reach pensionable age. If you have not received a form three months before you want to receive the pension, ask for one.

If the DSS tells you that you have not paid enough contributions, you may still be able to get your pension if you make up the missing contributions now. The DSS does not always tell you this, so it is worth asking specifically whether or not this rule applies to you.

Payments

Payments are usually made by giving you a book of orders which you may cash weekly in advance. However, you can choose to be paid by direct credit transfer into a bank account either four-weekly or quarterly in arrears if you prefer, in which case you should obtain a copy of Benefits Agency leaflet NI105 and complete the form attached to it.

Deferring your retirement pension

During the first five years after you reach pensionable age, you are allowed to defer entitlement to a Category A or Category B retirement pension. In return for doing so, you later become entitled to a higher rate of pension.

For each week you defer entitlement, the pension you eventually receive is increased by one-seventh of one per cent.[5] The same applies to graduated retirement benefit (see p99).[6] This means that, if you defer entitlement for the whole five-year period, you will then receive slightly over 37 per cent extra retirement pension each week.

The benefits which are increased in this way include any additional pension under the state earnings related pension scheme (SERPS), an invalidity increase and any increase resulting from your late spouse's deferment, but not increases for dependants or age addition.[7]

If you are a **widow** and your husband had deferred his entitlement to pension, you become entitled to the increase he would have gained through his deferment provided you do not remarry before you reach the age of 60. A **widower** can similarly become entitled to an increase resulting from his wife's deferment, but only if he was over pensionable age when she died.[8]

The rules for people who reached pensionable age before 6 April 1979 are different – in particular, you need eight weeks of deferment to gain a one per cent increase.[9]

It is important to realise that any day on which you receive any of the other benefits described in Chapters 2 to 6 of this guide will not be counted when your increased pension is calculated[10] – nor will any day for which you would have been disqualified from receiving a Category A or B retirement pension because you were in prison.[11] In the past, the DSS also applied this rule to graduated retirement benefit (see p99) so that, in particular, married women who were receiving that benefit but who were forced to defer their Category B retirement pension (see below) found that when their husbands reached pensionable age their Category B retirement pensions were not increased to reflect that deferment. In practice, this meant that an increment to the Category B pension worth many pounds was lost because of payments of graduated retirement benefit of as little as a few pence per week.

However, a recent Court of Appeal decision[12] means that the DSS was wrong to do this and many women are now entitled to substantial arrears and an enhanced rate of pension in the future. People who believe they may be affected and who have not already been approached by the DSS should immediately contact their local Benefits Agency office. If you claimed your pension before 19 January 1988, you may have difficulty in getting arrears before that date because of the 'anti-test-case' rules (see p225). Rather than seek a review (see p228), you should ask for leave to make a late appeal (see p242) against the decision to refuse or reduce your increment and get advice (see p259) if this is refused.

After the Court of Appeal's decision, the DSS changed the law again so that from 5 August 1992 receipt of graduated retirement benefit will again prevent you from receiving an increment to your pension.[13] So you should think carefully, and if necessary take advice, before claiming it unless you are claiming your pension at the same time (particularly since the graduated retirement benefit will itself be increased if you defer claiming it).

Many married women have no choice about whether to defer their Category B retirement pensions. This is because they cannot claim them until their husband reaches pensionable age and claims his own Category A retirement pension (see p96). As women reach pensionable age at 60 and men at 65, any married woman who is not at least five years younger than her husband is likely to find herself in this position for a time when she would otherwise become entitled to her pension.

Anyone who does have a choice should think very carefully before deferring their pension now that the earnings rules for retirement pensions have been abolished. Even if you can afford to live without the money from your pension at present, you may be better off claiming it now and investing it. Apart from anything else, if you die within five years of reaching pensionable age, any money you have claimed and invested will go to your family, but if you die before you claim only your spouse, and not other members of your family, can benefit from the deferment of your pension, and even then only in certain circumstances (see p91). Your entitlement to means-tested benefits such as income support, housing benefit and council tax benefit will not be affected as long as you do not allow your total capital to rise above £3,000.

One situation where you might want to consider not claiming your pension (or de-retiring – see below) is if you are a married man who is terminally ill and whose wife is over 60. This is because if you are not receiving a Category A retirement pension when you die, your widow may be able to receive the £1,000 lump sum widow's payment (see p84). And if you do not claim any other contributory benefit either, her widow's pension may also be increased to take account of the deferment of your Category A pension (see p90). But if you are in this position you should take advice before deciding to defer to ensure that you do not lose more in pension payments than your wife is likely to gain. One possibility – if you are under 70 – might be to prepare and sign an election to de-retire and authorise someone to send it to the Benefits Agency by recorded delivery post shortly before your death. The election takes effect as soon as it is posted.[14]

De-retirement

You can usually defer your retirement pension simply by not claiming it but, once you have become entitled, you may only defer by notifying the Benefits Agency of your intention on the proper form.[15] You may 'de-retire' in this way at any time during the first five years after you reach pensionable age.[16] You can also cancel your deferment at any time, but you cannot then de-retire a second time.[17]

You cannot de-retire if you are a man who is entitled to a Category A retirement pension and you have a wife who is entitled to a Category B retirement pension by virtue of your contributions unless your wife consents or withholds her consent unreasonably.[18]

Tax and other benefits

Retirement pensions are taxable except for increases for children.[19]

You can continue to receive invalidity pension or severe disablement allowance when over pensionable age. If you are entitled to these benefits, there may be tax advantages in not retiring. This is because, firstly, they are non-taxable, whereas retirement pensions are taxable; and secondly, because people receiving invalidity pension receive a higher rate of income support and some other means-tested benefits than most people with retirement pensions.

Retirement pensions are taken fully into account for income support purposes, but pensioners receive a higher rate of income support.[20]

2 Category A retirement pension

Conditions of entitlement[1]

- You must claim within the time limit (see below), but see see page 90 for exceptions).
- You satisfy the contribution conditions (see p187) on the basis of your own contribution record (unless you are a widow, a widower or divorced).
- You are over pensionable age.

Amount of payment[2]

	£pw
Claimant	56.10
Adult dependant	33.70
Child dependant	10.95

In addition, you may receive:

- **an age addition** of 25 pence a week if you are over 80;
- **graduated retirement benefit** based on earnings between 1961 and 1975 (see p99);
- **an additional pension** based on SERPS if you reached pensionable age after 5 April 1979 (see p188);
- **a higher pension** if you deferred entitlement to pension (see p90);
- **invalidity allowance** if you were receiving this within eight weeks of reaching pensionable age (see p61). If you were over pensionable age on 5 April 1979, the allowance is payable under the old rules and you receive the higher rate only if you were under 35 on the relevant date, and the middle rate only if you were under 45.[3] If you have an additional SERPS pension, any invalidity allowance to which you are entitled is set off against it;[4]
- **a Christmas bonus** (see p212).

You may receive less than the standard amount of pension if you only partially satisfy the contribution conditions (see p188).

Exceptions to the rule on claiming[5]

Provided you meet the other conditions of entitlement you need not claim your Category A retirement pension if *either*:

- you are a woman aged over 65 and receiving widowed mother's allowance; *or*

- you are a woman aged under 65 and receiving a widow's pension.

If you fall into either of these categories you should be paid your pension automatically when you either cease to receive widowed mother's allowance or reach the age of 65.

Special rules for divorced people

There are special rules which may help you qualify for a Category A retirement pension, if you cannot qualify on the basis of your own contributions.[6] These rules apply if:

- you have been divorced; or
- your marriage was voidable (not void) and has been annulled by a court; and either
- your decree absolute of divorce or nullity is dated after you reach pensionable age; or
- your decree absolute of divorce or nullity is dated before you reach pensionable age and you do not remarry before you reach that age.

Those rules mean that you will be treated as satisfying the first contribution condition (see p187) for a Category A retirement pension if your former spouse did so in any year of his/her working life (see p187) up to and including the year in which your marriage ended.[7]

In addition, you can use your former spouse's contribution record instead of your own in order to increase the number of years in which you satisfy the second contribution condition (see p187).[8]

To do this, you divide the number of years in which your former spouse met the second contribution condition by the number of years in his/her working life (in both cases up to but *excluding* the year in which your marriage ended). You can then *either*

- multiply the number of years in your own working life (up to and including the year in which your marriage ended) by this figure and then rounding up to the next whole number and adding the number of years after that year in which you satisfy the second contribution condition; or
- multiply the number of years for which you were married (including both the year in which you were married and the year in which your decree absolute was given) by this figure and then rounding up to the next whole number and adding the number of years – both before and after your marriage – in which you personally satisfied the second contribution condition.

You are then taken as having satisfied the second contribution condition for whichever number of years is higher.[9]

In practice this means that if your former spouse had a full contribution record, you can use it to replace your own either for all the years in your working life up to and including the one in which you were divorced or for all the years during which you were married. If your former spouse's contribution record was incomplete you will not be treated as satisfying the second contribution condition for all of those years – only some of them. But this may still be more than you would qualify for on the basis of your own contributions.

These rules may mean that if your spouse is continuing to work and pay contributions, it is to your advantage not to get divorced when your marriage breaks up, unless and until one of you wants to remarry.

If you are considering remarrying, have an incomplete contribution record, and are approaching pensionable age, you should think carefully about the timing of your wedding as it may be to your financial advantage to postpone it until after you have reached pensionable age. Conversely, in some cases there may be a financial advantage in bringing the wedding forward. This will depend both on whether you are male or female and on the contribution records of your former and your prospective spouses. You should take advice.

If you have been married more than once, only your most recent marriage counts for these purposes.[10]

These rules do not apply to you if:[11]

- you had already reached pensionable age by 5 April 1979 (ie, if you are now a woman aged 74 or over or a man aged at least 79); *and*
- your decree absolute is also dated on or before 5 April 1979.

Special rules for widows and widowers

The rules for divorced people (see above) also apply to all women who are widows on the day they reach pensionable age.[12] They apply to widowers in the following circumstances:

- your late wife died before you reached pensionable age and you did not remarry before you reached that age;[13]
- you are a man and were widowed after you reached pensionable age but before your late wife's sixtieth birthday[14] (a woman in the equivalent position would not need to use these rules because of her entitlement to Category B retirement pension at the widows' rate and the rules discussed below).

Widowers cannot benefit from the rules if they had already reached pensionable age by 5 April 1979 unless their late wife did not die until after that date.[15]

In addition if you are entitled to both a Category A pension at a reduced rate on your own contributions and a Category B pension on the contributions of your late spouse there are special rules which allow you to add the two together up to a maximum of £56.10 per week (see p209).[16] This rule only applies to widows and widowers – not if you are divorced.

3   Category B retirement pension for a married woman

Conditions of entitlement[1]

- You must claim within the time limit (see p90).
- Your husband satisfied the contribution conditions (see p187).
- You and your husband are both over pensionable age.
- Your husband has become entitled to a Category A retirement pension.

If your husband was receiving an increase of Category A retirement pension in respect of you before you receive this pension, that increase will be replaced by this pension, which will normally be paid at the same rate.

Amount of pension[2]

	£pw
Claimant	33.70
Child dependant	10.95

In addition, you may receive:

- **an age addition** of 25 pence a week if you are over 80;
- **a higher pension** from deferring entitlement to pension (see p90);
- **a Christmas bonus** (see p212).

You may receive less than the standard rate because your husband only partially satisfies the contribution conditions (see p187 but see also p209).

4   Category B retirement pension for a widow

Conditions of entitlement[1]

- You must claim within the time limit (see p76), but see page 81 for exceptions; *and either*
- your husband satisfied the contribution conditions (see p161); *or*
- your husband died as a result of an industrial injury or disease (see p68); *and either*
- you were 60 or over when he died; *or*
- you were a widow immediately before you reached the age of 60 *and* you are entitled to a widow's pension (or would be but for one or more of the reasons given below).

If you were under 60 when your husband died, but are not receiving a widow's pension, you are still entitled if the reason you are not receiving the widow's pension is one or more of the following:[2]

- you have failed to claim it; *or*
- you are receiving widowed mother's allowance instead; *or*
- you are cohabiting; *or*
- you have remarried (but only if after 4 April 1971); *or*
- you are disqualified under the 'overlapping benefits' rules (see p208) or for any other reason (other than being abroad); *or*
- you are over 65.

Effectively, only widows who fail to qualify because they were too young when their husband died, or when their children grew up, are not entitled.

Amount of payment[3]

	£pw
Claimant	56.10
Child dependant	10.95

In addition, you may receive:

- an **age addition** of 25 pence a week if you are over 80;
- **graduated retirement benefit** based on your husband's graduated contributions between 1961 and 1975 (see p99);
- a **higher pension** if your husband deferred entitlement to pension (see p90);
- an **additional pension** based on your husband's earnings after 5 April 1979 under SERPS (see p188);
- a **Christmas bonus** (see p212).

You may receive less than the standard amount of pension because your husband only partially satisfied the contribution conditions (see p187 but see also p209).

If you formerly received widow's pension which was reduced because you were under the age of 55 when your husband died, or when you ceased to be entitled to widowed mother's allowance, your Category B retirement pension will be reduced in the same way.[4] An identical reduction is made if you would have been receiving a widow's pension but you were disqualified (eg, while you were living with a man as his wife).[5]

Period of payment

The pension is paid indefinitely and does *not* cease if you remarry (as long as your remarriage was after 4 April 1971) or you live with a man as his wife.[6]

Exceptions to the rule on claiming

These are the same as for Category A retirement pension (see p93).

5   Category B retirement pension for a widower

Conditions of entitlement[1]

- You must claim within the time limit (see p90).
- Your wife satisfied the contribution conditions (see p187).
- You reached the age of 65 after 5 April 1979.
- Your wife died when you and she were both over pensionable age.

Amount of payment[2]

	£pw
Claimant	56.10
Child dependant	10.95

In addition, you may receive:

- **an age addition** of 25 pence a week if you are over 80;
- **graduated retirement benefit** on your wife's graduated contributions between 1961 and 1975 (see p99);
- **an additional pension** based on your wife's earnings after 5 April 1979 (see p188);
- **a higher rate pension** if your wife deferred entitlement to pension (see p90);
- **a Christmas bonus** (see p212).

You may receive less than the standard amounts because your wife only partially satisfied the contribution conditions (see p187 but see also p209).

Period of payment

The pension is paid indefinitely and does *not* cease if you remarry or live with a woman as her husband.[3]

6   Category D retirement pension

Conditions of entitlement[1]

- You must claim within the time limits (see page 90, but see also page 99 for exceptions).
- You satisfy the residence conditions (see p194).
- You are aged 80 or over.
- You are entitled either to no other retirement pension or to an amount of retirement pension less than the current rate of a Category D retirement pension.

Amount of payment[2]

	£pw
Claimant	33.70

In addition, you will receive:

- **an age addition** of 25 pence a week because you are over 80;
- **a Christmas bonus** (see p212).

Exception to the rule on claiming[3]

Provided you meet the other conditions of entitlement you need not claim Category D retirement pension if you were 'ordinarily resident' in Great Britain (see p196) on your 80th birthday and you are already receiving another retirement pension.

7 Graduated retirement benefit

Between 1961 and 6 April 1975, those paying flat-rate Class 1 contributions also paid graduated contributions. For every £7.50 contributed by a man, or £9 contributed by a woman during that period, that person is now entitled to 7.09 pence a week.[1]

If you are a **widow**, you may add half your husband's entitlement to your own. Similarly, a **widower** entitled to a Category B retirement pension (or who would be if he did not have a Category A retirement pension) may also add half his wife's entitlement to his own.[2]

Graduated retirement benefit may be paid even if you are not entitled to any retirement pension. But if you are entitled to only a very small amount, you will receive a lump-sum payment instead of weekly payments. It is increased if you defer entitlement to a retirement pension (see p90).[3]

The contribution conditions for graduated retirement benefit discriminate against women on the grounds of their sex and would appear to be against EC law (see p201). It is true that as far as contributions are concerned, the graduated pension scheme came to an end before the EC Directive on Equal Treatment of Men and Women[4] became operative, but payments are still being made on a discriminatory basis and the European Court of Justice has decided in the past that the current rules of the social security system may not perpetuate the effects of past discrimination.[5] Neither does the discrimination seem to come within the exception to the Directive which allows discrimination where this is the necessary consequence of having different pensionable ages for men and women. If you are a woman and receiving graduated retirement benefit you may like to ask your adviser to contact CPAG's solicitors for further details. Although the difference in the weekly rate of your graduated retirement benefit will be small, you may get a lump-sum payment of arrears. However, you must be prepared to appeal and await the outcome of a test case to the European Court.

CHAPTER SEVEN

Benefits for severely disabled people

This chapter covers:
1 Introduction
2 Disability living allowance mobility component
3 Disability living allowance care component
4 Attendance allowance
5 Matters common to both disability living allowance and attendance allowance

l Introduction

The benefits available to severely disabled people were reorganised from 6 April 1992. Unfortunately, the Benefits Agency was ill-prepared for the changes and the large volume of claims made under the new rules. Many claimants faced unacceptable delays. Only a trickle of cases have therefore been heard before disability appeal tribunals, and no cases have led to significant decisions by the commissioners on the new rules that were introduced. The existing case law on the provisions that duplicate those within the former attendance and mobility allowance remains valid.

- **Disability living allowance** is divided into two 'components' payable at different rates. The old mobility allowance, and attendance allowance for those under 65, were incorporated into this new benefit:
  - the **mobility component** extended and replaced mobility allowance; *and*
  - the **care component** extended and replaced attendance allowance for those under 65 years of age.
- Attendance allowance remains for those who are **aged 65 or more** when their care needs start.
- Mobility allowance became the **higher rate 'mobility component'**. Severely mentally impaired people may also qualify for this if they meet a series of stringent conditions.
- A new **lower rate 'mobility component'** was also introduced. This benefits people who can walk but need help getting about.
- The higher rate of attendance allowance became the **higher rate 'care component'**.
- The lower rate of attendance allowance became the **middle rate 'care component'**.
- A new **lower rate 'care component'** was introduced for those who have

limited attention needs or who are unable to cook for themselves. This benefits a substantial number of people who would not have previously qualified for attendance allowance.
* The rules about **qualifying periods** are the same for both components but do not apply to those who are terminally ill.
* The **claims and adjudication processes** for disability living allowance and attendance allowance were changed (see p118 and Chapter 16 for more detail):
    – Claimants now complete extensive 'self-assessment' claim forms and most claims are decided without any medical examination.
    – Decision-making is by adjudication officers, not doctors as in the past.
    – There is a right to review by a different adjudication officer, and, if still dissatisfied, a right of appeal to an independent disability appeal tribunal.

People who were receiving mobility allowance or attendance allowance were transferred into the new benefit structure from 6 April 1992 (see p121).

People entitled to these benefits may also qualify for other benefits mentioned elsewhere in this guide.

See Appendix One for benefits and services not usually regarded as social security benefits but which are available to people with disabilities (p261).

2 Disability living allowance mobility component

Conditions of entitlement[1]
* You satisfy the residence conditions (see p193).
* You are 5 or over but under 66 when you first claim.
* You are likely to be able to benefit from time to time from 'facilities for enhanced locomotion'.
* You satisfy the 'disability' conditions:
    – **For the higher rate** of the mobility component (the former mobility allowance):
    either you must be suffering from a physical disability such that you are unable to walk; *or*
    you are virtually unable to walk; *or*
    you are both deaf and blind; *or*
    you were born without feet or are a double amputee; *or*
    you are severely mentally impaired; *and* have severe behavioural problems; *and* qualify for the highest rate of the care component.
    – **For the lower rate** of the mobility component you need to show that although you are able to walk you are so severely disabled, physically or mentally, that, ignoring any familiar routes, you are unable to walk outdoors without guidance or supervision from another person most of the time.[2]

– **For both rates** you must have satisfied one of these conditions for at least the past three months and you must be likely to satisfy it for the next six months (unless you are terminally ill).

Amount of payment[3]

- The higher rate of mobility component is £31.40 per week.
- The lower rate of mobility component is £11.95 per week.

Rules about age

The mobility component cannot be paid to anyone under the age of five. However, the three months before the fifth birthday can be the qualifying period resulting in payment from the fifth birthday.

For the lower rate mobility component, those aged between 5 and 16 also have to show *either*:

- that they require substantially more guidance or supervision than persons of their age in normal physical and mental health would; *or*
- that persons of their age in normal physical and mental health would not require such guidance or supervision.[4]

The upper age limit for claiming either rate of the disability living allowance mobility component is normally 65. Those who are aged 65 but who have not yet reached 66 are able to claim if they can show that they had met the residence and presence test and that their disability had begun on the day before their 65th birthday. The three-month retrospective qualifying period runs from the date the disability began, provided that it was before the date of their 65th birthday. You cannot claim the mobility component for the first time once you have reached the age of 66.[5] But once you become entitled, it can then be paid for life.

Unable or virtually unable to walk

This is the commonest route to the higher rate mobility component. The regulations say that a person shall be treated as suffering from a physical disablement that makes him unable or virtually unable to walk *only if*:

'his physical condition as a whole is such that without having regard to circumstances peculiar to that person as to the place of residence or as to place of, or nature of, employment:

- he is unable to walk; *or*
- his ability to walk out of doors is so limited, as regards the distance over which or the speed at which or the length of time for which or the manner in which he can make progress on foot without severe discomfort, that he is virtually unable to walk; *or*
- the exertion required to walk would constitute a danger to his life or would be likely to lead to a serious deterioration in his health.'[6]

'Physical disablement'

To qualify for the higher rate of the mobility component the cause of your incapacity to walk must be physical and not psychological – ie, people with agoraphobia (who are frightened of going out) do not qualify for the higher rate mobility component (although they may qualify for the lower rate, see p106). To qualify as virtually unable to walk, you may need to show that 'behavioural problems' which limit your mobility have a physical cause. Often, what are referred to as behavioural problems are the result of a mental disability which has an organic, physical basis.

'Unable or virtually unable to walk'

Ability to walk is considered after taking into account any artificial aid you habitually wear or use, or which would be suitable for you.[7] You will not qualify if you are able to walk with a stick or crutches. However, the term 'walk' is important here. A man with one leg and no artificial limb may be able to get about with crutches but getting about in this way cannot mean the same thing as being able to 'walk'. He qualifies because he is simply unable to walk without it being necessary to consider whether he is virtually unable to walk.[8] Since April 1991 people who have no feet have qualified automatically.

'Out of doors'

The test is whether you can walk out of doors, not indoors. If you have problems with your balance on uneven pavements and roads, or you have a lung or other condition which has been worsened by wind or rain, these will be relevant factors in deciding your claim.[9]

'Distance'

The regulations do not say that if you are able to walk a certain distance you are automatically ineligible for the mobility component. In one case, a medical appeal tribunal's decision that a person who had walked less than 50 yards was not virtually unable to walk was upheld.[10] But other medical appeal tribunals have accepted that a person was 'virtually unable to walk' even when able to cover 300 yards or more. One relevant consideration may be how long it takes you to recover after walking a certain distance – eg, 50 yards. If you can walk another 50 yards after only a minute's rest, your walking ability is obviously greater than that of a person who has to lie down for an hour after walking such a distance.

'Without severe discomfort'

If, when you walk, you feel severe discomfort – eg, pain and breathlessness brought on by walking[11] – you should make this clear. The point of this part of the regulation is to ignore any walking that can be achieved only with severe discomfort when considering whether you are virtually unable to walk.[12] However, pain is difficult to measure, and may be as much a subjective phenomenon as an objective one.

'The exertion required to walk'

This provision has been explained in one case:

> 'It is "exertion required to walk" which must lead to the danger to life or a serious deterioration in health. The expression includes . . . a condition which might be induced or precipitated by walking. It then has to be shown as a matter of probability that the exertion would constitute a danger to life or lead to a serious deterioration in health.'[13]

It is unclear what distance has to be considered when applying this test.

It is not necessary for the possible serious deterioration in your health to be permanent or long-lasting.[14]

In practice, few claimants qualify under this route. Even those with heart problems, who might be thought most likely to do so, are rarely advised not to walk on medical grounds. However, it may well be that their walking tolerance is so limited by pain or breathlessness that they are virtually unable to walk.

'Without having regard to circumstances peculiar' to the claimant

Your personal circumstances are not taken into account. It is not, for instance, relevant that you do not have sufficient mobility to get to your nearest bus stop to go shopping,[15] or that you are no longer able to use public transport.

People without feet

From April 1991 people without feet are automatically treated as being unable to walk. A person needs to fit within this precise definition:

> 'he has both legs amputated at levels which are either through or above the ankle, or, he has one leg so amputated and is without the other leg, or is without both legs to the same extent as if it, or they, had been so amputated.'[16]

Blind and deaf claimants

You are treated as being unable to walk if:

- the degree of disablement resulting from your loss of vision is 100 per cent; *and*
- the degree of disablement resulting from your loss of hearing is 80 per cent on a scale where 100 per cent represents absolute deafness;[17] *and*
- the combined effects of the blindness and deafness mean that you are unable to walk to any intended or required destination while out of doors, without the help of another person.[18]

The legislation does not explain how your loss of vision and loss of hearing should be assessed. So, you should argue that 100 per cent loss of vision is to be assessed by reference to the scale used for severe disablement allowance and disablement benefit on which 100 per cent is the assessment for 'loss of sight to such an extent as to render the claimant unable to perform work for which eyesight is essential' (see p268). [19] That is something less than total blindness.

Since absolute deafness is assessed as 100 per cent on the same scale, the statutory test for industrial deafness cases can be used to decide whether your disablement from loss of hearing is 80 per cent. On that basis, you qualify if adding together the hearing loss in each ear due to all causes at 1, 2 and 3 kHz and dividing the result by two gives an average loss of at least 87 dB. [20] In practice, adjudication officers accept a person as having 80 per cent loss of hearing if s/he is unable to understand a question asked from a distance of one metre.

Claimants with severe learning difficulties

Prior to April 1992, those with severe behavioural difficulties had considerable problems in qualifying for mobility allowance. These problems were recognised by introducing a route to the higher rate mobility component of disability living allowance for this group.

A claimant qualifies if:

- s/he is severely mentally impaired; *and*
- s/he displays severe behavioural problems – ie:
  - s/he exhibits disruptive behaviour which is extreme; *and*
  - s/he regularly requires someone else to intervene and physically restrain them in order to prevent them causing injury to themselves or others, or damage to property; *and*
  - s/he is so unpredictable that another person has to be present and watching over them whenever they are awake; *and*
- s/he qualifies for the higher rate of the care component by meeting both a day and a night attention or supervision condition. [21]

Many people likely to pass this test may live in hospitals or other accommodation where the care component is not payable. They may, therefore, need to put in a claim for the care component and satisfy the Benefits Agency that they would qualify for it at the higher rate, (even though it will not be payable to them). They would then be able to receive the mobility component under these rules.

People with severe behavioural difficulties who are already in receipt of mobility allowance may have been awarded it for a short period only, at the end of which they will need to make a renewal claim in the standard way. They may not meet all of the elements of the test for the higher rate mobility component – for example, they may not be sufficiently unsettled at night to get the higher rate care component. However, if they qualified previously on the basis that they were virtually unable to walk, there is nothing to stop them continuing to qualify for the higher rate component via that route. The same applies to new claimants who might also be unable to fit themselves within the newer test. This will involve arguing that the claimant's disability prevents her/him from walking effectively, causing so many refusals to walk that the person can be said to be suffering from 'temporary paralysis' and thus be virtually unable to walk. [22]

The lower rate mobility component

Claimants who lacked 'directional mobility' – ie, people with disabilities such as blindness or learning difficulties – had problems with the previous mobility allowance. They had legs and could walk but for various reasons found it difficult to get about.

Some of these claimants will now meet the test of severe mental impairment and thus qualify for the higher rate mobility component. However, that test is restrictive and intended to benefit only those with severe behavioural problems. Not all people with learning difficulties qualify for the higher rate.

Many people with learning difficulties have problems finding their way on unfamiliar routes or lack road sense. Others may have behavioural difficulties but not receive the higher rate care component. They, and many blind and partially sighted people who cannot walk effectively out of doors with an aid (eg, a stick or guide dog), qualify for the lower rate mobility component. They can show that (ignoring any familiar routes) they are unable to walk outdoors 'without guidance or supervision from another person most of the time'.

People with dementia and similar conditions, who are not so severely disabled as to qualify for the higher rate mobility component, should also qualify under this test. People with agoraphobia, whose fear of going outside means that they need another person to be with them, and those who need to be accompanied because of the effect of unpredictable fits or blackouts, may also qualify.

'Guidance' would be most likely to cover people with visual disabilities, while 'supervision' would be more likely to cover those with mental disabilities.

'To benefit from enhanced facilities for locomotion'

This test applies to both rates of the component. Very few people fail it.

You should receive the disability living allowance if you are in hospital or in an institution such as a children's or old people's home, provided that you can still benefit from a trip out, even if, for instance, you have to be carried into a taxi for a ride. It is not essential that you be interested in or enjoy going out provided that it would be beneficial for you to do so. [23]

Even if, in practice, it would be very hard for the claimant to go out at all, because of behavioural problems or a very disabling physical condition, it should be argued that if there were a theoretical chance that they could do so if they had sufficient resources available to them, then they should not be excluded under this provision. The only people who should be excluded are those who are in comas or who cannot be moved because, for medical reasons, it would be dangerous for them.

Terminal illness

A terminally ill claimant is defined in the same way for the mobility component as for the care component (see p114). However, unlike the care component, a terminally ill person is not automatically deemed to satisfy the qualifying conditions for the mobility component. The only special treatment given is that where a claim is made specifically on the basis that the claimant is terminally ill, then s/he does not have to satisfy either the three-month retrospective or the six-month prospective qualifying conditions. [24] It is hoped that such claims will usually be processed within ten days.

The mobility component and invalid vehicles

The Benefits Agency used to provide invalid vehicles and help with car running costs for people with disabilities. Those schemes were first replaced (for new claimants) by mobility allowance and, from April 1992, by the mobility component of disability living allowance. If you still have a vehicle or assistance, the mobility component will not be paid. [25]

The only exception is if the Secretary of State certifies that: [26]

• you have purchased or obtained on hire, hire purchase or lease, a car of your own, or intend to do so; *and*
• you intend to keep the car for at least six months (or such other period as the Secretary of State determines) and to learn to drive within that time; *and*
• you are using the mobility component during that period to help obtain the car.

You may surrender a vehicle or end the assistance, and receive the higher rate of the mobility component instead. You can transfer onto the mobility component when you are over the age of 65. You will continue to receive the component provided that you continue to satisfy the residence and presence conditions, and provided that your physical condition does not improve to the extent that you would no longer have qualified for the vehicle. [27]

Motability

Motability is a charity incorporated by Royal Charter. It runs a scheme to help you lease or buy a car if you receive the higher rate mobility component.

You pay your disability living allowance mobility component direct to Motability. You may also have to make a down payment and if you drive more than 12,000 miles a year you may also have to make further annual payments. For further information write to Motability, Gate House,

Westgate, Harlow, Essex CM20 1HR. Motability produces leaflets on its schemes for car leasing and hire purchase of new cars, used cars and electric wheelchairs.

3 Disability living allowance care component

Conditions of entitlement[1]

- You must satisfy the residence conditions (see p193).
- You must not be resident in certain types of accommodation (see p101).
- You must also satisfy the 'disability' conditions:
- *either* you satisfy one or more of the attention or supervision conditions (see pp110 and 111); *or*
- you are over 16 and can pass the 'cooking test' (see p109); *and, in either case*:
  - you have done so for a continuous period of three months immediately before your claim;
  - you are likely to continue to satisfy those conditions for the next six months; *or*
- you are terminally ill (see p114).

Amount of payment[2]

The care component is paid at three weekly rates:

- the **lower rate** of £11.95 – for satisfying *either* the cooking test *or* the limited attention condition;
- the **middle rate** of £30.00 – for satisfying any one other disability condition;
- the **higher rate** of £44.90 – for satisfying *both* a day *and* a night disability condition *or* for being terminally ill.

Rules about age

There is no lower age limit for claiming the care component. However, as with other claimants, a baby has to meet the qualifying conditions for three months before the allowance becomes payable unless they are terminally ill.

Children (ie, those under the age of 16) cannot qualify for the lower rate care component via the cooking test. A child can otherwise qualify provided s/he meets one of the following additional conditions:

- s/he has attention or supervision requirements 'substantially in excess of the normal requirements of a person of his age'; *or*
- s/he has substantial attention or supervision requirements 'which younger persons in normal physical and mental health may also have but which persons of his age and in normal physical and mental health would not have'.[3]

The upper age limit for claiming the care component is normally 65, although those who are aged 65 are able to claim if they can show that their disability had begun and they had met the residence and presence test on the day before their 65th birthday. You cannot claim it once you have reached the age of 66. If you are above this age limit you have to claim attendance allowance.

There is no upper age limit for receipt of the care component once you qualify.

The rules about qualifying periods for those in receipt of disability living allowance care component above the age of 65 are the same as those for attendance allowance. Thus, those who are above the age of 65 and whose condition worsens have to show that they have met the qualifying conditions for the higher rate care component for six months before it can be awarded, not three months. Those aged over 65 who receive the middle rate component and whose condition improves, lose the allowance altogether. They cannot move down on to the lower rate component. [4]

The 'cooking test'

This test provides a gateway to the *lower* level of the allowance for those who can show that they are so severely disabled physically or mentally that they cannot prepare a cooked main meal for themselves if they have the ingredients. [5] This test does not apply to those under the age of 16. [6]

Satisfying the 'cooking test'

In parliamentary debate, a government spokesman said that this was 'an abstract test' – ie, you do not need physically to demonstrate that you are unable to cook. [7] It seems that the meal for the test is a traditional one, cooked in a conventional oven. You need to show that your disability makes you unable to perform the tasks that are needed to cook such a main meal. The claim form asks about your ability to peel and chop vegetables, use taps, cooking utensils, a cooker, cope with hot pans, and plan a meal.

Thus, you need to be able to manage both the physical tasks (eg, lifting, carrying, bending, and making fine movements), and the mental tasks (eg, concentrating and planning) examined in the test.

It may be argued that those with epilepsy and other conditions which prevent them from cooking a meal satisfy this test. Although they might physically and mentally be able to cook, in practice they would not because it would be potentially too dangerous an activity for them. Only those who could reasonably be expected to prepare a cooked main meal should be regarded as being able to do so.

In addition, the degree of stamina required to cook a main meal must be taken into account. It may be that there are disabled people able to undertake any one of the tasks involved in the test but that, overall, because of fatigue, they would be unable to prepare the meal.

The attention conditions

You need to show that you are so severely disabled physically or mentally that you require, in connection with your bodily functions, from another person: [8]

- attention for a significant portion of the day, whether during a single period or a number of periods; this is the new lower rate 'limited attention' condition; *or*
- frequent attention throughout the day; this is the day attention condition; *or*
- prolonged or repeated attention during the night in connection with your bodily functions; this is the night attention condition.

Attention in connection with bodily functions

The attention you require must be in connection with bodily functions. These include:

> 'breathing, hearing, seeing, eating, drinking, walking, sitting, sleeping, getting in or out of bed, dressing, undressing, eliminating waste products and the like, all of which an ordinary person who is not suffering from any disability does for himself. But they do not include cooking, shopping, or any of the other things which . . . generally . . . one of the household does for the rest of the family.' [9]

This list has now been extended by more recent decisions of the social security commissioners.

Although cooking is not directly a form of 'attention in connection with your bodily functions', the special selection and very precise weighing and measuring of a very specialised diet may qualify as such because it is part of your overall treatment. [10] Arguably, this approach could be extended to include the laundry needs of people who are incontinent.

If you are profoundly deaf and cannot speak properly you may qualify if you can show that you need attention from another person to enable you to communicate. [11]

The attention must be 'required'. This does not mean only 'medically required' – it simply means 'reasonably required'. [12] In the past this area was a source of disputes. The DSS would suggest that, for example, it was not medically necessary for someone to have their bedding frequently changed if they were incontinent, if they had adequate padding and their skin was not too vulnerable. However, this was unlawful. What mattered was that it was *reasonable* to change the bedding frequently.

The 'limited attention' condition

This test provides a route to the lower rate of the care component. You need to show that you need attention for a 'significant portion of the day'. This can be either during a single period or a number of periods.

People qualify for this lower rate care component who do not meet the attention conditions for the middle or higher rates of the component –

eg, those who need help with 'getting up' activities such as dressing and washing at the beginning of the day, and with 'going to bed' activities such as undressing and washing at the end of the day, but are otherwise able to care for themselves without help.

It remains unclear how long a 'significant portion of the day' is. A government spokesman said this was 'an hour or thereabouts' in the debate on this provision.[13]

Frequent attention throughout the day

To satisfy the day attention condition you need to show that attention is required frequently throughout the day. There is likely to be a thin line between some of those who meet the 'limited attention condition' and some of those who satisfy the 'frequency condition'. A 'frequent' need might include help with toiletting (whether that be to reach the toilet, use a commode, or deal with zips and buttons), or needing help to walk within your own home. For this test, it is the pattern of the needs across the day which is crucial. These are both examples of activities which most people would reasonably engage in with some frequency during the course of a normal day. However, most people who satisfy this test will have a range of care needs. These should be added together and looked at to see whether the person needs frequent help throughout the day.

Prolonged or repeated attention during the night

This night attention condition is more able to be clearly defined than the day attention condition. This is because the help that needs to be given in the night has to be either 'prolonged' or 'repeated' – both of which are more easily measured than the 'frequency' condition that must be met during the day (see above). The Benefits Agency usually regards 20 minutes of attention as 'prolonged'. 'Repeated' simply means twice or more. It is not necessary for the attention to be required every night or even on most nights, provided that it is a fairly regular feature. In fact, fewer people satisfy the night condition simply because most people sleep through the night and so do not require attention.

It should be noted that sleeping is a 'bodily function' (see p110). This means that soothing a child back to sleep counts as giving attention in connection with a bodily function.[14]

The supervision conditions

You need to show that you are so severely disabled physically or mentally that you require:

- continual supervision from another person throughout the day in order to avoid substantial danger to yourself or others; this is the day supervision condition; *or*
- another person to be awake for a prolonged period or at frequent intervals to watch over you in order to avoid substantial danger to yourself or others; this is the night supervision condition.

Continual supervision in order to avoid substantial danger

This provision applies to the amount of supervision that is required in the daytime. It has been held to consist of four parts. [15]

- There must be a substantial **danger to yourself or someone else as a result of your medical condition.** What constitutes a 'substantial danger' must be decided on the facts of each case.
- The substantial **danger must be one against which it is reasonable to guard.** This involves weighing the remoteness of the risk and the seriousness of the consequences should it arise. While the risk of a house catching fire may be remote (but not fanciful), the consequences of leaving a disabled person who is unable to move alone in a house which did catch fire would be catastrophic. Thus, it can be argued that such a person reasonably requires continual supervision. [16] In another case it was said:

  > 'If a small child, escaping the supervision of its mother, runs out of the house on to a public highway, that may well be an isolated incident. But it only requires one such incident for the child to be killed by passing traffic. In my view, the fact that the incidents in question were isolated is nothing to the point.'[17]

  In assessing the likelihood of danger, the adjudication officer must look not only at what has happened in the past but at what may happen in the future. [18]
- There must be a **need for the supervision.** As with the attention conditions, there have in the past been many arguments as to whether supervision need be 'medically required' or only 'reasonably required' (see p110). This is particularly important because it has often been suggested that a claimant is 'sensible' and could avoid risks. A person can avoid most risks by staying in a chair all day but that may be totally unreasonable. [19] In considering your need for continual supervision, the adjudication officer should regard the fact that such supervision is in fact provided as strong evidence that it is 'required'. As one Chief Commissioner said: 'Mothers would be unlikely to exhaust themselves by providing it unnecessarily for years.'[20] However, people may still qualify who, although they do not receive supervision (perhaps because they live alone), clearly require it.
- The supervision must be **continual.** This is something less than 'continuous', but supervision which is required only occasionally or spasmodically is insufficient. The 'characteristic nature of supervision is overseeing or watching over considered with reference to its frequency or regularity of occurrence'. [21] Supervision can be precautionary and anticipatory. It does not necessarily involve direct intervention. Some claimants liable to epileptic fits without warning may need continual supervision, although attention for the period between the fits is not required. [22] Even if you have warning of the fits so that you can prevent yourself from falling, you may require continual supervision if you suffer from prolonged periods of confusion afterwards. [23] A parent with a young child may need supervision so that there is someone to look after the child when the parent has a fit.

Watching over in order to avoid substantial danger

This provision applies to the amount of watching over that is required at night time. The person watching over you has to be awake for a prolonged period or at frequent intervals. A 'prolonged period' may well mean 20 minutes or more, similar to the night attention condition. 'Frequent intervals' probably means more than twice.

Night and day

An adult who needs help going to the toilet at 3am, a time when most people are asleep, clearly needs that help at night. Problems do sometimes arise when children need supervision or attention in the evening or where an adult requires assistance in the late evening or early morning.

'Night' has been rather unhelpfully defined as 'that period of inactivity, or that principal period of inactivity, through which each household goes in the dark hours' beginning when 'the household, as it were, closes down for the night'.[24] This may be somewhere between 11pm and 7am, but the pattern of activities of the particular household needs to be taken into account. The definition of 'night' for a child is the same as for an adult, so that attention given to a child in the evening before the adults have gone to bed will count only towards satisfaction of the day condition.[25]

Attention or supervision

The difference between, on the one hand, attention, and on the other, supervision or watching over, is often straightforward. 'Attention' involves some services of an 'active nature'[26] whereas supervision is passive and 'may be precautionary or anticipatory, yet never result in intervention'.[27]

However, where supervision does lead to intervention, the supervisor is providing 'attention', so you should not regard the two categories as completely separate. For example, if you need to be supervised because you are likely to fall and injure yourself, you receive attention every time your carer gives you a steadying hand or warns you of an obstacle you were about to trip over.[28] If that attention is 'frequent' you will qualify even if the supervision is not 'continual' throughout the day. And, sometimes, an act can be both supervision and attention.

It is therefore probably wise for advisers and claimants to emphasise the extent of the disabled person's disabilities and needs without trying to fit them neatly into either attention or supervision categories.

Renal dialysis

Special regulations apply if you are undergoing renal dialysis on a kidney machine.[29] To qualify, you need to have such treatment regularly for two or more sessions a week. You also need to show that either the dialysis is of a type which requires the attendance or supervision of another person or, that you, in fact, require attention or supervision from another person whilst you are dialysing. You will receive the middle rate care component. These rules also apply to those who dialyse in hospital and have no help from any member of the staff. Others who dialyse in hospital will not qualify by this special route. There is nothing to prevent those who undergo renal dialysis in a manner that will not qualify them under this route, from qualifying for the care component under the ordinary conditions.

Terminal illness

A terminally ill claimant is treated as satisfying the conditions for the higher rate care component and as having done so for the preceding three months.[30] So, all terminally ill claimants are entitled to disability living allowance except those excluded on such grounds as being abroad or in hospital or similar accommodation (see p116). The Benefits Agency is usually able to deal with claims within ten days. They are usually referred to as claims under the 'special rules'.

A person is regarded as 'terminally ill' if s/he is suffering from a progressive disease and can reasonably be expected to die within six months as a result of that disease.[31] Note that this does not mean that it must be more likely than not that the person will die within this period. It simply means that death within six months would not be unexpected.

The special rules only apply if the claim is made on that basis, or if an application for review or an appeal on an existing claim is made on that basis. Any notification to the Benefits Agency that a person is terminally ill should be treated as an application for a review or a claim, provided that the notification refers to disability living allowance. Someone else is allowed to make a claim or seek a review on behalf of a terminally ill person without her/his knowledge or authority.[32]

4   **Attendance allowance**

Attendance allowance is for people over the age of 65. The rules largely follow those for the higher and middle rates of the disability living allowance care component. The claims procedure and the structure of adjudication are described in section 5 below.

Conditions of entitlement[1]

- You satisfy the residence conditions (see p193).
- You are not resident in certain types of accommodation (see p116).
- You satisfy the disability conditions:
    - you meet one or more of the day or night attention or supervision conditions (see pp110 and 111); *and*
    - you have done so for a continuous period of six months immediately before your claim; *or*
    - you are terminally ill (see above).

Amount of payment[2]

Attendance allowance is paid at two weekly rates:

- the **lower rate** of £30.00 – for satisfying *either* the day or the night attention condition, *or* the day or the night supervision condition;
- The **higher rate** of £44.90 – for satisfying *both* the day attention or supervision condition, *and* the night attention or supervision condition, *or* for being terminally ill.

The attention and supervision conditions

These are the same as for the middle or higher rates of the disability living allowance care component. The guidance given above (see pp110-113) applies but there is no equivalent of the lowest rate care component.

The qualifying period

If you claim attendance allowance you have to show that you have met the conditions about needing attention and/or supervision for six months before the benefit can be awarded to you.

Renal dialysis

The same rules apply as for the disability living allowance (see p113).[3]

Terminal illness

A terminally ill claimant is deemed to satisfy the conditions for the higher rate of attendance allowance and to have done so for the preceding six months.[4] For the meaning of 'terminally ill', see p114.

5   Matters common to disability living allowance and attendance allowance

Tax and other benefits

- Attendance allowance is not taxable nor is any part of disability living allowance.[1]
- These benefits may be paid in addition to any other benefits paid in addition to any other benefits described in this guide *except that*:
  - attendance allowance and the care component of disability living allowance overlap with constant attendance allowance under the industrial injuries or war pensions schemes (see pp141 and 262); *and*
  - the mobility component of disability living allowance overlaps with the war pensioners' mobility supplement payable under the war pensions scheme.
- If you are receiving the higher or middle rates of the care component, or

attendance allowance, and someone regularly looks after you, that person may be entitled to **invalid care allowance** (see p125).

* Receipt of attendance allowance or any rate of disability living allowance will entitle you to a Christmas Bonus (see p212).
* Neither attendance allowance nor any part of disability living allowance is taken into account as income for the purposes of income support, family credit, housing benefit or council tax benefit (unless you receive the care component or attendance allowance and are in residential care or a nursing home).
* If you or a partner or a child in your family is entitled to attendance allowance or disability living allowance, income support, housing benefit and council tax benefit will be paid at a higher rate than usual, via the premiums for disabled adults, disabled children and disabled pensioners. There is a special premium, the severe disability premium, for people who receive attendance allowance or the higher or middle rates of the care component who are treated as living alone, or who live with someone else who is also receiving attendance allowance or that level of that component. For further information see CPAG's *National Welfare Benefits Handbook*, the companion work to this guide, which deals comprehensively with means-tested benefits.

Special rules for certain types of accommodation [2]

The mobility component of disability living allowance is unaffected by stays in either hospital or scheduled accommodation.

The rules for attendance allowance and for disability living allowance care component are the same. Neither can usually be paid once someone has been in hospital or scheduled accommodation for more than a set period.[3] For hospitals, this period is 28 days for adults and 84 days for children. For 'scheduled accommodation', it is 28 days for both adults and children. Two or more distinct periods, separated by 28 days or less, will be added together towards the 28 or 84 day limit as appropriate.[4] Only a complete period of 24 hours, midnight to midnight, counts as a day in hospital or specified accommodation.

Hospitals

Attendance allowance or the care component can no longer be paid once someone has been maintained free of charge and is receiving in-patient treatment in hospital for more than the set period.

Someone cannot be paid attendance allowance or the care component of disability living allowance on their first claim if they live in hospital. However, it may be worth claiming nevertheless, because the person will receive the initial 28-day concession payment if they spend even one day outside. Those who are moving into the community from residential care often start by spending limited periods outside of the hospital.

Accommodation provided out of public or local funds

The allowances cannot be paid where the accommodation is provided under Part III of the National Assistance Act 1948 (often referred to as 'Part III accommodation'), or, in Scotland, Part IV of the Social Work (Scotland) Act 1968 or section 7 of the Mental Health (Scotland) Act 1984.

Also excluded is any accommodation where the cost is or may be borne wholly or partly out of public or local funds under the above Acts or under any other enactments relating to 'persons under disability or to young persons or to education or training'.

A small number of people who appeared not to qualify under the former rules did receive attendance allowance as the Secretary of State had a discretion which he exercised in their favour. This discretion has now been removed, though it is the policy intention that the new regulations should not make anyone worse off.

These restrictions may affect local authorities changing the status or nature of accommodation provided to disabled people. They will take effect not only where the local authority funds the accommodation, but also where the local authority could do so but chooses not to, and even where the person now lives in a residential care home but has been encouraged to move there from some form of local authority provision.

These restrictions do not apply to children who are under the age of 16 and being looked after by a local authority, who have been placed by that local authority into a private dwelling. Nor do they apply to certain disabled young people in private dwellings, who are under 18 and to whom section 17(10)(b) of the Children Act 1989 applies or to whom section 17(10)(c) of that Act applies. Nor do they apply where anyone under 18 is being educated abroad and having the costs met by their local authority (eg, at the Peto Institute).

Where the person is living in accommodation where the cost is not but could be borne out of public or local funds, these restrictions do not apply if the claimant is:

- living in accommodation as a privately fostered child; *or*
- living in accommodation provided for homeless people by local authorities under section 65 of the Housing Act 1985.

The 'could be borne' provision also cannot usually be applied to anyone who lives in a private dwelling. However, it will apply where the private dwelling that the disabled person lives in is a residential care home with at least four other residents. It will also bite where the person was moved from somewhere where the costs were borne wholly or partly out of local funds, 'at the instigation of the body which bore the cost', into a residential care home.

From 1 April 1993 some of the rules in this area have changed following the introduction of community care policies. People have 'preserved rights' if they were living in these forms of accommodation on 31 March 1993, or were absent for only a limited period.[5]

Those with preserved rights who receive these allowances on the basis that they are terminally ill can continue to receive them if living not in Part III accommodation but in accommodation where the cost is not but could be borne out of public or local funds, or in accommodation where the cost is or may be borne wholly or partly out of public or local funds under any other enactments relating to 'persons under disability or to education or training'.

Those without preserved rights (essentially those who move in on or after 1 April 1993) who receive these allowances on the basis that they are terminally ill can continue to receive them if they are living in certain hospices only.[6]

Those with preserved rights can receive the allowances if living in accommodation where the cost may be borne wholly or partly out of public or local funds and they are paying the whole cost, and always have paid the whole cost, of the accommodation.

Those without preserved rights can receive the allowances in any form of accommodation where their rights to receive them would otherwise be restricted but only if they are not receiving income support or housing benefit and are paying the whole cost of their accommodation, either through their own resources or with the help of third parties or charities.

Respite care

Note that two periods separated by less than 28 days are linked and count as one period. This may particularly affect you if you need 'respite care'. If you go into hospital or residential care to give your carer a break more than once every four weeks the odd short periods when you are in such accommodation will be added together and, after 28 such days, your attendance allowance or disability living allowance care component is no longer paid while you are in such accommodation. This can be avoided if it is possible for you to remain at home for over four weeks at a time every now and then, because the link is then broken. If you are unable to break the link, it may be useful to have your allowance paid by direct credit transfer rather than by order book because the necessary adjustments can be made with less inconvenience both to the Benefits Agency and you.

You are paid the allowance at a daily rate of one-seventh of the weekly rate for odd days of entitlement between periods in hospital or other accommodation disqualifying you from the allowance.

Claims and decisions

All initial decisions on claims are made by an adjudication officer.[7] There is a Disability Living Allowance Advisory Board which gives guidance to adjudication officers and the Secretary of State but this body does not actually decide any cases.

A claim for attendance allowance or disability living allowance should be made on the relevant DSS claim form, either a DS2 or a DLA1. These forms have undergone a number of revisions and may well change again in the future. They are not generally available to the public. However, you can get one by ringing or visiting your local DSS office. Alternatively, you can ring the DSS Freephone benefit enquiry line for people with disabilities on 0800 882200 or send in the tear-off slip requesting a claim form from the leaflet DS702 for attendance allowance or DS704 for disability living allowance. You will then be sent a claim form. (It may be wise to keep a record of the date you asked for it.) The claim form will be date-stamped, and provided that you return it within six weeks, your claim will be treated as being made on the date you requested the form.[8]

The forms are also available through citizens' advice bureaux and other advice agencies. These will not be date-stamped. The date of claim will be the date the claim form is received by the DSS, in the normal way.

Completing the claim form

The disability living allowance claim pack is large and runs to 40 pages. The attendance allowance claim pack has over 20 pages. Both packs come in two parts. The first asks for various factual details about the person claiming the allowance, the second about the sort of help they need with personal care and/or getting around. If you find it difficult to complete the form, you can get help with this. The Benefits Agency can arrange to ring you to help you complete the form or in some circumstances send a visiting officer to do so. Most advice agencies will also willingly help you complete the form. It is the first part of the pack which is technically the benefit claim. If you are going to take a while to complete the second part, do not delay sending the first part back.

The process is similar for both benefits. In the second part of the form you are asked to assess your abilities across a range of tasks and activities and to describe the nature of your condition. You are also asked to give the names of two people who can confirm what you have said. One of these is a person who knows you well in a professional capacity, the other someone who knows you personally. These might be, therefore, your doctor and your carer. Your doctor will not charge you for completing that page of the form. If you are unable to get other people to complete the form you should send it in anyway, as the Benefits Agency will arrange for this to be done.

The disability living allowance claim form covers both mobility and care needs, but you do not need to complete both sections. It is quite possible, for example to complete the questions that only relate to mobility needs because you only want to claim for the mobility component.

When you complete the second part of the form you should look carefully at the descriptions of the qualifying conditions for the various rates of the allowances given earlier in this chapter.

If you are claiming for the higher rate mobility component of disability living allowance, be cautious whem completing the part of the form which asks you to say how far you can walk without experiencing 'severe discomfort'. It is often difficult to judge distances accurately. Get a relative or friend to check that any estimate you make is right. Make sure that if walking becomes painful after you have gone a short distance, or you have to stop after a short distance, it is that short distance that you put down, not the total distance that you can achieve. Remember that this is supposed to be a test of your ability to walk out of doors. If you have a walking problem which is worse when you are out of doors you should make this clear.

The attendance allowance and disability living allowance claim forms ask many detailed questions about your need for personal care, including dressing, undressing, getting in and out of bed, eating, drinking, toileting, etc. However, no form can be comprehensive. There is plenty of opportunity given for you to add your own comments, over and above replying to the set questions. Do give details of any needs you have which are not asked about on the form.

It is hard to complete the form accurately for someone who may qualify under the 'supervision' criteria, especially if they have a mental health problem. There are questions about being kept safe and about fits, blackouts and falls but there is an emphasis within them on the frequency with which help is required. Remember that someone can qualify under the supervision criteria if they need continual supervision to prevent an only occasional but nevertheless dangerous eventuality.

It is particularly difficult to complete the disability living allowance care component part of the form for a child. Remember that the test of their care needs involves a comparison with the amount of help that a non-disabled child of the same age would need. Again, the best approach may be to try to give as much detail as possible of the child's needs, over and above completing all of the boxes on the form.

For both care and mobility elements the form asks regularly about how many times a week you need help or have a walking problem. It is your overall pattern of needs or problems that will be looked at. Something is most likely to be taken into account if it happens more often than not, that is, on four days a week or more, or on most of the occasions when you try to walk outside.

Claiming for terminally ill people

If a claim is being made on the basis that a person is terminally ill, it may be made without the ill person's knowledge or authority. This applies equally to claims for attendance allowance, the care component of disability living allowance, or the mobility component of disability living allowance (although in this latter case, as explained above, terminal illness will only exempt the claimant from the rules about qualifying periods').[9]

These claims are known as claims under the 'special rules'. People claiming under these rules need to provide a form DS1500, completed by their GP or consultant, detailing their medical condition. They do not need to fill in the parts of the claim form relating to their need for personal care. If they wish to claim for the mobility component then they do need to fill in that part of the form.

It is possible for someone acting on behalf of a terminally ill person to request a review of an unfavourable decision, and even to appeal to a disability appeal tribunal, without the ill person's knowledge or authority. Such claims will normally be dealt with within ten days.

Renewal claims

If you have been awarded disability living allowance or attendance allowance for a limited period you will be invited to make a renewal claim before the current award runs out. Even if you fail to do so promptly you may still not lose out as benefit can be backdated to the end of the previous award provided that you submit a renewal claim within six months and throughout met all of the qualifying conditions.

The position is different where your award has ended for another reason than a failure to make a renewal claim, perhaps because your condition has improved. If you reclaim within two years you can be paid from the date of claim, without again having to serve the standard three- or six-month qualifying period, provided that you meet all of the other qualifying conditions.[10]

Transitional rules about claims

People who prior to April 1992 had mobility allowance or attendance allowance under the old system were transferred over into their equivalents in the new benefits structure. The details of these provisions were given in the 15th edition of this *Guide*.

It was possible, between April 1992 and April 1993, for people to make 'top-up' claims where they had either attendance or mobility allowance prior to April 1992, but not both, and wanted to try for the other element which they did not have. Such people were thus safeguarded against the unexpected loss of their existing component, as that would not normally have been considered afresh. Some claims of this type may still be outstanding. Note that they can be backdated to 6 April 1992 if they were received before 5 April 1993.[11]

The administration of claims

Claims are initially dealt with by regional disability benefit centres. A claim is first checked to see that it does not fail on grounds other than the claimant's disability, for example, that the claimant is abroad or the wrong age. If your claim fails on these grounds you have the right to challenge the decision by means of a review, although if you wish to take the matter any further your appeal will be to a social security appeal tribunal.

Your claim is then checked by the adjudication officer to see what information is needed to come to a decision on your case and if anybody needs to be contacted about it. S/he may choose to contact someone you have named on the form for more information, perhaps your doctor. S/he may also arrange for you to be given a medical examination by a doctor acting on behalf of the DSS.[12]

The Secretary of State does have the power to refer claimants to doctors for examinations either in order to monitor the operation of disability living allowance, or to provide the adjudication officer with further information in connection with the claim.[13] He may also direct that certain classes of case are always referred to doctors. The doctors themselves may refer such special cases to the Disability Living Allowance Advisory Board for advice.

If you refuse to attend a medical examination at the request of the adjudication officer or the Secretary of State 'without good cause to do so' then the adjudication officer will have to decide your claim against you.[14]

Period of payment

Either allowance can be awarded for limited periods or for life.[15] In practice, a limited period award is likely where the claimant is a child, or has a medical condition which is receiving active treatment, but limited period awards are in any event common on first claims. If you are aggrieved about the length of the award made to you, either because your condition is such that your care or mobility needs will not decrease, or because you needed a longer period award of the mobility component to take advantage of the Motability scheme, you should consider asking for a review (see p123). If the award is for a limited period you will be invited to make a renewal claim shortly before the award runs out.

Between April 1992 and April 1993 people who qualified for both the care and mobility components of disability living allowance, either by claiming them for the first time after April 1992, or because they had their previous equivalents, still technically had separate awards of the two components.[16] These could therefore be for different periods. From 5 April 1993 such beneficiaries will have their two separate awards terminated. They will be given a new combined award of both components. If one award was for life and the other for a limited period, then the new combined award will run until the award which is for a fixed period expires. Thereafter the beneficiary will have only a life award of the other component (although the component which has stopped may well become payable for a further fixed period, or for life, when a renewal claim is made). If both awards were for a fixed period, then the end date of the new combined award will always be the earlier of the end dates of the two previous awards.[17]

Payment to children

The care and mobility components of disability living allowance for a child (that is, someone under the age of 16) are usually paid to an adult with whom the child is living, whom the Secretary of State appoints to act on their behalf. This will normally be the child's mother or the child's father. If the child is not living with either parent, then whomever the child is living with may be appointed to act for them.

The allowance can continue to be paid even when the child and appointee are not living together, including during a temporary separation of up to twelve weeks, or when the child is absent at a boarding school, or when the child is in hospital. The allowance will cease to be paid immediately when the child is being looked after by a local authority or any similar arrangement, unless the arrangement is not intended to last for more than 12 weeks.[18]

Reviews

If you are dissatisfied with the decision that you receive on your claim, you can seek to have the decision reviewed. If you ask for the review within three months of the decision this can be **'on any ground'**, so it is enough that you simply think the decision is wrong.[19] Your request for a review should be made in writing to the disability living allowance unit or attendance allowance unit within three months of the decision being sent to you. This three-month limit can be extended if your request for a review was delayed in the post by industrial action.[20]

A review is carried out by a different adjudication officer from the one who took the original decision. The second adjudication officer is based at the relevant central unit, not the regional disability benefit centre where your claim was initially decided. The adjudication officer conducting the review decides what further evidence is needed in order to come to a decision, and how to collect this. Medical evidence, from a GP or consultant, may well be helpful at this stage. However, evidence from a carer, or a diary of your walking and/or care needs over a period, may be equally useful.

If you are refused at this review stage and you wish to take your case further this will normally be by way of an appeal to a disability appeal tribunal.

It is also possible for an adjudication officer's decision to be reviewed outside these time limits if the adjudication officer conducting the review accepts that:

- the earlier decision was made in ignorance of, or was based on a mistake about, some material fact; *or*
- there has been any relevant change of circumstances since that decision was made; *or*
- it is anticipated that there will be a relevant change of circumstances; *or*
- there was an error of law in the decision; *or*
- the decision was to make an award wholly or partly after the claim was made but on the basis that some condition would be fulfilled in the future and that condition has not been fulfilled; *or*
- the decision was that someone was terminally ill and there has been a change of medical opinion in relation to that.[21]

There are two groups who use this route to review. The first are adjudication officers. The second are those claimants whose condition has worsened, who are asking to be awarded a higher rate than they had before. If a claimant is dissatisfied with a decision on such a review application, typically because the adjudication officer takes the view that their condition has not worsened sufficiently to qualify them for the rate they were requesting, then they may seek a further review of that decision. If still dissatisfied, the claimant can then appeal against the decision on review to the disability appeal tribunal in the standard manner.[22]

You should think carefully before requesting a review. A review is a fresh hearing of your case. That means that your case is looked at completely anew. So there is a risk that, if you have been awarded a component of disability living allowance, or attendance allowance, at a particular rate, and you seek a review because you think you should have got more than you were awarded, you may lose what you had. This happens only rarely.

There is a further small risk in seeking a review, which arises from the combination of attendance and mobility allowance into disability living allowance in April 1992. Some people seeking a review may be doing so because they have not been awarded one component of the disability living allowance when they are already in receipt of the other. Or they may be seeking a review of the rate they have been awarded of one component when they are quite satisfied with the rate they receive of the other. In these circumstances the adjudication officer need not consider the component which is not the subject of the review, although s/he may. [23]

Further, if a person has been awarded a component of disability living allowance for life, then the adjudication officer should not consider the rate of that component, or the length of time for which it has been awarded, unless the review has been asked for on that basis, or 'information is available to the adjudication officer which gives him reasonable grounds for believing that entitlement to the component, or entitlement to it at the rate awarded or for that period, ought not to continue'. [24]

Appeals

You may appeal against the decision of the adjudication officer on your review. This is to a disability appeal tribunal, if your dispute relates to a 'disability question', otherwise it will be to a social security appeal tribunal (see p242). If you are still dissatisfied, you may then appeal to a social security commissioner against any decision of a disability appeal tribunal, but only on a point of law (see p249).

CHAPTER EIGHT

Invalid care allowance

I Introduction

Conditions of entitlement[1]

- You satisfy the residence conditions (see p193).
- You are caring for a person receiving either the higher or middle rates of the care component of disability living allowance (see p108), attendance allowance (see p114) or constant attendance allowance in respect of industrial or war disablement (see pp141 and 262).
- The care you give is regular and substantial (see p126).
- You are not gainfully employed or in full-time education (see p127).
- You are not under 16 nor over 65 (but see p127 for exceptions).
- You claim within the time limit (see below).

How to claim

You should claim the allowance from your local Benefits Agency office within 12 months of becoming entitled. If you claim later, only 12 months' arrears will be paid.[2]

A claim for income support or unemployment benefit *may* be treated as a claim for invalid care allowance (ICA).[3] This is a decision for the Secretary of State, so there is no right of appeal (see p227) and he does not have to treat the claim as one for ICA.[4] You will win if it is felt that a reasonably alert official, asking the proper questions, would have recognised that you were entitled to ICA. If you fail, consider complaining to the Ombudsman (see p240).

Amount of payment[5]

	£pw
Claimant	33.70
Adult dependant	20.15
Child dependant	10.95

While receiving ICA, you are credited with Class 1 contributions (see p157). You are entitled to a Christmas bonus (see p212).

Tax and other benefits

ICA is taxable except for any increase in respect of dependent children.[6]
There can be both advantages and disadvantages to claiming ICA

because of its effect on other benefits. There are a number of factors that you need to take into account.

If you are a married woman, your husband cannot claim an increase of his benefit in respect of you.[7] This may be important if he receives invalidity pension because an increase of invalidity pension in respect of a wife is not taxable. On the other hand, ICA now has a more generous earnings rule.

If you receive ICA you are not required to be available for work as a condition of entitlement to income support.[8] If you are not receiving ICA, but you are regularly and substantially caring for a person who receives or has claimed attendance allowance or the higher or middle rates of the care component of disability living allowance, you are likewise not required to be available for work.[9]

If you receive ICA, (or are entitled to it but do not receive it because of the effect of the overlapping benefit rules) you will get a carer's premium of £11.95 per week included in the calculation of your income support, housing benefit or council tax benefit.[10] However, if you actually receive ICA the person you care for will not be able to get the severe disability premium for the purposes of those benefits.[11] Your means-tested benefit will be reduced by the amount of any ICA you receive as it is taken into account in full as income for these benefits.[12]

ICA attracts a credited Class 1 contribution (but your contribution record may be protected anyway through home responsibilities protection (see p182).

'Regularly and substantially' caring

To qualify for the benefit you must be engaged in caring for your patient 'regularly and substantially'. You satisfy this requirement during any week in which you are (or are likely to be) engaged and regularly engaged in caring for her/him for 35 hours or more.[13] You can be treated as meeting this rule if some of the time you spend on caring in the week is time spent preparing for the disabled person to come to stay with you, or clearing up after their visit.[14] However, it is not possible to meet the rules if caring for 35 hours per week on average by caring for more than 35 hours in some weeks and less in others. The rules require that the carer cares for 35 hours per week in the week in question.[15]

Once you have been caring for your patient for a while, temporary breaks in your care do not lead to the loss of your benefit. You can have a break, provided that you *were* caring for your patient for 14 of the previous 26 weeks and that you *would have been* caring for 22 of those weeks but you or your patient was in hospital. That means you can have four weeks' holiday in any period of six months.[16]

ICA stops if your patient's attendance allowance or disability living allowance stops because they are in hospital. If your patient is an adult this will be after they have been an in-patient for more than four weeks. If your patient is under the age of 16 they do not lose their disability living allowance until they have been in hospital for 12 weeks.

'Gainfully employed'

You cannot qualify if you are gainfully employed or in full-time education. You are considered to be gainfully employed if your earnings are £50 a week or more (for the way earnings are calculated, see p210). Your earnings will be ignored if you are working during a period when you are not actually caring for the disabled person because s/he is in hospital or you are on your four weeks' holiday (see above). They will also be ignored during any week when you are on leave from work, even if that is a week of paid absence from work.[17]

'Full-time education'

If you are attending a university, college or school full-time, and the Secretary of State certifies that you are receiving full-time education, you will not be entitled to benefit. You will not be treated as being in full-time education unless the Secretary of State issues such a certificate.[18] You cannot appeal to a tribunal against the decision to issue a certificate because it is a decision of the Secretary of State (see p227).

People over pensionable age

Under British legislation, you are not entitled to ICA once you are over pensionable age (65 for men, 60 for women) unless you were entitled to it immediately before you reached that age (or you would have been but for the overlapping benefit rules, see p208).[19] However, the Court of Appeal has decided that the difference in the ages at which this rule applies amounts to sex discrimination which is unlawful under European Community law.[20]

The effect of this is that women as well as men are now able to claim ICA up to the age of 65 simply by satisfying the usual conditions. The Secretary of State is appealing to the European Court of Justice against this decision and, in the meantime, the DSS is refusing to make payments under it. The outcome will not be known until after this edition of the guide is printed. If you are in this position you should claim anyway and await the outcome of the appeal. If an adjudication officer decides against you, lodge an appeal to a tribunal (see p242) and ask an advice agency to contact CPAG's solicitors.

If you are over 65, you are entitled to ICA only if you were receiving it immediately before you reached *either* the age of 60 *or* the age of 65. These alternatives arise because the British legislation prescribes the two different pensionable ages and men can claim to be discriminated against by the choice of 65 and women can claim to be discriminated against by the choice of 60. Therefore both sexes can choose either age depending on which suits their claims.

If you are a woman entitled to ICA immediately before you reach the age of 65, you can continue to receive the benefit even if you have ceased to look after a disabled person and even if you start working full-time. Under British legislation this only applies to a man if you are entitled to

ICA immediately before you reach the age of 70.[21] However, it is arguable that European law again has the effect that the sexes should be treated equally so that men too may continue to receive ICA once over the age of 65, even if they have ceased caring for an invalid and have started full-time work.

The overall effect of this is as follows:

- if you are aged under 65, you are entitled now provided you satisfy the usual conditions;
- if you are aged over 65 and you were receiving ICA immediately before you reached 60 but not immediately before you reached 65, you are entitled now provided you satisfy the usual conditions;
- if you are aged over 65 and you were receiving ICA immediately before you reached 65, you are entitled now even if you have ceased caring for an invalid or have started full-time employment.

Unless you qualify under British legislation alone, you are likely to have to appeal in order to get benefit. Ask a local advice agency to contact CPAG's solicitors if you need further help.

CHAPTER NINE

Industrial injuries benefits

This chapter covers:

1 Introduction
2 Industrial accidents and diseases
3 Disablement benefit
4 Reduced earnings allowance
5 Retirement allowance
6 Industrial death benefit

I Introduction

Benefits under the industrial injuries scheme are paid to people who are disabled as a result of an accident at work or a disease caused by their job. The main benefit is **disablement benefit** (see p139). There are also a number of benefits which are paid as increases to disablement benefit of which the most important are constant attendance allowance (see p141) and exceptionally severe disablement allowance (see p141). There are three other benefits – reduced earnings allowance, retirement allowance and industrial death benefit – but these are being phased out and will only be relevant if your accident or disease occurred before October 1990 (for reduced earnings allowance and retirement allowance) or if your spouse died before April 1988 (for industrial death benefit).

For all these benefits (except industrial death benefit) you must show:

- *either* you have suffered a '**personal injury**' in an '**industrial accident**' (see p130); *or*
- you are suffering from a '**prescribed industrial disease or injury**'; (see p133); *and*
- as a result of that accident or disease you have suffered a '**loss of faculty**'; *and*
- as a result of that loss of faculty you are '**disabled**'; *and*
- you were an '**employed earner**'.

You are not covered by the scheme if your disability is caused by an industrial accident which happened before, or by a disease the onset of which was before 5 July 1948. However, you may still be able to claim allowances under either the Workman's Compensation (Supplementation) Scheme 1982 or the Pneumoconiosis, Byssinosis and Miscellaneous Diseases Scheme 1983. See leaflets WS1 and PN1, available from the DSS.

Note that you will also be able to receive full sickness or invalidity benefit even though you do not meet the usual contribution conditions if you are incapable of work as a result of an industrial accident or disease (see p57).

If you have been injured by your work you may also have the right to sue your employer. Legal aid and help under the green form scheme (pink form in Scotland) may be available and you may be able to get a free consultation with a solicitor under the ALAS scheme. Your right to compensation from your employer is separate from your rights to benefit under the industrial injuries scheme (although your compensation may be reduced if you have received benefits from the Benefits Agency, see p213).

2   Industrial accidents and diseases

A 'personal injury'

Defining a personal injury is not normally difficult. You will usually know whether you have been injured or not and if you are in doubt you should claim anyway. Personal injury includes the obvious, such as broken legs or arms,[1] but also covers the less obvious such as strains and psychological injury.[2] So an assault on a teacher causing slight physical injury might give a far greater injury to the mind by causing agoraphobia or a break-down. In difficult cases, the question is whether or not you have suffered a physiological or psychological change for the worse. It is not enough just to suffer pain if the pain is merely a symptom of an existing condition and does not make that condition substantially worse.[3] The damage must be to your body or mind but some permanent prostheses will be treated as part of your body even though they are not living tissue – eg, dislocation of an artificial hip joint counts as a personal injury,[4] but damage to a pair of spectacles[5] or an artificial leg,[6] does not.

An 'industrial accident'

An industrial accident is defined as 'an accident arising out of and in the course of your employment'.[7] It is important to realise that despite the name it is not only industrial workers who can suffer from industrial accidents – any accident while you are doing your job can qualify. For example, if you are an office worker and a badly loaded filing cabinet tilts and falls on you, that would count as an industrial accident.

'Accident'

The 'accident' must be an 'unlooked-for occurrence' or 'mishap'.[8] If you do a heavy or dangerous job where accidents are common, a resulting injury is just as much an accident as if your job is sedentary and compara-tively safe. If your heavy lifting causes a heart attack, it is the heart attack which is the accident, not the heavy lifting.[9] Deliberate acts by third parties can be accidents – for example, assaults on security workers or on staff in shops and hospitals.[10] However, if you start a fight at work and injure your hand punching somebody, that is not an industrial accident!

One of the most difficult questions in this area is the distinction between an 'accident', for which benefit is payable, and a 'process', for which it is not, unless it causes a 'prescribed disease' (see p133). Clearly, to fall from a ladder and break your leg is an accident – equally clearly, to work for many years as a heavy manual worker and have a sore back is a cumulative process.[11] However, sometimes a series of events, over a period of time, can be viewed as an accident for the purposes of the benefit.[12]

Example
Your job is trimming excess rubber from hot water bottles with a pair of scissors. A particularly hard batch of rubber comes through and each cut requires greater strength. Over two or three days you suffer a strain injury in your hand. The series of cuts constitutes a series of accidents that meets the definition.

It will be easier to establish the series of events as an accident if the period of time is fairly short,[13] or is noticed at an identifiable moment.[14] An accident is proved if you can establish that an identifiable occurrence must have happened, even if it is impossible to prove when.[15]

'In the course of . . . employment'

The accident must arise 'in the course of' employment. It has been said that 'an accident befalls a man in the course of his employment if it occurs while he is doing what a man so employed may reasonably do within a time during which he is employed, and at a place where he may reasonably be during that time to do that thing'.[16] Difficulties arise when work rules are broken, or when you do something not directly connected with work. The guidelines given below are literally only guidelines – there are exceptions to nearly every rule.

Generally speaking when you arrive at your employers' factory or shop, and are on their private property, you are in the course of your employment. You do not have to have clocked in or have reported to your actual workplace. If you arrive early to get ready for work, or to have a meal in the works canteen,[17] you are covered, though if you arrive early to fit in a game of billiards you are not.[18] You are probably covered during breaks from working if you remain on the employers' property,[19] but probably not if you go elsewhere. So if, during a tea-break, you go to a local shop to buy a snack, you are outside the course of your employment.[20] If you are allowed to have a snack either at home or at work while still on duty (such as may happen with a police officer) you are covered.[21]

While at work most activities are considered to be 'in the course of' work.[22] Smoking,[23] chatting,[24] or passing sweets[25] are all 'reasonably incidental' to the employment, provided they are not done in breach of instructions.[26] Even if you were doing something in breach of instructions you are still covered if what you were doing was done for the purposes of, or in connection with, your employment.[27]

Example
You work as a labourer in a paper factory where there is an absolute ban on riding on the load of a fork-lift truck. You are seen riding on the load, fall off and are injured. Usually you would not be covered, but you saw the load was slipping and rode on the truck in order to hold it on. This was done for the purposes of your employment and so, this time, you are covered.

Example 2
A supervisor works in an office where central heating has been removed, but not replaced or the holes patched. It is cold and her staff are threatening not to work in the draught. The employers do not respond to her pleas for help. She goes onto the roof to patch the holes with papers and falls through it. She is in the course of employment even though the employers would have stopped her activities.

As more people are injured on journeys to and from work than are injured at work itself, accidents while travelling have been a source of much dispute. You are not in the course of your employment during ordinary journeys to and from work unless you are travelling on transport operated by or on behalf of your employer or by arrangement with your employer and not in the ordinary course of public transport service.[28]

Many employees have no set place of work, eg, lorry drivers, local authority home-helps, gas and electricity board employees. Obviously a lorry driver is at work when driving her/his lorry, but gas board workers, travelling directly from home to their first job of the day are not always in the course of employment even if driving a gas board van. It depends on the circumstances, including the rules for the use of the van.[29] A home-help has been found to be in the course of her employment travelling between jobs, but not going to the first job or from the last. This is because she became engaged in her employment once she started at the first job and remained engaged until the end of the day.[30] However, a home-help who had to go out of her way to the first job to get special sugar for a diabetic client was in the course of her employment when injured travelling from the shop.

Some employees with no fixed hours of work may be regarded as covered from the moment of leaving home.[31] Recent cases have eased the rules on travelling, say to conferences or meetings. You must look at all the factors in a common-sense way when deciding whether or not you were in the course of your employment. So a police officer who had to travel about 40 miles from home to a training course was in the course of his employment while travelling.[32] Provided you go reasonably directly, with no marked deviation from a proper route, and do not embark on activities unrelated to the journey, you are covered. In considering whether to proceed with an appeal or not, you must look at all aspects of the employment, including the wording of your contract and the degree of flexibility in the arrangements between you and your employers.[33]

'Out of . . . employment'

As well as arising in the course of your employment, the accident must arise 'out of' your employment, so that it can be said that in some way the employment contributed to it. The fact that you suffered a displaced retina at work is not sufficient to show it arose 'out of' the employment, but medical evidence which shows that it was caused by sudden head movements while inspecting a production line will enable a finding of 'industrial accident' to be made. An unexplained fracture while walking at work is not an industrial accident;[34] but it is if you slip and the fracture occurs while you are falling onto the ground. You are covered even if you are more susceptible to injury because, for example, your bones are brittle[35] or your eyes are weak.

Example
A farm worker, doing his normal job of digging, suffers sudden pain in the groin. It is found that one testicle, which did not drop in childhood, has suddenly done so. The adjudication officer says that this *could* have happened at any time and so was not related to the employment. The claimant's doctor says it could have happened any time but probably did so at *that* time because of the heavy digging.
A tribunal awards him benefit.

An accident also arises out of your employment if it arises in the course of your employment, *and*:[36]

- it is caused by another's misconduct, skylarking or negligence, *or* by the behaviour or presence of an animal (including bird, fish or insect), *or* it is caused by your being struck by any object or by lightning; *and*
- you did not directly or indirectly induce or contribute to the happening of the accident by your conduct outside the employment or by any act not incidental to the employment.

An accident is deemed to be 'out of and in the course of your employment' if you are helping people in an emergency, or trying to save property at or near where you are employed.[37] A milkman was covered when he went to help at a bungalow which had caught fire and to which he was delivering milk.[38]

A 'prescribed industrial disease'

Not every disease you suffer because of your work will qualify you for benefit. It is necessary for the disease to be 'prescribed'. This means it is on a list, produced by the DSS, of diseases which are known to have an occupational link.[39] This list is reproduced in full in Appendix Three (see p270).
Whether or not you suffer from a prescribed disease is known as the

'diagnosis question' and is decided by a special procedure (see p226).

If the Benefits Agency accepts that you are suffering from a prescribed disease other diseases which result from it (eg, amnesia resulting from methyl bromide poisoning (C12)) will be included when assessing your loss of faculty and disablement.[40]

'Prescribed occupations'

Different diseases are 'prescribed' for different types of jobs because different jobs have different health risks. To qualify for benefit on this ground it is not enough to be suffering from a disease which happens to be on the list. You must also prove:

- that you have worked in one or more of the jobs for which that disease is prescribed; *and*
- that your job caused the disease.

It can sometimes be difficult to say whether a particular job is included on the list or not. Commissioners have recently had to decide whether workers suffering from **occupational deafness** (prescribed disease A10) who had respectively been employed in a steel rolling mill[41] and on the surface of a coal mine[42] had worked with a 'forging press plant engaged in the shaping of metal' and 'in mining coal'. The answers (no and yes respectively) are of less general importance than the fact that the decisions illustrate how complicated the questions can be. As can be seen from Appendix Three, the definitions are complex and you may need an expert's report to prove your case. If the Benefits Agency refuses to accept that you have worked in a prescribed occupation you should take advice, preferably from your union if you have one, or from a citizens' advice bureau.

For most prescribed diseases you do not have to have worked in a pre-scribed occupation for any minimum length of time as long as you can prove that the job caused the disease. Occupational deafness (A10) is an exception. To receive benefit for this disease you must have worked in pre-scribed occupations for a total of 10 years.[43] There are also special time limits for claiming benefits if you suffer from this condition (see p142).

Causation

You must prove that the disease is due to your occupation, but it is normally assumed that if you suffer the disease in the prescribed occupa-tion within a month of last working in that occupation, the occupation caused the disease.[44] With dermatitis (D4) and nasal cancer (D5) there is no such presumption. The connection has to be proved, so the Benefits Agency will investigate this, and you may need to ask your GP or consult-ant to help with a report linking the disease to your occupation. DSS guidance on the diagnosis of diseases is available (see Appendix Five, p291). However, it is not necessary to prove the link beyond any reason-able doubt and to rule out all other possibilities. It is necessary only to establish the link 'on a balance of probabilities'; in other words that it is more likely that there is a connection than there is not.

Example
A hospital cleaner uses a new cleaning material. A rash develops on his hands and he has to give up the job. The medical evidence shows that the cleaning material could have caused the problem but so could several things with which the cleaner had been in contact outside work. There is a strong argument that the cleaning material was what did cause the rash because the rash developed so soon after using it.

'Onset' and 'recrudescence'

The 'onset' (date of starting) of a prescribed disease is taken as the date of the first day you suffer the relevant loss of faculty (see p136). In deafness cases it is the later of either the date you first suffered the loss of faculty or the date you successfully claimed benefit.[45]

In diseases other than deafness, asthma and respiratory conditions, you can improve and then worsen again. It is important to know whether it is a 'recrudescence' (fresh outbreak) or a completely new attack. The first enables an immediate review;[46] with the second, a claim will have to wait for 15 weeks before disablement benefit can be claimed. If a further attack commences during a current period of assessment, it is assumed to be a recrudescence unless the contrary is proved. There is a special procedure (see p226) for deciding this recrudescence question.

Pneumoconiosis, byssinosis and diffuse mesothelioma

If you are suffering from pneumoconiosis, byssinosis or diffuse mesothelioma (or you are the widow or were another dependant of someone who died while suffering from one of those diseases) and you cannot get compensation from the employer, you may be able to get a lump-sum payment in addition to any industrial injuries benefit. For further details see Appendix One.

The disablement questions

In addition to showing the link between your injury or disease and your occupation, you also need to establish that you have suffered a loss of faculty and are disabled. There are three disablement questions:[47]

* Has the relevant accident or disease resulted in a loss of faculty?
* What is the extent of disablement resulting from a loss of faculty?
* What period is to be taken into account by the assessment?

These questions are decided not by adjudication officers but by adjudicating medical authorities (see p227) and on appeal by medical appeal tribunals (see p245). It is here that most disputes about disablement benefit arise. The DSS guidance for adjudicating medical authorities is available to the public (see Appendix Five).

Loss of faculty

A loss of faculty is simply an 'impairment of the proper functioning of part of the body or mind'.[48] A decision of an adjudication officer that there has been a personal injury resulting from an industrial accident does not itself prevent the medical authorities from finding that there is no loss of faculty but this will be rare.[49]

If you are turned down on the ground that there is no loss of faculty, ie, the accident has had either no effect on you, or only a very marginal effect (less than one per cent), you should be realistic as to whether this is true. If it is not, and you feel there has been a loss of faculty, you should appeal. You may not get to the 14 per cent 'barrier' for payment of disablement benefit, but, if your accident or disease occurred before 1990, you will need a finding of at least one per cent to claim for reduced earnings allowance (see p121) if there is any income loss. In addition, if you are unlucky enough to suffer another industrial accident, the percentages of disablement can be added together and may entitle you to benefit, even if neither accident would do so on its own.

Loss of faculty is *not* the same as disablement (see below).

Disablement

The extent of your disablement is assessed on a percentage basis. If the total disablement from all industrial accidents and diseases is more than 20 per cent, it is rounded to the nearest multiple of 10 per cent with multiples of five per cent being rounded upwards.[50] Any assessment between 14 per cent and 19 per cent is treated as 20 per cent (except for those entitled to disablement gratuities – see p140).[51]

Some degrees of disablement are laid down by regulations.[52] These include various amputations – eg, loss of a hand, or a leg – and degrees of hearing loss (see Appendix Two). However, even in these cases the adjudicating medical authorities must take into account the real disablement resulting from an injury[53] – for example, the loss of a right hand will be more disabling for a right-handed person than for a left-handed person. Apart from age, sex and physical and mental condition, the personal circumstances of a claimant must be ignored, so that particular problems you may have, like the location of your office, or the distance to the nearest bus stop, are ignored. Disablement is assessed by reference to a person of the same age and sex whose physical and mental condition   is   normal.[54]

When no degree of disability is laid down (and these form the vast majority of cases), the authorities must assess you on the basis of their experience and use the prescribed degrees as a guide.[55] In particular, you should note that 100 per cent is given to people who are far from totally disabled (eg, those with no disabilities other than total deafness) and other assessments should reflect this. The DSS *Industrial Injuries Handbook for Adjudicating Medical Authorities* gives further guidance based on medical appeal tribunal decisions (see Appendix Five).

It is important that you are very straightforward with the examining doctors. The authorities have checks to establish that your symptoms are consistent with the injury, and that your movements are consistent with the disablement you claim. Therefore how you walk into the room, and how you undress will be examined as carefully as how you respond to the examination.

The relationship between the industrial injury and any other disability is quite complex, depending on which arose first. If the other disability is congenital or arose *before* the industrial one, it is deducted from the total disability.[56]

Example
You lose a hand, which would normally be 60 per cent, but you had previously lost its index finger. So 14 per cent is deducted, leaving 46 per cent (rounded up to 50 per cent).

The reduction is often known as the 'offset'. Mistakes are sometimes made because the authority incorrectly bases your assessment on the loss of faculty instead of on the disablement resulting from the loss of faculty.

Example
You have a back injury as a result of an industrial accident. An authority has reduced your assessment by, say, five per cent on the ground of a pre-existing disability of which you knew nothing. Many people have spines that are slightly curved due to lifting things. The authority may have looked at an X-ray, correctly considered that your curved spine is not due to the relevant accident and then incorrectly reduced your assessment. What the authority should have done was consider whether the pre-existing loss of faculty (the curved spine) really has led to disablement which would have occurred even if the industrial accident had not happened. The authority should therefore have considered, among other things, whether the loss of faculty led to disablement before the industrial accident occurred. There was no physical disablement if you did not suffer any pain or restriction of movement (disfigurement is an exception) and it was therefore wrong to reduce your assessment unless there was some good reason for deciding that disablement would have arisen during the period of assessment even if the industrial accident had not occurred. You should appeal.

The authority also should bear in mind that even if you did have a pre-existing problem which caused a disability, the accident may worsen the effects of it, as well as causing a new problem. The assessment should reflect the increase in the original problem as well as the new disability.

No reduction is made if 100 per cent is a reasonable assessment for the industrial accident.[57]

If the other disability arose *after* the industrial accident then the authority has first to assess the purely industrial injury – if it is less than 11 per cent any disability from the other cause is ignored; if it is more than 11 per cent any extra disablement caused by the effect of the industrial injury on the other disability is added.[58]

Example 1
You lose a little finger in an industrial accident and are assessed as
seven per cent disabled as a result. You then lose the other fingers of
that hand in a non-industrial accident. You continue to be assessed
as seven per cent disabled due to the industrial accident.

Example 2
You lose the middle, ring and little fingers of one hand in an industrial accident and are assessed as 30 per cent disabled as a result. You
then lose the index finger of that hand in a non-industrial accident.
Your total disablement (assessed according to the Schedule) is now
50 per cent. But loss of the index finger only would have been 14 per
cent. The disablement resulting from your industrial accident is
therefore reassessed at 36 per cent (50 per cent – 14 per cent) which
is rounded up to 40 per cent.

In pneumoconiosis cases there are special rules. Any effect of tuberculosis
is assessed with the effects of the pneumoconiosis,[59] and if you are
assessed at 50 per cent due to the pneumoconiosis, any added disability
due to chronic bronchitis or emphysema will be added.[60]

Period of assessment

The authority or medical appeal tribunal makes an assessment for a
period 'during which the claimant has suffered and may be expected to
continue to suffer from the relevant loss of faculty'. It must begin on a
specified date and normally ends on a specified date. For assessments of
14 per cent or more these are usually six months, one year or two years,
or will be given for life.[61] For assessments under 14 per cent the
assessment will be given both as the actual percentage and as being 'at
least one per cent' for a period. This is to preserve the entitlement to
reduced earnings allowance.

An assessment will be either **final** or **provisional**.[62] It will be provisional when there is doubt as to what will happen in the future, and you
will be automatically called for assessment at the end of the period.[63] Life
assessments are of course final. An assessment of disablement benefit for
occupational deafness is always provisional for a period of five years.[64] If
the later assessment shows that your hearing loss is lower than the 50
decibels minimum loss for benefit to be paid, no benefit is then paid.[65]
This does not mean that your hearing has got better (the condition
generally worsens, in fact) but different means of testing give different
results. If a re-assessment does take you down to just under the 50 decibel
mark it is worth asking your GP or trade union to arrange for you to have
a further examination done to try to get grounds for appeal.

If your condition deteriorates during a period of assessment or, if you
still have a disability at the end of a period for which you have been given
a final assessment, you should apply for a review (see p232). If your

assessment was awarded by a medical appeal tribunal, you must ask a tribunal to give leave for such a review to take place.

Employed earner's employment

You can claim industrial injuries benefits only if you were an employed earner whose accident or disease was caused by your employed earner's employment.[66] This rule excludes the self-employed.[67] It also excludes most trainees on employment training and youth training schemes although they are likely to be covered by a similar scheme run by the Department of Employment.

If you pay, or ought to pay, Class 1 contributions as an employed earner (see p171) you are covered by the scheme. This includes those paying Class 1 (and, in the case of volunteer development workers, Class 2 – see p178) contributions while abroad.[68] You are also covered if your earnings are too low to pay contributions – mostly this is because of part-time work. Finally, you are treated as being in employed earner's employment if you are an apprentice, mine inspector or rescue worker, special constable, taxi-driver, office cleaner, agency worker, minister of religion, lecturer, member of an aircrew, mariner, or – in some situations – an offshore oil or gas worker.[69]

You are treated as *not* being an employed earner if:[70]

- you are employed by your spouse and *either* your employment is not for the purpose of her/his employment *or* your earnings are normally below the lower earnings limit (see p172). So a man employed by his wife to help run her shop, and earning £60 a week, is covered; *or*
- you are employed by a near relative (parent, step-parent, grandparent, son, daughter, step-child, grandchild, brother, sister, half-brother or half-sister) in a private house where you both live, and your employment is not for your relative's trade or business carried out there; *or*
- you are a member of visiting Armed Forces, or a civilian employed by them, unless you are normally resident in the United Kingdom.

3 Disablement benefit

Conditions of entitlement

- You suffer from loss of physical or mental faculty, as a result of one or more industrial accidents or prescribed diseases or injury.
- Your resulting disablement is assessed as being at least 14 per cent (one per cent in the case of pneumoconiosis, byssinosis and diffuse meso-thelioma).
- Ninety days (excluding Sundays) have elapsed since the date of the accident or onset of the prescribed disease or injury.

Amount of payment

The amount of benefit depends on the extent of your disablement (see p105).[1]

Extent of disablement	Benefit pw Claimant aged under 18 and not entitled to an increase in respect of a dependant	Benefit pw Any other claimant
100%	56.10	91.60
90%	50.49	82.44
80%	44.88	73.28
70%	39.27	64.12
60%	33.66	54.96
50%	28.05	45.80
40%	22.44	36.64
30%	16.83	27.48
11-20%	11.22	18.32
1-10%	5.61	9.16

There are also increases of benefit (see p141).

Since 1 October 1986, disablement benefit has been paid only if the assessment of disablement is at least 14 per cent,[2] except in the cases of pneumoconiosis, byssinosis and diffuse mesothelioma, when benefit is paid if the assessment is at least one per cent.[3]

Until 1 October 1986, disablement benefit was paid in respect of any assessment of disablement of at least one per cent. The old rules are still in force for assessments following claims made before that date.[4] That is most important where there have been a series of provisional assessments because any new assessment is then regarded as following from the original claim which may have been made some years ago.

Under these old rules, an assessment of less than 20 per cent results in entitlement to a lump-sum **disablement gratuity**.[5] The amount of the gratuity depends on the maximum disablement gratuity in force at the beginning of the period of assessment (rather than at the date of the award). The maximum is now £6,080 and is awarded if the assessment is 19 per cent disablement for life. The gratuity is reduced by five per cent for every one per cent by which the assessment is lower than 19 per cent. A life assessment is treated as equivalent to an assessment for seven years and, if the assessment is for a shorter period, the gratuity is reduced proportionately.

Example
A pre-1986 accident giving rise to an assessment of 10 per cent disablement for two years from 1 May 1992 results in a disablement gratuity of:

$$£6,080 \times 55\% \times {}^{2}/_{7} = £955.43$$

Before 1 October 1986, those entitled to special hardship allowance (now replaced by reduced earnings allowance) could choose to have a small weekly pension instead of a gratuity. That option has been abolished, but those already entitled to such pensions continue to receive them with their reduced earnings allowance.[6]

Tax and other benefits

Disablement benefit is not taxable.[7]

It is taken into account in full for income support purposes.

Increases of disablement benefit

Constant attendance allowance

You are entitled to constant attendance allowance if:[8]

- you are entitled to a basic disablement pension based on a degree of disablement assessed at 100 per cent; *and*
- you require constant attendance as a result of the relevant loss of faculty (see p136).

Disablement as a result of pre-1948 industrial accidents and diseases, war injuries and injuries suffered while on police or fire duty, may be taken into account in considering the degree of your disablement.[9]

Invalid care allowance may be paid to someone looking after you while you are receiving constant attendance allowance (see p125).

The **higher weekly rate**, £73.40, is paid if a person is 'so exceptionally severely disabled as to be entirely, or almost entirely dependent on (constant) attendance for the necessities of life, and is likely to remain so dependent for a prolonged period and the attendance so required is whole-time'.[10]

The **lower weekly rate**, £36.70, is paid if a person is 'to a substantial extent dependent on (constant) attendance for the necessities of life and is likely to remain so dependent for a prolonged period'. This may be increased up to £55.05 a week if 'the extent of such attendance is greater by reason of the beneficiary's exceptionally severe disablement'. If attendance is part-time only, the amount payable is 'such sum as may be reasonable in the circumstances' (usually £18.35 a week). Some claimants are better off claiming the care component of disability living allowance or the ordinary attendance allowance instead (see pp101 and 114).[11]

Exceptionally severe disablement allowance

This is paid at the weekly rate of £36.70 if you are entitled to a constant attendance allowance (or would be if you were not in hospital) at a rate in excess of £36.70 a week, and are likely to remain so permanently.[12]

Unemployability supplement

This was abolished in April 1987, except for claimants already in receipt of it. It is an increase of disablement benefit almost identical to invalidity benefit, including an increase like invalidity allowance and increases for dependants are all at the same rates as for invalidity benefit. However, it cannot be paid at the same time as reduced earnings allowance.[13]

Hospital treatment allowance

This was abolished in April 1987 except for existing claimants (see p205).[14]

Claims and reviews

Disablement benefit, including constant attendance allowance and exceptionally severe disablement allowance, should be claimed within three months of your becoming entitled. If you claim late, only three months' arrears can be paid, unless you have 'continuous good cause' for claiming late (see pp222-24).[15] The usual absolute bar on any payment in respect of a period more than 12 months before the date of your claim does *not* apply to disablement benefit.

You can apply for a declaration that you have had an industrial accident. You do this on form BI 95 from your local Benefits Agency office. This may be a wise precaution where you have had an accident but are not sure whether you wish to proceed with a claim to benefit

There are special rules for people suffering from occupational deafness (A10) or occupational asthma (D7). The old rule was that, for occupational deafness, you had to claim within five years of working in a prescribed occupation (see p134) and, for occupational asthma, within 10 years.[16] If you missed these time limits not only did you not get any arrears of benefit but you would not get benefit in the future either. In 1989 a Court of Appeal decision overturned the rule for occupational deafness and held that you could claim after the five-year limit had expired provided you had 'good cause' (see pp222-24) to do so.[19] By implication the ruling also applied to the occupational asthma time limit. Since then, the DSS has changed the law and claims that the old rule has been restored retrospectively.[18] But it is not yet clear whether this is right. It has been held that this change in the law cannot be used as the basis for reviewing awards made to those who had been awarded benefit in this situation before the retrospective legislation.[19] The validity of the retrospective legislation is due to be tested in the Court of Appeal in June 1993. If you are refused benefit because of these time limits you should seek immediate advice and ask your adviser to contact CPAG's Citizens' Rights Office for further information.

Any decision of an adjudicating medical authority or a medical appeal tribunal may be reviewed by a medical board (see p232) if satisfied by fresh evidence that the decision was given in ignorance of a material fact or was based on a mistake as to a material fact.[20] Furthermore, any assessment of the extent of disablement may also be reviewed by a medical board on the ground of 'unforeseen aggravation of the results of the relevant injury'.[21] This gives very wide powers to reopen cases – even long after the expiry of a final assessment of disablement.[22] But if the original decision was made by a medical appeal tribunal, an application for a review may be made only with the permission ('leave') of a medical appeal tribunal.[23] This restriction does not apply to a review following recrudescence of an attack of a prescribed disease or injury (see p135).[24] The period taken into account for a review on the ground of unforeseen aggravation may include any period not exceeding three months before the date of application for the review (or the date of claim leading to a 'recrudescence question' on which the review was based).[25] In order to succeed, you will need to show not only that your condition has worsened, but also that such deterioration was not allowed for in the original assessment. You may appeal against a decision by a medical board on review to a medical appeal tribunal (see p245).[26]

Disqualification

You may be disqualified for misconduct on the same grounds as for sickness and invalidity benefit (see p59), except that you are not liable to be disqualified for behaving in a manner likely to retard your recovery.[27]

4 Reduced earnings allowance

This has now been abolished except for those who had accidents, or started to suffer from diseases, prior to 1 October 1990.

Conditions of entitlement[1]

*   You suffer from loss of physical or mental faculty due to an industrial injury before 1 October 1990 or an industrial disease, the onset of which was before that date (see p135); *and*
*   your resulting disability is assessed as being at least one per cent (see p136); *and*
*   as a result of the relevant loss of faculty *either*:
    *   you are incapable and likely to remain permanently incapable of following your regular occupation *and* are incapable of following employment of an equivalent standard which is suitable in your case ('the permanent condition'); *or*
    *   you are, and have been at all times since the end of the 90-day qualifying period for disablement benefit, incapable of following your regular occupation or employment of an equivalent standard which is suitable in your case ('the continuing condition'); *and either*
*   you are under pensionable age; *or*
*   you have not given up regular employment (see p145); *and*
*   you have not been in receipt of reduced earnings allowance since 1 October 1990 and subsequently ceased to be entitled to it for at least one day (see p147).

In addition to those rules of entitlement, if you were entitled to reduced earnings allowance on either 10 April 1988 or 9 April 1989 and on that date you were over pensionable age and were retired, or were treated as retired, you remain entitled to the allowance for life. For the meaning of 'retired or treated as retired', see page 69 of the twelfth edition of this guide.

Reduced earnings

The fact that you are losing money as a result of an industrial injury is not, in itself, enough. You must meet either the permanent or continuing conditions, outlined below. Some people fall through the gap caused by the regulations – you can have gone back to work after the accident for long enough to miss out on the continuing condition, and are now losing money, but cannot show that you are likely to be *permanently* incapable of your regular occupation.

The permanent condition

Only incapacity at the time of claim and in the *future* are relevant. The phrase 'likely to remain permanently incapable' relates only to the 'regular occupation' and not to 'employment of an equivalent standard'. So you do not need to prove at a tribunal that you are likely to remain incapable of employment of an equivalent standard; just that you are not likely to be able to perform your normal job.

A person suffering from pneumoconiosis, who is advised not to work by a medical board, is deemed not to be able to work unless the adjudication officer proves otherwise.[2]

If your condition could be improved by an operation, and you refuse to have it, the adjudication officer may disqualify you, but only if the operation is a very minor one.[3] You have the right to refuse a more serious operation even if the result of not having it is permanent incapacity.

The continuing condition

Only incapacity at the time of claim and in the *past* are relevant, so there is less scope for argument than when assessing the future. However, if you returned to work but were 'sheltered' by your workmates, you can still argue that you were 'incapable' of following your regular occupation. Specific provision is made so that, if you have worked since the end of the 90-day period, but this work was approved by the Secretary of State or done on the advice of a doctor for rehabilitation, testing or training, it can be disregarded. So, also, is employment before obtaining surgical treatment, and six months of employment thereafter.[4] If you have given up work due to pneumoconiosis on the advice of a medical board you are deemed to have been continuously incapable of following that regular occupation.[5]

Regular occupation

This involves looking at your work history (part-time[6] as well as full-time) and the content of the job, as opposed to its title. For example, a docker, still employed to work as a docker but unable to earn as much because he is unable to do the full range of his duties, was found incapable of his regular occupation.[7]

If an accident happens when you have just started a new job your intentions and prospects will be relevant,[8] unless it was just a stop-gap occupation, say during ill-health.[9] If you are a full-time student, any part-time work will count as your regular occupation;[10] otherwise subsidiary employment will not count. If you would have been fairly sure to have been promoted by the time of your claim, but for the accident, then the promoted position may count as the regular occupation.

If you suffer from a prescribed disease and, because of this, gave up a job before you applied for benefit, it may count as the regular occupation.[11]

Employment of an equivalent standard which is suitable

Employment is of an equivalent standard if the normal earnings are the same as the normal earnings in your regular occupation.[12] If these earnings include a great deal of overtime, so that you have to do a lot more hours to earn the same, that is disregarded. It is the total earnings 'package' that matters, not how it is made up. Suitability is judged by looking at your education, experience, training, work history and general health.[13] Only employed earner's employment can be treated as suitable, so self-employed work will not be considered.[14]

If your regular occupation was part-time, full-time work is not of an equivalent standard even if you are medically fit to do it. Like must be compared with like. However, if there are no jobs of the same number of hours, different work for a similar number of hours may be regarded as equivalent.[15]

Giving up 'regular employment'

If you are over pensionable age, you lose entitlement to reduced earnings allowance if you give up 'regular employment' (unless you were entitled to the allowance on 10 April 1988 or 9 April 1989 and were then already over pensionable age and retired). Entitlement is regained by a return to regular employment since 1 October 1990.

'Regular employment' is now defined in this connection as employment for at least ten hours a week in a week within a period of five or more weeks of such employment. Hours are averaged over any period of five weeks but you are regarded as not having given up regular employment in any week in which you have one or more days of interruption of employment (ie, days of unemployment or incapacity for work – see pages 9 and 10).[16] This means that it may be important for you to defer entitlement to a retirement pension (see p90) when you reach pensionable age and claim unemployment benefit, sickness benefit or invalidity benefit instead.

There was no statutory definition of 'regular employment' before 1 April 1990.

In the light of the above it should be clear that in practice most people who lose reduced earnings allowance will do so because they reach retirement age. This is 65 for a woman, 70 for a man. It is arguable that there is no necessary connection between the overall rules about pensions and retirement age, and the discriminatory effect they have in this situation of withdrawing the benefit from women at an earlier age than men. This provision may therefore be in breach of the EC directive 79/7. If you are in this position you should seek advice.

During any period when you are not entitled to reduced earnings allowance because you have given up regular employment, you will receive retirement allowance instead (see p148).

Amount of payment

The amount of the allowance is the amount by which your current earnings, or earnings in a job which it is considered you could do, are less than the current earnings in your previous regular occupation.[17] Earnings include overtime. For most claimants this is a fairly routine calculation. However, if you are unemployed, the DSS's doctors are asked for your limitations; the Department of Employment's disablement resettlement officers are asked to say what job they think you could do; and the JobCentre is asked to quote a wage which such a job would command in your area. This leads to a number of possible areas of argument – they will be contrasting an income from the regular occupation, which may be an estimate, with the notional income of a notional job which the adjudication officer, advised from a number of sources, considers that you can do! You should look carefully at all the elements of the calculation, and assess whether the jobs quoted are realistic for you to do, whether the wages seem correct, and if a proper allowance has been given for you as an individual.

Example
You were employed as a 'silver service waitress' but injured your knee, and cannot manage walking very easily. You are unemployed, and there are few jobs of any description in the area for someone of your age (mid-50s) and physical restriction. You would have been earning £95 a week including tips. The disablement resettlement officer suggests that you could become a receptionist and quotes £70-£90 as a range. The adjudication officer usually takes an average and so allows you £95 – £80 = £15 a week. You argue that, given your disabilities and lack of experience, an employer would pay at the very bottom of the range. You find adverts for jobs offering less than £70. At worst you should be able to argue for £95 – £70 = £25 a week for at least a year or two.

Once the first assessment has been made the amount is usually increased in line with earnings in that industry or workplace, unless that 'regular occupation' has ceased to exist.[18] In that case, it is calculated as rising in line with the nearest 'occupational group' as defined by the Department of Employment. You can ask for a fresh assessment to take into account your normal prospects of advancement, though here you have to show that promotion would have happened, say at the end of a period of employment or training, not just that it may have happened if you had been particularly diligent.[19]

The maximum amount you may receive is £36.64 a week (£22.44 a week if you are under 18 and not entitled to an increase for a dependant).[20] You cannot receive more than this, plus a 100 per cent disablement pension, even for two or more industrial injuries.[21] If you were over pensionable age and retired before 6 April 1987 your allowance would be reduced if it would otherwise mean that you would be receiving more than 100 per cent disablement pension.[22]

A person who qualified for reduced earnings allowance, and was retired or treated as retired, on either 10 April 1988 or 9 April 1989 will continue to receive the allowance at the same rate. Its value will therefore erode over time.[23]

Tax and other benefits

Reduced earnings allowance is not taxable. It is taken into account in full as income for income support purposes.

The withdrawal of reduced earnings allowance

It is still possible for someone to make a first claim for reduced earnings allowance now, provided that they meet the standard qualifying conditions, and that the accident or disease occurred before 1 October 1990.

It is also possible to make a claim by showing good cause for not having claimed from an earlier date. The standard 12-month bar on the payment of arrears does not apply to reduced earnings allowance. Many claimants have been successful at tribunals because publicity for reduced earnings allowance (and special hardship allowance which it replaced) was so poor. The disablement benefit claim form, later redesigned, simply had a note saying that a leaflet was available, with no indication that a separate claim was needed. You should argue that this expected too much of claimants.[24] Further, it implied that help was available only to those who had at the time of making the claim lost earnings as a result of their accident. This would not have assisted those who were able temporarily to return to their regular occupation but might in future have become unable to do so because of the effect of their accident.

Because of the withdrawal of the allowance from those who were entitled prior to 1 October 1990 but who then failed to meet the qualifying conditions for one day or more, there are dificulties in advising those who have missed out on the allowance. Someone who might, for example, arguably be able to show good cause back to an accident in 1988, but who worked in 1991 for a few weeks in well-paid work, might be better off not raising the issue of good cause but merely claiming from now.

5 Retirement allowance

This is really a reduced rate of reduced earnings allowance for people over pensionable age. As reduced earnings allowance is phased out, so too will be retirement allowance.

Conditions of entitlement[1]

- You are over pensionable age.
- You have given up regular employment (see p145).
- You were entitled to reduced earnings allowance at a rate of at least £2 a week (in total, if you had more than one award) immediately before you gave up regular employment.
- You are not entitled to reduced earnings allowance.

(ii) Amount of payment[2]

The amount of payment is £9.16 a week or 25 per cent of the amount of reduced earnings allowance you were receiving, whichever is the lower.

Tax and other benefits

Retirement allowance is not taxable. It is taken into account in full for income support purposes.

6 Industrial death benefit

Introduction

Industrial death benefit is payable only in respect of deaths due to industrial accidents or diseases which occurred before 11 April 1988. The conditions of entitlement for **widows** are covered on page 87 and for **children** on page 159. The conditions for **widowers** are covered below.

If a man dies as a result of an industrial accident or disease after 10 April 1988, he is deemed to have satisfied the contribution conditions for widows' benefits and Category B retirement pension, so his widow is likely to be entitled to one or more of those benefits. Otherwise, there are now no special rules or benefits for people who die following industrial accidents and diseases.

Industrial death benefit for widowers

Conditions of entitlement[1]

- Your wife died before 11 April 1988 as a result of an industrial accident or disease (see p81).
- At the time of her death, you were being wholly or mainly maintained by her (or would have been but for the relevant accident or disease).

- At the time of her death, you were permanently incapable of self-support.

Amount of payment

Benefit is paid at the rate of £56.10 a week for life.[2] It does *not* stop if you remarry or live with a woman as man and wife.

CHAPTER TEN

Benefits for children

This chapter covers five benefits paid specifically in respect of children:

1 Child benefit
2 One parent benefit
3 Guardian's allowance
4 Child's special allowance
5 Industrial death benefit for children

Disability living allowance is also available for children (see Chapter 7).

I Child benefit

Conditions of entitlement[1]

- You and the child satisfy the residence conditions (see p193); *and either*
- the child lives with you; *or*
- you contribute to the maintenance of the child at the rate of at least the amount of child benefit for that child.

Amount of payment

Child benefit is payable at the weekly rate of £10.00 for the eldest child for whom benefit is payable and £8.10 in respect of each other child.[2]

A 'child'

A child is:[3]

- a person under 16; *or*
- a person under 19 receiving full-time secondary education either in a recognised educational establishment (or elsewhere if the Secretary of State is satisfied with the education); *or*
- a person under 18 who has ceased full-time education but is still within the 'extension period'.

Full-time education

A person is receiving full-time education if s/he is *either*:

- attending a course of education for more than 12 hours a week including instruction, tuition, supervised study, exams, practical work and experiments or projects provided for in the curriculum, but excluding meal breaks and unsupervised study.[4]

If your child's education is interrupted, the absence from school can be ignored for up to six months if it is 'reasonable in the circumstances', or for longer if it is because of illness or disability.[5] If your child leaves full-time education but returns after a period of work or unemployment, child benefit becomes payable again until your child is 19.

Child benefit is not payable if your child is doing an advanced course, ie, above A-level, OND, Scottish Higher Certificate or the equivalent level[6] or if s/he is on a youth training scheme and receiving a training allowance or if s/he receives income support in her/his own right.[7]

A child ceases to qualify for child benefit the week after becoming 19 or on the Sunday after the first of the following dates after leaving school or college – first Monday in January, first Monday after Easter Monday, first Monday in September. A child who has been entered for an external examination before ceasing full-time education at a school or college is treated as still being at the school or college until after the examination or until her/his name is withdrawn from entry.[8]

The 'extension period'

After a child becomes 16 or ceases full-time education, child benefit continues to be paid during an 'extension period' if s/he:[9]

* is under 18; *and*
* is registered as available for work or youth training; *and*
* is not in remunerative work for 24 hours a week or more; *and*
* is not receiving income support; *and*
* is not on a youth training scheme.

The extension period begins on the day s/he reaches 16 or is treated as leaving full-time education (whichever is later). If that first day is on or after the first Monday in September but before the first Monday in January, the extension period ends on the day before the first Monday in January. If it is on or after the first Monday in January but before the first Monday after Easter Monday, the extension period ends on the day before the 14th Monday of the year. If the extension period begins at any other time of the year, it ends on the 14th Monday after Easter of that year.[10]

Example
Your 16-year-old daughter leaves school in June 1993 She is treated as being in full-time education until 12 September 1993. The extension period then starts on the next day and continues until 2 January 1994.

Child benefit is payable during the extension period *only if* it was payable immediately before the period started *and* you apply in writing.[11]

Children in care

If a child is away from home in the care of a local authority (or, in Scotland, subject to supervision and residing in residential accommodation under the Social Work (Scotland) Act 1968), child benefit is not payable after the first eight weeks of absence.[12]

However, if the child stays with you while subject to a care order (or, in Scotland, supervision), child benefit is payable if:[13]

- the child 'actually' lives with you throughout the week; or
- the child 'actually' lives with you for part of a day in that week and then for the whole of the next six days; or
- the child 'actually' lives with you for a *whole day* in that week and for the whole of the six previous days; or
- the child ordinarily lives with you for at least *one whole day each week* even if the child is not actually at home in that particular week.

A 'week' means seven days beginning with a Monday.[14] A 'day' means from midnight to midnight.[15] This effectively means that the child has to stay with you for two nights to be regarded as living with you for one day.

Example
Your child is in care and comes home for half-term from Friday night in one week until Tuesday morning 10 days later. You are entitled to three weeks' child benefit because your child stayed with you for a whole week, with a day in both the week before and the week after.

The requirement that a child 'actually' be living with you is regarded very strictly, and even one night's absence by a child in hospital can result in benefit being lost. On the other hand, absence by you for two nights or so may be regarded less severely.[16] This is not a problem if the child 'ordinarily' lives with you at least one day a week because it then does not matter if the child is away during any particular week.

If you qualify for child benefit under these rules, you will still not receive it if you are receiving a boarding-out allowance from the local authority, unless the child has been placed with you for adoption and you were entitled to child benefit before 6 April 1987.[17]

Entitlement to child benefit is not affected by private fostering arrangements.

Other children for whom child benefit is not payable

Child benefit is not payable in respect of a child who is:

- married[18] (unless the child is not living with her/his spouse or her/his spouse is in full-time education. A spouse can never be the claimant even in these circumstances[19]); or
- in remunerative work for at least 24 hours a week;[20] or

- receiving severe disablement allowance (see p64) or income support in her/his own right;[21] *or*
- receiving an allowance under the youth training scheme;[22] *or*
- in prison or other custody (see p208).[23]

A child 'living with' you

To be living with you, the child 'must live in the same house or other residence as [you] and also be carrying on there with [you] a settled course of daily living'.[24] This does not mean the same as 'residing together' or 'presence under the same roof'.[25] A child may be 'living with' you even while temporarily away.

An absence for *any* reason of up to 56 days in 16 weeks is ignored.[26]

A child is still treated as living with you while receiving full-time education at a boarding school.[27]

You remain entitled to child benefit for a total of 12 weeks when a child goes into hospital, or into certain other forms of residential accommodation for medical purposes.[28] After this period, the child is treated as living with you only if you are regularly incurring expenditure in respect of her/him.[29] As long as you are making visits, this condition is likely to be satisfied.

Contributing to the maintenance of a child

To satisfy this condition you must contribute at the rate of at least the current rate of child benefit.[30]

Contributions must be regular although the odd hiccough may be ignored.[31] Payments may be in kind rather than cash.[32] If a husband and wife are residing together, any contribution by one may be treated as a contribution by the other.[33] Similarly, if you and another person each contribute less than the relevant rate to the maintenance of a child but your total contributions are greater than that amount, one of you will be treated as contributing the whole of it. If you do not agree on which one of you it is to be, the Secretary of State will decide.[34]

See page 165 for the way the amount of contribution is calculated in difficult cases.

Priority between claimants

It is sometimes possible for more than one person to claim child benefit for the same child. For example, the child may be living with one parent and maintained by the other. There is an order of priority which governs who receives child benefit when two or more people would otherwise be entitled.

No one is entitled without making a claim for child benefit and this must be done before the priority rules apply.[35] Even if the new claim carries priority over an existing claim, child benefit continues for the next three weeks on the original basis.[36]

After that, claimants take priority in the following order:[37]

- person having the child living with her/him;
- wife, where husband and wife are 'residing together' (see below);
- a parent (this includes a step-parent, adoptive parent and both parents of an illegitimate child)[38];
- mother, where the parents are unmarried and are residing together (see below);
- in any other case, a person agreed by those entitled;
- a person selected by the Secretary of State.

If someone else has priority over you, the result is not just that child benefit cannot be *paid* to you. You are not *entitled* to benefit even if you fulfil all the other conditions of entitlement. So, for example, if your claim is refused because the child is living with someone else and s/he then comes to live with you, you must make a new claim even if you have been contributing to her/his maintenance at the appropriate rate all the time s/he was not living with you.

A person who has claimed child benefit and has priority can agree that someone else with lower priority should receive it by writing to the local Benefits Agency office.[39] It may be important to concede priority to a person looking after a child so that s/he can claim home responsibility protection (see p183). A couple may also think that it is fair for the person looking after the child to receive the child benefit.

A married couple are regarded as residing together:[40]

- while one or both are temporarily or permanently in hospital or a similar institution; *or*
- until they are legally separated or divorced; *or*
- where there is no legal separation, until they have been apart for at least 13 weeks and the separation is likely to be permanent. This waiting period applies even if the couple have never lived together.[41]

An unmarried couple are regarded as residing together during any period of temporary absence, but not during any absence which is likely to be permanent.[42]

Claims

You make a claim for child benefit on forms CB2 and CB3 obtainable from your local Benefits Agency office.

Child benefit is administered from the Child Benefit Centre, PO Box 1, Newcastle upon Tyne, NE88 1AA. The public telephone number is 091-417 9999 but it is often engaged so it is best to send queries in writing, except in emergencies.

If you claim late, you may receive up to six months' arrears of benefit [43] unless someone else was receiving child benefit in respect of the same child.[44] That person's entitlement will usually continue for three weeks after your claim and then the benefit will be paid to you if you have priority over that person (see p153).

You cannot claim before a child is born because you will not know the precise date of birth. In other situations you can claim up to three months before you expect to be entitled to benefit, eg, when a child is returning from care, or when you have made an agreement over future receipts of child benefit.[45] On a first claim you will be asked to send the child's birth or adoption certificate.[46]

Payment

Child benefit is generally paid four-weekly in arrears either by order book or by credit transfer into your bank account (see p234).[47]
Weekly payments can be made only if:

* you were receiving child benefit before 16 March 1982, and you applied in writing before, or within 26 weeks after, your first four-weekly payment[48] (or from your return from abroad as a member or the partner of a member of the Forces[49]); or
* you are entitled to one parent benefit;[50] or
* you or your spouse or the person with whom you are living as husband and wife are entitled to income support or family credit;[51] or
* the Secretary of State is satisfied that four-weekly payment 'is causing hardship'.[52]

Weekly payment of benefit can be particularly important if you are receiving income support or family credit or are otherwise on a low income. Even if you are in one of these categories, you need to inform the Benefits Agency in writing that you want to receive the benefit weekly. In an urgent case you should contact your local Benefits Agency office; otherwise write to the Child Benefit Centre.

Tax and other benefits

Child benefit is not taxable.[53]
If you are a single parent, you may be entitled to one parent benefit on top of child benefit (see below).
If you are entitled to other social security benefits, you may be entitled to an increase in respect of a child for whom you receive child benefit (see p163).
Child benefit is taken into account as income for the purposes of income support.[54] If you have a child and are in full-time work but have a low income, you should ask your Benefits Agency office about family credit. Despite its misleading name, this is a weekly benefit and *not* a loan. Your child benefit order book gives you an indication how much family credit a person with your earnings should receive so you can decide whether it is worth applying.
If your child is living with you, s/he will continue to be treated as your dependant for the purpose of means-tested benefits during the child benefit extension period (see CPAG's *National Welfare Benefits Handbook*).

2   One parent benefit

Conditions of entitlement[1]

- You must be entitled to child benefit for a child who is living with you (see p153).
- You must not be residing together with your spouse if you are married (see p165) or living with anyone else as husband or wife (see p79).
- You must not be 'residing with' (see p165) a parent of the child (unless you are entitled in respect of another child and are not residing with the parent of that child).

There are certain limitations if you are in receipt of other benefits (see below). Also, you cannot qualify for one parent benefit for a child if you qualify for child benefit only on the grounds that you contribute towards maintaining her/him – the child must be 'living with' you.

Amount of payment

One parent benefit is £6.05 a week.[2]
  It is payable as an addition to child benefit in respect of the eldest child who qualifies.

Tax and other benefits

One parent benefit is not taxable[3] but is taken into account as income for income support purposes.[4]
  One parent benefit is not payable while you are receiving certain other benefits, in particular guardian's allowance, child's special allowance or an increase of retirement pension, a widow's benefit or invalid care allowance in respect of the same child.[5] If you receive an increase of any other benefit in respect of the child, the increase will be reduced by the amount of your one parent benefit.[6]

Claims and payments

You claim on a form which is contained in DSS leaflet CH11. The benefit is paid as part of your child benefit.

3   Guardian's allowance

Guardian's allowance is a benefit paid to those looking after children who are effectively orphans.

Conditions of entitlement[1]

- The residence conditions must be satisfied; and
- you must be entitled to child benefit for the child; and
- the child must be a qualifying child (see p157); and either

- the child must be living with you (see p153); *or*
- you must contribute to the maintenance of the child at the rate of at least £10.95 a week in addition to any payment you are making to qualify you for child benefit (see p165).

Amount of payment

Guardian's allowance is £10.95 a week in respect of each child.[2]

Tax and other benefits

Guardian's allowance is not taxable[3] but is taken into account as income for income support purposes.[4] It is not payable if you are receiving an increase of a social security benefit in respect of the child.[5]

Claims

You claim on form BG1 – see DSS leaflet NI14 for details.

You should claim within six months of being entitled to guardian's allowance. If you claim later, only six months' arrears will be paid.[6] If you are looking after a child of whom you are not a parent, and you do not qualify for guardian's allowance, you might consider approaching the local authority social services department for a fostering fee.

Children who qualify

A child will qualify if:[7]

- both the child's parents have died; *or*
- one of the child's parents has died and the whereabouts of the other parent are unknown and were unknown at the time of the death of the first parent (you must show that you have taken reasonable steps to find the missing parent, including asking known relatives and friends and checking on old addresses[8]); *or*
- one of the child's parents is dead and the other is sentenced to a term of imprisonment greater than five years (see below).

A **step-parent** does not count as a parent and so may be entitled to guardian's allowance in respect of a step-child.[9]

If a child is adopted, her/his adoptive parents are the ones who count as parents.[10] Guardian's allowance will be payable if both the adoptive parents have died or if one has died and the other has disappeared or is in prison. If a child is adopted by one person only, a claim can be made for guardian's allowance if that one person dies. If a child's adoptive parents have died, the child's natural parents may claim guardian's allowance.[11] However, adoptive parents may continue to receive guardian's allowance if they were entitled to it immediately before the adoption.[12]

If a child is illegitimate, guardian's allowance is payable after the death only of the mother, provided that paternity has not been clearly established or admitted by the father.[13]

If a child's natural or adoptive parents were divorced, and one parent has died and the other did not have custody of the child (and was neither maintaining the child nor liable under a court order to do so), guardian's allowance is payable to a claimant other than the surviving parent.[14]

Prison sentences

The rules for calculating the length of a parent's prison sentence[15] are complicated. They apply to other custodial sentences (such as detention in a young offenders' institution).

No period before the death of the other parent is taken into account.

Any period on remand (after the death of the other parent) is added to the sentence. This is despite the fact that the sentence will be treated as reduced by the period on remand for the purpose of calculating the date for the prisoner's release and not for the purposes of guardian's allowance. The result is that a person sentenced to four and a half years' imprisonment after being in custody on remand for nine months counts, whereas a person who receives the same sentence after being on bail does not. This is even more surprising because no benefit is payable for a period before sentence is passed and the person who has been in custody on remand can expect to be released sooner than the person who was on bail.

Consecutive sentences are added together but, if they are not imposed on the same date, any part of a short sentence served before the imposition of a later sentence (which takes the total to over five years) is ignored.

The allowance ceases to be payable when the parent is released from prison unless the release is only temporary. If the parent is transferred to hospital or escapes, guardian's allowance continues to be payable until the date when the sentence would have been served (without remission). If s/he is then returned to prison after the allowance has ceased to be payable, s/he is treated as serving a sentence equal to the remainder of the original sentence (plus any further consecutive sentence).

4   Child's special allowance

Child's special allowance, designed to provide some assistance to a woman who did not receive widowed mother's allowance because she was divorced from her ex-husband before he died, was abolished on 6 April 1987.[1] However, if you were receiving it on that date you will continue to be paid until:[2]

- you cease to be entitled (or to be treated as entitled – see p164) to child benefit for a child; *or*
- you remarry; *or*
- you and a man live together as husband and wife (see p79).

The rate of payment is £10.95 a week for each child.[3]

5   **Industrial death benefit for children**

This is not payable if the death was after 10 April 1988. However, usually either an increase of widowed mother's allowance or guardian's allowance is payable instead.

Conditions of entitlement[1]

* The deceased person died before 11 April 1988.
* The deceased person died as a result of an industrial accident or disease (see p81).
* At the time of her/his death, the deceased was entitled to (or, treated as entitled to) child benefit in respect of the child.
* The widow of the deceased is entitled to industrial death benefit.
* The claimant is entitled to (or, may be treated as entitled to – see p164) child benefit in respect of the child.
* *Either* the claimant is the widow; *or* the widow was, immediately before the claim, entitled to death benefit at the higher permanent rate (see p87) *and* she has not ceased to reside with the child.

The effect of this last condition is that industrial death benefit for a child continues to be paid if a widow lives with a man as husband and wife. The reason for this is that the widow remains *entitled* to industrial death benefit in respect of herself even though it is not *payable* while she is cohabiting.[2] The benefit may be claimed by the man with whom she is living.

Children who qualify

Benefit is paid for a child in respect of whom the deceased was entitled to child benefit. The deceased is also treated as if s/he had been entitled to child benefit if the child:[3]

* was a child of the deceased and either the deceased or his wife was either living with (see p153) the child or contributing to the child's maintenance (see p153) at the appropriate rate (or would have been but for the relevant accident or onset of the disease); *or*
* was a posthumous child of the deceased; *or*
* was wholly or mainly maintained by the deceased at the time of her/his death (or would have been but for the relevant accident or onset of disease); *or*
* was a child living with or maintained by the deceased's wife if she had been widowed before and her previous husband had been living with or maintaining the child when he died.

Amount of payment

Death benefit is paid at the rate of £10.95 a week in respect of each child.[4]

CHAPTER ELEVEN

Increases for dependants

This chapter covers:

1 Introduction
2 Extra money for your wife
3 Extra money for your husband
4 Extra money if you are not married
5 Extra money for your children
6 Residence and maintenance
7 The earnings rules
8 Trade disputes
9 Tax
10 Miscellaneous rules

I Introduction

If you are getting:

- invalid care allowance;
- invalidity benefit;
- severe disablement allowance;
- Category A or C retirement pension;

or if you are over pensionable age and are getting:

- unemployment benefit; *or*
- sickness benefit;

you may get extra money for your dependants (ie, your wife, husband, child or someone who looks after your child for you) on top of the basic benefit.

If you are getting:

- Category B retirement pension; *or*
- widowed mother's allowance (or the corresponding non-contributory benefit);

you may be able to get extra money for any children who you look after (but not for any adult dependant).

If you are getting:

- maternity allowance;

or if you are under pensionable age and are getting:

- unemployment benefit; *or*

• sickness benefit;

you may be able to get extra money for an adult dependant (but not for any child).

2 Extra money for your wife

Conditions of entitlement[1]

• You must be entitled to the basic benefit; *and*
• even if you have already claimed the basic benefit, you must also make a separate claim for the increase within the time-limits (see p222);[2] *and either*
• you are 'residing with' your wife (see p165); *or*
• you are 'contributing to the maintenance' of your wife (see p165) at a weekly rate equal to or greater than the standard amount of the increase (see below).

If you are getting **invalid care allowance** you must 'reside with' your wife to get the increase. You cannot qualify just by contributing to her maintenance.

Even if you meet these conditions there is an **earnings rule** (see p166) which may disqualify you from being paid an increase if your wife is working or has an occupational pension of her own.

The **overlapping benefits** rules (see p208) apply if your wife is claiming a benefit in her own right

Amount of benefit

Increases are paid only for some benefits. The rates are as follows:[3]

	£
Unemployment benefit (claimant not over pensionable age)	27.55
Unemployment benefit (claimant over pensionable age)	33.70
Sickness benefit (claimant not over pensionable age)	26.40
Sickness benefit (claimant over pensionable age)	32.30
Invalidity benefit	33.70
Severe disablement allowance	20.15
Maternity allowance	26.40
Invalid care allowance	20.15
Category A retirement pension	33.70
Category C retirement pension	25.50

3 Extra money for your husband

If you are a woman, you can get an increase for your husband in the same
circumstances and at the same rates as a man can get one for his wife. But
there are two exceptions:

- a woman cannot ever get an increase in her Category C retirement pension to cover her husband; and
- a woman can only get an increase in her Category A retirement pension
  to cover her husband if:
  - immediately before she became entitled to the basic pension she was
    entitled to unemployment benefit, sickness benefit or invalidity
    benefit including an increase for him; and
  - she has not stopped residing with her husband or contributing to his
    maintenance at the appropriate weekly rate for a single day since she
    became entitled to the basic Category A pension. [1]

These rules discriminate directly against women, but a commissioner has
held that the rule on Category A retirement pension is not unlawful discrimination because it falls within an exception to the EC Equal Treatment Directive (see p201) which allows discrimination where it is the
consequence of setting different retirement ages for men and women. [2]
However, in the light of the *Thomas* cases (see p201) this decision may
well be incorrect as the commissioner did not consider the question of
'proportionality' as required by EC law. [3] If you are a woman and are
refused an increase which you would get if you were a man, you should
appeal and ask your local advice agency to contact CPAG's solicitors for
advice.

4 Extra money if you are not married

Even if you are not married (or are married to someone else) you may get
an increase if your dependant is looking after a child for whom you are
responsible.

   Most people who benefit under these rules are living together as husband and wife with one partner looking after the child rather than
working.

   But other people can benefit as well. In particular, it is not necessary
for you and your dependant to be of different sexes, so gay or lesbian
couples may be entitled as may, for example, two widows with children
who live together for mutual support.

Conditions of entitlement [1]

- You must be entitled to the basic benefit; and
- even if you have already claimed the basic benefit you must also make
  a separate claim for the increase within the time limits (see p221); [2] and
- your dependant has care of a child; and either
- you are entitled to child benefit for that child; or

- you are treated as entitled to child benefit for that child (see p164); *and*
- you reside with your dependant (see p165); *or*
- you contribute to the maintenance (see p165) of your dependant at a rate equal to at least the standard rate of the increase; *or*
- you employ your dependant at a cost to you of at least the standard rate of the increase and the employment started before you became unemployed, incapable of work or retired, (whichever applies to you) unless the need for you to employ your dependant arose afterwards; *and*
- you do not also get an increase for your husband or wife.

If you are getting **invalid care allowance** you must 'reside with' your dependant to get the increase. You cannot qualify just by contributing to her/his maintenance or employing her/him.

There is the same **earnings rule** as for dependent wives and husbands (see p166) except that any money which you pay your dependant for caring for the child is ignored.

If your dependant is claiming benefit in her/his own right the **overlapping benefits** rules apply (see p208).

If you are getting **Category A** or **Category C retirement pensions** your dependant must be a woman.[3] You may be able to argue that this rule is indirect discrimination and unlawful under EC law (see p201). If you are a woman with a male dependant and would be entitled to an increase if he were female; you should appeal and ask your local advice agency to contact CPAG's solicitors for further advice. You should do this as soon as possible because you will have to prove as a fact that more men have female dependants to whom they are not married and who look after their children than vice versa. This will have to be done at your appeal to the SSAT (see p241) because social security commissioners only have jurisdiction to decide questions of law (see p249).

Amount of benefit

The increase is paid for the same benefits and at the same rates as for spouses (see p161).[4]

5   Extra money for your children

Conditions of entitlement[1]

- *Either* you are entitled to invalidity benefit, severe disablement allowance, invalid care allowance, a Category A, B or C retirement pension, widowed mother's allowance (or the corresponding, non-contributory benefit); *or*
- you are over pensionable age (see p89) and entitled to unemployment benefit or sickness benefit; *and*
- you must make a separate claim for the increase within the time limits (see p222) even if you have already claimed the basic benefit;[2] *and either*

- you are entitled to child benefit for a child; *or*
- you are treated as entitled to child benefit for the child (see below); *and either*
- the child lives with you; *or*
- you contribute to the maintenance (see p165) of the child at a rate of at least £10.95 a week in addition to the amount you must contribute in order to entitle you to child benefit (see p153).

There is an **earnings rule** (see p166) which may stop you getting the increase if you are living with your husband or wife or cohabiting and your partner has a job or occupational pension.

If you are getting an increase in widow's benefit, retirement pension or invalid care allowance for a child, you cannot also get one parent benefit. In addition, the **overlapping benefits** rules (see p208) mean that if you are getting one parent benefit for a child, an increase in any other benefit for that child will be reduced by the amount of the one parent benefit. They also mean that guardian's allowance cannot be paid if there is an increase for the child. Only one increase may be paid for any individual child even if more than one person meets the conditions of entitlement.

Amount of benefit

The increase is payable for invalidity pension, severe disablement allowance, invalid care allowance and Category A, B and C retirement pensions. It is also payable for unemployment and sickness benefit but only if you are over pensionable age (see p89). Widowed mother's allowance and the corresponding non-contributory widow's benefit are increased only for 'qualifying children' (see p85).

The basic rate of the increase is £10.85 for each child[3] but this will be reduced by £1.15 for the eldest child because of the 'overlapping benefits' rules (see p210).

When can you be treated as entitled to child benefit?

If you do not yourself receive child benefit for a child, you will still be treated as doing so if:[4]

- you are residing with (see below) a parent of a child who is receiving child benefit; *and either*
- you are also a parent of the child; *or*
- you are 'wholly or mainly maintaining' the child (see p166).

This means that if a child lives with both parents and the mother receives child benefit, the father may still claim an increase for the child. But a stepfather can only claim the increase if he is 'wholly or mainly maintaining' the child.

If you do not benefit from these rules you may still qualify for an increase if you arrange for child benefit to be transferred to you (see p154).

6 Residence and maintenance

'Residing with'

'Residing with' means that you and your husband, wife or other dependant have a common household. This rarely causes difficulties in practice.

Temporary absences do not stop two people from being treated as residing with each other[1] and you are also treated as residing with your husband or wife when either or both of you are in hospital, even if the stay in hospital is likely to be permanent.[2]

It does not mean the same as 'living with' (see p166).

'Contributing to the maintenance'

'Contributing to the maintenance' means that you are making **regular** payments to or on behalf of a person. Generally, a payment covers you only for the week after it is made, but payments will be spread over a longer period if that is what you originally intended.[3] For example, you can make regular monthly payments and they will be treated as covering the month beginning with the week after they were made. Payments may be in kind.[4]

If you make a regular payment **for more than one person**, the total payment will be allocated between your dependants in the way that is most advantageous to you (even if you pay under a court order which specifies the amounts in respect of each person).[5] If the payment includes an element of arrears it is ignored.[6]

Example
You receive invalidity benefit and pay under a court order £60 a week representing £10 to your wife, £20 for each of your two children and £10 off outstanding arrears. You will be treated as paying £50 a week which will be allocated as £33.70 to your wife and £10.95 to your first child so as to enable you to claim increases for them. You, therefore, receive £44.65 a week by way of increases rather than just £21.90 a week for two children.

If you have stopped maintaining a person, you cannot later cover yourself by making a payment in arrears.[7] A broad view is taken of an interruption in otherwise regular payments.[8] If you are not paying enough, but think you are, a payment of arrears may be taken into account.[9] A woman entitled to an increase of unemployment or sickness benefit who becomes entitled to a higher increase is deemed to have been contributing at the higher rate if she was contributing sufficient to be entitled to the lower increase.[10]

If more than one member of a household contributes to the household income, the extent to which any member of the household supports any other is calculated using the **family fund test**.[11] To apply this, you calculate the unit cost of each member of the family by dividing the household income by the number of members of the family (treating each child as half an adult). Each person who contributes more than her/his unit cost is then treated as contributing to the maintenance of all the others. The amount of the contribution to any individual is calculated by dividing that individual's deficit proportionately between those providing a surplus.

This calculation is made before you became unemployed, incapable of work or retired.[12] Subsequent changes are ignored but you must contribute the amount of the increase to remain entitled to it.[13]

If you are contributing to the family fund out of income support which you are claiming, you are still treated as making the contribution from your own funds.[14] Remember, the conditions of entitlement for the increases mean that it is *never* necessary to prove that you are 'contributing to the maintenance' of an adult dependant if you are 'residing with' her/him.

'Living with'

'Living with' means the same as for entitlement to child benefit (see p153).

'Wholly or mainly maintaining'

'Wholly or mainly maintaining' means that:[15]

- while you are on benefit you are contributing towards the maintenance of your dependant at a weekly rate equal to or greater than the amount of the increase; *and*
- before you claimed benefit you contributed more than half the actual cost of maintaining your dependant (unless your dependant did not become dependent until after you claimed benefit).

If two or more people are 'wholly or mainly maintaining' someone between them, they may agree by a majority that one of them will get the increase. The agreement must be in the form of a signed letter to the Secretary of State.[16]

If there is no agreement the increase will be paid to the person who contributes most (even if, on her/his own s/he contributes less than half the cost of maintaining the dependant) or, if everyone contributes equally, to the eldest.[17]

It may be necessary to use the 'family fund test' (see p165) to decide who is contributing what to whom.

7   The earnings rules

Adult dependants

If you are **residing with** your dependant *and* are claiming an increase in invalidity benefit, severe disablement allowance or Category A or C retirement pension, your increase will not be paid if, in the previous week, your dependant earned more than £44.65.[1] This limit does not apply if you have been entitled to an increase continuously since 14 September 1985, although in that case if your dependant's earnings exceed £45 the increase will be reduced by 5 pence for each complete 10 pence above that figure up to £49, and 5 pence for each complete 5 pence your dependant earns after that.[2] This is obviously more favourable than the normal rule where you could lose all your increase (up to £33.70 per week) if your dependant's earnings went a penny over £44.65.

In any other case (ie, if you are not residing with your dependant or if you are claiming an increase in any other benefit), your increase will not be paid if your dependant's earnings in the previous week were more than the standard rate of the increase which you have claimed (see p161).[3]

Because the earnings rule is more generous for invalidity than for sickness benefit, you may not have been entitled to an increase while you were receiving sickness benefit but may qualify after you transfer to invalidity pension. It is then necessary to make a separate claim for the increase.

For how earnings are calculated, see page 211.

If your dependant's earnings fluctuate, you will not automatically lose your entitlement to the increase every time your dependant earns too much in a particular week (although you will have no right to be paid benefit during the following week if that happens).[4] This is important. It means that you do not have to make a fresh claim every time your dependant's earnings exceed the limit. It also means that if you were claiming on 14 September 1985 you can continue to benefit from the more generous earnings rules which were in force before that date (see above).

A recent decision of the Court of Appeal[5] means that many claimants whose adult dependants had an occupational pension but no job and whose increases were refused or reduced because of the earnings rule may be entitled to substantial arrears. You are affected if:

* You are a man and at any time between 11 March 1988 and 5 December 1992 you were entitled to a Category A or C retirement pension; *and*
  - your wife was under 60; *and*
  - you were 'residing with' her (see p165); *and*
  - she had an occupational pension; *but*
  - she had no job.
* You are a man and at any time between 11 March 1988 and 5 December 1992 you were entitled to invalidity benefit or severe disablement allowance; *and*
  - you were 'residing with' your wife; *and*
  - she had an occupational pension; *but*
  - she had no job.
* You are a woman and at any time between 11 March 1988 and 5 December 1992 you were entitled to a Category A retirement pension and an increase of that pension for your dependent husband; *and*
  - your husband had an occupational pension; *but*
  - he had no job.

People who receive an unemployability supplement to their disability pension (see p141) may also benefit.

The DSS is seeking leave to appeal against the decision to the House of Lords, but anyone who is affected should take advice immediately. You should be prepared to appeal as the DSS are relying on the 'anti-test-case' rules (see p225) to refuse to pay arrears. However, you should argue that this is wrong as those rules do not apply when, as in this case, a decision of a commissioner is reversed on appeal by a higher court (see p226).

The Court of Appeal decision has also raised the possibility that there has been no legal basis for an earnings rule for any dependants' increases for the claimants of any benefit (except invalid care allowance) between 16 September 1985 and 4 December 1992 – even in those cases when the dependant was working. If so, many more claimants would be entitled to arrears. A further test case will be brought to clarify the position and developments will be reported in the *Welfare Rights Bulletin*.

Child dependants[6]

If you are living with your husband or wife or cohabiting, you will not get an increase for your first child for any week, if in the previous week your partner earned more than £120 and for each complete £16 per week s/he earns, in addition to £120, you lose entitlement for another child. So if you have three children and your partner earns £136 a week, you will only get an increase for one child.

8 Trade disputes[1]

If your dependant is disqualified from unemployment benefit because of a trade dispute (see p37) (or would have been disqualified if s/he had claimed unemployment benefit) you are not entitled to an increase.

9 Tax[1]

Increases of unemployment benefit and retirement pensions for adult dependants are taxable. Other increases (including all increases for children) are not.

10 Miscellaneous rules

Increases may be affected if you or your dependant go into hospital (see p205) or to prison (see p207). It is important to note that your increase may not be affected in the same way as your basic benefit. Increases are also treated separately under the overlapping benefits rules (see p208).

PART THREE

Contributions and earnings-related pensions

CHAPTER TWELVE

Contributions and earnings-related pensions

This chapter covers:

1 Introduction
2 Payment of contributions
3 Credits and home responsibility protection
4 Contribution conditions for benefits
5 The State Earnings Related Pension Scheme (SERPS)

I Introduction

As was mentioned in Chapter 1, many of the benefits described in this guide are financed from the national insurance fund which is made up of the social security contributions paid by employees, their employers, the self-employed and other people who choose to make them.

In turn, entitlement to those benefits – and, for long-term benefits, the amount paid – depends upon the contribution record of the claimant or, in the case of widows' benefits, of her husband. For the contribution conditions for benefits, see page 185.

Fixed percentages of social security contributions go towards the cost of the National Health Service. The rest is paid into the national insurance fund.[1]

Most contributions are collected for the DSS by the Inland Revenue but the ultimate responsibility for ensuring that contributions are paid correctly lies with part of the DSS called the Contributions Agency. The Contributions Agency also keeps the records of your contributions throughout your working life.

Classes of contribution

There are five different classes of contribution.[2] The class you pay depends upon whether you are an **employee, self-employed** or a **voluntary contributor**. The class is also important because the contribution conditions of contributory benefits are satisfied only by contributions of the relevant class.[3] Not all contributions count for all benefits.

Class of contribution	Payable by	Giving entitlement to
Class 1	employed earners and their employers	all benefits with contribution conditions
Class 1A	employers of employed earners	no benefits
Class 2	self-employed earners	all benefits with contribution conditions except unemployment benefit (but see p178)
Class 3	voluntary contributors	widows' benefits and retirement pensions
Class 4	self-employed earners	no benefits

The amount of Class 1 or Class 4 contributions you pay depends upon your earnings. However, you do not necessarily gain more benefit by paying higher contributions and Class 4 contributions represent an earnings-related payment to the national insurance fund giving no entitlement at all, although, of course, those paying Class 4 contributions normally pay Class 2 contributions as well.

Employed earners and self-employed earners

The distinction between being employed and being self-employed is usually clear but there are sometimes grey areas.

An **employed earner** is defined as 'a person who is gainfully employed in Great Britain either under a contract of service, or in an office (including elective office) with emoluments chargeable to income tax under Schedule E.'[4]

A **self-employed earner** is anyone 'gainfully employed in Great Britain otherwise than in employed earner's employment'.[5] If you have two jobs it is possible to be both employed and self-employed.

There is not usually much dispute over whether you hold an office or not. Office-holders are such people as company directors, registrars of births, deaths and marriages and so on.

The usual area of dispute is whether you are employed under a contract *of* service or a contract *for* services. This can be a complicated question and the Secretary of State must take into account a number of factors such as how closely your work is supervised, whether you can employ a substitute to do your job for you, the method of payment, whether the contract is for a fixed period, whether you have to provide your own equipment, where you work and the amount of freedom you have to decide when you work and how much work you must do. No one criterion is conclusive and different aspects may have different weight attached to them in different cases.[6]

Certain people are deemed to be employed earners.[7] These are office cleaners, many agency workers, people employed by their spouses for the purposes of their spouses' employment, lecturers, teachers and instruct-ors (but not if the instruction is for no more than three days in any three months or is given as public lectures) and most ministers of religion. Con-versely examiners, moderators and invigilators are deemed to be self-employed. [8]

The following employment is disregarded altogether: [9]

- employment in your home by a close relative if you *both* live in the home *and* the employment is not for the purposes of any trade or business carried on there. Close relatives are parent, grandparent, step-parent, son, daughter, step-son, step-daughter, brother, sister, half-brother or half-sister;
- employment by your spouse if it is not for the purposes of your spouse's employment;
- employment as a self-employed earner if you are not ordinarily self-employed;
- employment as a returning officer (etc) at an election;
- employment by certain international organisations or foreign armed forces (but only in certain circumstances).

Upper and lower earnings limits

Contributions are now paid by reference to the tax year (ie, 6 April to 5 April).[10] For each tax year there is an upper earnings limit and a lower earnings limit.[11] Employees are liable to pay Class 1 contributions on weekly earnings between those limits. The figure for the *lower earnings limit* is also used in other contexts where contributions are concerned. Since the present system was adopted in 1975, the earnings limits have been as follows:

Year	Lower earnings limit	Upper earnings limit
1975-76	£11.00	£69.00
1976-77	£13.00	£95.00
1977-78	£15.00	£105.00
1978-79	£17.50	£120.00
1979-80	£19.50	£135.00
1980-81	£23.00	£165.00
1981-82	£27.00	£200.00
1982-83	£29.50	£220.00
1983-84	£32.50	£235.00
1984-85	£34.00	£250.00
1985-86	£35.50	£265.00
1986-87	£38.00	£285.00
1987-88	£39.00	£295.00
1988-89	£41.00	£305.00
1989-90	£43.00	£325.00
1990-91	£46.00	£350.00
1991-92	£52.00	£390.00
1992-93	£54.00	£405.00
1993-94	£56.00	£420.00

Earnings factors

The amount of earnings upon which your Class 1 contributions have been paid is said to be the 'earnings factor' derived from those contributions. Each Class 2 and Class 3 contribution gives rise to an earnings factor equal to that year's lower earnings limit.[12]

Earnings factors are relevant not only for the calculation of entitlement to basic benefits, but also for the calculation of the additional pension payable under SERPS (see p188).

Decisions relating to contributions

These are made by the Secretary of State[13] and not by an adjudication officer, which means that you cannot appeal to a tribunal, although there are other ways of contesting a decision (see p227). One issue the Secretary of State must decide is whether you are employed or self-employed. Disputes can also arise over a person's contribution record. The Secretary of State relies heavily on a Contributions Agency computer at Newcastle upon Tyne but will often accept that the computer is not perfect if you can explain why you think the computer record is wrong.

2 **Payment of contributions**

Age limits

Contributions are intended to be paid during a normal working life. They are not therefore payable by those under the minimum school-leaving age of 16,[1] nor by those over pensionable age (65 for men, 60 for women).[2] The DSS should send you a certificate of age exemption when you reach pensionable age. Ask at your local office if it does not. Employers of employees over pensionable age still have to pay contributions at the full (contracted-in) rate.

Residence and presence in Great Britain

Class 1 contributions must usually be paid by employees who are employed in Great Britain[3] and either resident or present (except for temporary absence) or ordinarily resident in Great Britain at the time of the employment.[4] However, if you are employed by an overseas employer and are not ordinarily resident or employed in the United Kingdom, you are not liable for Class 1 contributions until you have been resident in Great Britain for a year.[5] This also applies to certain foreign students and apprentices.[6]

If you are working abroad, you must still pay Class 1 contributions for the *first year* if your employers have a place of business in Great Britain, you were resident in Great Britain before your employment started and you are still ordinarily resident in Great Britain.[7] After that year you are entitled, but not obliged, to pay Class 3 contributions.[8]

Class 2 contributions are compulsory if you are self-employed in Great Britain and are either ordinarily resident in Great Britain, or have been resident here for at least 26 weeks during the last year.[9] If you are present in Great Britain, they may be paid voluntarily if you are not required to pay them.[10] If you are self-employed outside Great Britain, you may pay Class 2 contributions if you wish, provided you were employed or self-employed immediately before you left Great Britain and, *either*:

- you have been resident in Great Britain for a continuous period of at least three years at some time in the past; *or*
- you have paid contributions producing an earnings factor of at least 52 times the lower earnings limit in each of three years in the past. Each set of 52 flat-rate contributions paid before April 1975 counts as satisfying that condition in respect of one year.[11]

You may also pay Class 2 contributions if you are a **volunteer development worker** resident in Great Britain but employed outside Great Britain and not liable to pay Class 1 contributions. These are paid at a special rate and give entitlement to unemployment benefit, but are payable only if the Secretary of State certifies that it would be consistent with the proper administration of the legislation to allow you to do so.[12]

Class 3 contributions are always voluntary. They may be paid if you are resident in Great Britain during the course of the year in respect of which you wish to pay the contributions. They are payable while you are abroad if you satisfy either of the conditions which would allow you to pay Class 2 contributions but it is not necessary for you to have been employed or self-employed before you left Great Britain. You may also pay them if you have been paying Class 1 contributions while abroad.[13]

Class 4 contributions are payable only if you are resident in the United Kingdom for income tax purposes.[14]

For those who pay Class 2 or 3 contributions, the old system of buying stamps at the post office each week has been abolished from April 1993. Instead, the Contributions Agency will send you a bill each quarter or you may ask to pay by direct debit. For more details, see DSS leaflet CA05 – *Self-Employed and Voluntary Contributors* – 'Payment by Quarterly Bill'.

If you wish to pay contributions while abroad, obtain DSS leaflet NI38 which contains an application form.

When you return to Great Britain, it is a good idea to notify the Contributions Agency so that you can be told of any deficiency in your contribution record that you might remedy, and so that your future contribution record is accurately tied in with your past record.

The meaning of the terms 'resident' and 'present' are explained on pages 195 and 196. Members of the Armed Forces are deemed always to be present in Great Britain and there are special rules for aircrew, mariners, share fishermen and offshore workers on the continental shelf. The DSS takes the view that you are 'ordinarily resident' in Great Britain if you are likely to return within the next three to five years, although facts such as whether you keep a home or bank account in Great Britain are also relevant.

It should also be noted that Northern Ireland and Isle of Man contributions count towards British benefits and so can contributions paid in other countries in some circumstances. Also you may be entitled to benefits from other countries while you are in this country (see Chapter 13).

Reduced liability for married women and widows

Newly married or widowed women now pay the same level of contributions as anyone else. Until 5 April 1977 they could choose to pay a reduced Class 1, or no Class 2, contribution. Women who had done so were able to choose to continue payment at this reduced level of contribution.[15] The disadvantage is that there is no later entitlement to any benefit except for industrial injury and no right (except for widows) to receive credits when these would otherwise be made, eg, during sickness.[16]

A married woman whose husband dies while she is taking advantage of this provision loses her right to continue to do so unless she is receiving a widow's benefit. The right is lost at the end of the tax year in which her husband dies or the end of the next year if he dies after 30 September.[17]

The right to opt for reduced liability is also automatically lost:[18]

- on divorce or annulment of marriage;
- at the end of the tax year in which she stops receiving a widow's benefit;
- after two tax years with no earnings;
- at the end of a tax year in which a Class 1 contracted-out contribution (see p176) is paid by mistake but the woman wishes to pay such contributions;
- when a Class 1 contracted-in contribution (see below) is paid by mistake but the woman wishes to continue paying it, has asked for no refund, has not since paid any reduced or contracted-out rate contributions and confirms to the Secretary of State that she wishes to pay the full rate before the end of the calendar year after the tax year in which she starts to pay the full contributions, eg, 31 December 1993 for the tax year 1991-92.

It is worth thinking carefully about your position if you are currently taking advantage of the reduced liability. Once lost, the right cannot be reclaimed. On the one hand, if you continue with the reduced liability, you are not accumulating entitlement to contributory benefits. On the other hand, you can still receive widows' benefits and Category B retirement pension on your husband's record, non-contributory benefits (such as attendance allowance or mobility allowance), and means-tested benefits (such as income support). Bear in mind the extent to which your pension entitlement will be improved by paying contributions now, but remember that home responsibility protection (see p183) is only available if the election to pay the reduced amount is revoked. Also you could gain an additional pension under SERPS if you start paying full Class 1 contributions now, but you could consider putting the money into a private scheme instead.

It is very difficult to give general advice in this field. Quite a lot depends on individual circumstances, such as the amount you earn, the security of your employment, your state of health, your age and whether you are sufficiently well-off to be disqualified from income support. Ask your union or local citizens' advice bureau for advice.

To revoke your election, fill in the form in DSS leaflet NI1 for married women or NI51 for widows.

Class I contributions

Class 1 contributions are paid both by **employed earners** (see p171 – known as primary contributors) and their **employers** (secondary contributors).[19] Both your liability and your employers' liability depend upon the amount of your earnings in relation to the lower and upper earnings limits (see p172). These earnings limits are currently £56 and £420 a week. If your earnings are monthly, the earnings limits are multiplied by $4^{1}/_3$ to give monthly equivalents.[20]

If you are **not contracted out of SERPS** (see p189), the rate of your contribution is two per cent of earnings below the lower earnings limit plus nine per cent of your earnings between the lower and upper earnings limits.[21]

Example
If your weekly earnings are £176, your Class 1 contribution is:

2% of £56 + 9% of £120 = £1.12 + £10.80 = £11.92

The most anyone can have to pay is £33.88 a week (ie, two per cent of £56 plus nine per cent of £364).

If you are **contracted out of SERPS** (see p188), the rate of your contribution is two per cent of earnings below the lower earnings limit plus 7.2 per cent of your earnings between the lower and upper earnings limits.[22] So, the most anyone can have to pay is £27.33 a week.

Although your contributions to the national insurance fund are lower if you are contracted out, you probably pay more than two per cent of your earnings into your occupational pension scheme instead.

If you are a member of an **appropriate personal pension scheme** (see p189), you pay Class 1 contributions at the contracted-in rate but the Secretary of State then pays to the scheme a sum equal to the difference between the contracted-in and contracted-out rates.[23]

If you are **a married woman or widow with reduced liability** for contributions (see p175), you pay 3.85 per cent of your earnings up to the upper earnings limit but your employers pay at the usual rate.[24]

There are also **special rates** for members of the armed forces and the employers of certain mariners employed on foreign-going ships.[25]

If you have **more than one job**, obtain DSS leaflet NP28 which gives details of the arrangements which apply. Basically, contributions are payable on all earnings up to a maximum figure which is equal to the maximum that would be payable if you had only one employment.[26]

Your employers' liability is calculated differently from yours. Again, there is no liability if your earnings are below the lower earnings limit. If they are above that, your employer pays a contribution calculated as a percentage of your earnings. There are reduced rates if you earn below £190 a week but, unlike you, your employers must pay the same rate on your earnings below the lower earnings limit and on any earnings above the upper earnings limit (unless you are contracted out of SERPS).[27]

Weekly earnings £pw	Rate of contribution
56.00- 94.99	4.6%
95.00-139.99	6.6%
140.00-194.99	8.6%
195.00 and above	10.4%

If you are contracted out of SERPS, your employers pay 3 per cent less on that part of your earnings between the lower and upper limits.[28]

Example

If you are contracted out of SERPS and your weekly earnings are £120, your employers' contribution is:

6.6% of £56 + 3.6% of £64 = £3.70 + £2.30 = £6.00

If you are contracted out of SERPS and your weekly earnings are £475, your employers' contribution is:

10.4% of £56 + 7.4% of £344 + 10.4% of £55 = £5.82 + £25.46 + £5.72 = £37.00

Your employers should deduct your Class 1 contributions from your earnings and pay them with their own contributions to the Inland Revenue.[29] See page 179 for what happens if they do not.

Class 1A contributions[30]

Class 1A contributions are paid by **employers**. They are only payable if an employee has the use of a company car and is charged at 10.4 per cent of the 'cash equivalent' of the benefit to the employee of the car and any fuel. This is calculated in the same way as for income tax.

Class 2 contributions

Class 2 contributions must be paid by **self-employed earners** (see p171) unless you have a certificate of exception on the grounds of income below a certain level (£3,140 in 1993-94; £2,900 in 1991-92; £3,030 in 1992-93).[31]

You must apply for a certificate as soon as possible because it can only be backdated up to 13 weeks before the date of application,[32] although repayment of contributions is now possible – see below. The application form is included in DSS leaflet NI27A. It is sometimes possible to have the calculation of your earnings deferred until the end of the year (see DSS leaflet NP18) and thus wait and see if you do or do not have sufficiently low earnings. Usually your earnings are estimated; your earnings will be estimated as below the minimum level if they were below that level in the previous year and there has been 'no material change of circumstances'. Expenses are excluded from earnings.[33]

You *must* pay contributions unless you have a certificate; you *may* pay them even if you do have a certificate.[34] Married women and widows with reduced liability for contributions (see p175) are not liable for Class 2 contributions.

Class 2 contributions are payable at a flat rate.[35] The current and recent rates are:

1991-92	£5.15 a week
1992-93	£5.35 a week
1993-94	£5.55 a week

Volunteer development workers overseas (see p174) and **share fishermen** pay contributions at special rates (£3.70 and £7.00 a week respectively) which count towards unemployment benefit, unlike other Class 2 contributions.[36]

The methods of payment are set out in DSS leaflet NI41. If you are self-employed part of the time and also have a job as an employed earner you pay both Class 1 and Class 2 contributions, subject to a maximum (see DSS leaflet NP18).[37]

If you have paid Class 2 contributions, you can apply to have them repaid to you if your earnings in that year were in fact low enough to entitle you to exception. The application must be made in writing after the end of the relevant contribution year (5 April) and no later than 31 December of the same calendar year.[38]

Class 3 contributions

Class 3 contributions are purely **voluntary**.[39] They give entitlement only to widows' benefits and retirement pensions and are not payable if your earnings factor is otherwise sufficient in that tax year to meet the second contribution condition for those benefits (see p187).[40] Any accidental overpayment of contributions should be refunded if you make a written application.[41]

Class 3 contributions are paid at a flat rate. The current and recent rates are:[42]

1991-92	£5.05 a week
1992-93	£5.25 a week
1993-94	£5.45 a week

The introduction of home responsibility protection (see p183) has lessened the need for payment of Class 3 contributions. However, if your contribution record for long-term benefits would otherwise be imperfect (eg, because you have been abroad or in prison) you may still consider it a good idea to pay them. Ask at your local Benefits Agency office if you are in doubt.

Class 4 contributions

Class 4 contributions are paid by **self-employed earners** (see p171). They are levied at a percentage of profits or gains between certain sums.[43] The current and recent rates are:

Year	Payable on earnings between	Percentage
1991-92	£5,900 and £20,280	6.3
1992-93	£6,120 and £21,060	6.3
1993-94	£6,340 and £21,840	6.3

The profits and gains are those chargeable to income tax under Schedule D, and Class 4 contributions are usually collected with your income tax by the Inland Revenue. You may apply for permission to defer payment for a specified period if the amount to be paid has not yet been established.[44]

If you are liable to pay both Class 1 and Class 4 contributions, the total is limited to the maximum which could be paid under one class only.[45]

Pre-1975 contributions

The present contribution system was introduced on 6 April 1975. Between 5 July 1948 and 5 April 1975, there were no Class 4 contributions and Class 1 contributions were paid by way of a flat-rate 'stamp' in the same way as Class 2 and Class 3 contributions. Graduated contributions giving entitlement to graduated retirement benefit (see p99) were introduced in 1961 but were collected separately.

Before 6 April 1975, contribution years were not the same as tax years – as they are now. Instead each person was allocated a contribution year which might have begun in December, March, June or September depending on the last letter of your national insurance number. There were complicated transitional arrangements in both 1948 and 1975 so that you may well have had a contribution year which was not 12 months long. That may explain what would otherwise be anomalies in your contribution record.

Before 5 July 1948, there was a contributory scheme under the Widows', Orphans' and Old Age Contributory Pension Acts 1936-41, which may still give entitlement to an enhanced rate of pension (see p187).

Non-payment or late payment of contributions

It is an offence not to pay contributions on time (unless, of course, they are voluntary).[46] As far as Class 1 contributions are concerned, it is your employers' responsibility to make sure that contributions are deducted from your earnings and then paid to the Inland Revenue. But if you connive with your employers in order to avoid paying contributions, you too could be prosecuted. In practice, the Contributions Agency is usually more interested in collecting the appropriate contributions than in prosecuting people.

If your employers have deducted Class 1 contributions from your earnings but have failed to pay them to the Inland Revenue, you are treated as though they had been paid unless you have been negligent, or consented to or connived in that arrangement.[47]

Class 2 contributions should technically be paid in the week in respect of which they are due.[48] In practice, payment is by quarterly bill or direct debit. (See Contributions Agency leaflet CA-OS.) At the end of the tax year you will know whether or not it is necessary to pay Class 3 contributions if you want to fill any gap in your record.

In any event, contributions may still count for benefit purposes if paid late provided that they are paid within two years (Class 1) or six years (Class 2 or Class 3) after the end of the tax year in which they were due.[49] Students, apprentices and prisoners may pay Class 3 contributions to cover their period of education, apprenticeship or imprisonment at any time before the end of the sixth complete tax year after that period finished.[50] However, contributions give no entitlement to benefits, until they have actually been paid (and, in the case of unemployment or sickness benefit, until six weeks *after* they have been paid).[51]

Voluntary contributions may be paid on behalf of a contributor after her/his death provided they are paid no later than s/he would have been allowed to pay them.[52]

3   Credits and home responsibility protection

When you are not required to pay social security contributions, there will be gaps in your contribution record. However, in a large number of circumstances you will be 'credited' with a contribution. A credited contribution is usually known simply as a 'credit'.

Credits help you satisfy the second contribution condition for those benefits with two contribution conditions, but they do not count towards other contribution conditions. You are credited with an amount of earnings equal to the lower earnings limit (except in the case of starting credits, in which case you are given a Class 3 credit).

You receive only sufficient credits in any tax year to meet the contribution condition which allows credits to count.[1] For example, if you earn £4,000 as an employee between April and October 1993 you receive no credits during the rest of 1993-94 because you have already paid contributions with an earnings factor of more than £2,912 (the minimum required to count for long-term benefits; 52 times the lower earnings limit of £56).

Married women currently opting for reduced liability for contributions (see p150) are not entitled to credits other than starting credits.[2]

Home responsibility protection (see p183) helps you satisfy the second contribution condition for long-term benefits by removing years of home responsibility from the number of years for which you would otherwise have to satisfy the contribution condition.

Credits for weeks of unemployment or incapacity for work

You get one Class 1 credit for,[3] *either*:

- each week of six days of unemployment or incapacity for work; *or*
- each week of five days of unemployment, provided that on the other day you do not earn more than the current lower earnings limit (see p172); *or*
- each week of six days where you are working, provided that this is for less than eight hours a week and you are still available for work. The work must be *other* than your usual main occupation unless done for, or organised through, a charity or public body for a similar purpose.

The week runs from Monday. Days count if you claim late or if you are receiving **income support** because you are either incapable of work or unemployed.

Credit entitlement is one reason why you might continue to sign on at the unemployment benefit office, even though you are getting no immediate benefit from doing so. Therefore, if you do not have a good enough contribution record to claim unemployment benefit or your entitlement to unemployment benefit has run out and you are unable to claim unemployment benefit or income support in your own right, you should consider whether it is still worth signing on to protect your right to benefits.

You are also entitled to credit if you are receiving **statutory sick pay**, and not otherwise paying contributions, for that week. But, unlike other credits, these are not awarded automatically. You should send a copy of your medical certificate to your local office to claim them.

These credits will only help you towards qualification for **unemployment benefit** and **sickness benefit** if, during the relevant contribution year, *either*:

- you have an earnings factor of at least 25 times the lower earnings limit in one of the two years before the beginning of the relevant benefit year (see p185). For unemployment benefit this must have been derived from Class 1 contributions; *or*
- you were entitled to invalidity benefit, invalid care allowance or unemployability supplement for at least one day; *or*
- you claimed and satisfied the contribution conditions for unemployment benefit, sickness benefit or maternity allowance; *or*
- you were credited with a contribution for approved training (see below); *or*
- you received the credits on the ground of unemployment or incapacity for work after you had exhausted your right to unemployment benefit or sickness benefit or while in receipt of statutory sick pay.[4]

Credits for caring for an invalid

You receive a Class 1 credit for each week you receive **invalid care allowance** (see p125).[5] You also receive credits if the only reason that you do not receive invalid care allowance is that it overlaps with a **widow's benefit**.

If you are looking after an invalid but are not entitled to credits under these provisions, you may receive **home responsibility protection** instead (see p183).

Starting credits

You receive Class 3 credits for the contribution year in which you were 16 and for the next two years if you would otherwise have an insufficient contribution record for long-term benefits.[6]

This is intended to help those who have stayed on at school after the minimum school-leaving age. No credits are made under this provision in respect of years before 6 April 1977.

Education and training credits

You receive Class 1 credits for the purposes only of **unemployment benefit** and **sickness benefit** for any week of a course of full-time education or full-time (or, for a person who is registered as disabled, part-time – at least 15 hours a week) training to acquire occupational or vocational skills or apprenticeship provided that:

- in one of the two contribution years in which you must satisfy the second contribution condition for the benefit, you have an earnings factor of 50 times the lower earnings limit without recourse to this provision; *and*
- you were under 21 when the course started. [7]

You also receive Class 1 credits for the purposes of **all benefits** for each week you are undertaking an approved training course[8] provided that:

- the training is full-time unless either you are disabled or it is an introductory course; *and*
- the training is not part of your job; *and*
- the training is intended to run for less than one year (except in certain circumstances if it is a course for disabled people); *and*
- you were 18 or over at the beginning of the contribution year in which the credit is claimed.

All courses run by the Training Enterprise and Education Directorate count. Other courses are considered on their merits. You should apply through your local DSS office on form CF55C.

Credits for maternity pay period

You are entitled to a Class 1 credit for each week of the maternity pay period (see p72) for which you receive statutory maternity pay.[9] This will be important only if you are receiving maternity pay at a rate less than the lower earnings limit (currently £56 a week). You must claim these credits in writing before the end of the 'benefit year' (see p184) following the tax year in which the week falls, but the time may be extended if it is reasonable to do so.

Credits for jury service

You are entitled to a Class 1 credit for each week after 6 April 1988 when you spend part of the week on jury service.[10] Again, you must claim these credits in writing before the end of the benefit year (see p184) following the tax year in which the week falls (or such further period as is reasonable).

Credits for widows

If you are a widow, you may receive credits to enable you to satisfy the second contribution condition for unemployment benefit or sickness benefit. This is, of course, important only if you are not receiving widowed mother's allowance or widow's pension at the full rate.

You receive Class 1 credits for each year in which widow's allowance (a benefit abolished in April 1988) or widowed mother's allowance was paid, if the payments have ceased for a reason other than remarriage or cohabitation.[11] Since a widow in this position is deemed to satisfy the first contribution condition for unemployment benefit or sickness benefit,[12] the effect of this provision is effectively to waive the contribution conditions for widows altogether.

Credits for men aged 60 or over

Women are not entitled or required to pay contributions once they are 60 or over. Men aged over 60 must continue to pay contributions if they are liable even if their contribution records are already sufficient to qualify them for a full Category A retirement pension. This rule discriminates against men on grounds of their sex but is *not* contrary to EC law because it is a 'necessary consequence' of having a differential retirement age.[13]

Men receive Class 1 credits for the contribution year in which they become 60 and for the next four years if credits are needed to allow the year to count for the purposes of the second contribution condition for any benefit.[14] This means that if you take early retirement at 60 you will still have the last five years of your 'working life' counted in full towards satisfaction of the second contribution condition for your retirement pension when you reach 65.

Home responsibility protection

A year of home responsibility is one:[15]

• throughout which you receive child benefit in respect of a child aged under 16; *or*

- throughout which you are allowed to receive income support without being required to be available for work because you are looking after an invalid; *or*
- in 48 weeks of which you spend 35 hours looking after someone receiving either the higher or middle rates of disability living allowance care component, attendance allowance (see p114) or constant attendance allowance (under the industrial injuries or war pensions schemes, see pp129 and 261).

A year should be automatically recorded as a year of home responsibility if you qualify because you receive child benefit or you receive income support while caring for an invalid. If you qualify only on the third of the above grounds, or you qualify for part of the year on one ground and the rest on another, you should apply at your local DSS office. This should be done at the end of any contribution year when your earnings do not exceed 50 times that year's lower earnings limit. Ask your local office for Form CF411.

Note that for the first of the above grounds, *you* have to be entitled to child benefit. If you are a man looking after children and their mother is receiving child benefit, you should ask her to stop claiming the child benefit so that you can claim it instead. When you claim the child benefit, you should include a letter from her saying that she no longer wishes to claim. It is not enough for you to say that your name is or should be on the child benefit order book *together* with hers.

A year in which a woman has elected reduced liability for contributions cannot be a year of home responsibility.[16] It may be worth revoking such an election (see p175).

No year before 6 April 1978 can be a year of home responsibility.

Home responsibility protection helps towards satisfaction of the second contribution condition for the long-term benefits (see p187). Years of home responsibility in which you do not satisfy the contribution conditions are deducted from the number of years for which you would otherwise have to satisfy the contribution conditions.[17]

Example
You left school at age 16 in 1976. You will be 60 in 2020. Your working life for retirement pension purposes will be 44 years and the number of years in which you would normally have to satisfy the contribution conditions is 39 (see p162). The effect of home responsibility protection for 10 complete years of looking after children, and three of looking after a disabled relative receiving attendance allowance, is to reduce the requisite number of years in which you must satisfy the contribution conditions for a retirement pension on the basis of your own contributions to 26 (ie, 39 – 13).

Home responsibility protection can reduce the requisite number of years to 20 or half what it would otherwise be, whichever is lower.[18]

4 Contribution conditions for benefit

Contributory benefits have two contribution conditions *except* in the case of maternity allowance and widow's payment. To help you satisfy the second condition, you may be credited with contributions to fill gaps in your record (see p180). However, the first contribution condition must always be satisfied by contributions which have actually been paid.

Unemployment benefit and sickness benefit

The first condition

You must have actually paid, in one contribution year, the appropriate class of contributions producing an earnings factor (see p173) at least 25 times that year's lower earnings limit (eg, £1,350 in 1992-93, 25 times £54).[1] For sickness benefit, they may have been paid in any tax year; but for unemployment benefit they must have been paid in one of the last two complete tax years before the 'relevant benefit year' (see below).

The contributions may be either Class 1 or 2 for sickness benefit; they must be Class 1 for unemployment benefit (except for share fishermen and volunteer development workers, see p178).[2] They must be paid before a claim for unemployment benefit or sickness benefit is made.

Benefit years are almost the same as calendar years and run from the first Sunday in January.[3] The 'relevant benefit year' is the benefit year in which begins the period of interruption of employment that contains the claim (see p202).[4]

A **widow** who loses her entitlement to widow's allowance or widowed mother's allowance for some reason other than remarriage or cohabitation (eg, she loses her widowed mother's allowance because her children grow up) will be deemed to have satisfied this contribution condition (and may well be credited with contributions to satisfy the second condition – see p183).[5]

For sickness benefit, this condition is satisfied by 25 flat-rate contributions of the kind payable before 6 April 1975.[6]

The second condition

You must have either paid or been credited with contributions producing an earnings factor (see p173) equal to 50 times the lower earnings limit in each of the last two complete contribution years ending before the relevant benefit year (see above).[7]

Thus, if your period of interruption of employment starts on Saturday 2 January 1993, the relevant contribution years are 1989-90 and 1990-91. If your period of interruption of employment starts on Monday 4 January 1993, the relevant contribution years are 1990-91 and 1991-92.

In rare cases, this may mean that you should delay a claim so that you can draw on a different year's contribution record. This is because the relevant contribution year(s) for unemployment benefit or sickness benefit depend(s) on the benefit year in which falls the *first* day of your period of interruption of employment (see p202). Thus, if you claim after 4 January 1993, the relevant contribution years for unemployment benefit purposes will be 1990-91 and 1991-92, whereas if you claim on or before 2 January 1993 they would be 1989-90 and 1990-91. Any day for which you do not claim does not count as a day of unemployment or incapacity for work,[8] so it is easy to postpone your period of interruption of employment. However, if you claim and are refused benefit because the contribution conditions is not satisfied, your period of interruption of employment will have started.[9] You would then have to stop claiming for more than eight weeks and make a fresh claim after that period. The eight-week gap would reak the period of interruption of employment.

Example
During 1989-90, you spent time at home looking after your children and have only done paid work and made contributions since April 1990. In 1992 you are made redundant and (after payments in lieu of notice were taken into account), your period of interruption of employment is due to start on 16 December 1991. Your husband is in full-time employment so you are not entitled to income support. It is plainly in your interest to wait until Monday 4 January 1993, before you claim unemployment benefit.

Maternity allowance

The only contribution condition for maternity allowance is that you must, in respect of at least 26 weeks in the 52 weeks ending at the *end* of the 15th week before the expected week of confinement, have actually paid Class 1 or Class 2 contributions. The earnings factor is immaterial, but contributions paid by a married woman or widow at the reduced rate do not count.[10]

Widow's payment

The only contribution condition for widow's payment is that your husband must have actually paid, in any one tax year before his death, contributions of Classes 1, 2 or 3 producing an earnings factor (see p148) of at least 25 times the lower earnings limit (eg, £1,350 in 1992-93, 25 times £54).[11]

Any paid contributions may be counted if he became liable to pay contributions only in the tax year in which he died or the previous tax year, or if he had ever successfully claimed unemployment or sickness benefit.[12] The payment of 25 flat-rate contributions in a contribution year prior to 6 April 1975 satisfies this condition.[13]

Widowed mother's allowance, widow's pension and Category A and B retirement pensions

The first condition

The contributor must have actually paid in any one tax year before death or pensionable age, contributions with an earnings factor of 52 times that year's lower earnings limit (eg, £2,808 in 1992-93, 52 times £54).[14]

This condition is deemed to be satisfied if the contributor was receiving invalidity benefit in the year of death or of reaching pensionable age, or in the preceding year.[15] Fifty flat-rate payments in a contribution year before 6 April 1975 also satisfy this condition.[16]

The second condition

The contributor must have paid or been credited with contributions with an earnings factor of at least 52 times that year's lower earnings limit for each of the requisite number of years.[17]

The number of years you need to satisfy this condition depends on the length of your 'working life'. This is the period inclusive of the tax year in which you reach the age of 16 up to but exclusive of the year in which you reach pensionable age or in which you die.[18]

If you were over 16 on 5 July 1948, your working life is taken as having started either on 6 April 1948 or on 6 April of the year between 1936 and 1948 that you first started paying contributions, if you paid contributions before 5 July 1948.[19]

A year of home responsibility looking after a child or invalid does not count as a year of your working life unless your earnings factor in that year was at least 52 times the lower earnings limit (see p159 for exactly how this works).

The requisite number of years is then calculated as follows:[20]

Length of 'working life'	Requisite number of years
1-10 years	Length of working life minus 1
11-20 years	Length of working life minus 2
21-30 years	Length of working life minus 3
31-40 years	Length of working life minus 4
41-50 years	Length of working life minus 5

Since contributions paid before 6 April 1975 do not produce an earnings factor (see p173), the number of years before that date in which the contribution condition is satisfied is calculated by adding together all the contributions paid or credited before 6 April 1975, and dividing the answer by 50. If that does not produce a whole number the result is rounded up, as long as that would not produce a number greater than the number of years of the working life before 6 April 1975. A credit is given for each of the 13 weeks between 6 April and 4 July 1948 if those form part of your working life but you did not contribute then.[21]

Example
You are a man who reached pensionable age in July 1993. You did
not contribute to any pre-1948 scheme and paid or had credited
1,200 contributions between 1948 and 1975. For every year from 6
April 1975 to 5 April 1992 you paid contributions with earnings
factors above the minimum level of 52 times the lower earnings
limit. Your working life began on 6 April 1948 and ended on 5 April
1993 – a total of 45 years. The requisite number of years is therefore
40. You have satisfied 16 years since 1979. Between 1948 and 1975
you paid or had credited 1,200 contributions, which equals 24 years
(1,200 divided by 50). You therefore satisfy the condition for 41
years, one more than the requisite number that you need.

Note that widows, widowers and divorcees may be able to combine their
own contribution records with those of their late or former spouses in
order to claim a Category A retirement pension (see p94).

Insufficient contributions

Benefits are paid at a reduced rate if the second contribution condition is
not satisfied for the requisite number of years, provided it is satisfied in at
least 25 per cent of the requisite number. The benefit is paid at a
percentage of the amount which would otherwise be paid; the percentage
is calculated by expressing the number of years in which the condition is
satisfied as a percentage of the requisite number of years and rounding it
up to the nearest whole number.[22] Thus, if you are a widow and your
husband's working life was 12 years, so that the requisite number of years
is ten years, and if he only satisfied the condition in eight years, you
receive 80 per cent of the standard rate of widowed mother's allowance.

Any increase in respect of an adult dependant is reduced in the same
proportion as the basic benefit, but an increase in respect of a child
dependant is always paid at the standard rate.[23]

5   The State Earnings Related Pension Scheme (SERPS)

The State Earnings Related Pension Scheme (SERPS) provides for
earnings-related pensions to be paid to those who have paid Class 1
contributions in excess of the minimum required for entitlement to basic
retirement pensions. It provides similar pensions for widows and
widowers and for invalidity pensioners.

Everyone who has paid Class 1 contributions before April 1991 is in
SERPS for invalidity benefit purposes.

For the purposes of widows' benefits and retirement pensions you are *not*
in SERPS if you either are contracted out by your employers (see below) or
are a member of an appropriate personal pension scheme (see below).

Contracting out

You may be contracted out of SERPS by your employers if your service counts for the purpose of either a salary-related occupational pension or if your employers make certain minimum payments to a 'contracted-out money purchase' scheme. To enable you to be contracted out, either sort of scheme must be covered by a certificate from the Occupational Pension Board.[1]

The effect of being contracted out is that you and your employers pay national insurance contributions at a lower rate than other employees and their employers (see p176).[2] This means that you do not build up any entitlement to pensions under SERPS (although, until April 1991, you did as an addition to invalidity pension).[3] However, you will have to contribute to your employers' scheme and will receive a benefit from that.

An employer cannot compel you to be a member of any particular scheme, so you can opt out and join an appropriate pension scheme of your choice (see below).[4]

The Secretary of State will make an extra contribution to any newly contracted out pension scheme.[5] This amounts to two per cent of your earnings or £1 (whichever is the greater) for each week until 5 April 1993. It is to encourage schemes to contract out.

Appropriate personal pension scheme

If a personal pension scheme satisfies certain conditions, the trustees or managers of the scheme may obtain an 'appropriate scheme certificate' from the Occupational Pension Board.[6]

If you then choose to become a member of an appropriate personal pension scheme, the Secretary of State will pay to the scheme the difference between your contracted in national insurance contributions and those you would have paid had you been contracted out[7] and, if you are over 30 at the beginning of the tax year in question, an additional sum representing one per cent of your income between the upper and lower earnings limits.[8] The effect of this is to place you in much the same position as a person in a contracted out money purchase scheme[9] or, if you are over 30, to give you an incentive to opt out of SERPS. The main difference is that it is your decision to join the scheme and not your employers'.

You are then treated as not contributing to SERPS and must look to your personal pension scheme instead.

For any week up to 5 April 1993 the Secretary of State will make an extra contribution to your scheme of two per cent of your earnings or £1 (whichever is greater) to encourage people to join appropriate personal pension schemes.[10]

Calculating the additional pension

The method of calculating additional pensions will change in 1999.[11] Only the present system is explained here and, of course, only for those in SERPS. For the calculation from 1999, see DSS leaflet NP46.

Until 5 April 1991, everyone was regarded as being in SERPS in order to calculate additional pensions for invalid pensioners. However, no year after 1990-91 will count as a relevant year (see below) for invalidity pension purposes. [12]

For invalidity pension or Category A retirement pension, the additional pension depends on your 'earnings factor' (see p173) in each 'relevant year' in which you have paid contributions. For widows' benefits or Category B retirement pensions, the additional pension depends upon your spouse's 'earnings factor' in each 'relevant year' in which s/he has paid contributions. [13]

'Relevant years' are:

- in the case of invalidity pension, contribution years from 1978-79 up to, but excluding, the year in which you became entitled to invalidity pension or to 1990-91, whichever is earlier;
- in the case of Category A retirement pension, contribution years from 1978-79 up to, but excluding, the year in which you reached pensionable age;
- in the case of widowed mother's allowance, widow's pension or Category B retirement pensions, contribution years from 1978-79 up to, but excluding, the year your spouse reached pensionable age or died under that age.

For each relevant year, you take the 'earnings factor' and increase it by the appropriate percentage to take account of inflation. The appropriate percentages are those coming into force during the final relevant year. If the last relevant year was 1992-93, the percentages are: [14]

1978-79	291.0%	1985-86	76.6%
1979-80	244.8%	1986-87	62.2%
1980-81	188.2%	1987-88	51.1%
1981-82	141.6%	1988-89	38.9%
1982-83	119.3%	1989-90	25.8%
1983-84	103.3%	1990-91	17.3%
1984-85	88.2%	1991-92	6.5%

You deduct, from each of those figures, 52 times the lower earnings limit in force in the *last* relevant year. You then add together the resulting figures and multiply the total by 1¼ per cent to give the total additional pension you will receive for a year. [15] You divide that figure by 52 to obtain a weekly figure.

Once that calculation has been done for the first time, it is not repeated each year. Instead, the additional pension is simply increased in line with inflation. [16] Thus, any additional pension paid up to April 1992 was then increased by 4.1 per cent.

Example
You retire in May 1993 and claim Category A retirement pension. You were self-employed until July 1984 and then became employed. In 1984-85 your earnings factor was £6,032, and in 1985-86 it was £7,134. You were made redundant in March 1986 and remained

unemployed until May 1989. Your earnings factor in 1989-90 was £8,835, in 1990-91 it was £9,916, in 1991-92 it was £10,527 and in 1992-93, your last relevant year, it was £11,209.

For each of the years when you were wholly self-employed or wholly unemployed, your earnings factor will not be higher than the lower earnings limits for those years. So they do not count towards an additional pension.

For the remaining years, the calculation is as follows:

	1984-85 £	1985-86 £	1989-90 £	1990-91 £	1991-92 £	1992-93 £
earnings factor	6,032	7,134	8,835	9,916	10,527	11,209
increased for	×1.882	×1.766	×1.258	×1.173	×1.065	×1.000
inflation	11,352	12,598	11,114	11,631	11,211	11,209
Less 52 × £54	2,808	2,808	2,808	2,808	2,808	2,808
	8,544	9,790	8,306	8,823	8,403	8,401

Adding those together gives £52,267.

$$1\tfrac{1}{4}\% \text{ of } £52,267 = £653.33$$
$$£653.33 \div 52 = £12.56$$

So your weekly additional pension is £12.56.

If you do not have all the necessary figures available to you, or if you wish to check the Contributions Agency records, you should fill in the form on leaflet NP38 and the Contributions Agency will tell you the amount of additional pensions they believe you are entitled to at current values and their estimate of the amount of additional pension which you will receive if you continue working.

In certain circumstances, a **widow** or **widower** may be entitled to an additional pension based both on her/his own contributions and on those of her/his spouse (see p208).

Invalidity allowance is reduced by the amount of any additional pension (see p209).

CHAPTER THIRTEEN

Residence conditions and going abroad

This chapter covers:

1 Introduction
2 Residence and presence conditions
3 Absence from Great Britain
4 Northern Ireland, the Isle of Man and the Channel Islands
5 The European Community
6 Reciprocal agreements

l   Introduction

If you spend time outside Great Britain (ie, England, Wales and Scotland) your benefits may be affected in three different ways, none of them advantageous:

- all *contributory* benefits depend on your contributions record and the rules for paying contributions depend in turn on your being resident or present in Great Britain. These rules are set out in Chapter 12 and if, as a result of going abroad, you do not meet them, it may mean either that you are not *entitled* to the contributory benefit you are claiming (because you do not satisfy the contribution conditions) or, in the case of long-term benefits, that your benefit may be *paid* at a reduced rate;
- all *non-contributory* benefits have residence or presence conditions attached to them. This means that before you can become *entitled* to them you must have been resident or present in Great Britain in the past. These conditions are covered in section 2 of this chapter;
- even once you have become *entitled* to a benefit, there is a general rule which means that it will not be *paid* to you for any period during which you are absent from Great Britain. This applies to all benefits, contributory *and* non-contributory.

However, there are a large number of exceptions to these general rules. In particular:

- for some, but not all, benefits, absence abroad may not disqualify you from being paid benefit to which you would otherwise be entitled, as long as the absence is *temporary*. The rules for this are discussed on page 197;
- there are special rules for other parts of the United Kingdom (see p198);

- European Community (EC) law may mean that periods of residence and/or presence in another EC country count as residence and/or presence in Great Britain. EC law also has rules which may allow you to 'export' your claim for benefit so that it can be paid in another EC country (see p199);
- there are special agreements with some, but not all, other countries which allow you to claim benefits while you are there (see p201).

Matters affecting the payment of benefit while you are abroad, or when you have recently come from abroad, are dealt with by the Benefits Agency Overseas Branch, Newcastle upon Tyne NE98 1YX. Adjudication officers there make decisions, but appeals are held wherever in Great Britain is convenient for you.

The Overseas Branch will answer questions that you may have and it also advises local Benefits Agency offices when necessary. Write to them if you want information.

2 Residence and presence conditions

Severe disablement allowance

You are entitled if *either*:[1]

- you are ordinarily resident in Great Britain (see p196); *and*
  - you are present in Great Britain (see p195) and have been present for at least 26 weeks in the past year; *or*
- you were entitled to severe disablement allowance on any day between 30 March and 5 April 1992 (inclusive); *and*
  - you are present (see p195) in Great Britain and have been present for at least 24 weeks in the last 28 weeks; *and*
  - you have been resident (see p196) in Great Britain for 10 out of the last 20 years. If you are under the age of 20, you must have been resident in Great Britain for at least 10 years since your birth.

Once you satisfy these residence conditions you are not subject to continuing residence conditions on subsequent days of incapacity during the same period of interruption of employment (see p202).[2]

The rules are relaxed for members of the armed forces.

Invalid care allowance, disability living allowance and attendance allowance

You are entitled if:[3]

- you are 'ordinarily resident' in Great Britain (see p196); *and*
- you are present in Great Britain (see p195); *and*
- you have been present in Great Britain for a total of 26 weeks, in the last 12 months.

People who make a claim for attendance allowance or disability living allowance, or apply for a review, on the basis that they are terminally ill, are exempted from the rule that they have to have been present in Great Britain for the last 26 weeks.[4] If claims are made for disability living allowance for babies who are less than six months' old they only have to have been present for 13 of the last 26 weeks.[5]

For **disability living allowance** and **attendance allowance**, you are treated as present during any temporary absence of less than 26 weeks, and during any further absence for the purpose of treatment. (You must obtain a certificate from the Secretary of State to the effect that the further absence is reasonable.[6])

For **invalid care allowance** you are treated as present during any temporary absence of up to four weeks. You are also treated as present during any temporary absence for the purpose of caring for your patient provided, of course, that your patient's disability living allowance care component, attendance allowance or constant attendance allowance is still payable.[7]

Non-contributory widows' benefits

To obtain the non-contributory benefits corresponding to widow's pension and widowed mother's allowance:[8]

- you must have been resident in Great Britain for a total of at least ten years during the period from 5 July 1948 to 1 November 1970; *and*
- you must have been ordinarily resident (see p196) in Great Britain on 2 November 1970; *and*
- your husband must have died on or before 1 November 1970 and been ordinarily resident in Great Britain at the date of his death.

If your husband died on or before 2 November 1970, your own residence is irrelevant and the only condition is that your husband should have been entitled to a Category C retirement pension (or its predecessor under the National Insurance Act 1970) at any time during his life.[9]

Category D retirement pension

You are entitled if:[10]

- you have been resident (see p196) in Great Britain for at least ten of the last 20 years; *and*
- you were ordinarily resident (see p196) in Great Britain either on the day you reached the age of 80, or on the date of your claim.

Child benefit and guardian's allowance

For **child benefit**, there are separate conditions for the child, the claimant and, if different, the child's parents.

- The child must generally be in Great Britain.[11] However, the child may be abroad where:[12]

- someone was entitled to receive child benefit immediately before the absence; *and*
- the absence, when it began, was intended to be temporary and continues as such; *and*
- *either* the child has not been abroad for more than eight weeks; *or*
the child has not been abroad for more than 156 weeks receiving full-time education at a recognised education establishment; *or*
the child is abroad during a period agreed by the Secretary of State which is for the specific purpose of medical treatment for a condition which existed before s/he left.

There are special rules if a child was born abroad during a temporary absence of the mother.[13]

• The claimant must be in Great Britain.[14] However, someone already receiving child benefit may continue to do so for eight weeks while abroad on an absence which was intended when it began, and continues, to be temporary.[15]

• The claimant *and either* the child *or* one of the parents must have been in Great Britain for more than 182 days in the last year.[16] There are complicated exceptions to this.[17] In particular, if the claimant is now in Great Britain and is likely to remain here for a total of at least 183 consecutive days (disregarding up to 28 days' temporary absence), s/he is treated as satisfying this condition if *either*:

- s/he has worked and been liable for Class 1 or 2 national insurance contributions during that period of 183 days but before the start of the week for which the claim for benefit is made;[18] *or*
- s/he has been entitled to child benefit within the past three years;[19] *or*
- her/his spouse was entitled to child benefit within the past three years; *and either* the spouse is residing with (see p165) the claimant at present; *or* the spouse was residing with the claimant at the time when the spouse was entitled to benefit.[20]

Entitlement to **guardian's allowance** depends upon entitlement to child benefit, so the above conditions must be satisfied. However, if the only bar to your entitlement to child benefit and, therefore, guardian's allowance is that neither the child nor either of her/his parents had been in Great Britain during the last year, that condition is waived.[21]

A further condition of entitlement to guardian's allowance is that at least one of the child's parents was born in the United Kingdom or had, at some time after reaching the age of 16, spent a total of 52 weeks in any two-year period in the United Kingdom.[22]

'Present' and 'absent'

To be 'present', subject to the special rules below, you must be physically present. To satisfy a presence condition, you must prove that you were present throughout any day in question.[23] 'Absent' is the opposite of present. If the adjudication officer seeks to disqualify you because you are absent from Great Britain, the burden is upon her/him to prove that you were absent throughout any day in question.[24]

For the purpose of satisfying presence conditions, you are treated by special rules[25] as being in Great Britain if you are:

- a member of the armed forces serving abroad;
- a spouse, son, daughter, parent or parent-in-law of a member of the armed forces serving abroad and living with her/him;
- a master, member of crew or other person employed on board a ship under a contract entered into in the United Kingdom;
- a pilot or member of crew or other person employed on board an aircraft under a contract entered into in the United Kingdom;
- a person employed on an oil or gas rig on the continental shelf.

The rules do not always apply in the case of guardian's allowance: members of the family of a serving member of the armed forces are not covered. In the case of child benefit, the circumstances in which the rules apply are also limited.

A worker on an oil or gas rig on the continental shelf is not disqualified from benefit if s/he is in the area of an oil or gas field or is travelling to it from another such area or from Norway or a member state of the EC (see p175).[26]

Under EC law presence in another EC member state may count as presence in Great Britain (see p199).

'Resident' and 'ordinarily resident'

You are usually 'resident' in the country where you have your home for the time being.[27] It is possible to be resident in more than one place at a time but it is unusual.[28] You can remain resident in a place during a temporary absence but this depends on the circumstances.[29] So if you go abroad to work on one particular project of limited duration, intending to return on its completion, you remain resident in Great Britain. But if you go abroad for a considerable period, you may not remain resident in Great Britain even if you do expect to return eventually. Important factors in deciding the issue are where the rest of your family live, the sort of accommodation you have – a hotel does not suggest residence – and where your furniture and other personal effects are kept. If you move intending to settle at your new address, you are regarded as resident there from the very first day.

You are 'ordinarily resident' if there is some degree of continuity about your residence.[30] So if you live mostly in Great Britain but also live elsewhere from time to time, you remain ordinarily resident in Great Britain throughout the shorter periods of residence elsewhere. The Benefits Agency does not usually regard people as ordinarily resident in Great Britain unless they have been or are likely to be in Great Britain for at least three years.

The burden of proof lies on you to show that you are or were resident in Great Britain at the relevant time.[31]

Under EC law residence in another EC member state may count as residence in Great Britain (see p199). Some reciprocal agreements with other countries contain similar rules.

3 **Absence from Great Britain**

The general rule is that you are disqualified from receiving benefit while you are absent from Great Britain.[1] Various exceptions are set out below. Note, however, that there are special arrangements with other countries (see pp198, 199 and 201). There are also limited exceptions for aircrew, mariners, members of the armed forces and offshore oil and gas workers.[2]

Sickness benefit, invalidity benefit, severe disablement allowance and maternity allowance

These are payable during a temporary absence if the Secretary of State has certified that payment would be 'consistent with the proper administration of the Act' *and*:[3]

- your absence from Great Britain is for the specific purpose of being treated for an illness which began before you left this country; *or*
- in the case of sickness or invalidity benefit arising from an industrial injury or disease, your absence is for the specific purpose of receiving treatment which is appropriate for that injury or disease; *or*
- when you left this country you had been continuously incapable of work for six months and you have been continuously incapable of work since your departure; *or*
- in the case of severe disablement allowance, you are absent only because you are living with a member of the armed forces and you are that member's spouse, son, daughter, parent or parent-in-law.

A temporary absence is one which is 'not permanent' and this is a question which depends on the circumstances of each individual case. An absence which is, or has become, indefinite does not necessarily cease to be temporary as long as you intend to return to Great Britain eventually *and* it is still possible for you to do so.[4]

Widows' benefits, retirement pensions, and guardian's allowance

These are payable while you are abroad, but you are not normally entitled to upratings of benefit after you have ceased to be 'ordinarily resident' (see p196) in Great Britain.[5] You cannot de-retire (see p90) while abroad.[6]

In the case of **widow's payment**, two further conditions are that:[7]

- you or your husband were in Great Britain when he died; *or*
- the contribution conditions for widowed mother's allowance or widow's pension are satisfied.

Attendance allowance, disability living allowance, invalid care allowance and child benefit

These are all payable while you are abroad provided that you continue to satisfy the residence and presence conditions described on pages 193-94 and 195.[8]

Disablement benefit and reduced earnings allowance

Disablement benefit (except constant attendance allowance and exceptionally severe disablement allowance) is unaffected while you are abroad.[9]

Constant attendance allowance and exceptionally severe disablement allowance are payable during a temporary absence for up to six months, or such further period as the Secretary of State may allow.[10]

Reduced earnings allowance is payable during a temporary absence if:[11]

- you have been away less than three months, or such further period as the Secretary of State may allow; *and*
- your absence is not for work purposes; *and*
- you claim before you go; *and*
- you are entitled before you go.

If your accident occurs abroad or your disease is contracted abroad, your entitlement to disablement benefit or reduced earnings allowance arises only from the date of your return to Great Britain.[12]

Increases for dependants

If your **spouse** is abroad, you remain entitled to an increase during any period your spouse is 'residing with you' (see p165).[13] No increase is paid while another adult dependant is abroad.

If your **child** dependant is abroad, you remain entitled to an increase while you are entitled to child benefit (see above and p194). If you are not entitled to child benefit, but you would be if you were not abroad, you are still entitled to the increase if there is no one else who is entitled to child benefit in respect of the child.[14]

4   Northern Ireland, the Isle of Man and the Channel Islands

The rules described in this guide apply only to Great Britain (ie, England, Wales and Scotland). However, although Northern Ireland and the Isle of Man have their own social security legislation, any contributions paid there count as though paid in Great Britain and vice versa; and for most practical purposes the systems may be treated as identical. You will not lose any benefit by moving between Northern Ireland or the Isle of Man and Great Britain.[1]

Jersey and Guernsey (including Alderney, Herm and Jethou), have their own social security systems but there is a reciprocal agreement under which you can receive British benefits while on those islands (see DSS leaflet SA4, from the Overseas Branch, see p193).[2] You will also remain entitled to benefits under British legislation while in any other part of the Channel Islands.[3]

5 The European Community

The European Community (EC) consists of Belgium, Denmark, Germany, France, Greece, the Irish Republic, Italy, Luxembourg, the Netherlands, Portugal, Spain and the United Kingdom (including Gibraltar).

You may qualify for benefit while abroad within the EC because the basic rules about going abroad apply. However, you may also qualify for benefit either under EC law (which overrides British law if there is a conflict) or under a reciprocal agreement. If EC law does apply to you, you cannot rely on a reciprocal agreement even if that would be more favourable to you.[1]

The main EC legislation applies only to employed people, self-employed people, those who were formerly employed or self-employed and the families of such people. You are counted as employed or self-employed if you are insured under a national social security scheme (ie, you either pay contributions or ought to do so as an employed or self-employed person).[2] If the EC legislation does not apply to you, you may benefit from one of the reciprocal agreements.

All the benefits covered in this guide used to be within the scope of this EC legislation. But the law changed on 1 June 1992 and, from that date on, attendance allowance (see p114), invalid care allowance (see p125) and disability living allowance (see pp101 and 108) are excluded.[3]

EC social security law provides only for the 'co-ordination' of different national schemes and not for their 'harmonisation'.[4] In very general terms, this means that while the benefits available may differ from country to country, periods of residence or contributions paid in one EC country count towards entitlement to benefits in others and that benefits from one country can be paid in any of the others.

The general rule is that you can receive benefit only from the last country where you were insured, but it is a matter of controversy whether that prevents you from gaining entitlement to benefit from another country under national law alone. In one case, the European Court of Justice has made a decision which would have the effect that you could not qualify for, say, disability living allowance under British law if you happened to have been last insured in France and were accordingly entitled to French invalidity benefit.[5] However, that decision was made by a court of only three judges and it is arguable that it is not consistent with an earlier decision where, in a different context, it was decided that the removal of rights acquired under national law alone was inconsistent with the EC Treaty.[6] If you need further advice about this, ask a local advice agency to contact CPAG's solicitors.

Wherever you claim, the claim is referred to the relevant social security institution in the country where you were last insured. Only that institution calculates the amount of benefit due.[7] The calculation of benefit involves treating periods of insurance or residence in other countries as though they were periods in the country where you were last insured. The detailed rules are much too complicated to be covered here. Benefit is usually paid through the relevant social security institution in the country where you are living and that institution carries out medical examinations etc.

So, if you last worked in Italy but are now ill and living in Great Britain, you can claim through your local Benefits Agency office and you will receive benefits calculated by the Italian authorities but paid through the Benefits Agency. Similarly, if you last worked in Great Britain but are now abroad, you can claim British benefits in the country where you are now. For the purpose of satisfying time limits for claims, your claim is treated as made when you send it to the relevant institution in the country where you are living.[8]

Once you have acquired (whether under national law or EC law) the right to invalidity benefit, severe disablement allowance, widow's benefit, a retirement pension, an industrial injuries benefit or guardian's allowance, you are entitled to travel anywhere within the EC without losing it – provided, of course, that you continue to satisfy any conditions other than residence conditions.[9] Residence conditions are perfectly legitimate for the purpose of deciding whether or not you acquire entitlement to the benefit in the first place.

An unemployed person retains the right to unemployment benefit while looking for work in another country only in quite limited circumstances. You must register as available for work under the local procedures in each country where you go and the maximum period for which you retain the right to unemployment benefit is three months.[10] If you fail to register, you are disqualified even if the failure was due to the Department of Employment not having advised you properly before you went.[11] In some countries, it was necessary to satisfy additional conditions. Thus, in Spain, it was necessary, until 31 December 1992, to have obtained permission to seek work there from the authorities before you go. The Overseas Branch (see p193) will deal with specific queries and will send you the relevant guide from a series published by the Commission of the European Communities. These guides cover:

No. 1 *People going to work for an employer in another member country.*
No. 2 *People going for temporary stays in another member country.*
No. 3 *People sent by an employer in the United Kingdom to work in another member country.*
No. 4 *Pensioners living in one member country and entitled to benefit from another.*
No. 5 *People living in one member country and dependent on a person working in another.*

You must say which country is relevant, so that the appropriate edition is sent to you.

European Community law on social security benefit for people moving between countries within the EC will be covered in detail in CPAG's *Ethnic Minorities' Benefits Handbook*, to be published later this year.

In addition to the legislation described above, there are directives issued by the Council of the European Communities of which the most important is one requiring equal treatment of men and women.[12] This directive is not confined to people moving within the EEC but applies to the whole working population including self-employed people and those whose working life has been interrupted by illness, unemployment or old age. British social security law has been amended in an attempt to comply with it, but it overrides British law where there are still conflicts. Widows' benefits are excluded from its scope and so is the fixing of pensionable ages, but it has been decided that fixing the age limits for other benefits by reference to unequal pensionable ages is not legitimate.[13] This particular case was concerned only with severe disablement allowance and invalid care allowance, but it is arguable that it also applies to unemployment benefit, statutory sick pay, sickness benefit and invalidity benefit, all of which have rules discriminating between the sexes once people reach pensionable age (see pp39, 50, 59 and 62).

6 Reciprocal agreements

There are several countries with which Great Britain has reciprocal agreements. These mean that you receive some British benefits while in the other country and *vice versa*.

There are agreements between Great Britain and Australia, Austria, Barbados, Bermuda, Canada, Cyprus, Finland, Iceland, Israel, Jamaica, Malta, Mauritius, New Zealand, Norway, the Philippines, Sweden, Switzerland, Turkey, and the United States of America. There are also agreements with all the EC countries but these cannot help you if you are covered by the EC legislation (see p199).

The agreement with the former Yugoslavia is being honoured by the remaining regions of what was the Federal Republic of Yugoslavia and by the newly independent states of Croatia, Slovenia and Bosnia-Herzegovina.

The arrangements are described in leaflets available from the Overseas Branch (see p193). Child benefit arrangements are explained in DSS leaflets CH5 and CH6.

CHAPTER FOURTEEN

Other general provisions

This chapter covers:
1 Periods of interruption of employment
2 Hospital in-patients
3 People in legal custody
4 Overlapping benefits
5 Calculating earnings
6 Christmas bonus
7 Recovery of benefit from compensation payments
8 Deductions from benefit
9 Criminal offences

I Periods of interruption of employment

The rules on periods of interruption of employment are relevant for unemployment benefit, sickness benefit, invalidity benefit and severe disablement allowance.

Unemployment benefit (see Chapter 2) is paid for days on which you are unemployed, and sickness and invalidity benefits and severe disablement allowance (see pp57, 60 and 64) are paid for days on which you are too ill to work. But even if you satisfy all the other conditions of entitlement, you may not get benefit if you are only sick or out of work for a short period. Single days have to be joined together to form a 'period of interruption of employment' before benefit can be paid.

The minimum length of time which can count as a period of interruption of employment is *either*:

* two 'days of unemployment' (see p203). These need not be consecutive as long as they are within a period of six consecutive days of each other;[1] *or*
* four consecutive 'days of incapacity for work' (see p203);[2] *or*
* if you are having regular weekly kidney dialysis, plasmaphoresis, chemotherapy or radiotherapy, two days of incapacity for work. Again, these days do not have to be consecutive as long as they are within the same period of six consecutive days.[3]

Example
You are unemployed on Friday for two consecutive weeks and Thursday in the third week. The first two Fridays do not form a period of interruption of employment as the period in which they both fall – Friday and Saturday of the first week and Monday-Friday

in the second – is seven days long, not six. But the second Friday and the Thursday do make up a period of interruption of employment because, when you ignore Sunday, they are within the same period of six consecutive days. (Note, however, that the rules on waiting days may mean that you will not actually be paid unemployment benefit for these two days unless you have been out of work or sick in the recent past and the 'linking rule' applies – see below.)

The length of a period of interruption of employment can, of course, be much longer than two or four days. So, for example, if you are out of work for four of the six days in the week or ill for three weeks – or even three years or more – all the days will count as part of a period of interruption of employment.

Days of unemployment

A 'day of unemployment' is a day upon which you satisfy the conditions of entitlement for unemployment benefit (see p8) and are not disqualified from receiving that benefit for any of the reasons set out in Chapter 2.[4] Some days are 'deemed' to be days of unemployment when your period of interruption of employment is worked out even though you will not be paid unemployment benefit for them. These are:

* days upon which you attend certain training courses;[5]
* days upon which you are entitled to income support without being required to be available for work because you are 60 or over;[6]
* days between the first day (6 April) of the tax year during which you reach 60 and the day before your 70th birthday (or your 65th birthday if you are a woman) when you cannot receive unemployment benefit because:
  - you have exhausted your entitlement (see p9); *or*
  - you do not satisfy the contribution conditions (see p185); *or*
  - your occupational pension is too high.[7]

Days of incapacity for work

As its name suggests, a 'day of incapacity for work' is a day on which you are incapable of work (see p43) *and* on which you are not disqualified from receiving benefit for any of the reasons on pp59 and 60.[8] Days on which you are entitled to maternity allowance (see p75) also count as days of incapacity[9] so that, for example, if you are still unable to go back to work after the maternity allowance period (see p76) ends, you may be able to claim either sickness benefit, invalidity benefit or severe disablement allowance immediately as long as you meet the other conditions of entitlement.

If you work at night

There are special rules to help people who work night shifts. If you work a shift that starts before midnight on one day and ends the following day, then:

- if the time spent working before midnight is longer than the time spent after it, you are treated as having worked only on the first day;[10]
- if the time spent working after midnight is the same as or longer than the time spent working before it, you are treated as having worked only on the second day.[11]

In either case, the day on which you are treated as not working can be a day of unemployment or incapacity for work if you are sick or do no other work apart from your night shift during it.[12]

Sundays

Sundays cannot normally count as days of unemployment or incapacity for work and are ignored when working out any period of consecutive days.[13] For unemployment benefit (but not any other benefit) there are two exceptions to this rule:

- if you normally work on Sunday and have another day (or days) off instead;[14] *or*
- if you do not normally work on Sunday but object to working some other day on religious grounds and do not mind working on Sunday;[15]

then as long as you claim unemployment benefit for Sunday and satisfy the conditions of entitlement on that day, the other day is disregarded instead of Sunday.

The linking rules

Two or more periods of interruption of employment are joined together to form a single period unless they are separated by at least eight consecutive weeks.[16] This is known as the 'linking rule'. It has a number of important conesquences:

- If you become unemployed within eight weeks of a previous spell of unemployment or illness, you do not have to serve a further period of three 'waiting days' before unemployment benefit is paid (see example on p9).
- The question of whether or not you satisfy the contribution conditions for unemployment benefit or sickness benefit is decided once and for all at the beginning of the period of interruption of employment. For this reason, it may sometimes be in your interest to delay a claim for unemployment benefit (see pp185-86).
- The 168 days of incapacity needed to qualify for invalidity benefit must be in the same period of interruption of employment, but because of the linking rule, they do not need to be consecutive.
- Your entitlement to invalidity allowance (see p61) is based on your age on the first day of incapacity for work in the period of interruption of employment, not the day (168 days of incapacity later) when you

become entitled to invalidity benefit. If you have been ill sporadically, this may have been some years previously and this may entitle you to invalidity allowance at a higher rate.

Provided that they are not more than eight weeks apart, you can link two periods of interruption of employment even if one is made up of days of unemployment and the other days of incapacity. An example of how this works is given on page 9.

There is also an extended linking rule for people receiving invalidity benefit or severe disablement allowance which is intended to encourage them to try to go back to work. If you do try, but find that ill-health forces you to give up, your period of interruption of employment can be linked back for up to two years provided that you have been continuously entitled to disability working allowance (see CPAG's *National Welfare Benefits Handbook*) while you were working. This means that you can go straight back onto invalidity benefit or severe disablement allowance without having to wait a further period of 168 or 196 days.[17]

2 **Hospital in-patients**

The amount of benefit which you receive may be affected by the fact that you are spending a period in hospital receiving continuous free in-patient treatment. The amount may also be affected if an adult dependant or child for whom you are claiming is in hospital. Two periods separated by less than 28 days are counted as one period; periods of less than a full day (midnight to midnight) do not count.[1] Benefit should be paid in full during short periods at home during treatment, but you will need to tell the Benefits Agency that you are out of hospital.

Sickness and invalidity benefit, severe disablement allowance, widows' benefits and retirement pensions

All these benefits are unaffected by your first six weeks in hospital. The effect of a longer stay in hospital depends on whether you have dependants. Your dependants for these purposes are:[2]

• people for whom you are entitled to an increase of benefit or would be but for the overlapping benefits rules (see p208);
• your spouse, if temporarily abroad for the treatment of an illness which began before departure from Great Britain.

After six weeks in hospital:[3]

• if you have no dependants, your benefit is reduced by £22.40 a week;
• if you have dependants, your benefit is reduced by £11.20 a week.

The reduction will be less if you would otherwise be left with less than £11.20 a week (not including increases for dependants).

After 52 weeks in hospital:[4]

- if you have no dependants, your benefit is reduced *to* £11.20 a week;
- if you have dependants, your benefit is reduced *by* £22.40 a week. £11.20 a week of that is paid to *you*. The balance, with any increases for dependants, is paid to your dependants or someone else on their behalf. You have to agree to the money being paid to your dependants or another person but, if you do not, the money is kept by the Benefits Agency and you still do not receive more than £11.20 a week.

However, **after a year** in hospital all payment of benefit to you may cease if:

- you are unable to act for yourself; *and*
- the benefit is payable on your behalf to the hospital board or other authority in control of the hospital where you are staying; *and*
- the doctor treating you certifies that no sum of money, or only a part of what you would otherwise receive, can be used for your personal comfort or enjoyment.[5]

Disability living allowance

The mobility component of disability living allowance is unaffected by any period spent in hospital, whether by an adult or a child. It will remain payable unless you become unable to benefit from 'enhanced facilities for locomotion' (see p106).

The care component of disability living allowance stops after four weeks in hospital for an adult or 12 weeks in hospital for a child (anyone under the age of 16).[6]

Attendance allowance

This ceases after four weeks.[7]

Disablement benefit

Disablement benefit (including exceptionally severe disablement allowance but not other increases) is unaffected. Constant attendance allowance ceases after four weeks.[8] Unemployability supplement is treated like invalidity benefit (see p205). If you were already entitled before 6 April 1997, you continue to receive **hospital treatment allowance**, which was equal to the difference between the amount of disablement benefit (excluding increases) paid and what would have been paid if the extent of disablement were 100 per cent.[9]

Other benefits for adults

There are no specific rules governing other benefits. So, maternity allowance, reduced earnings allowance and retirement allowance are unaffected. Entitlement to invalid care allowance depends on whether you are still treated as 'regularly and substantially caring' for your patient (see p126). Unemployment benefit inevitably ceases to be payable as you are no longer available for work. Sickness or invalidity benefit is payable instead.

Increases for adult dependants

While you are in hospital, these continue to be paid at the usual rate even if your basic benefit is reduced, but you need to make a special application after 52 weeks.

If your wife or husband goes into hospital there is no reduction in the increase paid in respect of her/him during the first six weeks. After this period, the following rules apply.[10]

After six weeks, the increase is reduced by £11.20 a week, but it does not drop below £11.20 a week.

After 52 weeks, the increase is reduced to £11.20 a week. That is payable *only* if you are regularly incurring expenditure for the dependant (eg, by visiting, buying presents).

An increase for any other adult dependant ceases as soon as s/he goes into hospital, as s/he will not be caring for a child, and so does not meet the requirements for the increase (see p162).

Benefits for children

Child benefit, one parent benefit, guardian's allowance and increases of other benefits paid in respect of children are all affected in the same way. If your child is living with you (see p153), there is no reduction during the first 12 weeks the child is in hospital. **After 12 weeks** the benefits stop altogether, unless you are regularly incurring expenditure for the child (eg, by visiting, buying presents, etc) *and* are satisfying the other requirements for the benefit.[11] In practice, the benefits continue, since a child is treated as continuing to live with you as long as you are regularly incurring expenditure by visiting. That is enough to entitle you to both child benefit and increases of other benefits.

3   People in legal custody

Legal custody means imprisonment, or detention in a young offenders' institution, and includes remands in custody before trial.

The general rule is that you are disqualified from benefit while in legal custody,[1] but there are exceptions.

Adults

Most benefits are payable if you are in custody **on remand** (awaiting trial), unless you receive a custodial sentence at the end of your case. These benefits are sickness and invalidity benefit, attendance allowance, disability living allowance, child's special allowance, severe disablement allowance, maternity allowance, widows' benefits, retirement pensions, disablement benefit, reduced earnings allowance and retirement allowance.[2]

They are suspended while you are on remand and you are then paid arrears if you do not receive a sentence of imprisonment (including a suspended sentence[3]), youth custody or detention. If you do not receive a custodial sentence, you should also check that the Contributions Agency has credited you with contributions for the time you were on remand.

Disablement benefit (other than increases) is paid for up to a year in addition to any period on remand when the increases are payable.[4]

If you are transferred to a mental hospital while serving a sentence and are detained in the hospital, the disqualification ends on the date on which you would otherwise have been released.[5] Others detained in mental hospitals are always treated as being hospital in-patients (see p205) rather than being 'in legal custody'.

If your husband or wife is in legal custody, you cannot receive an increase in respect of her/him. If your spouse is *remanded* in custody, your increase is merely suspended, and is paid if no custodial sentence is awarded.[6]

You are treated as residing with your husband or wife even though one of you is in prison, unless your marriage has broken down and your separation is likely to be permanent.[7]

You will not receive an increase for any other adult dependant while that adult is in custody.[8]

Children

You can still claim child benefit[9] and guardian's allowance while you are in legal custody.[10]

If your child goes into legal custody, child benefit ceases after eight weeks, so guardian's allowance and any increase of benefit for the child also stops.[11] However, as with adults, arrears will be paid at the end of any period of remand if your child does not receive a custodial sentence.[12]

If you are looking after the child of someone in legal custody and the child's other parent is dead, you may be entitled to guardian's allowance (see p156).

4   **Overlapping benefits**

You cannot receive two or more *earnings replacement* benefits (see p4) at the same time. There are also overlapping provisions covering some other benefits.

Personal benefits

You cannot usually receive more than one of the following benefits for the same period. You receive the one paid at the greatest rate[1] (but see below and p63 if you are entitled to invalidity benefit and widows' benefits).

Unemployment benefit	Invalid care allowance
Sickness benefit	Widowed mother's allowance
Invalidity pension	Widow's pension
Severe disablement allowance	Non-contributory widow's benefit
Maternity allowance	Retirement pension

A **training allowance** paid by a government department or training agency causes any of those benefits to be reduced by the amount of the training allowance.[2]

Unemployability supplement (under the industrial injuries scheme or war pensions scheme, see pp141 and 261) causes any of those benefits except maternity allowance to be reduced by the amount of the unemployability supplement.

Death benefit paid to an adult (under the industrial injuries scheme or war pensions scheme – see pp87, 159 and 262) does not affect unemployment benefit, sickness benefit or maternity allowance but causes any of the other personal benefits to be reduced by the amount of the death benefit (except in the case of an invalidity pension or Category A retirement pension which is not reduced below the amount of the basic component based on your own contributions – ie not including any additional pension under SERPS or any part of the pension based on your former spouse's contributions or the fact that you are a widow or widower).[3]

You cannot receive more than one **retirement pension** at a time.[4] But there are special rules if you would otherwise be entitled to both a Category A (see p93) *and* a Category B retirement pension (see pp96-98) *and* your Category A pension would be paid at a reduced rate because you have not paid enough contributions (see p187). In this case your Category A pension will be increased either:

- by the amount of a basic Category B pension; *or*
- to the full amount of a basic Category A pension;

whichever is less.[5]

If you are a widow or widower, you will then also be entitled to both an additional pension on your own contribution record and one on your spouse's record, subject to a maximum equal to the maximum additional pension a person could theoretically receive on one contribution record.[6]

A **widow** entitled to both invalidity pension and either widowed mother's allowance or widow's pension may receive both basic benefits subject to a maximum of £56.10 a week.[7] She will also be entitled to both additional pensions subject to a maximum equal to the amount one person could theoretically receive on top of one benefit. Usually, the widow's benefit is paid in full with any additional benefit being paid as invalidity pension. As invalidity pension is not taxable, it is advantageous to apply for the full invalidity pension to be paid, with widow's benefit merely topping it up.[8]

Additions to benefits

Increases for dependants are covered below.

Invalidity allowance is treated as part of invalidity pension and similarly the age-related addition of severe disablement allowance is treated as part of the basic benefit. Invalidity allowance is reduced by an additional pension under SERPS,[9] and guaranteed minimum pensions under occupational pension schemes.

The increase of retirement pension equivalent to invalidity allowance counts merely as part of the pension but it may be paid with a Category B retirement pension if you are receiving such a pension because it is payable at a higher rate than the Category A retirement pension you would otherwise have.[10] An age addition overlaps only with another age addition.[11]

Additional pensions under SERPS, and graduated retirement benefit, do not overlap with basic benefits. However, if two or more benefits would otherwise be payable with an additional pension and graduated retirement benefit, only the higher or highest total of additional pension and graduated retirement benefit payable in addition to one of the basic benefits is due.[12]

There are exceptions to this rule for Category B retirement pensioners whose own contribution records would entitle them to Category A retirement pensions and for widows who receive invalidity benefit (see p209).

Benefits for people with disabilities

Disability living allowance care component and attendance allowance overlap with constant attendance allowance.[13] Otherwise attendance allowance, disablement benefit, reduced earnings allowance and retirement allowance do not overlap with any of the other benefits described in this guide. You may therefore receive, say, invalidity pension, both components of disability living allowance, disablement benefit and reduced earnings allowance all at once.

Increases in respect of adult dependants

Only one person may receive an increase of benefit in respect of the same dependant, except when one of the claimants receives an increase because the dependant is a woman employed by her/him to look after a child. Equally, you may only receive one increase in respect of an adult dependant. If, apart from those rules, more than one increase would be payable, only the higher or highest total is paid.[14]

An increase for an adult dependant also overlaps with any basic benefit payable to that dependant. If the increase is less than the basic benefit payable to the dependant, the increase will not be paid. If the increase is greater than the basic benefit, it is paid at a rate equal to the difference between the two rates of benefit.[15]

Benefits in respect of children and for child dependants

Only one person may receive child benefit or an increase for a child dependant for the same child (see p153 and 164)

The basic rate of child benefit does not overlap with any other benefit but if you are receiving the extra £1.90 per week payable for the eldest child, any other benefit or increase paid for the same child will be reduced by £1.15. [16]

You cannot get **one parent benefit** if, for the same child, you get guardian's allowance (see p156), child's special allowance (see p158), industrial death benefit for children (see p159) or an increase in widow's benefit, disablement benefit, invalid care allowance or a retirement pension. [17] Increases in invalidity benefit, severe disablement allowance, unemployment benefit or sickness benefit will be reduced by the same amount of any one parent benefit that is paid for the same child. [18]

All increases for children and child's special allowance overlap with guardian's allowance and industrial death benefit for children. [19]

5 Calculating earnings

These rules apply whenever earnings have to be calculated for social security purposes. [1]

The important figure will be your earnings *before* tax but after the deduction of national insurance contributions and certain other expenses.

All items provided by your employer count as earnings except: [2]

* meals provided by your employer at your place of work;
* accommodation in which you are required to live as a condition of employment;
* food or produce provided for your normal needs;
* luncheon vouchers up to a maximum of 15 pence per day;
* a Christmas bonus.

Payments from an occupational pension count as 'earnings' for the earnings rules for increases for dependants (see p166).

The following expenses can be deducted from your earnings: [3]

* national insurance contributions;
* trade union subscriptions;
* fares to and from work;
* the cost of making reasonable provision for looking after another member of your household (for example, childminding fees);
* overalls and the cost of cleaning them;
* tools and equipment including, in the case of the self-employed, the cost of business premises other than your home;
* any other reasonable expense.

The basic principle is that any expense incurred because of your work is deductible.

It is *your* responsibility to report any earnings over an earnings limit in a given week to the local Benefits Agency office. Note that these rules are different from the rules governing the calculation of earnings for the purposes of income support and other means-tested benefits.

6 Christmas bonus

A Christmas bonus of £10 is payable to those receiving one or more of the qualifying benefits in respect of at least part of the 'relevant week' (even if the benefit is paid later).[1] The 'relevant week' is usually the week beginning with the first Monday in December.

The qualifying benefits are:

- invalidity benefit
- severe disablement allowance
- invalid care allowance
- widowed mother's allowance
- widow's pension
- retirement pension
- disability living allowance
- attendance allowance
- disablement benefit (but only if unemployability supplement or constant attendance allowance is payable)
- industrial death benefit for widows or widowers
- war disablement pension
- war widow's pension
- income support (but only if you reach pensionable age before the end of the 'relevant week')

You may also claim an **extra bonus** for your husband or wife (or someone who you live with as husband or wife) if:[2]

- you are both over pensionable age at the end of the 'relevant week'; *and*
- s/he has not received a bonus in her/his own right; *and*
- you are entitled, or may be treated as entitled, to an increase of benefit in respect of her/him.

You are treated as entitled to a benefit if you are not receiving it because some other payment is being made from public funds. Similarly, you are treated as entitled to an increase in respect of your wife if the reason for it not being paid is either that some other payment is being made from public funds or that she earns too much.[3]

The bonus is tax free and has no effect on other benefits. A claim is not necessary in most cases, but if you have not obtained it within a year, your right is lost.[4]

7 Recovery of benefits from compensation payments

The general rule

The general rule is that damages are awarded by courts to compensate for loss so that if, as the result of the defendant's action, a plaintiff has had to claim benefit, the amount of damages to be awarded is reduced by the amount of benefit received by the plaintiff.

Thus, in a wrongful or unfair dismissal case, the claim for loss of earnings is reduced by the amount of unemployment benefit received.[1] The Secretary of State is able to recover an equivalent sum from the employer if it is an unfair dismissal case dealt with in an industrial tribunal[2] (see p27), but *not* if there is a settlement (see p28), or it is a wrongful dismissal case dealt with by a court.

Personal injury cases

These rules apply to the victims of an accident or injury suffered on or after 1 January 1989 or to a person who first claimed benefit in respect of a disease on or after that date. They apply to out of court settlements as well as to payments ordered by the courts. A compensator may not make a payment (unless it is 'exempt' – see below) to the victim of the accident, injury or disease before obtaining a 'certificate of total benefit' from the Secretary of State. The compensator must deduct from the payment the amount required by the 'certificate of total benefit' and must then provide the victim with a 'certificate of deduction'. The 'certificate of total benefit' should require the deduction of the amount of 'relevant benefits' paid, or likely to be paid, during the 'relevant period' to the victim in respect of the accident, injury or disease.[3]

'Relevant benefits' are unemployment benefit, sickness benefit, invalidity benefit, severe disablement allowance, disability living allowance (both components), attendance allowance, industrial injuries benefits, income support, family credit and statutory sick pay.[4] The 'relevant period' is the period of five years from the date of any accident or injury or from the date the victim first claimed a 'relevant benefit' in respect of the disease, unless the compensator makes a final payment before the end of that period, in which case the 'relevant period' ends when the payment is made.[5]

'Exempt payments' are any payments under £2,500 and also any made in a Fatal Accident Act case or by criminal courts. Payments made under the Vaccine Damage Act 1979 (see Appendix One, p264), the National Health Service industrial injury scheme and redundancy payments are also exempt, as are payments from certain trusts and insurance companies.[6]

The Secretary of State may review a 'certificate of total benefit' if satisfied that it was issued in ignorance of, or was based on a mistake as to, a material fact or if there was an error in its preparation, eg, a miscalculation.[7] The compensator and the victim (or intended recipient) can both appeal against the certificate but not until the payment has been made. Appeals are heard by social security appeal tribunals (see p241) but questions as to whether a person suffered a particular injury, sickness or disease, or for what period, are referred to a medical appeal tribunal (see p245) instead. Further appeals lie to a commissioner in the usual way (see p249).[8] You should appeal if deduction has been made of benefits you would have been receiving even if the accident or disease had not occurred.

Details of the procedures to be followed and other advice can be obtained from: Compensation Recovery Unit, Department of Social Security, Reyrolle Building, Hebburn, Tyne and Wear NE31 1XB (Tel: 091-489 2266). An excellent guide to the procedures called *Deduction from Compensation* is available free from the DSS leaflets unit (see Appendix Five, p281).

Old cases

Different rules apply to the victim of an accident or injury suffered before 1 January 1989 and also to any case where a person first claimed benefit in respect of a disease before that date.

Most social security benefits, including attendance allowance and mobility allowance, reduce the amount of damages payable by the person who caused the injuries leading to the payment of the benefits.[9] However, there are two major exceptions:

- In a personal injury case, only half of any sickness benefit, invalidity benefit, severe disablement allowance or disablement benefit is taken into account when assessing loss of earnings for the five years after an accident or onset of a disease or disablement.[10] After that five-year period, those benefits are ignored entirely.[11]
- In a fatal accident case, any widows' benefit, death benefit or other benefit resulting from the death is ignored.[12]

8   Deductions from benefit

Overpayments of non-means-tested benefits

If any of the benefits covered in this guide are overpaid and the overpayment is recoverable (see p235), it is usually recovered by making deductions from future payments of benefit. It can also be recovered by deductions from or by stopping any of the other benefits covered in this guide except statutory sick pay or statutory maternity pay.[1] The only exceptions are that child benefit or guardian's allowance cannot have deductions made from them except to recover an overpayment of the same benefit.[2] Deductions can also be made from income support or family credit but there are limits to the rate at which deductions can be made from income support (see CPAG's *National Welfare Benefits Handbook*).

Overpayment of means-tested benefits

Overpayments of income support and family credit which are recoverable can also be recovered from any of the benefits covered in this guide, except statutory sick pay, statutory maternity pay, child benefit, guardian's allowance or attendance allowance for a child.[3] So can overpayments of housing benefit or council tax benefit, but only if the overpayment was due to a misrepresentation or failure to disclose.[4] (The circumstances in which those two benefits can be recovered by other methods are quite wide.) Overpayments of those two benefits are recovered from social security benefits only when a local authority is unable to recover them from housing benefit or council tax benefit.

Social fund loans

These are recoverable from any of the benefits covered in this guide, except statutory sick pay, statutory maternity pay, widow's payment, disability living allowance, attendance allowance, child benefit, guardian's allowance or child's special allowance.[5]

9 **Criminal offences**

When dealing with the DSS **you must not:**

- make any statement or representation which you know to be false; *or*
- provide documents or information which you know to be false; *or*
- knowingly cause or allow anyone else to provide documents or information which you know to be false.[1]

If you do so you are guilty of a criminal offence and can be fined up to £5,000 and/or imprisoned for up to three months. In addition, you may have to repay any overpaid benefit (see p235). It does not make any difference whether it is you or someone else that is actually claiming benefit, so, for example, an employer who gave false reasons for having dismissed a former employee would be committing an offence (and s/he might also have to repay the Benefits Agency any benefit overpaid as a result – see p235). Neither does it matter if you were not successful in being paid benefit. Simply giving false information is a crime. These offences can be tried only in a magistrates' court (in Scotland, a sheriffs' court), and the prosecution must be commenced within 12 months of the commission of the offence or within three months of sufficient evidence coming to light, whichever is later.[2]

To prove that you have made a statement or representation that you knew to be false, the prosecution must show that you knew both that you were making the statement and that it was false. It is usual for the prosecution to rely on your signing the statement on the giro or order book to the effect that you are entitled to the money and have reported all relevant changes of circumstances. You must sign that statement when cashing the Giro or order. It is a defence if you believed that you were entitled to the money and had reported everything necessary. You are only guilty if you are *dishonest*.[3] On the other hand, it is not necessary for the prosecution to show that you intended to defraud the DSS rather than someone else. If you knew the statement was false, it does not matter why you made it.[4]

For more serious frauds, the prosecution usually brings charges of deception under section 15 of the Theft Act 1968, which carry very much heavier penalties.

Because the signing of each Giro or order may be a separate offence, the prosecution usually brings charges in relation to just two or three weeks.

For a deliberate and prolonged fraud, such as claiming unemployment benefit while working full-time, a sentence of imprisonment may be considered even for a person with no previous convictions. However, it has been emphasised that such offences are non-violent, non-sexual or non-frightening crimes so that custodial sentences are by no means inevitable.[5]

A court may order compensation to be paid in addition to or instead of any sentence imposed on a convicted defendant. If this is for a sum less than the overpayment, the Benefits Agency may still recover the balance from you (see p235).

If you are charged with an offence of this nature you should apply for legal aid and see a solicitor, even if you are thinking of pleading guilty.

Fraud in relation to contributions attracts the same penalties as the fraudulent claiming of benefits.[6] Again, more serious offences may be charged under the Theft Acts.

Non-payment of Class 1 or Class 2 contributions within the time limits renders a person liable to a fine of up to £1,000.[7] Failure to comply with other contribution regulations may also lead to a fine of £1,000, but in this case there may be a further £40 fine for each day the contravention continues.[8]

The Secretary of State may appoint inspectors to investigate possible fraud, and it is an offence wilfully to delay or obstruct an inspector in the exercise of her/his powers or to refuse or neglect to answer any questions or to furnish any information or to produce any document when required to do so under the Social Security Act 1975. Again, the maximum penalty is £500, and there can be a further daily penalty of £40 for refusing to answer questions or produce documents.[9] However, you are not required to answer any questions or give any evidence which might incriminate you or your spouse.[10]

PART FOUR

Administration and appeals

CHAPTER FIFTEEN

Administration

This chapter covers:

1 Claims
2 Decisions
3 Reviews
4 Payments
5 Recovery of overpayments
6 Complaints

I Claims

The Benefits Agency

The benefits covered in this guide (and also the main means-tested bene-fits) are administered by part of the DSS called the Benefits Agency. Most benefits are dealt with at your local Benefits Agency office. However, there are exceptions to this. For example, if you live in certain parts of London, your claim will be processed by special Benefits Agency offices in Glasgow (although you should still claim at the local office) and all claims for certain benefits are processed centrally. For example, child benefit is administered in Washington, Tyne and Wear – see p154. Unemployment benefit is administered by the Employment Service, part of the Depart-ment of Employment, on behalf of the DSS – claims are dealt with at local unemployment benefit offices and payments are made from a central computer.

All enquiries about social security benefits should first be made at the appropriate local office, which you will find listed under 'S' in the tele-phone directory.

Every Benefits Agency office has a 'customer service manager' whom you can contact if you are unhappy about the service you are receiving and cannot resolve the problem with the reception supervisor. Benefits Agency leaflet BAL1 (*Have Your Say*) contains a form for you to write to the cus-tomer service manager but you do not have to use it if you prefer to write your own letter, or speak to her/him in person. If you are still dissatisfied after the customer service manager has looked into your case, you should write to either the district manager or to the Chief Executive of the Bene-fits Agency, Mr Michael Bichard, Benefits Agency, 286 Euston Road, London NW1 3DN, marking your letter for his personal attention.

As part of the government's 'Citizen's Charter' initiative, the Benefits Agency has produced a 'customer charter'. This sets out standards of service which cover matters such as the prompt and accurate payment of your benefits. There are specific targets set for processing your claim – eg, in the case of sickness benefit, 65 per cent of claims should be processed within 10 working days, and 95 per cent within 30 working days. You can get a copy of the customer charter from your local office or from the customer service branch of the Benefits Agency at the address above. If you have to complain, it may help you if you can show that the Benefits Agency has failed to meet its published standards in your case.

Whenever you write to the Benefits Agency, you should be sure to quote your national insurance number and, if you are not writing to the office which is handling your claim, the name and address of that office.

Making a claim

A claim must be made for almost all benefits. You become entitled to benefit only when you submit a claim. This is the case, even if you satisfy all the other conditions,[1] although, in some instances, claims can be backdated (see pp222-24). (The only exceptions to this rule are retirement allowance and certain retirement pensions which do not have to be claimed if you are already receiving certain other retirement pensions or widows' benefits.[2])

Claims for benefit should normally be made on the appropriate DSS form. However, the Secretary of State *may* decide to treat any letter or other written communication as being a valid claim.[3]

Example

You were claiming sickness benefit and wrote to the Benefits Agency office to say that your husband had died. You were unaware that you could claim a widow's payment. Two years later, you find out about widow's payment. You can ask the Secretary of State to treat your letter as being a claim for widow's benefit. Write to your local Benefits Agency office arguing that you should have been given proper advice two years ago.

Because the decision is formally made by the Secretary of State (see p227), you cannot appeal. However, it is only the question whether the manner of a claim was sufficient (eg, whether your letter gave enough information to make it obvious that you were entitled to a benefit) that has to be decided by the Secretary of State. Any question as to whether a claim has been made (eg, if the Benefits Agency have no record of your letter and suggest you never wrote it) and, if so, when it was received by the Benefits Agency are questions to be decided by an adjudication officer, so you can appeal to a tribunal.[4]

A claim for unemployment benefit must be made *in person* at the unemployment benefit office, unless the Secretary of State directs you otherwise.[5]

An appropriate claim form is generally found at the back of the DSS leaflet describing the benefit. Personal interviews are rarely required, but medical examinations may be. Since backdating is possible only to a limited extent, you should claim as soon as you think that you *might* be entitled to a benefit, even if it will take you some time to collect all the information required by the form. Very occasionally, it may be in your interests to wait for the next calendar year to claim on the basis of a better record of national insurance contributions (see pp185-86).

You can amend your claim form by writing to the local office and, if this is received before a decision is made, the Secretary of State can treat the claim as amended from the date it was initially made.[6] A claim form submitted without a proper signature or certification may be treated in a similar way, provided you correct this within a month of the form being returned to you.[7]

If the claimant is a child or is otherwise unable to act on her/his own behalf, another person may apply in writing to be appointed to take all the necessary steps in relation to a claim, unless a court has already appointed someone else.[8] Even if you could act on your own behalf, there is nothing to prevent you asking someone else to act for you (except in the case of a claim for unemployment benefit[9]) provided that you write a letter to the Benefits Agency telling them. However, you must still take reasonable steps to make sure that time limits are kept to.[10]

The Secretary of State may require you to provide documentation and evidence relevant to the claim and you can be asked for an interview if one is reasonably required.[11] You may be able to claim travelling expenses for this.[12] However, personal interviews (other than for unemployment benefit) are relatively rare and most claims for social security benefits are administered by post. Once completed, the claim should be referred forthwith to the adjudication officer (see p224) for decision.[13] If you do not provide the evidence asked for by the Secretary of State, or you do not attend an interview, your claim still has to be referred to an adjudication officer who is not entitled to withhold a determination until you have complied with the Secretary of State's request.[14] The adjudication officer must make a decision on the available evidence and so must a tribunal if you appeal. Obviously an adjudication officer or tribunal is unlikely to decide in your favour if you fail to provide evidence which would be available to you if your claim were justified.

Even if the Secretary of State does not ask for further documents, you should make sure that the adjudication officer has all the evidence that might be relevant. If you were sacked and there is a dispute over whether you lost your job through misconduct, you might ask your former workmates to write statements for you to send to the adjudication officer to back up your version of events.

Until the claim is passed to the adjudication officer to decide, there has been no decision on it against which you can appeal. See page 225 for suggestions as to what to do if you think there is unreasonable delay in processing your claim or an unreasonable demand for further information or evidence.

Interchange of claims

If you have claimed the wrong benefit but are in fact entitled to another benefit, your original claim can be treated as a claim for the right benefit. This is a matter for the Secretary of State's discretion, but it will usually apply when the circumstances of your claim should have made it obvious to the Benefits Agency that you had made a mistake. Not all benefit claims are interchangeable. A claim for unemployment benefit may be treated as a claim for any incapacity benefit (ie, sickness benefit, invalidity benefit or severe disablement allowance), maternity allowance or invalid care allowance. A claim for invalidity benefit may be treated as a claim for any other incapacity benefit or maternity allowance but not for unemployment benefit. A claim for maternity allowance may be treated as a claim for any incapacity benefit. A claim for widow's benefit may be treated as a claim for retirement pension and vice versa. A claim for income support may be treated as a claim for invalid care allowance but not as a claim for other benefits.[15]

In the case of claims for children, a claim for child benefit may be treated as a claim for one-parent benefit, guardian's allowance, an increase of other benefits for the child or even maternity allowance for the period since the child's birth and vice versa. A claim for guardian's allowance may also be treated as a claim for an increase of another benefit for the child if you are not entitled to guardian's allowance.[16]

If a person claims a benefit (other than child benefit) but is not entitled to it, the claim may be treated as a claim by someone else for an increase in his/her benefit for the person who originally claimed. If a person claims an increase of benefit for a child or adult dependant but is not entitled to it, the claim may be treated as a claim by someone else who would be entitled.[17]

Time limits for claims

Benefits may be claimed up to three months *before* you actually become entitled to them, except for maternity allowance (which may be claimed no earlier than 14 weeks before the expected date of confinement), retirement pension (which may be claimed up to four months in advance), and attendance allowance.[18]

Once you have made your initial claim, benefit is awarded for an indefinite period, except for unemployment benefit which is usually awarded for a fortnight at a time.[19] An award is reviewed if your circumstances change or you cease to satisfy the conditions for entitlement (see p228).

There are strict time limits for claiming benefits. These may be extended for 'good cause' in the case of some benefits only (see pp222-24). Otherwise a benefit must be claimed within a specified period after the day for which the claim is made.

The specified periods are:[20]

Unemployment benefit	This must be claimed on the very day for which the claim is made unless you have been told to claim on another particular day.[21] In practice, after your first claim, you will usually be told to claim fortnightly.

Sickness and invalidity benefit
and severe disablement allowance:

• on the first claim ever made by a claimant	1 month
• on any other initial claim	6 days
• on any continuation claim	10 days

Industrial injuries benefits	3 months

Child benefit, guardian's allowance and any increase of benefit for a dependant	6 months

Retirement pensions, widows' benefits, maternity allowance and invalid care allowance	12 months

Disability living allowance
and attendance allowance:

• on any initial claim	The very day for which benefit is claimed[22]
• on any continuation claim	6 months[23]

The time limits for unemployment, sickness and invalidity benefit and for severe disablement allowance may be increased to one month if the Secretary of State certifies that to do so would be consistent with the proper administration of the legislation.[24]

The time limits for widows' benefits may be extended in some cases (see p83).

Failing to claim within the time limit does not usually mean that you do not receive any benefit at all for the period of your claim; but benefit will be backdated only to a limited extent. So, if you claim industrial injuries benefits five months after becoming entitled to them, and you have no good cause for the delay, you will receive three months' arrears only. That is because your claim will have been in time for the last three months. The exceptions to this are disablement benefit for occupational deafness (prescribed disease A10) or occupational asthma (prescribed disease D7) where missing the time limits may mean that you lose your right to benefit altogether (see p142).

'Good cause' for a late claim

If you claim outside the time limit, you will still be entitled to arrears of some benefits if you can show that there has been 'good cause' for not claiming throughout the period of the delay.[25] However, this applies only to unemployment benefit, sickness benefit, invalidity benefit, severe disablement allowance and industrial injuries benefits.

Even if you have 'good cause' for a late claim, you will still not receive any benefit other than industrial injuries benefits due more than 12 months before the date of your claim.[26] It may be possible to argue that a claim for one benefit may be treated as a claim for another, or that any written document may be treated as a claim (see pp220 and 221).

It is not always easy to show good cause for a late claim. Clearly, ill health can amount to good cause in some circumstances. If you are a hospital in-patient, you are assumed to have good cause for not claiming sickness or invalidity benefit or severe disablement allowance until either 13 weeks after your admission or three weeks after your discharge, whichever date comes sooner.[27] Ill health, whether physical or mental, may also amount to good cause in other cases.[28]

Claimants frequently say that they did not know that they could claim. Adjudication officers usually reply that ignorance is no excuse. That is an oversimplification of the law. It has been held that good cause means 'some fact which, having regard to all the circumstances (including the claimant's state of health and the information which he had received and that which he might have obtained), would probably have caused a reasonable person of his age and experience to act (or fail to act) as the claimant did'.[29] So, there is a general duty to find out your rights, but your age and experience are taken into account in deciding whether you have acted reasonably. If you claim late because you were ignorant of your rights, the first thing you need to explain is why.[30] You are expected to make enquiries by looking at the relevant DSS leaflets[31] or asking the DSS,[32] a solicitor[33] or a citizens' advice bureau.[34] Merely relying upon the advice of friends,[35] or even a doctor,[36] is not enough.

If you have made enquiries, you will have good cause for a late claim if you were misinformed, or insufficiently informed of your rights or were accidentally misled.[37] The enquiries need not necessarily have been in connection with that particular claim, and people have succeeded where they have simply misunderstood the system. So, a person who had once made enquiries about the rights of the self-employed to unemployment benefit and who had thought that the answers applied equally to sickness benefit succeeded in showing good cause.[38] People who know that certain benefits depend upon contributions paid while working, and who leave work not realising that they are covered for benefit by their contributions for up to two years afterwards (due to the rules relating to periods of interruption of employment) have also succeeded.[39] While language difficulties, illiteracy and unfamiliarity with technical documents do not in themselves amount to good cause for not claiming, they obviously increase the likelihood of confusion and are important matters to be taken into consideration.[40]

If you have made no enquiries at all it is more difficult to show good cause. You must show that your ignorance was due to a mistaken belief 'reasonably held', so you must explain exactly how you came to be under the wrong impression.[41] The general rule is that you cannot be expected to claim something if you have no reason to suspect you have a right to claim it. Being unaware that you have an industrial disease is good cause,[42] but if you know you have the disease, and you suspect it was caused at work, you are expected to enquire whether it was a prescribed industrial disease. You are likely to be excused ignorance of detailed changes in the law which give you new rights.[43]

If a person has been *formally* appointed by a court or the Secretary of State to act on your behalf, the question is whether the appointee has good cause for any late claim – not whether you have had.[44] If someone is *informally* acting on your behalf, the question is whether *you* have good cause and you must show that the delegation of the claim was reasonable, and that reasonable supervision was exercised.[45]

The good cause must continue up to the date of claim. Although the odd day may be overlooked, a substantial break in the good cause for not claiming will result in only the later period counting.[46]

If you are prevented from receiving benefit because your claim was more than 12 months late due to an error on the part of the DSS, it may still be possible to persuade the DSS to meet its moral obligation and make an *ex gratia* payment to you even though it is not strictly obliged to do so. The intervention of an MP or the Ombudsman (see p240) may help in these circumstances.

2 Decisions

It is important to know who is making the decision on any particular question in your case because that determines how you can challenge the decision. There are three separate bodies who may be responsible for making initial decisions.

The adjudication officer

The adjudication officer makes most initial decisions on claims for social security benefits.[1] The exceptions to this general rule are:

- decisions which have to be taken by the Secretary of State (see p227);
- disablement questions in relation to severe disablement allowance and disablement benefit, which are referred to adjudicating medical authorities (see p227).
- forfeiture questions (if you have killed your husband), which are decided by a social security commissioner (see p251)

Adjudication officers are civil servants either in the Benefits Agency or, in relation to unemployment benefit, the Employment Service of the Department of Employment. A Chief Adjudication Officer is appointed to give them advice and keep the adjudication system under review.[2] A decision should be taken on your claim within 14 days of receiving your papers so far as practicable.[3] Sometimes the decision will take longer than this. In the interim, you may be able to claim income support if you have inadequate resources. The amount of any income support paid to you may be deducted from arrears of social security benefits which you subsequently receive.[4]

If you need to contact the adjudication officer, you can write to her/him at the local office. A relatively common problem is a delay in making a decision. To remedy this, you can quote the statutory time limit of 14 days. You can also threaten to complain to the Ombudsman (see p240) or to write to the Chief Adjudication Officer (at the address in Appendix Four – see p279). In an extreme case it might be possible to make an application for judicial review, but you would need to see a solicitor (see p279). In one case, where there had been a four month delay in deciding an unemployment benefit claim, a decision was made within 24 hours of the claimant being granted legal aid for judicial review!

It is not possible to sue an adjudication officer for negligence in the way s/he decides your claim.[5] If the decision is wrong, the only thing you can do is appeal against it. But the position is different if you are given *wrong* advice by an employee of the Benefits Agency (see p240).

There is a special procedure for the 'diagnosis' and 'recrudescence' questions for industrial diseases (see p226).

In all other cases, the adjudication officer may decide the case for you, or against you, or may decide to refer it to a social security appeal tribunal (see p241).[6] It is uncommon to refer cases to a tribunal unless an appeal is already pending on the claim, but it is a procedure used when there is a clear conflict on the papers between, say, the employers and a claimant over the circumstances of a dismissal.

If you are not happy with the adjudication officer's decision on your case, you may appeal to a social security appeal tribunal (see p241). Alternatively, the decision may be reviewed (see p228).

The 'anti-test-case' rules

The adjudication officer must make decisions in accordance with the law, including commissioners' decisions (see p256). However, there are rules which say that some decisions should be ignored when adjudication officers are considering claims for periods before the decision was given. This is intended to prevent claimants from taking advantage of test cases brought against the DSS, but it goes rather wider.

If a commissioner or court has recently held that a tribunal (or, in limited circumstances explained below, an adjudication officer) in a totally different case has made an error of law, the adjudication officer must decide any part of your claim which relates to the period before the decision of the commissioner or court as if that decision of a tribunal 'had been found by the commissioner or court in question not to have been erroneous in point of law'.[7] That appears to mean that the adjudication officer in your case must make exactly the same error as the tribunal had made. However, that interpretation could lead to absurd results. Unless it is in your favour, you should argue instead that the effect of this provision is that the decision of the commissioner or court should simply not be taken into account by the adjudication officer. This would limit the effect of the provision to situations where a commissioner or court overrules a previous binding decision because, in other cases, the adjudication officer would be free to, and so likely to, reach the same result as the commissioner or court anyway.[8]

Note that this applies only to that part of your claim which relates to a period before the decision of the commissioner or court. Also it means that the decision of the commissioner or court has to be disregarded for that period only if the tribunal has been held to have been wrong; not if it has been upheld.

This rule applies if the high court (in Scotland, the court of session) has found an adjudication officer to have been wrong on an application for judicial review but not in cases where a commissioner or court has disagreed with an adjudication officer but has agreed with a *tribunal* which allowed a claimant's appeal.

The rules may not apply where a claimant has *successfully* appealed to the Court of Appeal against an adverse decision of a commissioner. This is because they only apply if a decision of an 'adjudicating authority' has been held to be erroneous and commissioners are not included in the definition of 'adjudicating authority'.[9] A recent commissioner's decision[10] throws some doubt on this argument but this will be appealed to the Court of Appeal. The *Welfare Rights Bulletin* will report developments as they occur.

If there is an *unsuccessful* appeal from a commissioner to the Court of Appeal (in Scotland, the court of session) in another case, it is unclear whether the tribunal's error has to be applied to the whole period before the commissioner's decision. If the error is helpful to you, you should argue that the relevant date is the date of the court's decision because that decision replaces the commissioner's decision. If the error is unhelpful to you, you should argue that the relevant date is the date of the commissioner's decision because that decision is not quashed by the court and so is left standing. The latter argument is the better one, but it is worth trying the other if it is more helpful, particularly if the court has reached the same result as the commissioner for totally different reasons.

It is important to note that these provisions apply only when an adjudication officer is considering a new claim or a review on the ground of error of law. They do not apply to reviews on other grounds or if you are given leave to make a late appeal (see p242).

Industrial disease cases

The 'diagnosis' and 'recrudescence' questions for industrial diseases (see pp134 and 135) are decided by a special procedure.

First, the adjudication officer must obtain a medical report, unless a suitable one is already available.[11] Then the case may be decided by the adjudication officer or may be referred to a medical board (see p227) for its decision.[12] These references are much more common than those to tribunals – particularly in industrial disease cases (where there must always be a reference if a disablement question (see p135) arises[13]).

If the case is decided by an adjudication officer, you may appeal to a medical board. The appeal must be in writing and must be given to the local office within three months.[14] The time may be extended by the chairperson of the medical board if there are special reasons.[15] See page 228 for the procedure before medical boards. Alternatively, the decision may be reviewed (see p228).

The Secretary of State

The legislation specifies that some matters are to be decided by the Secretary of State. In practice, they are taken by specially authorised officials who are called Secretary of State's representatives. A Secretary of State's decision cannot be appealed to a tribunal.

A large number of matters – many of them procedural but others dealing with substantive matters such as whether benefit is to be paid while a person is abroad – are decided entirely at the Secretary of State's discretion. You can always ask the Secretary of State to reconsider the decision by writing to your local office giving reasons.[16] There is no other remedy against an unsatisfactory decision other than an application to the high court for judicial review, which will rarely be possible.

However, certain matters are dealt with by a special procedure.[17] These are to do with contributions and a person's employment, for example, whether a person is an 'employed earner' for the purposes of paying contributions or entitlement to industrial injuries benefits, or satisfies the contribution conditions for a benefit or the conditions for receipt of home responsibility protection. Also included are questions concerning the calculation of earnings factors, and certain questions concerning occupational pensions and personal pension schemes. Decisions on these matters may be taken first by the adjudication officer if it appears that they are not in dispute. You are notified of the decision and the reasons and invited to reply if dissatisfied.[18] On receipt of your reply, the adjudication officer certifies that the matter is for determination by the Secretary of State and you are invited to apply for a formal decision.[19]

The Contributions Agency will investigate the facts and reach a provisional decision. If you are not happy with this, the question is then determined by an oral hearing before someone appointed by the Secretary of State, generally a DSS solicitor.[20] The decision is given in writing.[21] You may appeal to the high court (in Scotland the court of session) and can apply for a statement giving the grounds of the decision which will enable you to decide whether or not you want to do this.[22] Alternatively, you may ask for a review of the decision (see p232).

Adjudicating medical authority

An adjudicating medical authority is a doctor, known as an **adjudicating medical practitioner**, or a **medical board** which consists of two or more doctors. Cases involving some prescribed diseases (B6, C15, C17, C18, C22(b), D1, D2, D3, D7, D8, D9 or D10 – see Appendix Three, p270) are determined by specially qualified medical boards.[23]

The questions dealt with by adjudicating medical authorities are:

- the 'diagnosis' and 'recrudescence' questions relating to industrial diseases where medical boards hear appeals and references from adjudication officers (see p226);
- the 'disablement questions' relating to severe disablement allowance and disablement benefit (see pp68 and 135) which are referred to adjudicating medical authorities for their initial decision. These questions are usually dealt with by a single adjudicating medical practitioner. If it is an industrial disease case or if the Secretary of State so directs, the questions are referred to a medical board;[24]
- an application for a review of any decision on the above questions. This is referred to a medical board for its initial decision.[25]

The adjudicating medical authorities do not hold hearings in the same way as tribunals. You have no right of representation before them, although, with your consent, the presence of anyone 'likely to assist them' to make the decision can be allowed.[26] The doctor or board is there to give you a medical examination and is not concerned with other aspects of your case. The doctor will probably take a statement of your condition from you, so make sure you are clear in your mind about what your symptoms are. This is particularly important if your condition is fluctuating or if you want to describe an aspect of your condition that the doctor will not be able to see for her/himself. One way of making sure that you give the doctor all the relevant information is to write it down before you go so that you can just hand it to the doctor when you attend the examination (remembering to keep a copy for yourself). However, you should still talk to the doctor about your symptoms because that makes it easier for any uncertainties to be cleared up.

The decision will be sent to you in writing.[27] You may appeal against a decision of an adjudicating medical authority to a medical appeal tribunal (see p245).

3   Reviews

Any decision affecting entitlement to benefit may be reviewed if certain conditions are met. Following the review, the decision may be revised either to increase or to decrease your entitlement to benefit. This enables decisions to be altered if they were wrong or to take account of new circumstances without appeals being necessary. (Reviews and appeals are compared on page 233.)

Reviews can be considered if you ask for one (in writing to your local Benefits Agency office) or because an adjudication officer or the Secretary of State feels that one is needed. A review may be considered at any time. In some cases decisions are reviewed several years after they were originally made.

Reviews of decisions on disability living allowance or attendance allowance are considered on page 123.

Review by an adjudication officer

An adjudication officer may review any decision of an adjudication officer (except in the case of the 'diagnosis' or 'recrudescence' questions for industrial diseases), or a social security appeal tribunal or a commissioner. Reviews usually arise if new information comes to the attention of the adjudication officer or because there is a change in the law. A decision may be reviewed only if: [1]

- it was given in ignorance of, or was based on a mistake as to, a material fact; *or*
- there has been any relevant change of circumstances; *or*
- the original decision must be changed to take account of a new decision of the Secretary of State or the adjudicating medical authorities (eg, to increase the amount of disablement benefit after a new assessment of disablement by a medical board); *or*
- the original decision was made by an adjudication officer (not a tribunal or commissioner) and was wrong in law;
- in the case of an advance award of benefit, that the claimant no longer satisfies the requirements for entitlement to the benefit.

It is open to an adjudication officer to review a case on the ground of, say, ignorance of a material fact but then decide not to revise the decision because the 'new' fact would not have affected it.

'Ignorance of, or mistake as to, a material fact'

If a decision is reviewed on this ground, any revision will take effect from the beginning of the period covered by the original decision. If it is in your favour, you will receive arrears (but see p231 for the limits). If it is not in your favour there may have been an overpayment so the adjudication officer will decide whether or not you should pay it back (see p235). You would then want to consider whether the adjudication officer really had the power to review the decision.

It is only ignorance of, or a mistake about, a primary (or specific) fact which justifies a review. [2] This means that an adjudication officer does not have the power to review a decision on this ground merely because a doctor has expressed a different view about your capacity for work. A doctor's opinion is not itself a primary fact; it is a conclusion drawn by the doctor from a number of primary facts.

Example
You are a plumber claiming reduced earnings allowance. The doctor examines you and records his findings, including the results of his examination of your ability to bend your legs at the knees. He decides that you are permanently incapable of performing your regular occupation. You are awarded benefit. A second doctor then decides that you are not incapable of performing your regular occupation. That does not permit the adjudication officer to review the original decision on the ground of ignorance or mistake. However,

the adjudication officer could do so if there was evidence that you had been misleading the first doctor so that there had been a mistake by him as to the extent of your disability or, if the first adjudication officer had been under a misapprehension as to the nature of your regular occupation.

It is often difficult to draw the line between medical opinion and primary fact and it is not often that adjudication officers review decisions based on medical evidence on the ground of ignorance or mistake.

A different medical opinion may allow an adjudication officer to review a decision on the ground that the requirements for entitlement to the benefit are no longer satisfied (see below) but such a review will have effect only from the date of the review and will not be retrospective.

'Relevant change of circumstances'

If a decision is reviewed on this ground, it takes effect from the date of the change.

Again, a difference of medical opinion does not necessarily mean there has been a change of circumstances[3] but an adjudication officer can review a decision on the ground that the requirements for entitlement to the benefit are no longer satisfied (see below).

'Requirements for entitlement ... are not satisfied'

This power to review decisions is entirely separate from the power to review on grounds of ignorance or mistake of a material fact or change of circumstances.[4] It applies where benefit is awarded in advance and most claims for benefit are now regarded as made in advance for indefinite periods. However, whereas the burden of proving entitlement to a benefit rests on the claimant in the beginning, once an award is made, the burden of proving that the requirements for entitlement are no longer satisfied rests on the adjudication officer.[5]

A review on this ground takes effect from the date of the adjudication officer's decision (or the next pay day). That is because the adjudication officer is terminating an award and has no power to do that retrospectively.

Error of law

An adjudication officer can review a decision based on an error of law made by her/himself or by another adjudication officer but cannot correct such an error on the part of a tribunal.[6] S/he must appeal or ask for the decision to be set aside in the same way as a claimant.

The 'anti-test-case' rules affect these reviews in the same way as they affect decisions on new claims (see p225). So, if a commissioner or court in another case has held a tribunal (or an adjudication officer) to have made an error of law in that case, the adjudication officer reviewing your case on the ground of error of law must decide your case as though the decision of the tribunal (etc) 'had been found... not to have been erroneous in point of law' insofar as the review covers a period before the date of the decision of the commissioner or court.[7] See pages 225-26 for further discussion of the problems caused by this provision.

One possible effect is that if a commissioner or court decides that a tribunal made an error and that error would assist you, you should ask the adjudication officer to review the original decision awarding you benefit and to apply that error for the whole period before the date of the commissioner's or court's decision. CPAG will try and publicise suitable cases. The amount of arrears you receive may be limited to 12 months' (see below) but may nevertheless be a useful windfall.

Although these rules affect reviews, they do *not* apply to appeals (see Chapter 16). So, if you hear of a test case which might benefit you, you should appeal (asking permission for a late appeal if necessary – see p242) and only ask for a review if permission to appeal late is refused.

Arrears of benefit

If the review results in an award of benefit, or an increase in the amount of benefit to be paid, there will be only a limited backdating of benefit for the period before the date when you applied for the review or, if you did not apply, before the adjudication officer decided upon the review.

Unless you had 'good cause' for not applying earlier for the review, the arrears will be limited as follows:[8]

* no arrears of unemployment benefit and maternity allowance will be paid;
* only two weeks' arrears of sickness benefit, invalidity benefit or severe disablement allowance will be paid;
* only three months' arrears of widows' benefits, invalid care allowance, guardian's allowance or retirement pension will be paid;
* only a maximum of 12 months' arrears of child benefit will be paid.

'Good cause' in this context is the same as for late claims (see pp222-24).

If you did have 'good cause' for not applying earlier for the review, you will be entitled to a maximum of 12 months' arrears[9] unless *either:*

* the review is based on evidence which was before the adjudicating authority (ie, adjudication officer, SSAT or commissioner) at the time of the original decision but which was not taken into account; *or*
* the original decision was made by an SSAT or by a commissioner and the review is based on a document which was in the possession of the officer of the DSS or Department of Employment who made a submission to the adjudicating authority but was not included in that submission; *or*
* the review is based on evidence which did not exist at the time of the original decision but which was produced to the DSS, Department of Employment or to the adjudicating authority as soon as practicable after it became available to the claimant; *or*
* the original decision was made by an adjudication officer and the

review is for error of law because s/he overlooked or misinterpreted an Act of Parliament, Regulations or a decision of a commissioner or a court.

In these cases arrears will be paid either from the date of claim or the date upon which the new evidence was made available.[10]

Appeal

You may appeal to a social security appeal tribunal against a decision of an adjudication officer to review or not to review an earlier decision (see p242).[11]

Review by the Secretary of State

Questions which are determined at the discretion of the Secretary of State may be reconsidered by him at any time on any ground.[12]

On other questions (ie, those decided by the special procedure described on p227), the Secretary of State may review a decision only if:[13]

• new facts have been brought to his notice;
• the original decision was given in ignorance of, or based on a mistake as to, a material fact;
• the original decision was wrong in law.

Review by a medical board

A medical board may review a decision of:

• an adjudication officer on the 'diagnosis' and 'recrudescence' questions for industrial diseases (see pp227-28);
• an adjudicating medical practitioner;
• a medical board;
• a medical appeal tribunal.

The grounds upon which a decision may be reviewed depend upon the type of benefit under consideration and the body which made the original decision.

Any decision may be reviewed if the medical board is satisfied that it was given in ignorance of, or was based on a mistake as to a material fact.[14] The test is the same as for an adjudication officer (see p229) but the limitations are more important here because there is no alternative basis of review on the ground that the requirements of entitlement are no longer satisfied. Furthermore, there is another important limitation; the decision may be reviewed only if there is 'fresh evidence'.[15] That means evidence that could not reasonably have been obtained and produced to the body making the first decision.[16]

Any decision concerning the disablement questions for severe disablement allowance or disablement benefit may be made on the ground of unforeseen aggravation of your disability.[17] That implies a change of circumstances leading to an increase in your disablement. A change of circumstances leading to an improvement in your condition cannot be grounds for a review but, of course, when your current period of assessment comes to an end, any further assessment will be based upon your improved condition. If you wish to apply for a review of a decision of a medical appeal tribunal (but not an adjudicating medical practitioner or medical board), on the ground of unforeseen aggravation, you must first apply to the tribunal for leave.[18] Write to your local Benefits Agency office.

Any decision of a medical board may be reviewed on the ground that it was wrong in law.[19] (An adjudicating medical practitioner can review a decision of another adjudicating medical practitioner on the same ground.)

'Relevant change of circumstances'

A difference of medical opinion does not necessarily mean there has been a change of circumstances.[20] The burden of proving a change of circumstances rests on the medical board. It will be possible to show a change only if the new medical board has found different 'primary' facts upon which to base their opinion when compared with the original medical board's primary findings of fact, noted in their report of the examination.

Arrears of benefit

If a medical board reviews a decision, it will be necessary for the adjudication officer to review her/his decision about the amount of benefit you are to receive. Any increase of disablement benefit or reduced earnings allowance will be paid from the date of your application for the review 'or from such earlier date as appears . . . to be reasonable in the circumstances'.[21] In the case of a review on the grounds of unforeseen aggravation, the amount of arrears will be limited to the period of the new assessment which will not begin more than three months before the date of the application for review.[22]

Appeal

You may appeal to a medical appeal tribunal (see p245) against a decision of a medical board to review or not to review a decision.[23]

Reviews and appeals

Reviews and appeals are both ways of challenging decisions and in cases where it is suggested that the original decision was made in ignorance of, or was based on a mistake as to, a material fact, either method may be used. Indeed, if you appeal, your appeal will often be treated as an application for a review and a decision may be reviewed before it ever reaches a tribunal. However, there are occasions when it is necessary to choose your method of challenge with care.

The main advantages of applying for a review are that it is simpler than appealing and you receive a decision more quickly. You also get two bites at the cherry because, if your application is turned down, you can always appeal against that decision.

However, there is a major disadvantage in applying for a review in some cases because you may not be paid all the arrears due to you even if you are successful. In considering whether or not to ask for a review, you have to take into account all the factors that might lead to arrears of benefit being limited. These include the length of time since the original decision, the type of benefit, whether or not you have 'good cause' for the delay in asking for the review, whether the original decision was simply an administrative error on the part of the Benefits Agency, whether the 'anti-test-case' rules apply to you and so on (see pp225 and 230). If you think there is a risk that you will not obtain all the arrears, you should appeal instead of asking for a review.

There is not usually any risk attached to an appeal. The only problem is that you have to obtain leave from the tribunal chairperson if you wish to appeal against a decision more than three months after it has been made (see p245). If you have a good reason for the delay, you will usually be given leave to appeal. In theory there is a risk that you might lose arrears of benefit by delaying an application for a review while making an unsuccessful application for leave to appeal. However, you can then ask for your application for leave to appeal to be treated as an application for a review and the Benefits Agency will usually agree to do this.

4   **Payments**

Method of payment

Benefit is paid by individual Girocheques or order books. Payment is made at nominated post offices. Unemployment benefit is payable fortnightly in arrears. Sickness benefit, invalidity benefit, severe disablement allowance and maternity benefit are payable weekly in arrears. Child benefit is usually paid at four-weekly intervals, although there are circumstances in which you can have it paid weekly (see p155). Other benefits are payable weekly in advance.[1]

Alternatively you can choose to be paid some benefits by direct credit transfer into a bank account either four-weekly or quarterly in arrears. An overpayment of benefit due to the credit transfer arrangement itself is recoverable by the Benefits Agency, but not when the Secretary of State confirms that it would be inappropriate, or where it is not materially due to the credit transfer arrangement itself (unless you have misrepresented or failed to disclose a material fact – see p237.[2]

If the claim is for a child or any other person unable to act for her/ himself, or if a person has died since the claim was originally made, another person may be appointed to receive the benefit and take any necessary actions on the claim.[3] Benefit may also be paid to a third party if you are entitled to an increase of benefit on condition that payments are made to someone and you do not make those payments or, if the benefit is payable together with income support and you are in debt.⁴

For rules preventing the duplication of payments, see page 208.

Interim payment

An interim payment may be made, usually when a reference, review, application or appeal is pending, but also when it is impractical either for the claimant to claim the benefit or for the Benefits Agency to pay it.⁵ Interim payments are very rare in practice.

Any interim payment is offset against or deducted from the eventual award of benefit.⁶ If no benefit is eventually awarded on the claim or the amount is less than the interim payment, the balance of the interim payment is treated as an overpayment.⁷

Suspension of payment

When a review is being considered, or when an appeal or reference by the Secretary of State or an adjudication officer is awaiting consideration by a medical appeal tribunal or a commissioner, the payment of benefits may be suspended. If you win an appeal to an SSAT, payment may be suspended pending an appeal to the commissioner, provided that you are given written notice within 30 days from when the adjudication officer was told of the tribunal's decision that an application for leave to appeal has been made.⁸ The standard Benefits Agency letter saying that it is 'considering' an appeal is *not* sufficient.

Benefit may also be suspended if a question of law arises on your claim and the same question is being appealed to the commissioner or a court in a different case, or if it is to be considered by the high court on an application for judicial review.⁹

5 Recovery of overpayments

You have to pay back an overpayment 'in respect of a benefit' *only* if it was due to *either*:¹

* a misrepresentation as to a material fact; *or*
* a failure to disclose a material fact.

The misrepresentation or failure to disclose may be entirely innocent but the Secretary of State is still entitled to recover the overpayment.

The overpayment may be recovered either from the claimant or from whoever made the misrepresentation or failed to disclose the material fact.² If it is to be recovered from that other person s/he has an independent right of appeal against any decision that there has been an overpayment or that it is recoverable.³ The method of recovery is explained below.

A payment is only recoverable when the decision awarding the benefit has been revised on either a review or an appeal and an adjudication officer, social security appeal tribunal or commissioner has ruled that the payment is recoverable.[4] Even if you accept that there has been an overpayment, you still have a separate right of appeal against the decision that you should repay it. The burden of proving that any overpayment was due to a misrepresentation or failure to disclose rests on the adjudication officer.[5]

Misrepresentation

Any positive statement by you is a representation, and if it turns out to be wrong it is a misrepresentation. Thus, if you are asked 'are there any changes in your circumstances?' and you answer 'No' and it is later discovered that, unknown to you, your spouse's earnings have increased, there will have been a misrepresentation by you. But if you had answered 'Not to my knowledge', there would have been no misrepresentation.[6]

Furthermore, a written representation may be qualified by an oral one so that, if you fill in a form incorrectly but explain the situation to an officer when handing the form in, the explanation has to be taken into account when deciding whether what is stated on the form amounts to a misrepresentation. If you say you have no income on the form but, when handing it in, ask whether you should have mentioned your occupational pension, you should be treated as having mentioned the occupational pension on the form.[7]

Adjudication officers sometimes rely on the statement you sign on each order from your order book which says:

> 'I declare that I have read and understood all the instructions in this Order Book, that I have correctly reported any facts which would affect the amount of any payment and that I am entitled to the above sum. I acknowledge receipt of the above sum.'

However, to say 'I have correctly reported any facts' is not a representation as to a 'material fact' for the purposes of benefit. If you have not reported all the material facts, the overpayment is likely to be recoverable on the ground of your failure to disclose but, if it is not (because, say, you could not have known of the relevant fact – see below), the adjudication officer cannot rely on your signing the order so as to succeed on the ground of misrepresentation.[8]

If you sign that 'I am entitled to the above sum', that also is not a representation as to a material *fact*; it is a representation of *law* because it is a conclusion based on the facts of the case. Again, if you have not reported all the relevant facts the payment is likely to be recoverable on that ground, but, if it is not, the adjudication officer cannot rely on you having signed the order.[9] The exception to this is when you have been asked to return your order book and you cash one last order before doing so. In those circumstances, the signing of the order to the effect that you are entitled to the payment has been held to be a misrepresentation 'by conduct'.[10] It is not clear from that decision what the 'material fact' was that the commissioner considered had been misrepresented. In any event, that decision is binding on adjudication officers and tribunals, but it could be argued before a commissioner that payments cashed after benefit has been stopped following a review or a suspension are not payments 'in respect of a benefit' and can be recovered only through the courts.

Failure to disclose

You cannot be said to have 'failed to disclose' a fact that you did not know about unless there is some reason why you should have been aware of it. [11] Nor can you be said to have failed to disclose something unless you were *either* asked to disclose it *or* you should have realised that it was relevant and so had to be disclosed. [12]

An adjudication officer can often point to warnings and instructions at the back of an order book that you should have read. [13] On the other hand, the adjudication officer ought not to rely on warnings on forms you were asked to sign without having a proper chance to read. [14]

It has been said that there is a failure to disclose only if disclosure 'was reasonably to be expected'. [15] On the other hand the legislation makes it quite clear that an innocent failure to disclose will nonetheless make any overpayment recoverable. [16] Difficulties may arise if a person is mentally ill or 'vague'. If you are, or have been, aware of a fact (such as that your spouse has received an increase in her/his occupational pension) and have been told to report that fact to the Benefits Agency (perhaps through the notes in an order book), then if you do not tell the Benefits Agency about the increase, and benefit is overpaid as a result, that overpayment will inevitably be recoverable. Even if you did not read the notes in the order book, the adjudication officer can say that you ought to have done so or to have had someone else read them to you. But your mental state would be relevant in deciding whether you ever knew your spouse had an increase in the pension. [17] It would also be relevant in deciding whether you ought to have realised the significance of the occupational pension increase if you had been aware of the increase but had not been specifically told to report it.

Disclosure does not have to be in writing and it does not have to be made by the claimant personally. But it does have to be made to the right part of the Benefits Agency and you cannot assume that mentioning a fact to the Child Benefit Centre means that the local office will hear about it and adjust any other benefit. On the other hand, you cannot be expected to understand exactly how the Benefits Agency works so that making a disclosure to the office where your claim is being handled and making specific reference to your claim will be enough because you can then reasonably expect the person receiving the information to pass it on to the right person. [18]

Once a disclosure has been made *to the right person*, any continued overpayment due to the Benefits Agency not acting on it will not be recoverable. However, if you do not make the disclosure to the right person but make it to someone else in the reasonable expectation that it will be passed on, you will have satisfied the duty to disclose only for a while. The duty to disclose is then a continuous one and if it later becomes obvious to you that the information has not filtered through to the right person, you should disclose the facts again and if you fail to do so there will be a further recoverable overpayment.[19] It is unclear whether this applies only if you actually realise that you are being over-paid or whether it is enough that you should have realised. You should argue that since the Benefits Agency also ought to have realised that you were being overpaid and since the legislation does not require the recovery of an overpayment in a case where you have disclosed every-thing to the right person even if you should have realised later that you are being overpaid, only actual knowledge that you are being overpaid gives rise to a further duty to disclose in a case where you expected the information to be passed on.

If it is suggested that an overpayment is recoverable because someone other than the claimant failed to make a disclosure, it is extremely important for the adjudication officer to establish that disclosure was reasonably to be expected from that person.

The amount to be recovered

The amount of benefit to be recovered is only that sum arising from the misrepresentation or failure to disclose a material fact. Also deducted from the amount to be recovered is the amount of any other social security benefit (including income support) which would have been payable if you had not received the overpayment.[20]

Overpayments made before 6 April 1987

Before 6 April 1987, overpayments were not recoverable unless a claimant had failed to use due care and diligence to avoid overpayment. In most cases, overpayments recoverable under the present law would have been recoverable under the old test too, but in some cases the results would have been different. The old law tended to be more favourable to claimants although sometimes it would work the other way round.

The Court of Appeal has ruled that the new test applies even if the overpayment was made before 6 April 1987. CPAG takes the view that that decision was wrong.[21] However, it was not appealed to the House of Lords because the Secretary of State undertook not to ask the claimant to repay the overpayment even though she had lost her case. CPAG now has another case which raises the same point and expects to petition the House of Lords for leave to appeal in the near future. See the *Welfare Rights Bulletin* for updates on this appeal.

If this is relevant to you, you should try and delay any tribunal hearing your case (although make sure you lodge your appeal in time). CPAG's solicitors will let you know the progress of their case so that you can inform the tribunal. If the tribunal hears your case, ask for leave to appeal to the commissioner, saying that you are awaiting the outcome of CPAG's case.

The method of recovery

Whether or not the Secretary of State is entitled to recover benefit from either the claimant or someone else is decided by the adjudication officer, with the usual rights of appeal. However, if it is decided that he is entitled to recover the benefit, it is still up to the Secretary of State to decide whether or not he will do so.[22] He does not always do so and may be persuaded that it would be unduly harsh in a particular case.

Benefit may be recovered by stopping payment of any of the benefits covered in this guide or equivalent benefits payable under EC legislation or the legislation of Northern Ireland or any income support or family credit, although there are limits to the extent by which income support may be reduced.[23]

Otherwise, any benefit may be recovered by enforcement proceedings in the county court in England and Wales or the sheriffs' court in Scotland.[24] Once the decision of the adjudication officer, social security appeal tribunal or commissioner is produced, the court has to enforce it unless you persuade the court to delay enforcement ('grant a stay of execution') while you appeal against the relevant decision.

Criminal proceedings

Sometimes the DSS commences criminal proceedings (see p215) at the same time as attempting to recover overpaid benefits. There is no general rule as to which proceedings should be determined first. If you are in this position, it is open to you to request either the tribunal or the magistrates' court to adjourn whilst the other body decides the issue. It is generally better for the tribunal to deal with any appeal before any criminal trial because tribunals have a better understanding of social security law than courts and also because they tend to be more sympathetic to claimants' confusion about the social security system (although that is not always the case). Also, any conviction by a court carries great weight in a tribunal whereas the fact that you were unsuccessful in your appeal would probably not be mentioned in any criminal court.

An acquittal on the criminal charge does not prevent the Benefits Agency recovering the overpayment.[25] Nor will conviction on the criminal charge necessarily prevent you from showing that an overpayment is not recoverable, or even that you have an entitlement to the benefit.[26] The right of the Benefits Agency to reclaim money paid to you is independent of the powers of the court to fine you or to order compensation.

6 Complaints

The Benefits Agency will sometimes pay compensation if you can show that you have lost out through their error or delay and the loss cannot be made good by an appeal or review. For instance, if you failed to claim guardian's allowance because you were misled by the Benefits Agency, you could not have the benefit back-dated more than six months. Even when you can get arrears on a review, you still receive them at the original rates with no interest to make up for the effects of inflation.

The Benefits Agency

You should first complain to the customer service manager of the local office. If that does not work, write to the district manager. If you are still dissatisfied try writing for the personal attention of Michael Bichard, Chief Executive, Benefits Agency, 286 Euston Road, London NW1 3DN. If you are still unsuccessful, you can try the Ombudsman.

The Ombudsman

The Ombudsman (technically known as the Parliamentary Commissioner for Administration) investigates complaints about civil service administration and publishes reports on them. A report in your favour by the Ombudsman may help to persuade the Benefits Agency to pay compensation. You cannot contact the Ombudsman direct but must apply through a Member of Parliament.

Compensation

This obviously varies from case to case but there is a general rule which applies in cases where benefit has been delayed due to an error by the DSS.

If the total delay in making payment is 52 weeks or more and at least some of it was due to DSS error, compensation is paid in the form of interest. However, the interest is payable only from the beginning of the second year of delay. In calculating that date, any time your case was in the hands of any appeal tribunal is ignored as is any period of three months or more due to excessive delay on your part. This formula has been agreed with the Ombudsman.

In some cases there may be a legal obligation to pay compensation wich can be enforced against the DSS in the courts if necessary. Although you cannot sue an adjudication officer if s/he negligently decides your claim wrongly and you lose out as a result, the situation is probably different if you are given wrong advice about your entitlement to benefit. This is because the DSS holds itself out (in its leaflets and in the public statements of some ministers) as being a competent source of advice on social security and, as a result, a court is likely to say that it must take reasonable care to get that advice right. So, for example, if you ask about your entitlement to a retirement pension and are told that you have not paid enough contributions and it subsequently turns out that you could have topped up your contributions and become entitled, you should see a solicitor or a law centre (see p260) if the DSS refuse to pay you full arrears. In practice such claims for compensation are almost always settled without need for a court hearing.

CHAPTER SIXTEEN

Appeals

This chapter covers:
1 Social security appeal tribunals
2 Medical appeal tribunals
3 Disability appeal tribunals
4 Social security commissioners
5 How to prepare an appeal

If you are dissatisfied with a decision of an adjudication officer or an adjudicating medical authority (including a medical board), you can appeal to an independent tribunal (although it is sometimes worth applying for a review instead – see p228). If you are claiming disability living allowance (see pp101 and 108), or attendance allowance (see p114) appeals on a question about your disability will be heard by disability appeal tribunals.

Appeals from adjudication officers are heard by social security appeal tribunals. Appeals from adjudicating medical authorities are heard by medical appeal tribunals.

If you are dissatisfied with the decision of a tribunal, you can appeal to a social security commissioner if there is a point of law involved.

1 Social security appeal tribunals

The tribunal

Social security appeal tribunals are independent of the DSS. There is a President of Social Security, Medical and Disability Appeal Tribunals and he has overall responsibility for them.[1] They are grouped together into regions, each of which has a regional chairperson who is responsible for the administration of the tribunals in his region.[2] The names and addresses of the President and regional chairpersons are given in Appendix Four (p279).

Each region has a panel of chairpersons and a panel of lay members for social security appeal tribunals. The chairpersons are always lawyers.[3] The lay members are required to have knowledge or experience of conditions in their area and to be representative of people living in it.[4] If you want to be a member, write to the regional chairperson.

The tribunals' administration is dealt with by clerks who are civil servants assigned to the tribunals by the President.[5] They are based at the offices of the regional chairpersons. In practice, there are 'indoor clerks' who stay in the office and 'outdoor clerks' who travel to the various towns and cities where tribunals sit. They have purely administrative duties and do not take part in the making of any decisions by the tribunals.

A tribunal may hear up to about a dozen cases a day. For each hearing, there should be a lawyer chairperson and two lay members. Decisions are made by a majority vote so the lay members can, and often do, out-vote the chairperson.[6] If only the chairperson and one other member are present, the tribunal can still hear your case provided that you agree, but the chairperson then has a second vote.[7]

Very occasionally, a tribunal may sit with an expert assessor to advise it on the evidence. The expert is not a member of the tribunal and the tribunal still has to make its own decision.[8]

How to appeal

Social security appeal tribunals hear appeals from adjudication officers on all matters except for a few concerning disability living allowance, attendance allowance, and industrial accidents and diseases (see pp245 and 247).[9] They also hear appeals from the Secretary of State concerning the recovery of benefits from compensation payments (see p212).[10]

To appeal, you can either complete an appeal form provided by the Benefits Agency or you can simply write a letter. In either case, you should try to make sure it gets to your local Benefits Agency office within three months of the date of your being sent notice of the adjudication officer's decision against which you are appealing. If your appeal is outside the three-month time limit, a chairperson may still allow it to go ahead but only if there are 'special reasons'.[11] This does not just mean special reasons for why the appeal was late (although this may be enough on its own). Any good reason will be considered, so you should explain any delay or argue that you will suffer hardship if the appeal is not heard.[12]

Your letter of appeal should contain your reasons for appealing and make it clear which decision you are appealing against. If you are unsure of your position, you can always send in a short letter of just two or three lines, to keep within the time limit, and follow it up with more details (or withdraw it) later. The adjudication officer or chairperson can ask for more details.[13] In any case, it is a good idea to give as much detail as possible in your letter of appeal. Include any documents which are relevant such as medical reports. Such detail may lead the adjudication officer to review the decision in your favour (see p228), in which case it would not be necessary to attend a hearing. If not, your letter and documents will be included in the papers sent to the tribunal members and read by them before the hearing.

When your letter of appeal is received, the adjudication officer prepares a written submission, explaining the reasons for her/his decision. Your letter of appeal and accompanying documents, the adjudication officer's submission and any documents such as your claim form, medical certificates or employer's statements which the adjudication officer considers relevant are all sent to the tribunal clerk. Copies of this bundle of papers are then sent to the members of the tribunal and to you. If there are any more documents you would like the tribunal to see, send them to the clerk if there is time before the hearing. Otherwise, you can produce them for the tribunal on the day.

For advice on how to prepare a case and where to find further advice or representation, see pages 254-60.

If an adjudication officer has decided that you are entitled to statutory sick pay or statutory maternity pay, your employer has the same right of appeal to a tribunal as you. [14]

A tribunal chairperson may dispose of the appeal without a hearing if s/he is satisfied that the tribunal has no power to hear the case (eg, if you are trying to appeal against a Secretary of State's decision on a contribution question and should have appealed to the high court – see p228). [15] This does not allow a chairperson to dispose of an appeal merely because s/he thinks it looks hopeless.

Your appeal lapses if an adjudication officer reviews the decision you are appealing against so that you get everything you would have got had your appeal been successful. [16] If the review only gives you part of what you are appealing for, your appeal will still be heard.

Cases referred by the adjudication officer

Sometimes – particularly where there is a dispute about the facts between a claimant and, say, an employer in a case of dismissal due to alleged misconduct – the adjudication officer does not make any decision at all but simply refers the case to a tribunal. [17] In such cases, the procedure is the same as it is on an appeal except that the bundle of papers does not include a letter of appeal from you.

The hearing

When the bundle of papers is sent to you, you will also be sent a form to return saying whether or not you intend to attend the hearing and also whether you want to abandon the appeal. It is vital to complete and return this form in good time. You will then be told when and where the hearing will take place. You will be given 10 days' notice. [18] If you want to put off the appeal to another day, ask for an adjournment and explain why. It is for the chairperson or the tribunal to decide whether your request should be granted. One adjournment is usually accepted (although this cannot be guaranteed) but you need good reasons for more than one.

If you do not attend and you have not asked for an adjournment or your request is not accepted, the tribunal will hear your case in your absence. You are much more likely to succeed if you attend the hearing.

If you are disabled, check that there is proper access to the building where the hearing will take place, and that facilities are suitable. If the premises are not suitable, ask for the hearing to be held elsewhere.

You should be directed to a waiting room or area. The tribunal clerk will meet you there and will ask whether you have any representative or witnesses. The clerk will also take details of your travel expenses and loss of earnings and those of any witness. You are usually paid those in cash there and then but sometimes they are paid later by Girocheque.

When the tribunal is ready to hear your case, you are taken into their room with the presenting officer. The presenting officer is usually an adjudication officer but not the one who made the decision in your case. S/he is there to represent the adjudication officer.

The three members of the tribunal sit on one side of a large table. The clerk sits at a separate table to one side. You are shown where to sit. Usually you and the presenting officer both sit directly opposite the tribunal.

The proceedings are open to the public, but it is very rare for anyone to attend unless they are either involved in the case or are civil servants or tribunal members undergoing training. Of course, the right of the public to watch does mean that you can watch the case before yours to see what happens. If intimate personal or financial matters are involved in your case, you can ask the tribunal to exclude any members of the public. [19]

There are no strict rules of procedure. Usually the chairperson starts by introducing the members of the tribunal and everyone else who is present. The presenting officer then summarises the adjudication officer's written submission and you are asked to explain your reasons for disagreeing with it. You can call any witnesses and can ask questions of any witnesses called by the presenting officer. Usually the presenting officer does not say very much and the tribunal members ask questions. The chairperson takes a note of the evidence and arguments.

When both you and the presenting officer have put your cases, everyone, except the tribunal and its clerk, leaves the room and the tribunal members discuss the evidence and law and reach a decision.

Your case may be adjourned unfinished to be heard on another day because, for instance, more evidence is wanted or there is insufficient time. If this happens, the new tribunal hearing your case must rehear your case from the beginning unless it has the same three members as before or you agree to it being heard by two members of the previous tribunal without the third. [20]

The decision

The tribunal decides by a majority. If there are only two members of the tribunal, the chairperson has a second vote (see p242). [21] The chairperson has the duty of writing up the decision including the findings of fact and the reasons for the decision. [22]

Usually, you are asked to wait while the tribunal makes its decision so that you can be told the result of your appeal straight away. If you are unsuccessful, you can immediately ask the chairperson for leave to appeal to a commissioner (see p250). [23] However, unless there has been a dispute about the law (as opposed to the facts) during the course of the hearing, it is usually better to wait until you receive the written decision.

The written decision is sent to you a couple of weeks later with a note about your right of appeal to a commissioner [24] (see p249).

In certain circumstances, a decision of a social security appeal tribunal may be reviewed by an adjudication officer (see p228).

Correcting and setting aside decisions

The tribunal may correct an accidental error in its written decision.[25]

A tribunal may also set aside a decision of its own or of another social security appeal tribunal if a relevant document went astray or any party to the proceedings or a representative was absent. It may also do so if 'the interests of justice so require' because of any other procedural irregularity.[26]

These provisions are most relevant to tribunals, but also apply to other adjudicating authorities.

If you make an application to have a decision set aside, it must be in writing to the local office of the Benefits Agency or the office of the tribunal or other body giving the decision within three months of your being given notice of the decision. A late application may be accepted if there are 'special reasons'.[27] This procedure is not often used but can be helpful where something has gone wrong or a case was decided in your unavoidable absence and you now wish to give evidence.[28] If you are able to use it, it can also be very much quicker than an appeal to the commissioners.

2 Medical appeal tribunals

The tribunal

Medical appeal tribunals are also independent of the DSS. They are organised by the same President and regional chairpersons as social security appeal tribunals (see p241) and, again, their clerks are based in the offices of the regional chairpersons.

Each tribunal consists of a lawyer chairperson and two consultants. Neither is necessarily an expert in the field of medicine relevant to your case. The tribunal cannot proceed if any member is absent.[1]

How to appeal

Medical appeal tribunals hear all appeals by claimants against decisions of adjudicating medical authorities, including medical boards (see p227).[2] They also hear some appeals from the Secretary of State concerning the recovery of benefits from compensation payments (see p214).[3]

To appeal, you must write to your local Benefits Agency office within three months of being notified of the decision of the adjudicating medical authority. A chairperson may allow a late appeal if there are 'special reasons'.[4] As with appeals to social security appeal tribunals, it is a good idea to give as much detail as possible when appealing. If you obtain an independent medical report, send that to the tribunal clerk before the hearing, if possible. Before the hearing, you are sent a bundle of documents containing the Secretary of State's submission and the records of all the medical examinations you have had in connection with the claim (or previous claims for the same benefit).

See page 252 for advice about preparing a case and finding further advice or representation.

Any benefit payable by virtue of the adjudicating medical authority's decision may be suspended until the appeal is heard.[5] This may include the payment of reduced earnings allowance.

A tribunal chairperson may dispose of the appeal without a hearing if s/he is satisfied that the tribunal has no power to hear the case (eg, if you are trying to appeal against an adjudication officer's decision and have appealed to the wrong tribunal).[6] This does not allow a chairperson to dispose of an appeal merely because s/he thinks it looks hopeless.

References on behalf of the Secretary of State

If the Secretary of State considers that a decision of an adjudicating medical authority is wrong, s/he can ask the adjudication officer to refer the case to a medical appeal tribunal.[7] Such a reference is rather like a claimant's appeal and is usually made because the Secretary of State considers that the adjudicating medical authority was too generous. However, it can be because the award is thought to be too low, or because it is believed that the adjudicating medical authority made an error of law. The procedure on a reference is the same as on an appeal and, again, any benefit payable by virtue of the adjudicating medical authority's decision is usually suspended until the hearing.

The hearing

The arrangements for the hearing are similar to those for social security appeal tribunals (see p243) but hearings take place only where there are facilities for the doctors to examine claimants. Where a claimant is very ill, the tribunal sometimes go to the claimant's home.

When you go into the tribunal's room, the chairperson introduces the members of the tribunal. If it is your appeal, the chairperson usually asks you to present your case first. The Secretary of State's representative is usually asked to go first if it is a reference. It is very rare for a Secretary of State's representative to say much. They usually rely on the written submission.

If you think there are mistakes in the tribunal papers, point them out. It is important to explain how the injury (if any) occurred and your subsequent treatment. Where the extent of your disablement is at issue, it is also necessary to convey to the tribunal how your disability affects you at work or in your daily life at home. You should be completely straightforward with the tribunal, neither diminishing nor exaggerating your symptoms. If you feel better on some days than others, explain in what ways and give them an idea as to whether they are seeing you on a 'good' day or a 'bad' one.

The tribunal members tend to ask a lot of questions. After the main hearing, the medical members often examine you in a separate room in the absence of everyone else, including the chairperson and your representative, although you can have someone with you as a chaperone or to help you if you need assistance undressing. When you are examined, make sure you tell the members of the tribunal if you are in pain or suffering discomfort. It is also a good idea to give the tribunal a full list of any medicines you are taking.

After the hearing and any examination, the tribunal members discuss the evidence and the law by themselves.

The decision

The tribunal decides by a majority.[8]

You may be asked to wait while the tribunal reaches its decision. You are then told the result but, should you wish to appeal, you have to wait for the written decision before applying for leave to appeal.[9] The written decision must contain a statement of the reasons for the decision and record all relevant findings of fact.[10] It is sent to you with a note of your right of appeal on a point of law to a social security commissioner (see below).[11]

The rules for correcting and setting aside decisions are the same as for social security appeal tribunals (see p245).

In certain circumstances, a decision of a medical appeal tribunal may be reviewed by a medical board (see p232).

3 Disability appeal tribunals

The tribunal

Disability appeal tribunals hear appeals about the disability questions within disability living allowance, attendance allowance, and also disability working allowance (which is covered in CPAG's *National Welfare Benefits Handbook*).

Like social security and medical appeal tribunals, disability appeal tribunals are independent of the Benefits Agency and are organised by the same President and regional chairpersons. There is a national disability appeal tribunal office in Nottingham.

There are three members of a disability appeal tribunal: a lawyer chairperson, a doctor, and someone drawn from a panel made up of people experienced in dealing with the needs of people with disabilities, either in a professional or voluntary capacity or because they themselves have a disability.[1] People who receive invalidity benefit or severe disablement allowance are still treated as incapable of work if they serve on the tribunal for no more than one day a week.[2]

No one may act as a tribunal member on a case where they would be affected by the outcome, or where they have already been involved in the case in some capacity.[3] This means your own doctor cannot be the medical member.

The tribunal cannot proceed if any one of the three members is absent.[4]

The jurisdiction of the disability appeal tribunal

A disability appeal tribunal hears appeals about the disability conditions referred to in Chapter 7, including matters concerning the period during which the claimant satisfies those conditions and the rate at which the relevant allowance is payable.

Very occasionally a tribunal also deals with a non-disability question relating to disability living allowance or attendance allowance.[5]

A tribunal chairperson may refer the claimant to a doctor for a medical examination and report where s/he thinks that the appeal cannot be properly decided unless there is such an examination and report.[6]

Some people appealing to the tribunal may be appealing about not being awarded one component of the disability living allowance when they are already in receipt of the other. Or they may be appealing against the rate of one component when they are quite satisfied with the rate they receive of the other. In these circumstances the tribunal need not consider the component which is not the subject of the appeal, although it can if it wishes to.

If a person has been awarded a component of disability living allowance for life, then the tribunal should not consider the rate of that component, or the length of time for which it has been awarded, unless either the appeal is expressly about one of those questions, or 'information is available to the tribunal which gives it reasonable grounds for believing that entitlement to the component, or entitlement to it at the rate awarded or for that period, ought not to continue'.[7]

These provisions may raise some problems for claimants and their advisers. For example, take a case where someone has a serious accident and is awarded the higher rate mobility component because of walking difficulties, but is only awarded the lower rate care component. That person may then challenge the decisions on the care component by an appeal. If the award of the mobility component is for life, then the tribunal may not remove that unless it becomes clear to the tribunal that there is not entitlement to it at that rate, or at all, or for such a period. In the course of its deliberations, the tribunal will, typically, be considering medical evidence and discussing the claimant's disabilities. It is precisely this process which might point to information that could threaten the existing mobility component award. This problem is more acute if the award of the mobility component is for a limited period only. In this case, a tribunal is entitled to reconsider the mobility component award, although it may choose not to do so.

The hearing

The procedure at a disability appeal tribunal hearing is similar to that at a social security appeal tribunal.

The adjudication officer who made the decision which is the subject of the appeal is represented by a presenting officer.

The tribunal holds an oral hearing of the case. The independent tribunal system tries to ensure that there are sufficient accessible tribunal venues to enable claimants to get into the buildings where their cases will be heard. Nevertheless, there are likely to be a number of people appealing who will be unable to get to a hearing. It may, therefore, be not unusual for hearings to be held in a claimant's home.

The tribunal listens to claimants and asks questions about their disability, examines medical reports and medical evidence, and other evidence relevant to the case. However, there is no physical examination of the claimant, nor any 'walking test' for the mobility component. [8]

The decision

If the tribunal is unable to come to a unanimous decision, it makes a majority decision which may be announced after the hearing and is, in any event, sent in writing to the claimant and any representative. The written decision should include findings on all questions of fact material to the decision, and give reasons for the decision. It is sent out with a note explaining the further right of appeal to a social security commissioner on a point of law. [9]

4 Social security commissioners

Social security commissioners are professional judges of the same standing as circuit judges who sit in the crown court and county courts. Indeed, some commissioners do also sit in those courts.

Commissioners hear appeals from social security appeal tribunals, medical appeal tribunals and disability appeal tribunals. In all cases, you can only appeal to a commissioner on a point of law. [1]

Point of law

A commissioner allows an appeal only if the tribunal has made an error of law. An error of law has been made if the tribunal: [2]

- has made a decision based on a mistake as to what the relevant law is; or
- has failed to give an adequate statement of the reasons for its decision and the findings of fact on which it is based; or
- has made a decision based on a finding of fact for which there is no evidence; or
- has made a decision which no tribunal, acting judicially and applying the relevant law, could reasonably have made on the basis of their findings of fact; or
- has broken its obligations to act fairly (sometimes called the rules of 'natural justice').

The most common error of law is a breach of the requirement to give adequate reasons for the decision.

'The obligation to give reasons for the decision . . . imports a requirement to do more than only to state the conclusion . . . the minimum requirement must at least be that the claimant looking at the decision should be able to discern on the face of it the reasons why . . . evidence has failed to satisfy the authority.'[3]

On the other hand, when looking at a decision it is often quite clear what is meant, even if it is not expressly stated, and in such a case there will be no error of law.[4] A tribunal needs to record findings of fact only on matters in dispute, but it should remember that points may arise by implication, and those should be dealt with too.[5]

A tribunal is under a duty to employ a fair procedure when hearing your appeal. In particular, the rules of 'natural justice' mean you must be allowed to present your case properly and that the tribunal must consider what you say without bias. But 'natural justice' does not mean that there is an error of law if the tribunal reaches a decision which seems unfair or anomalous. On the contrary, the tribunal has to apply the regulations however unfair the result may be to you.

How to appeal

You must first obtain permission (known as 'leave') to appeal.[6] This procedure is designed to weed out hopeless cases. It means that you have to show that there has *possibly* been an error of law and that you have the beginnings of a case.

If you wish to appeal from a **social security or disability appeal tribunal**, you should first apply to the chairperson of the tribunal.[7] You may do this either orally, at the end of the hearing when you are told the decision, or by writing to the clerk of the tribunal within three months of being sent the decision of the tribunal. If the application is made in writing, it will almost invariably be considered without any further hearing, usually, but not always, by the chairperson who heard your case originally.[8]

If the chairperson refuses leave to appeal, do not be discouraged. You may make a fresh application for leave to appeal direct to a commissioner within six weeks of being sent the decision refusing you leave.[9] The addresses of the offices of the commissioners are set out in Appendix Four (see p279). The commissioners will often give leave to appeal even though the chairperson has refused to do so.

If you wish to appeal from a decision of a **medical appeal tribunal**, the rules are the same except that there is no right to make an oral application at the end of the hearing.[10]

In all cases, if you miss any time limit, you may still apply for leave to appeal but any application must then be made direct to a commissioner who will give you leave only if there are 'special reasons' (see p242).[11]

If you are given leave to appeal by the chairperson, you have six weeks in which to send in notice of the appeal itself.[12] You are sent a form on which to do this. The time may, again, be extended for 'special reasons'. If your application for leave was considered by a commissioner, you will be told that your notice of application for leave has been treated as a notice of appeal. There is no need to send in another form or letter.[13]

If a commissioner refuses you leave to appeal there is no further appeal against that decision. The only course open to you is to apply to the high court (the court of session in Scotland) for a judicial review of the commissioner's decision. It is vital that before you take this step you obtain expert legal advice and apply for legal aid. If you do not do this, you may end up paying the DSS's legal costs if you lose. The time limits for applying to the court are very short so you should act without delay as soon as you receive the commissioner's decision.

Adjudication officers and the Secretary of State have the same rights of appeal as you. So too does your union or an 'association which exists to promote the interest and welfare of its members'.[14] Your employer may appeal against a decision concerning statutory sick pay or statutory maternity pay.[15] The procedure is always the same. If an adjudication officer or the Secretary of State appeals, your benefit may be suspended (see p235).

If the decision against which you have appealed is reviewed and revised so as to give you everything you are appealing for, your appeal lapses.[16] If you are dissatisfied with the review decision, you must launch a new appeal against that review decision. Commissioners are sympathetic to claimants who are confused by this technical requirement and are likely to allow you to make a late appeal if the delay was caused because you thought your original appeal was still effective.

References in forfeiture cases

Apart from appeals, commissioners decide all cases concerning the forfeiture rule (see pp81-2) and if any question of forfeiture arises, the adjudication officer or Secretary of State must refer the question to the commissioner.[17] References are dealt with in the same way as appeals.

The written procedure

At this level, all adjudication officers' cases are taken over by adjudication officers at the office of the Chief Adjudication Officer (see Appendix Four, page 279). A bundle of documents is prepared by the commissioners' office who then send copies to each party, and the adjudication officer and/or Secretary of State are directed to make a submission in response to the appeal within a time limit of 30 days. This is often late. If you have not heard anything from the commissioners' office after a month write to them and ask what is happening.

Once the submission of the adjudication officer or Secretary of State has been received, you will be given 30 days in which to reply (although the commissioner may extend the time limit). If you have nothing to add and do not want to reply at any stage, tell the commissioners' office. A commissioner has the power to strike out an appeal that appears to have been abandoned, although you can apply for it to be reinstated.[18]

When the commissioner has all the written submissions, s/he decides whether or not there should be an oral hearing of the appeal. If you ask for an oral hearing, the commissioner will hold one unless s/he feels that the case can properly be dealt with without one. [19] It is not usual for a commissioner to refuse a claimant's request for an oral hearing unless s/he is going to decide the case in the claimant's favour. Occasionally, the commissioner decides to hold an oral hearing even if you have not asked for one.

If there is no oral hearing, the commissioner reaches a decision on the basis of written submissions and other documents.

Because of the length of time you have to wait before your case is dealt with, you should consider making a fresh claim for benefit. This is particularly important in attendance allowance or disability living allowance cases because there is no power to backdate a claim and if your appeal is unsuccessful you will get no benefit at all, even if your condition has deteriorated while you have been waiting.

The hearing

If the commissioner decides to hold an oral hearing, the appeal is heard either at the commissioners' offices in London or Edinburgh or at the law courts in Cardiff, Leeds or Liverpool. You are told the date in good time and your fares are paid in advance if you want to attend. At least half a day is set aside for each case.

Usually, one commissioner hears your case but, if there is a 'question of law of special difficulty', the hearing may be before a tribunal of three commissioners. [20] The procedure is still the same.

The hearing is a little more formal than those before social security, disability or medical appeal tribunals but the commissioner will still be concerned to try and make sure that you say everything you want. Commissioners usually intervene a lot and ask questions so you need to be prepared to argue your case without your script. A full set of commissioners' decisions and the 'Blue Volumes' (see p256) are available for your use. The adjudication officer or Secretary of State is usually represented by a lawyer, so you should consider trying to obtain representation as well (see p259). The commissioner may exclude members of the public if intimate personal or financial circumstances or matters of public security are involved. [21] This is not usually necessary because it is rare for anyone not involved in the case to attend.

The decision

The decision is always given in writing [22] – often at some length.

After a successful appeal against a decision of a social security or disability appeal tribunal, the case is usually sent back to a differently constituted tribunal with directions as to how the tribunal should go about reconsidering the issues. [23] However, if the commissioner feels that the record of the decision of the original tribunal contains all the material facts, or s/he feels that it is 'expedient' to make findings on any extra factual issues necessary to the decisions, the commissioner will make the final decision. [24] It is unusual for a commissioner not to send a case back to a tribunal if there is a dispute about facts not determined by the original tribunal, unless all the evidence points in one direction. [25]

After a successful appeal against a decision of a medical appeal tribunal, the case is always sent back to a tribunal (which is usually differently constituted).

A commissioner may correct or set aside a decision in the same way as a tribunal (see p245). [26]

In certain circumstances, an adjudication officer may review a commissioner's decision (see p229).

Decisions of commissioners establish precedents and so may affect many cases other than your own (see p256).

Appeals from social security commissioners

You may appeal against a decision of a commissioner to the Court of Appeal (in Scotland, the court of session). Again, the appeal is only on a point of law and you must first obtain leave to appeal. [27]

Although the staff of the Court of Appeal do their best to be helpful, the procedure in the court is strict, formal and far less flexible than the procedure before a tribunal or a commissioner. The Chief Adjudication Officer or Secretary of State will certainly be represented by a barrister at the hearing. You should therefore obtain legal advice and apply for legal aid before appealing. If you are unable to get help and have to represent yourself, the procedure is as follows.

The application for leave to appeal must first be made to a commissioner, in writing within three months of the date when you were sent the commissioner's decision. The commissioner may extend the time limit for 'special reasons' (see p242). [28] If you do not apply to the commissioner within the time limit and the commissioner refuses to extend it, the Court of Appeal (or court of session) cannot hear your appeal and you can only proceed by applying to the high court (in Scotland, the court of Session) for judicial review of the refusal to extend the time allowed for the appeal (see p251). [29]

Applications to a commissioner for leave to appeal are almost invariably considered without an oral hearing. If the commissioner refuses to give you leave to appeal (for reasons other than being outside the time limit), you can apply to the court for leave. [30] If your appeal is to the Court of Appeal, your notice of application should be lodged with the Civil Appeals Office within six weeks of notification of the commissioner's refusal being sent to you. [31] The court may extend the time but you must explain the reasons for your delay and file a sworn statement (called an 'affidavit') in support of an application for an extension of time. [32] Generally, the Court of Appeal will first consider your application without an oral hearing. If leave is refused, you may renew your application in open court within seven days. Similarly, if leave is granted, the Chief Adjudication Officer or the Secretary of State has seven days in which to ask for an oral hearing. [33]

If leave to appeal was granted by a commissioner, you must serve a notice of appeal on the relevant parties within six weeks of being sent notification of the commissioner's grant of leave. [34] If leave was granted by the Court of Appeal, the notice of appeal must be served within the same six-week period or within seven days of the grant of leave whichever is later (unless your notice of application for leave was lodged outside the six week time limit, in which case a time limit for lodging the notice of appeal should be contained in the court's order). [35] The solicitor to the DSS will accept service at New Court, 48 Carey Street, London WC2A 2LS on behalf of the Chief Adjudication Officer or the Secretary of State.

You cannot appeal to the Court of Appeal against a decision of a commissioner refusing you leave to appeal *to* a commissioner (against a decision of a tribunal), but you can apply to the high court for judicial review of such a decision. [36]

If the Court of Appeal refuses you leave to appeal after an oral hearing, you cannot appeal further, nor apply for a judicial review.

The procedures in Scotland are similar.

The Chief Adjudication Officer or the Secretary of State has the same rights of appeal as you.

5   How to prepare an appeal

Appeals are taken on all sorts of issues so the advice given here can only be fairly general.

Cases may concern disputes of fact or disputes about the law or both. You usually need to think about both the facts and the law because they are connected. The law tells you which facts are relevant and the facts tell you which bits of the law you need to consider.

Establishing the facts

You are likely to know more than anyone else about the facts of your case. Your key task is to pass your knowledge (and the knowledge of others who know something about the facts) on to the tribunal.

Tribunals decide cases on the evidence presented to them. The evidence may consist of oral evidence (what they are actually told during the hearing) and written evidence (contained in statements and other documents shown to them). What you yourself say during the hearing is perfectly good evidence. [1] It does not have to be backed up by any other evidence. On the other hand, a tribunal is not bound to believe you or to accept your opinion on, say, a medical matter. It is therefore a good idea to obtain additional evidence, if possible, of those facts likely to be in dispute.

When you appeal, you are likely to have some idea of the main areas in dispute. However, it is vital that you study the adjudication officer's or Secretary of State's submission when it arrives. That tells you what bits of your case are not disputed. You then know what facts are not agreed and so what you have to prove. Any evidence you collect must deal with the matters really in dispute.

For example, in a case where you have to prove that you are incapable of work, the adjudication officer may well accept that you are not fully fit and that you have, say, difficulty in bending down. S/he may simply be saying that this does not prevent you from working at some *suitable* employment. In this instance, a medical report which says that you are disabled and cannot bend down would not be a great deal of help to you because it does not answer the adjudication officer's point. You need evidence which shows either that you are more disabled than the adjudication officer believes, or that the type of employment suggested by the adjudication officer would involve bending down or is unsuitable for some other reason. Such evidence might come from a number of sources. You can try and obtain a more detailed medical report. You can tell the tribunal yourself about the effect of your disabilities. You can also ask someone working in the relevant employment to say what the work really involves.

Evidence given orally by people who actually attend the hearing is always the best. That is why it is so important for you to be there. It enables a tribunal to assess the reliability of the person giving the evidence and it also enables the witness to answer any questions. But it is not always possible to persuade people to attend hearings although expenses are paid not only for travel costs and a small subsistence allowance but also for loss of earnings up to £38.50 (for over four hours). Then the next best evidence is a detailed signed written statement. This may be more persuasive if it is a sworn statement (called an 'affidavit'). A solicitor may be able to help you with this at no charge under the 'green form' scheme (see p260).

Medical evidence is almost invariably in the form of written reports. As already mentioned, it is essential that they deal with the points in dispute if that is possible. Sometimes, a doctor does not really know much about the effect of a disability on a person's everyday life, in which case your evidence or that of a friend or relation may well be of more use. However, where a medical report is required, there are two ways of obtaining one apart from simply writing to the doctor yourself. Either a solicitor can obtain one for you (see p260); or the tribunal (or an adjudication officer) can refer you for an examination and obtain a report if the medical issue in your case is one of 'special difficulty'. [2] If the lack of a report is causing you difficulties at a tribunal hearing, you could remind the tribunal of this power to obtain one itself.

If you do obtain statements or reports, you should send copies to the tribunal clerk in advance if there is time. The clerk will send a further copy to the adjudication officer or the Secretary of State who might then decide to support your appeal.

If you are appealing to a commissioner, remember that commissioners have only very limited powers to deal with questions of fact. However, if you have new evidence, it might enable you to apply for a review (see p228) of the tribunal's decision and you can do that while the appeal is pending. Reviews are usually quicker than appeals but you may receive a lower amount of arrears (see pp231 and 233).

Checking the law

It is not usual for there to be a major dispute about the law. Do not worry if you do not have the time or resources to follow all the advice given here. The vast majority of cases involve parts of the law which tribunals are likely to know well.

However, the Benefits Agency does not always get the law right and you might well want to emphasise a point that the adjudication officer or Secretary of State has overlooked. Also, if you know what the law says, you will know what facts you have to prove.

The primary sources of social security law are **statute law** and **case law** (decided by commissioners and the courts). As explained below, it is fairly easy to find both sorts of law once you know what you are looking for.

The notes in this guide are intended to point you in the right direction. You should also look carefully at the submission of the adjudication officer or Secretary of State as that refers to the statute law and case law which s/he thinks is relevant. There are also a number of books which can help by explaining the law and referring you to relevant legislation and cases (see Appendix Five – p281).

Statute law

There are a number of important Acts of Parliament. The one which sets out the basic rules is the Social Security Contributions and Benefits Act 1992. The Act sets out the main framework and empowers the Secretary of State to make regulations covering the details. These regulations are laid before Parliament as 'statutory instruments'. Appendix Six (see p283) contains a list of Acts and regulations.

They can be purchased individually from HMSO bookshops. However, both Acts and regulations are amended from time to time which can lead to difficulties when you are trying to discover the current state of the law or chase up a reference. It is therefore much easier to refer to the looseleaf book, *The Law Relating to Social Security* (unless your case is a very old one and the law has changed since the relevant time). This is in ten volumes known as the 'Blue Volumes' or the 'Blue Book'. It is published by HMSO and is kept up to date by regular supplements. Most large reference libraries have a copy. In addition, your local Benefits Agency office has a copy which you are allowed to look at.

Less unwieldy is a single volume, published annually, which contains all the most important Acts and regulations with comprehensive notes explaining them. This is *Non-Means-Tested Benefits – The Legislation* edited by Bonner *et al* (see p281).

Case law

When a commissioner or a court decides a question of principle, the decision sets a precedent. An adjudication officer, adjudicating medical authority, social security appeal tribunal, medical or disability appeal tribunal deciding a similar case must follow that precedent.[3] The vast majority of relevant cases on social security law are commissioners' decisions.

All commissioners' decisions have file numbers. One example is CU/255/1984. The last numbers indicate the year in which the appeal was lodged. The second letter indicates the type of benefit involved in the decision. Each year, the most important cases are chosen by the Chief Commissioner to be reported. These are given a new number. CU/255/1984 became R(U) 3/86. Again, the second letter denotes the type of benefit. The last numbers indicate the year in which the case was reported. All reported cases since 1951 begin with an 'R'. There used to be an intermediate category of 'numbered' cases with references such as CG 2/70; reported cases before 1951 have such references. An extra 'S' or 'W' after a 'C' denotes a Scottish or Welsh case, as in CWG 3/78. In all cases, the type of benefit is indicated as follows:

A   attendance allowance
F   family allowance (now child benefit)
FC   family credit
FIS family income supplement
G   general (all benefits not covered in other categories)
I   industrial injuries benefits
IS   income support
M   mobility allowance
P   retirement pensions
S   sickness and invalidity benefit and severe disablement allowance
SB   supplementary benefit
SMP statutory maternity pay
SSP statutory sick pay
U   unemployment benefit

Individual reported decisions may be purchased from HMSO bookshops, as may bound volumes, although all the early ones are out of print. However, each local Benefits Agency office has a set which you are allowed to look at. If a commissioner's decision is challenged in the courts, the decision of the court is usually reported as an appendix in the series of reported commissioners' decisions.

Unreported decisions may be obtained from the offices of the commissioners (see p280) for £1.00 each. If one is to be used at a tribunal hearing by an adjudication officer or the Secretary of State, a copy should be supplied to you. Similarly, if you wish to use one, you should supply copies to everyone, preferably by sending one to the tribunal clerk in advance of the hearing. Unreported decisions must be followed by appeal tribunals in the same way as reported ones.[4]

It is worth checking the decisions relied on by adjudication officers and the Secretary of State. Sometimes, they rely on part of a decision only and fail to mention another part which is more favourable to you. To find other cases relevant to your own, you can use the notes in this guide or any of the books listed in Appendix Five (see p281). A particularly useful publication is *Neligan's Social Security Case Law: a Digest of*

Commissioners' Decisions published by HMSO in two volumes. This sets out summaries of decisions under subject headings. Again, your local Benefits Agency office has a copy which you may look at and your local reference library probably has one too.

Case law appears less precise than statute law and frequently cases seem to contradict each other. Very often there are small differences in the facts of the cases which justify the different results. You need to find cases where the facts are similar to yours. If cases appear to be against you, look at the facts of those cases and see whether any differences justify a different decision in your case. This is known as 'distinguishing' cases. One distinction may simply be that what seemed reasonable in the 1950s does not seem fair in the 1990s. [5] It should also be remembered that most old cases were decided when there was a right of appeal to commissioners on questions of fact as well as law so tribunals may not necessarily be erring in law if they take a different view from the commissioner's.

Where there is an irreconcilable conflict between cases, a tribunal has to choose which decision to follow. It *normally* follows a reported decision in preference to an unreported one, and *must* follow a decision of a tribunal of commissioners (see page 252) in preference to a decision of a single commissioner. [6] Decisions of the House of Lords, the Court of Appeal or of the high court on an application for judicial review (or, in Scotland, the court of session) take precedence over all commissioners' decisions. [7]

Commissioners have more freedom and do not have to follow the decision of another single commissioner if satisfied that the earlier decision was wrong. [8] However, a single commissioner must follow a decision of a tribunal of commissioners (see p252) although, if s/he thinks it may be wrong, s/he can ask the Chief Commissioner to appoint another tribunal to reconsider the point. A tribunal of commissioners does not have to follow the decision of another tribunal but will usually do so. [9]

Debates in Parliament

The House of Lords has recently decided [10] that, where the law is ambiguous, the courts – which will include SSATs and the commissioners' – can look at statements made to Parliament by ministers when the law was first made. It may therefore be worth checking the House of Commons and House of Lords official reports (known as *Hansard*) to see what was said in Parliament when the rules which apply to your case were first introduced.

Hansard can be difficult to find but the House of Commons Public Information Office publish a leaflet called 'APRILL' (Access to Parliamentary Resources and Information in London Libraries). This will tell you where you can find *Hansard* if you live in or near London and an updated leaflet covering the whole country should be available shortly after this guide is published. If you need a copy of APRILL or want more detailed help, ring the Public Information Office on 071-219 4272.

Hansard can be a confusing publication. To begin with, you need the volumes which deal with Parliamentary Debates and Written Answers rather than those covering the proceedings of Standing Committees. Then each volume has two sets of numbering – one for Parliamentary debates and one for Written Answers. There are two columns on each page, each of which has a separate number, so, for example, a single volume may have two columns numbered 609. The best way of finding what you want is to use the comprehensive index which is updated fortnightly. Again references in the index are to column numbers and those relating to Written Answers are pre-fixed by the letter 'W'. The ones you may need for your appeal are the ones which relate to Parliamentary Debates and have no prefixes.

Presenting your case

Each case is different and hearings are informal so there is no set pattern for presenting cases.

As already suggested, it is a good idea to send in a detailed submission and any medical reports before the hearing. Some claimants like to use a written submission at the hearing and to read directly from it. However, tribunals usually ask questions so it is necessary to be able to talk about your case without the script.

The tribunal will decide whether you or the presenting officer speaks first. It is helpful to make it clear at the beginning of the hearing which bits of the adjudication officer's or Secretary of State's submissions are in dispute. In most cases, much of those submissions are agreed and it is only a small, but vital, part which is not. It is, then, usually best to tell the tribunal about the facts first and to call any witnesses before turning to legal arguments.

It is the tribunal's job to help you to say everything you want by putting you at your ease and asking the right questions. If you forget to say something when it is your turn to speak, do not hesitate to add it at the end of the hearing.

Advice and representation

There are a number of agencies which can advise you about social security matters and can help you prepare cases for tribunal hearings. Some can also represent you at hearings if you feel that someone else can put your case better than you can.

Most areas have a citizens' advice bureau. The nearest one to you should be in the telephone directory, but you can also obtain its address from the National Association of Citizens' Advice Bureaux, Myddleton House, 115/123 Pentonville Road, London N1 9LZ (tel: 071-833 2181). If there are more specialist advice agencies in your area, the citizens' advice bureau or your local library or town hall will be able to tell you and every Benefits Agency office also has a list of advisers.

Many local authorities have good welfare rights advisers. Ask your town hall.

If you have been a member of a union, the union may be able to help you, particularly in industrial injuries cases.

Different groups of claimants have different sorts of problems. If you are unemployed, you could contact your local centre for the unemployed. A list of such centres can be obtained from the Trades Union Congress, Great Russell Street, London WC1B 3LS (tel: 071-636 4030). If you are disabled, you may be able to get help from the Disability Alliance, First Floor East, Universal House, 88-94 Wentworth Street, London E1 7SA (tel: 071-247 8776), or Network for the Handicapped, 16 Princeton Street, London WC1R 4BB (tel: 071-831 8031) or the Disablement Income Group, Millmead Business Centre, Millmead Road, London N17 9QU (tel: 081-801 8013). Pensioners can obtain advice from Age Concern, Astral House, 1268 London Road, London SW16 4ER (tel: 081-679 8000).

Many of these agencies will provide free representation or can put you in touch with a tribunal representation unit. However, it is easier to find free representation in large cities than in the country.

Advice from lawyers is not always easy to find either. Network for the Handicapped employs one and so do some unions. Many citizens' advice bureaux have evening sessions when you can obtain free legal advice, but their non-lawyer advisers are often better at dealing with social security problems. On the other hand, a citizens' advice bureau will be able to tell you which solicitors in its area will handle social security cases as part of their ordinary work.

Legal aid does not cover representation before tribunals or even the commissioners. However, the 'green form' scheme (in Scotland, the 'pink form' scheme) of free legal advice and assistance covers not only advice but also preparatory work for a hearing such as obtaining medical reports and writing submissions. Using it, a solicitor can obtain counsel's advice on a difficult point. If you have a solicitor acting for you in an industrial injury claim against your employer, s/he may have medical and other reports and evidence which you can use for your benefit claim.

If you are not eligible for 'green' (or 'pink') form advice and assistance, or you want to be represented by a lawyer at hearing, you are likely to have to pay. If your claim is worth hundreds of pounds, it may be a worthwhile investment. But, remember that many non-lawyer advisers know more about social security law than most lawyers.

Legal aid is available for cases in the Court of Appeal, the high court and the court of session and you should certainly obtain legal advice and representation. The legal aid authorities have, in the past, taken the view that an application to a commissioner for leave to appeal to the Court of Appeal cannot be covered by legal aid. However, it is arguable that such an application is a step 'preliminary to' proceedings in the Court of Appeal and is thus work for which legal aid is available. [11]

You should always consult a solicitor if you are taking a social security case to a court rather than to a tribunal or a commissioner.

Miscellaneous benefits for the disabled

This appendix covers various schemes providing money for those disabled by particular causes and it also very briefly deals with the Department of Employment's services for the disabled.

It does *not* cover forms of assistance provided by local authority social services departments, the National Health Service or district health authorities.

If you want to know more about rights, benefits and services for the disabled, obtain the *Disability Rights Handbook* (18th edn, 1993-94, £7.95 post-free) published by the Disability Alliance of which CPAG is a member organisation. You can obtain this from CPAG Ltd, 1-5 Bath St, London EC1V 9PY. Also very helpful is *Disability or Health Problems: A Guide to Employment Services and Schemes*, published by Youthaid and available from them at 409 Brixton Road, London SW9 7DG price £5 post-free.

I War pensions

There are a number of different schemes providing benefits for those disabled, or for the dependants of those killed, in the First World War and in all conflicts since 3 September 1939. The most important schemes are those covering members of the Armed Forces, but there are others covering auxiliary personnel, civil defence volunteers, merchant mariners and also ordinary civilians. Many of the benefits are similar to those provided under the industrial injuries scheme but there are important differences.

(i) Scope of the schemes

This varies from scheme to scheme but, generally, servicemen and servicewomen are covered if their disablement arises out of their service even if not due to the conflict itself, whereas civilians are covered only if their disablement is due to a 'war injury'.

(ii) Disablement benefit

The basic disablement benefit is assessed in the same way as for industrial injuries benefits (see p139). For those at least 20 per cent disabled it is paid at the same rate as industrial disablement benefit (£91.60 a week for someone assessed as 100 per cent disabled), although there are small additional components for those above the rank of ordinary seaman, private or aircraftsman (or their equivalents).

If the assessment is below 20 per cent, a lump-sum gratuity is paid even if the assessment is less than 14 per cent.

A claimant's assessment can be increased if her/his disability worsens at any time.

(iii) Increases of disablement benefit

Unemployability allowance is like invalidity benefit and includes equivalent increases for dependants and invalidity allowances.

Allowance for lowered standard of occupation is similar to reduced earnings allowance paid under the industrial injuries scheme (see p143). The most important difference is that it is limited so that the total of the basic disablement pension and the reduced earnings allowance cannot exceed £97.20 a week. Otherwise the maximum is £36.64 a week.

Constant attendance allowance is again like that paid under the industrial injuries scheme (see p141) except that it is payable if the assessment of disablement is 80 per cent or 90 per cent as well as 100 per cent.

Exceptionally severe disablement allowance is payable only to those receiving constant attendance allowance – again, as in the industrial injuries scheme (see p141).

Severe disablement occupational allowance is paid at the rate of £18.35 a week to those entitled to constant attendance allowance at more than the lower rate but who are nonetheless ordinarily employed in gainful employment.

Comforts allowance is payable to those receiving constant attendance allowance and who *either* receive unemployability allowance *or* who are assessed as 100 per cent disabled. The rate is either £15.70 or £7.85 a week.

Mobility supplement is payable to those who have amputations of both legs or who satisfy conditions similar (but not identical) to those for the mobility component of disability living allowance (see p101). The rate is £34.90 a week.

Age allowance is payable to those aged over 65 who are assessed as at least 40 per cent disabled. The rates are £6.50 a week (40 or 50 per cent), £10 a week (60 or 70 per cent), £14.30 a week (70 or 80 per cent) and £20 a week (90 or 100 per cent).

Other allowances are made for clothing for those with artificial limbs and for the education and maintenance of dependants.

(iv) Awards in respect of death

Widows may be paid a pension at a rate depending on her age and her husband's rank. A private's widow aged over 80 may receive £96.85 a week. A widow under 65 with a child receives £72.90 *plus* £15 for each child (except the first for whom only £13.85 is payable) *plus* up to £27.75 rent allowance a week. Those widows whose husbands were in the Armed Forces on or after 1 January 1973 receive a further earnings-related pension under the service pensions scheme.

Widowers may be paid up to £72.90 a week. A widower must have been incapable of self-support when his wife died if he is to be entitled to the benefit.

An unmarried dependant who was living as the spouse of the deceased and caring for a child of the deceased may receive up to £70.85 a week. Again a rent allowance of up to £27.75 is also payable.

Orphan's pension is payable at the rate of £15.45 a week for the first child and £16.60 a week for each other child under 16. An adult incapable of self-support may be paid up to £56.10 a week.

(v) Decisions

Claims should be made to The Controller, Central Office (War Pensions), DSS, Norcross, Blackpool FY5 3TA.

Decisions are taken by the Secretary of State who has a great deal of discretion. If there is a dispute as to whether disablement or death was due to service or a war injury (as the case may be) since 3 September 1939, or as to the extent of disablement, the claimant may appeal to the Pension Appeal Tribunal. There is a further right of appeal to the High Court (in Scotland, the Court of Session).

(vi) Further information

The DSS publish a number of leaflets about war pensions. There are also local war pensions committees in each area which may be able to assist with claims. The Royal British Legion also provides experienced advice and representation.

2   Criminal Injuries Compensation

Criminal injuries compensation is payable if you suffer personal injury directly resulting from a crime of violence or from trying to stop someone committing a crime or from trying to apprehend a suspected criminal. A dependant of someone killed in those circumstances may also make a claim.

(i) The compensation

This is paid as a tax-free lump sum. It is the amount that would be received if the claimant were to sue in the courts, so it varies from case to case. The spouse of someone killed (or the parents if the deceased was under 18 and unmarried) may claim a flat-rate bereavement award of £7,500 instead (£3,500 if the accident was before 1 April 1991).

(ii) Disqualification

Payments are not made if the award would be less than £1,000. Nor are they made for *road traffic accidents* except deliberate runnings down.

Payments may also be withheld or reduced if the claimant did not make sure the police were notified or did not co-operate with them.

More controversially, payments may be withheld or reduced if the claimant's conduct connected with the injury, or past convictions or conduct, make it appropriate that an award should not be made.

(iii) Decisions

Claims should be sent to the Criminal Injuries Compensation Board, Blythswood House, 200 West Regent Street, Glasgow G2 4SW (tel: 041-221 0945).

Decisions are made by the Board. It consists of senior lawyers. The first assessment is made by a single member. If a claimant is dissatisfied (or if the single member decides to refer the case) a hearing is held before three members of the Board. There is a right of appeal on a point of law to the High Court (in Scotland, the Court of Session).

(iv) Further information

The Board publish quite a full guide with a separate leaflet giving examples of the amounts that might be claimed for different sorts of injuries. Legal advice may be a good idea in these cases. A claimant can obtain advice and assistance (but not representation) under the green form scheme (in Scotland, the pink form scheme).

3 Vaccine damage payments

These are payable if a person is now over two years old and is assessed as at least 80 per cent disabled (see pp136-38) as a result of vaccination for diphtheria, tetanus, whooping cough, polio, measles, rubella (German measles), tuberculosis or smallpox. Except in the case of polio or rubella, the vaccination must have been carried out when the person was under 18.

(i) The payment

A lump sum of £30,000 tax free.

(ii) Decisions

Claims should be made to the Vaccine Damage Payments Unit, DSS,

North Fylde Central Offices, Norcross, Blackpool FY5 3TA within six years of the vaccination.

The Secretary of State makes the initial decision. An appeal may be made to the Vaccine Damage Tribunal which is a medical appeal tribunal (see p245) under a different name. A decision of the tribunal can be challenged on a point of law in the High Court (in Scotland, the Court of Session).

4   The Pneumoconiosis etc. (Workers' Compensation) Act 1979

This provides for lump-sum payments to those disabled, and the dependants of those who have died while disabled, as the result of pneumoconiosis, byssinosis or diffuse mesothelioma incurred through employment. The Act allows payments if no action for damages has been brought before the courts or settled and none can be now because the employer has ceased to carry on business. Actions dismissed on technical grounds do not count as having been brought. The claimant must be entitled to disablement benefit (or an equivalent payment under schemes for those employed before 5 July 1948). If the disabled person has died, either s/he must have been receiving disablement benefit (or an equivalent) when s/he died or death benefit or widow's benefit must be payable as a result of the disease.

(i) The compensation

Lump sums of up to £47,890 for disabled claimants and £21,740 in the event of death are awarded. The precise amount in any case depends upon the age and the extent of disablement of the claimant or the deceased.

(ii) Decisions

Claims should be made to the Department of Employment, HS1, Level 2, Caxton House, Tothill Street, London SW1H 9NF (tel: 071-273 5248) within 12 months of the claimant first becoming entitled to disablement benefit (or an equivalent) or within 12 months of the disabled person's death. The time limit may be extended if it is 'appropriate, having regard to the circumstances of the case'. Decisions are made by the Secretary of State in the same way as for contributions (see p227) and there is the same right of appeal to the High Court (in Scotland, the Court of Session). A guide for claimants is obtainable from the Department of Employment at the above address.

5   Department of Employment services

(i) Assessment, training and sheltered employment

The disablement resettlement officer at your local JobCentre may be able to
help you obtain further education or training or simply work experience if
you are finding it difficult to obtain employment. In particular, s/he can
give you advice about Employment Rehabilitation Centres which assess
your employment potential through talking to you and giving you written
and practical exercises. Two of the centres run residential courses and
lodgings can be arranged near the others if they are too far away for you to
travel to them daily. These courses provide both assessment and
rehabilitation following an injury, disease or illness (either physical or
mental). Training allowances and travel expenses are usually paid and
your benefits are unaffected during the assessment.

The disablement resettlement officer can also advise you about the
availability of sheltered employment.

(ii) Special aids and adaptations

The Employment Service provides all sorts of special aids to enable disabled people to take up employment. These include specially adapted
typewriters, computer equipment, tape recorders, amplifiers and
specially designed tools, chairs and wheelchairs. For a person who is
registered as blind or partially sighted, there may be a grant through the
Personal Reader Service to pay for someone to give part-time reading help
at work. Also available are grants of up to £6,000 for employers who
wish to adapt their premises and equipment for disabled employees. You
can advise your employer to ask the local JobCentre for further
information.

(iii) Fares for interviews and travelling to work

If you are eligible for registration under the Disabled Persons
Employment Act 1944 you can apply for help towards the travelling costs
to any job interview arranged by the JobCentre.

Once you have obtained a job, if you are on the JobCentre's Disabled
Persons Register and you incur extra costs getting to work because of your
disability, you can obtain grants either amounting to three-quarters of the
cost of taxi fares or by way of a mileage allowance for a friend or relative
who drives you to work. If you receive mobility allowance, the grant is
reduced by £9.70 a week (or by £1.94 a day if fewer than five days a week
are worked).

(iv) Help for employers

The Employment Service publishes pamphlets for employers with guidance about employing disabled people and, in particular, those suffering
from blindness or visual impairment, deafness or hearing impairment,

epilepsy, haemophilia, mental handicap, mental illness or multiple sclerosis.

An employer can be paid £45 a week for up to six weeks (or up to three months in exceptional circumstances) towards your wages during a trial period to see whether you can manage the job. There are also grants under the Pathway Employment Service run by MENCAP for those who offer trial periods or training for mentally handicapped people. The JobCentre can provide details.

Prescribed degrees of disablement

Schedule 2 to the Social Security (General Benefit) Regulations 1982

Description of injury	Degree of Disablement %	Description of injury	Degree of Disablement %
1 Loss of both hands or amputation at higher sites	100	**Amputation cases – lower limbs**	
2 Loss of a hand and a foot	100	18 Amputation of both feet resulting in end-bearing stumps	90
3 Double amputation through leg or thigh, or amputation through leg or thigh on one side and loss of other foot	100	19 Amputation through both feet proximal to the metatarso-phalangeal joint	80
4 Loss of sight to such an extent as to render the claimant unable to perform any work for which eyesight is essential	100	20 Loss of all toes of both feet through the metatarso-phalangeal joint	40
5 Very severe facial disfiguration	100	21 Loss of all toes of both feet proximal to the proximal inter-phalangeal joint	30
6 Absolute deafness	100	22 Loss of all toes of both feet distal to the proximal inter-phalangeal joint	20
7 Forequarter or hindquarter amputation	100	23 Amputation at hip	90
Amputation cases – upper limbs (either arm)		24 Amputation below hip with stump not exceeding 13 cms in length measured from tip of great trochanter	80
8 Amputation through shoulder joint	90	25 Amputation below hip and above knee with stump exceeding 13 cms in length measured from tip of great trochanter, or at knee not resulting in end-bearing stump	70
9 Amputation below shoulder with stump less than 20.5 cms from tip of acromion	80		
10 Amputation from 20.5 cms from tip of acromion to less than 11.5 cms below tip of olecranon	70	26 Amputation at knee resulting in end-bearing stump or below knee with stump not exceeding 9 cms	60
11 Loss of a hand or of the thumb and 4 fingers of 1 hand or amputation from 11.5 cms below tip of olecranon	60	27 Amputation below knee with stump exceeding 9 cms but not exceeding 13 cms	50
12 Loss of thumb	30	28 Amputation below knee with stump exceeding 13 cms	40
13 Loss of thumb and its metacarpal bone	40		
14 Loss of 4 fingers of 1 hand	50		
15 Loss of 3 fingers of 1 hand	30		
16 Loss of 2 fingers of 1 hand	20		
17 Loss of terminal phalanx of thumb	20		

Description of injury	Degree of Disablement %	Description of injury	Degree of Disablement %
Amputation cases – lower limbs *(cont.)*		43 2 phalanges	6
29 Amputation of 1 foot resulting in end-bearing stump	30	44 1 phalanx	5
		45 Guillotine amputation of tip without loss of bone	2
30 Amputation through 1 foot proximal to the metatarso-phalangeal joint	30	**Loss of toes of right or left foot:** Great toe:	
31 Loss of all toes of 1 foot through the metatarso-phalangeal joint	20	46 Through metatarso-phalangeal joint	14
		47 Part, with some loss of bone	3
Other injuries		Any other toe:	
32 Loss of 1 eye, without complications, the other being normal	40	48 Through metatarso-phalangeal joint	3
33 Loss of vision of 1 eye, without complications or disfigurement of the eyeball, the other being normal	30	49 Part, with some loss of bone	1
		2 toes of 1 foot, excluding great toe:	
		50 Through metatarso-phalangeal joint	5
Loss of fingers of right or left hand Index finger:		51 Part, with some loss of bone	2
34 Whole	14	3 toes of 1 foot, excluding great toe:	
35 2 phalanges	11	52 Through metatarso-phalangeal joint	6
36 1 phalanx	9	53 Part, with some loss of bone	3
37 Guillotine amputation of tip without loss of bone	5	4 toes of 1 foot, excluding great toe:	
Middle finger:		54 Through metatarso-phalangeal joint	9
38 Whole	12	55 Part, with some loss of bone	3
39 2 phalanges	9		
40 1 phalanx	7		
41 Guillotine amputation of tip without loss of bone	4		
Ring or little finger:			
42 Whole	7		

The degree of disablement due to occupational deafness is assessed using tables and a formula to be found in regulation 34 of and Schedule 3 to the Social Security (Industrial Injuries) (Prescribed Diseases) Regulations 1985 as amended.

Prescribed industrial diseases

Part I of Schedule I to the Social Security (Industrial Injuries) (Prescribed Diseases) Regulations 1985 as amended

Prescribed disease or injury	*Occupation*
A Conditions due to physical agents	**Any occupation involving:**
A1 Inflammation, ulceration or malignant disease of the skin or subcutaneous tissues or of the bones, or blood dyscrasia, or cataract, due to electro-magnetic radiations (other than radiant heat), or to ionising particles	Exposure to electro-magnetic radiations (other than radiant heat) or to ionising particles.
A2 Heat cataract	Frequent or prolonged exposure to rays from molten or red-hot material.
A3 Dysbarism, including decompression sickness, barotrauma and osteonecrosis	Subjection to compressed or rarified air or other respirable gases or gaseous mixtures.
A4 Cramp of the hand or forearm due to repetitive movements	Prolonged periods of handwriting, typing or other repetitive movements of the fingers, hand or arm.
A5 Subcutaneous cellulitis of the hand (Beat hand)	Manual labour causing severe or prolonged friction or pressure on the hand.
A6 Bursitis or subcutaneous cellulitis arising at or about the knee due to severe or prolonged external friction or pressure at or about the knee (Beat knee)	Manual labour causing severe or prolonged external friction or pressure at or about the knee
A7 Bursitis or subcutaneous cellulitis arising ator about the elbow due to severe or prolonged external friction or pressure at or about the elbow (Beat elbow)	Manual labour causing severe or prolonged external friction or pressure at or about the elbow
A8 Traumatic inflammation of the tendons of the hand and forearm, or of the associated tendon sheaths	Manual labour, or frequent or repeated movements of the hand or wrist.
A9 Miner's nystagmus	Work in or about a mine.
A10 Sensorineural hearing loss amounting to at least 50dB in each ear, being the average of hearing losses at 1, 2 and 3 kHz frequencies, and being due in the case of at least one ear to occupational noise (occupational deafness)	(*a*) The use of powered (but not hand-powered) grinding tools on cast metal (other than weld metal) or on billets or blooms in the metal-producing industry, or work wholly or mainly in the immediate vicinity of those tools whilst they are being so used; *or* (*b*) the use of pneumatic percussive tools on metal, or work wholly or mainly in the

Prescribed disease or injury

Occupation

immediate vicinity of those tools whilst they are being used; *or*

(*c*) the use of pneumatic percussive tools for drilling rock in quarries or underground or in mining coal, or work wholly or mainly in the immediate vicinity of those tools whilst they are being used; *or*

(*d*) work wholly or mainly in the immediate vicinity of plant (excluding power press plant) engaged in the forging (including drop-stamping) of metal by means of closed or open dies or drop hammers; *or*

(*e*) work in textile manufacturing where the work is undertaken wholly or mainly in rooms or sheds in which there are machines engaged in weaving manufactured or natural (including mineral) fibres or in the high speed false twisting of fibres; *or*

(*f*) the use of, or work wholly or mainly in the immediate vicinity of, machines engaged in cutting, shaping or cleaning metal nails; *or*

(*g*) the use of, or work wholly or mainly in the immediate vicinity of, plasma spray guns engaged in the deposition of metal; *or*

(*h*) the use of, or work wholly or mainly in the immediate vicinity of, any of the following machines engaged in the working of wood or material composed partly of wood, that is to say: multi-cutter moulding machines, planing machines, automatic or semi-automatic lathes, multiple cross-cut machines, automatic shaping machines, double-end tenoning machines, vertical spindle moulding machines (including high-speed routing machines), edge banding machines, bandsawing machines with a blade width of not less than 75 mm and circular sawing machines in the operation of which the blade is moved towards the material being cut; *or*

(*i*) the use of chain saws in forestry.

A11 Episodic blanching, occurring throughout the year, affecting the middle or proximal phalanges or in the case of a thumb the proximal phalanx, of:

(*a*) in the case of a person with 5 fingers (including thumb) on one hand, any 3 of those fingers; *or*

(*b*) in the case of a person with only 4 such fingers, any 2 of those fingers; *or*

(*a*) The use of hand-held chain saws in forestry; *or*

(*b*) the use of hand-held rotary tools in grinding or in the sanding or polishing of metal, or the holding of material being ground, or metal being sanded or polished by rotary tools; *or*

(*c*) the use of hand-held percussive metal-working tools, or the holding of metal being

Prescribed disease or injury	Occupation
(c) in the case of a person with less than 4 such fingers, any one of those fingers, or, as the case may be, the one remaining finger (Vibration White Finger)	worked upon by percussive tools, in riveting, caulking, chipping, hammering, fettling or swaging; or (d) the use of hand-held powered percussive drills or hand-held powered percussive hammers in mining, quarrying, demolition, or on roads or footpaths, including road construction; or (e) the holding of material being worked upon by pounding machines in shoe manufacture.

B   Conditions due to biological agents

B1 Anthrax	Contact with animals infected with anthrax or the handling (including the loading or unloading or transport) of animal products or residues.
B2 Glanders	Contact with equine animals or their carcases
B3 Infection by leptospira	(a) Work in places which are, or are liable to be, infested by rats, field mice or voles, or other small mammals; or (b) work at dog kennels or the care or handling of dogs; or (c) contact with bovine animals or pigs or their meat products
B4 Ankylostomiasis	Work in or about a mine
B5 Tuberculosis	Contact with a source of tuberculous infection
B6 Extrinsic allergic alveolitis (including farmer's lung)	Exposure to moulds or fungal spores or heterologous proteins by reason of employment in: (a) agriculture, horticulture, forestry, cultivation of edible fungi or malt-working; or (b) loading or unloading or handling in storage mouldy vegetable matter or edible fungi; or (c) caring for or handling birds; or (d) handling bagasse
B7 Infection by organisms of the genus brucella	Contact with: (a) animals infected by brucella, or their carcases or parts thereof, or their untreated products; or (b) laboratory specimens or vaccines of, or containing, brucella
B8 Viral hepatitis	Close and frequent contact with: (a) human blood or human blood products; or (b) a source or viral hepatitis infection by reason of employment in the medical treatment or nursing of a person or persons suffering from viral hepatitis, or in a service ancillary to such treatment or nursing

Prescribed disease or *injury*	*Occupation*
B9 Infection by *Streptococcus suis*	Contact with pigs infected by *Streptococcus suis*, or with the carcases, products or residues of pigs so infected
B10 (a) Avian chlamydiosis	Contact with birds infected with chlamydia psittaci, or with the remains or untreated products of such birds
B10 (b) Ovine chlamydiosis	Contact with sheep infected with chlamydia psittaci, or with the remains or untreated products of such sheep
B11 Q fever	Contact with animals, their remains or their untreated products
B12 Orf	Contact with sheep, goats or with the carcases of sheep or goats
B13 Hydatidosis	Contact with dogs
C Conditions due to chemical agents	
C1 Poisoning by lead or a compound of lead	The use or handling of, or exposure to the fumes, dust or vapour of, lead or a compound of lead, or a substance containing lead
C2 Poisoning by manganese or a compound of manganese	The use or handling of, or exposure to the fumes, dust or vapour of, manganese or a compound of manganese, or a substance containing manganese
C3 Poisoning by phosphorus or an inorganic compound of phosphorus or poisoning due to the anti-cholinesterase or pseudo anti-cholinesterase action of organic phosphorus compounds	The use or handling of, or exposure to the fumes, dust or vapour of, phosphorus or a compound of phosphorus, or a substance containing phosphorus
C4 Poisoning by arsenic or a compound of arsenic	The use or handling of, or exposure to the fumes, dust or vapour of, arsenic or a compound of arsenic, or a substance containing arsenic
C5 Poisoning by mercury or a compound of mercury	The use or handling of, or exposure to the fumes, dust or vapour of, mercury or a compound of mercury, or a substance containing mercury
C6 Poisoning by carbon bisulphide	The use or handling of, or exposure to the fumes or vapour of, carbon bisulphide, or a substance containing carbon bisulphide
C7 Poisoning by benzene or a homologue of benzene	The use or handling of, or exposure to the fumes of, or vapour containing benzene or any of its homologues
C8 Poisoning by a nitro- or amino- or chloro-derivative of benzene or of a homologue of benzene, or poisoning by nitrochlorbenzene	The use or handling of, or exposure to the fumes of, or vapour containing, a nitro- or amino- or chloro-derivative of benzene, or of a homologue of benzene, or nitrochlorbenzene
C9 Poisoning by dinitrophenol or a homologue of dinitropheno or by substituted dinitrophenols or by the salts of such substances	The use or handling of, or exposure to the fumes of, or vapour containing, dinitrophenol or a homologue or substituted dinitrophenols or the salts of such substances

Prescribed disease or injury	*Occupation*
C10 Poisoning by tetrachloroethane	The use or handling of, or exposure to the fumes of, or vapour containing, tetrachloroethane
C11 Poisoning by diethylene dioxide (dioxan)	The use or handling of, or exposure to the fumes of, or vapour containing, diethylene dioxide (dioxan)
C12 Poisoning by methyl bromide	The use or handling of, or exposure to the fumes of, or vapour containing methyl bromide
C13 Poisoning by chlorinated naphthalene	The use or handling of, or exposure to the fumes of, or dust or vapour containing, chlorinated naphthalene
C14 Poisoning by nickel carbonyl	Exposure to nickel carbonyl gas
C15 Poisoning by oxides of nitrogen	Exposure to oxides of nitrogen
C16 Poisoning by gonioma kamassi (African boxwood)	The manipulation of gonioma kamassi or any process in or incidental to the manufacture of articles therefrom
C17 Poisoning by beryllium or a compound of beryllium	The use or handling of, or exposure to the fumes, dust or vapour of, beryllium or a compound of beryllium, or a substance containing beryllium
C18 Poisoning by cadmium	Exposure to cadmium dust or fumes
C19 Poisoning by acrylamide monomer	The use or handling of, or exposure to, acrylamide monomer
C20 Dystrophy of the cornea (including ulceration of the corneal surface) of the eye	(*a*) The use or handling of, or exposure to, arsenic, tar, pitch, bitumen, mineral oil (including paraffin), soot or any compound, product or residue of any of these substances, except quinone or hydroquinone; *or* (*b*) exposure to quinone or hydroquinone during their manufacture
C21 (*a*) Localised new growth of the skin, papillomatous or keratotic (*b*) squamous-celled carcinoma of the skin	The use or handing of, or exposure to, arsenic, tar, pitch, bitumen, mineral oil (including paraffin), soot or any compound, product or residue of any of these substances, except quinone or hydroquinone
C22 (*a*) Carcinoma of the mucous membrane of the nose or associated air sinuses (*b*) primary carcinoma of a bronchus or of a lung	Work in a factory where nickel is produced by decomposition of a gaseous nickel compound which necessitates working in or about a building or buildings where that process or any other industrial process ancillary or incidental thereto is carried on
C23 Primary neoplasm (including papilloma, carcinoma-in-situ and invasive carcinoma) of the epithelial lining of the urinary tract (renal pelvis, ureter, bladder and urethra)	(*a*) Work in a building in which any of the following substances is produced for commercial purposes: (i) alpha-naphthylamine, beta-naphthylamine or methylene-bis-orthochloroaniline; (ii) diphenyl substituted by at least one

Prescribed disease or injury	*Occupation*
	nitro or primary amino group or by at least one nitro and primary (including benzidine); (iii) any of the substances mentioned in sub-paragraph (ii) above if further ring substituted by halogeno, methyl or methoxy groups, but not by other groups; (iv) the salts of any of the substances mentioned in sub-paragraphs (i) to (iii); (v) auramine or magenta; *or* (*b*) the use or handling of any of the substances mentioned in sub-paragraph (*a*) (i) to (iv), or work in such a process in which any such substance is used, handled or liberated; *or* (*c*) the maintenance or cleaning of any plant or machinery used in any such process as is mentioned in sub-paragraph (*b*), or the cleaning of clothing used in any such building as is mentioned in sub-paragraph (*a*) if such clothing is cleansed within the works of which the building forms a part or in a laundry maintained and used solely in connection with such works
C24 (*a*) Angiosarcoma of the liver (*b*) Osteolysis of the terminal phalanges of the fingers (*c*) Non-cirrhotic portal fibrosis	(*a*) Work in or about machinery or apparatus used for the polymerization of vinyl chloride monomer, a process which, for the purposes of this provision, comprises all operations up to and including the drying of the slurry produced by the polymerization and the packaging of the dried product; *or* (*b*) work in a building or structure in which any part of that process takes place
C25 Occupational vitiligo	The use or handling of, or exposure to, para-tertiary-butylphenol, para-tertiary-butylcatechol, para-amyl-phenol, hydroquinone or the monobenzyl or monobutyl ether of hydroquinone
C26 Damage to the liver or kidneys due to exposure to carbon tetrachloride	The use of or handling of, or exposure to the fumes of, or vapour containing carbon tetrachloride
C27 Damage to the liver or kidneys due to exposure to trichlormethane (chloroform)	The use of or handling of, or exposure to the fumes of, or vapour containing trichloromethane (chloroform)
C28 Central nervous system dysfunction and associated gastro-intestinal disorders due to exposure to chloromethane (methyl chloride)	The use of or handling of, or exposure to the fumes of, or vapour containing chloromethane (methyl chloride)
C29 Peripheral neuropathy due to exposure to n-hexane or methyl n-butyl ketone	The use of or handling of, or exposure to the fumes of, or vapour containing, n-hexane or methyl n-butyl ketone

Prescribed disease or injury	*Occupation*

D Miscellaneous conditions

D1 Pneumoconiosis

[*Occupations specified in reg 2(b) of, and Part II of Schedule 1 to, the Social Security (Industrial Injuries) (Prescribed Diseases) Regulations 1985 which are too numerous to set out here. They are all occupations involving exposure to dust, such as mining, quarrying, sand blasting, grinding, making china or earthenware, boiler-sealing and other work involving the use of stone, asbestos, etc.*]

D2 Byssinosis

Work in any room where any process up to and including the weaving process is performed in a factory in which the spinning or manipulation of raw or waste cotton or of flax, or the weaving of cotton or flax, is carried on

D3 Diffuse mesothelioma (primary neoplasm of the mesothelium of the pleura or of the pericardium or of the peritoneum)

(*a*) The working or handling of asbestos or any admixture of asbestos; *or*

(*b*) the manufacture or repair of asbestos textiles or other articles containing or composed of asbestos; *or*

(*c*) the cleaning of any machinery or plant used in any of the foregoing operations and of any chambers, fixtures and appliances for the collection of asbestos dust; *or*

(*d*) substantial exposure to the dust arising from any of the foregoing operations

D4 Inflammation or ulceration of the mucous membrane of the upper respiratory passages or mouth produced by dust, liquid or vapour

Exposure to dust, liquid or vapour

D5 Non-infective dermatitis of external origin (including chrome ulceration of the skin but excluding dermatitis due to ionising particles or electro-magnetic radiations other than radiant heat)

Exposure to dust, liquid or vapour or any other external agent capable of irritating the skin (including friction or heat but excluding ionising particles or electromagnetic radiations other than radiant heat)

D6 Carcinoma of the nasal cavity or associated air sinuses (nasal carcinoma)

(*a*) Attendance for work in or about a building where wooden goods are manufactured or repaired; *or*

(*b*) attendance for work in a building used for the manufacture of footwear or components of footwear made wholly or partly of leather or fibre board; *or*

(*c*) attendance for work at a place used wholly or mainly for the repair of footwear made wholly or partly of leather or fibre board

D7 Asthma which is due to exposure to any of the following agents:

Exposure to any of the agents set out in column 1 of this paragraph

Prescribed disease or injury	*Occupation*
(a) isocyanates	
(b) platinum salts	
(c) fumes or dusts arising from the manufacture, transport or use of hardening agents (including epoxy resin curing agents) based on phthalic anhydride, tetrachlorophthalic anhydride, trimellitic anhydride or triethylenetetramine	
(d) fumes arising from the use of rosin as a soldering flux	
(e) proteolytic enzymes	
(f) animals including insects and other anthropods used for the purposes of research or education or in laboratories	
(g) dusts arising from the sowing, cultivation, harvesting, drying, handling, milling, transport or storage of barley, oats, rye, wheat or maize, or the handling, milling, transport or storage of meal or flour made therefrom	
(h) antibiotics	
(i) cimetidine	
(j) wood dust	
(k) ispaghula	
(l) castor bean dust	
(m) ipecacuanha	
(n) azodice-bonamide	
(o) animals including insects and other arthropods or their larval forms, used for the purposes of pest control or fruit cultivation, or the larval forms of animals used for the purposes of research, education or in laboratories;	
(p) glutaraldehyde;	
(q) persulphate salts or henna;	
(r) crustaceans or fish or products arising from these in the food processing industry;	
(s) reactive dyes;	
(t) soya bean;	
(u) tea dust;	
(v) green coffee bean dust;	
(w) fumes from stainless steel welding;	
(x) any other sensitising agent (occupational asthma)	
D8 Primary carcinoma of the lung where there is accompanying evidence of one or both of the following: (a) asbestosis; (b) bilateral diffuse pleural thickening	(a) The working or handling of asbestos; or any admixture of asbestos; or (b) the manufacture or repair of asbestos textiles or other articles containing or composed of asbestos; or (c) the cleaning of any machinery or plant used in any of the foregoing operations and of any chambers, fixtures and applicances for the collection of asbestos dust; or

Prescribed disease or injury	*Occupation*
	(*d*) substantial exposure to the dust arising from any of the foregoing operations
D9 Bilateral diffuse pleural thickening	(*a*) the working or handling of asbestos or any admixture of asbestos; *or*
	(*b*) the manufacture or repair of asbestos textile or other articles containing or composed of asbestos; *or*
	(*c*) the cleaning of any machinery or plant used in any of the foregoing operations and of any chambers, fixtures and applicances for the collection of asbestos dust; *or*
	(*d*) substantial exposure to the dust arising from any of the foregoing operations
D10 Lung cancer	(*a*) work underground in a tin mine; *or*
	(*b*) exposure to bis(chloromethyl) ether produced during the manufacture of chloromethyl methyl ether; *or*
	(*c*) exposure to zinc chromate, calcium chromate or strontium chromate in their pure forms.

Social security adjudication

I The Chief Adjudication Officer

Mr K. Bellamy, Room 541, New Court, 48 Carey Street, London WC2A 2LS, tel: 071-962 8000

Central Adjudication Services
Quarry House, Quarry Hill, Leeds LS2 7UA, tel: 0532 324000

2 Social Security Appeal Tribunals, Disability Appeal Tribunals and Medical Appeal Tribunals

The President

His Honour Judge Thorpe, City Centre House, 39-45 Finsbury Square, London EC2A 1UU, tel: 071-814 6500

The Regional Chairpersons

Midlands
Mr I.G. Harrison, Albion House, 5-13 Canal Street, Nottingham NG1 7EG, tel: 0602-472869

North Eastern
Mr J.W.Tinnion, York House, York Place, Leeds LS1 2ED, tel: 0532-451246

North Western
Mr R.S.Sim, 36 Dale Street, Liverpool L2 5UZ, tel: 051-236 4334

Scotland
Ms L.T. Parker, Blytheswood House, 200 West Regent Street, Glasgow G2 4SS, tel: 041-248 2442

South Eastern
Mr R.G. Smithson, Whittington House, 19-30 Alfred Place, London WC1E 7LW, tel: 071-580 3941

Wales and South Western
Mr C.B.Stephens, Oxford House, Hills Street, Cardiff CF1 2DR, tel: 0222-378071

3 Social Security Commissioners

England and Wales   Harp House, 83 Farringdon Street, London
EC4A 4DH, tel: 071-353 5145

Scotland   23 Melville Street, Edinburgh EH3 7PW, tel:
031-225 2201

Cases are also heard in the Law Courts in Cardiff, Leeds and Liverpool
but administration in all English and Welsh cases is dealt with in London.

Books, leaflets and periodicals

Many of the books listed here will be in your main public library – the official publications probably being in the reference section.

You can get books published by HMSO from the six HMSO Bookshops but also from many others. Alternatively, they may be ordered by post, telephone or fax from HMSO Books, PO Box 276, London SW8 5DT (tel: 071-873 9090, fax: 071-873 8463). Enquiries should be addressed to PC51D, HMSO Books, 51 Nine Elms Lane, London SW8 5DR (tel: 071-873 0011).

I Textbooks

The Law of Social Security by A.I. Ogus and E.M. Barendt (Butterworths, 3rd Edition, 1988). This is the standard textbook on social security law.

Compensation for Industrial Injury by R. Lewis (Professional Books, 1987). This is an excellent and detailed study of industrial injuries benefits.

Claim in Time by M. Partington (Legal Action Group, 2nd edition, 1989). This is a detailed study of the rules for claiming benefits and, in particular, what amounts to 'good cause' for a late claim. It is available, price £8.50 including postage and packing, from Legal Action Group, 242 Pentonville Road, London N1 9UN.

Social Security Taxation by D. Williams (Sweet & Maxwell, 1982), an excellent book on contributions, but there have been changes since it was written.

Tolley's National Insurance Contributions 1992-93 (Tolley Publishing Company), a drier but more up-to-date book on contributions.

2 Case law and legislation

Social Security Case Law – Digest of Commissioners' Decisions by D. Neligan (HMSO, looseleaf in two volumes). This consists of summaries of Commissioners' decisions grouped together by subject.

The Law Relating to Social Security (HMSO, looseleaf in ten volumes). This consists of *all* the legislation but without any comment.

Non-Means Tested Benefits: The Legislation by D. Bonner, I. Hooker and R. White (Sweet & Maxwell, 1993). This contains the most useful legislation with a detailed commentary. The 1992 edition will be available from July, price £29.95, post-free from CPAG Ltd, 1-5

Bath Street, London EC1V 9PY (for CPAG members). A supplement will be similarly available from December, price £7.50. If you order both the main work and the supplement from CPAG before 31 May, the total cost is £33.50 (£37.45 post-May).

Medical and Disability Appeal Tribunals: The Legislation by Mark Rowland (former editor of this *Guide*) 1st edition (Sweet & Maxwell, 1993/4). This contains the rules on the new disability benefits, DATs and MATs with a detailed commentary on the law. It will be available in July 1993, price £29.95 post-free from CPAG Ltd at the above address (for CPAG members). (If you ordered this publication when it was originally announced, your copy will be supplied this year at the cheaper price originally advertised.)

3   Official guidance

Adjudication Officers' Guide (HMSO, looseleaf in ten volumes).

Industrial Injuries Handbook for Adjudicating Medical Authorities (HMSO, looseleaf).

Handbook for Delegated Medical Practitioners (HMSO, 1988).

Notes on the Diagnosis of Occupational Diseases (except pneumoconiosis and related diseases and occupational deafness) (HMSO, 1983 with 1985 addendum).

4   Tribunal handbooks

Social Security Appeal Tribunals: A Guide to Procedure (HMSO, 2nd edition, 1988).

Medical Appeal Tribunals: A Guide to Procedure (HMSO, 1987).

5   Leaflets

There are innumerable leaflets published by the DSS which cover particular benefits or particular groups of claimants or contributors. They have been greatly improved in recent years and contain quite detailed information. The bigger ones are really 48-page booklets. They are free from your local DSS office or from DSS Information Division, Leaflets Unit, Block 4, Government Buildings, Honeypot Lane, Stanmore, Middlesex HA7 1AY.

6   Periodicals

The *Welfare Rights Bulletin* is published every two months by CPAG for welfare rights advisers. It covers developments in social security law and so updates this *Guide* between editions. The annual subscription is £15 but it is sent automatically to CPAG Rights and Comprehensive members.

Articles on social security are also to be found in *Legal Action* (Legal Action Group, monthly), the *Journal of Social Welfare Law* (Sweet & Maxwell, bi-monthly) and *EAGLE – The Journal of the Exchange on Ageing, Law and Ethics* (Age Concern, England, bi-monthly).

Legislation

This list of legislation is not exhaustive. Only those statutes and statutory instruments to which reference is made in this *Guide* are included. It is anticipated that most readers who wish to look up the legislation will do so either in *The Law Relating to Social Security* (the 'Blue Volumes') or in *Non-Means-Tested Benefits – The Legislation* (see p281) where it is all set out in amended form. For that reason, legislation which simply amends earlier legislation is not listed here.

The abbreviations used in the notes in this *Guide* are not officially recognised, so it is better to use the proper title of legislation when writing letters.

Abbreviations used in the Notes

Acts of Parliament

EP(C)A 1978	Employment Protection (Consolidation) Act 1978
FA 1982	Forfeiture Act 1982
ICTA 1988	Income and Corporation Taxes Act 1988
LAA 1988	Legal Aid Act 1988
NIA 1965	National Insurance Act 1965
SB(D)A 1992	Still-Birth (Definition) Act 1992
SSA 1975	Social Security Act 1975
SSA 1979	Social Security Act 1979
SSA 1985	Social Security Act 1985
SSA 1986	Social Security Act 1986
SSA 1990	Social Security Act 1990
SSA 1993	Social Security Act 1993
SSAA 1992	Social Security Administration Act 1992
SSCBA 1992	Social Security Contributions and Benefits Act 1992
SSPA 1975	Social Security Pensions Act 1975

Regulations

Each set of regulations has a statutory instrument (SI) number and a date. You ask for them by giving their date and number.

CB Regs	The Child Benefit (General) Regulations 1976 No. 965
CB(Amdt) Regs	The Child Benefit (General) Amendment Regulations 1987 No. 35
CB(RPA) Regs	The Child Benefit (Residence and Persons Abroad) Regulations 1976 No. 963

CB&SS(FAR) Regs	The Child Benefit and Social Security (Fixing and Adjustment of Rates) Regulations 1976 No. 1267
CTB Regs	The Council Tax Benefit (General) Regulations 1992 No. 1814
EP(RUB&SB) Regs	The Employment Protection (Recoupment of Unemployment Benefit and Supplementary Benefit) Regulations 1977 No. 674
EP(VL)O 1992	The Employment Protection (Variation of Limits) Order 1992 No. 312
HB Regs	The Housing Benefit (General) Regulations 1987 No. 1971
IS Regs	The Income Support (General) Regulations 1987 No. 1967
IT(E) No 13 Regs	The Income Tax (Employment) (No. 13) Regulations 1982 No. 66
MA(VSB) Regs	The Mobility Allowance (Vehicle Scheme Beneficiaries) Regulations 1977 No. 1229
NHS(GMPS) Regs	The National Health Service (General Medical and Pharmaceutical Services) Regulations 1974 No. 160
SF(RDB) Regs	The Social Fund (Recovery by Deductions from Benefits) Regulations 1988 No. 35
SFM&FE Regs	The Social Fund Maternity and Funeral Expenses (General) Regulations 1987 No. 481
SMP Regs	The Statutory Maternity Pay (General) Regulations 1986 No. 1960
SMP(ME) Regs	The Statutory Maternity Pay (Medical Evidence) Regulations 1987 No. 235
SS(AA) Regs	The Social Security (Attendance Allowance) Regulations 1991 No. 2740
SS(Adj) Regs	The Social Security (Adjudication) Regulations 1986 No. 2218
SS(C1CCP)O	The Social Security (Class 1 Contributions – Contracted-out Percentages) Order 1992 No. 795
SS(C&P) Regs	The Social Security (Claims and Payments) Regulations 1987 No. 1968
SS(CatE) Regs	The Social Security (Categorisation of Earners) Regulations 1978 No. 1689
SS(CE) Regs	The Social Security (Computation of Earnings) Regulations 1978 No. 1698
SS(Con) Regs	The Social Security (Contributions) Regulations 1979 No. 591
SS(Con) Amdt 4 Regs	The Social Security (Contributions) Amendment (No. 4) Regulations 1992 No. 668
SS(Cr) Regs	The Social Security (Credits) Regulations 1975 No. 556
SS(DLA) Regs	The Social Security (Disability Living Allowance) Regulations 1991 No. 2890

SS(EEEIIP) Regs	The Social Security (Employed Earners' Employment for Industrial Injuries Purposes) Regulations 1975 No. 467
SS(EF) Regs	The Social Security (Earnings Factor) Regulations 1979 No. 676
SS(GA) Regs	The Social Security (Guardian's Allowance) Regulations 1975 No. 515
SS(GB) Regs	The Social Security (General Benefits) Regs 1982 No. 1408
SS(GRB) No 2 Regs	The Social Security (Graduated Retirement Benefit) (No. 2) Regulations 1978 No. 393
SS(HI) Regs	The Social Security (Hospital In-Patients) Regulations 1975 No. 555
SS(ICA) Regs	The Social Security (Invalid Care Allowance) Regulations 1976 No. 409
SS(IDLA) Regs	The Social Security (Introduction of Disability Living Allowance) Regulations 1991 No. 2891
SS(II&D)MP Regs	The Social Security (Industrial Injuries and Diseases) Miscellaneous Provisions Regulations 1986 No. 1561
SS(IIPD) Regs	The Social Security (Industrial Injuries) (Prescribed Diseases) Regulations 1985 No. 967
SS(IIRE) Regs	The Social Security (Industrial Injuries) (Regular Employment) Regulations 1990 No. 256
SS(IoM)O	The Social Security (Isle of Man) Order 1977 No. 2150
SS(J&G)O	The Social Security (Jersey and Guernsey) Order 1992 No. 1735
SS(MA) Regs	The Social Security (Maternity Allowance) Regulations 1987 No. 416
SS(MAP) Regs	The Social Security (Maximum Additional Pension) Regulations 1978 No. 949
SS(MB) Regs	The Social Security (Mariners' Benefits) Regulations 1975 No. 529
SS(ME) Regs	The Social Security (Medical Evidence) Regulations 1976 No. 615
SS(NIRA) Regs	The Social Security (Northern Ireland Reciprocal Arrangements) Regulations 1976 No. 1003
SS(OB) Regs	The Social Security (Overlapping Benefits) Regulations 1979 No. 597
SS(PAOR) Regs	The Social Security (Payments on Account, Overpayments and Recovery) Regulations 1988 No. 664
SS(R) Regs	The Social Security (Recoupment) Regulations 1990 No. 322

SS(SDA) Regs	The Social Security (Severe Disablement Allowance) Regulations 1984 No. 1303
SS(SDA) Amdt Regs	The Social Security (Severe Disablement Allowance) Amendment Regulations 1992 No. 704
SS(STB)(T) Regs	The Social Security (Short-Term Benefits) (Transitional) Regulations 1974 No. 2192
SS(US&IB) Regs	The Social Security (Unemployment, Sickness and Invalidity Benefit) Regulations 1983 No. 1598
SS(US&IB) Amdt Regs	The Social Security (Unemployment, Sickness and Invalidity Benefit) Amendment Regulations 1992 No. 2913
SS(WB&RP) Regs	The Social Security (Widow's Benefit and Retirement Pensions) Regulations 1979 No. 642
SS(WB&RP) Amdt Regs 87	The Social Security (Widow's Benefit and Retirement Pension) Amendment Regulations 1987 No. 1854
SS(WB&RP) Amdt Regs 92	The Social Security (Widow's Benefit and Retirement Pensions) Amendment Regulations 1992 No. 1695
SS(WBRP&OB)(T) Regs	The Social Security (Widow's Benefit, Retirement Pensions and Other Benefits) (Transitional) Regulations 1979 No. 643
SS(W&WIP) Regs	The Social Security (Widow's and Widower's Invalidity Pensions) Regulations 1978 No. 529
SSA86(Comm 5)O	The Social Security Act 1986 (Commencement No. 5) Order 1987 No. 354
SSB(Dep) Regs	The Social Security Benefit (Dependency) Regulations 1977 No. 343
SSB(Dep) Amdt Regs	The Social Security Benefit (Dependency) Amendment Regulations 1987 No. 355
SSB(MF) Regs	The Social Security (Benefit) (Members of the Forces) Regulations 1975 No. 493
SSB(MW&WSP) Regs	The Social Security (Benefit) (Married Women and Widows' Special Provisions) Regulations 1974 No. 2010
SSB(PA) Regs	The Social Security Benefit (Persons Abroad) Regulations 1975 No. 563
SSB(PRT) Regs	The Social Security Benefit (Persons Residing Together) Regulations 1977 No. 956
SSBU(No 2)O 1991	The Social Security Benefits Up-rating (No. 2) Order 1991 No 2910
SSBUO 1993	The Social Security Benefits Up-rating Order 1993 No. 349
SSCP Regs	The Social Security Commissioners Procedure Regulations 1987 No. 214

SSFA(PM) Regs	The Social Security and Family Allowances (Polygamous Marriages) Regulations 1975 No. 561
SSP Regs	The Statutory Sick Pay (General) Regulations 1982 No. 894
SSP(HR&MA) Regs	The Social Security Pensions (Home Responsibilities and Miscellaneous Amendments) Regulations 1978 No. 508
SSP(MAPA) Regs	The Statutory Sick Pay (Mariners, Airmen and Persons Abroad) Regulations 1982 No. 1349
SSREFO	The Social Security Revaluation of Earnings Factor Order 1992 No. 1102

Notes

References such as CS/50/1950 and R(U) 2/80 are references to Commissioners' decisions. See pages 256-8 for an explanation.

Decisions of courts are referred to by the names of the parties and there follows a reference to the volume and page of a series of law reports unless the case is unreported or reported only in *The Times* newspaper. *Clear v Smith* [1981] WLR 399(DC) is to be found reported in volume 1 of the Weekly Law Reports at page 399 and it was a decision of the Divisional Court. The abbreviations used in these notes are in general use and are as follows:

AC	Appeal Cases
All ER	All England Reports
CMLR	Common Market Law Reports
Crim App R(S)	Criminal Appeal Reports (Sentencing)
ECR	European Court Reports
FLR	Family Law Reports
ICR	Industrial Cases Reports
QB	Queen's Bench
WLR	Weekly Law Reports

(DC), (CA), (HL) and (ECJ) indicate decisions of the Divisional Court, Court of Appeal, House of Lords and European Court of Justice respectively.

References such as s14(1) SSA 1975 and reg 3 SS(C&P) Regs are references to legislation. A list of the titles of the legislation with a key to these abbreviations will be found in Appendix Six on page 283. Other abbreviations are:

Art	Article
Dir	Directive
O	Order
para	paragraph
r	rule
reg	regulation
RSC	Rules of the Supreme Court
s	section
ss	sections
Sch	Schedule

Chapter 2: Unemployment benefit

1 Conditions of entitlement
(p8)
1 ss25 and 57(1) SSCBA 1992

2 Payment
(pp8-10)
1 s25(4)-(6) and Sch 4 para 1 SSCBA 1992
2 s25(7) SSCBA 1992

3 Reg 24(1) SS(C&P) Regs
4 s25(3) SSCBA 1992
5 s26(1) SSCBA 1992
6 s26(2) and (3) SSCBA 1992
7 s122(1) SSCBA 1992
8 s26(2)(a) and (b) SSCBA 1992
9 s26(3) SSCBA 1992; reg 6A SS(US&IB) Regs
10 Reg 6A(2)(a)-(c) SS(US&IB) Regs
11 Reg 6A(2)(d) SS(US&IB) Regs
12 Reg 6A(3) SS(US&IB) Regs
13 s26(5) SSCBA 1992
14 R(U) 7/86 disapproving R(U) 6/83

15 Reg 16 SS(US&IB) Regs

3 How to claim
(pp11-12)
1 Reg 19(1) and Sch 4 para 1 SS(C&P) Regs
2 Reg 19(1) and Sch 5 para 1 SS(C&P) Regs
3 Reg 8 SS(C&P) Regs

4 Availability for work
(pp12-19)
1 s57(1)(a)(i) SSCBA 1992
2 R(U) 1/82; *Ali v Chief Adjudication Officer* (CA) reported as an appendix to R(U) 1/85
3 s57(1)(a)(i) SSCBA 1992
4 R(U) 44/53
5 Reg 7B(1) SS(US&IB) Regs
6 Reg 7B(2) SS(US&IB) Regs
7 Reg 7B(4)(c), (5) and (6) SS(US&IB) Regs
8 Reg 7B(6) SS(US&IB) Regs
9 Reg 7B(4)(b) SS(US&IB) Regs
10 Reg 7B(4)(a) SS(US&IB) Regs
11 Reg 12 SS(US&IB) Regs
12 Reg 9(a) SS(US&IB) Regs
13 Reg 9(b) SS(US&IB) Regs
14 Reg 10 SS(US&IB) Regs
15 Reg 11 SS(US&IB) Regs
16 Reg 7(1)(i) SS(US&IB) Regs
17 Reg 12A(1), (2) and (3)(b) SS(US&IB) Regs
18 Reg 12A(1), (2) and (3)(a) SS(US&IB) Regs
19 Reg 12D(2) SS(US&IB) Regs
20 R(U) 4/66
21 Reg 19, Sch 4 para 1 and Sch 5 para 1 SS(C&P) Regs

5 Actively seeking employment
(pp19-23)
1 s57(1)(a)(i) SSCBA 1992
2 Reg 12B(1) SS(US&IB) Regs
3 Reg 12B(3) SS(US&IB) Regs
4 Reg 12B(4) SS(US&IB) Regs
5 Reg 12B(4)(a) SS(US&IB) Regs
6 Reg 12B(4)(b) SS(US&IB) Regs
7 Reg 12B(4)(c) SS(US&IB) Regs
8 Reg 12B(4)(d) SS(US&IB) Regs
9 Reg 12B(2) SS(US&IB) Regs
10 Reg 12B(2) SS(US&IB) Regs
11 Reg 12D(1)(a) SS(US&IB) Regs
12 Reg 12D(1)(b) SS(US&IB) Regs
13 Reg 12D(3) SS(US&IB) Regs
14 Reg 12D(1) SS(US&IB) Regs
15 Reg 12D(2)(a) SS(US&IB) Regs

16 Reg 12D(2)(c) SS(US&IB) Regs as amended by reg 2 SS(US&IB) Amdt Regs
17 Reg 12D(2)(b) SS(US&IB) Regs
18 Reg 12D(1)(d) SS(US&IB) Regs
19 Reg 12D(1)(e) SS(US&IB) Regs
20 Reg 12D(1)(f) SS(US&IB) Regs
21 Reg 12C(1)(a) SS(US&IB) Regs
22 Reg 12C(2) and (3) SS(US&IB) Regs
23 Reg 12C(1)(b) SS(US&IB) Regs
24 Reg 12C(4) SS(US&IB) Regs
25 Reg 37(1)(a) SS(C&P) Regs
26 Reg 22 IS Regs

6 Special rules if you work part-time
(pp23-27)
1 Sch 8 IS Regs
2 s124(1)(c) SSCBA 1992; reg 5 IS Regs
3 Reg 7(1)(o) SS(US&IB) Regs
4 Reg 7(1)(g) SS(US&IB) Regs
5 Reg 3(3) SS(CE) Regs
6 s57(1)(b) SSCBA 1992
7 Reg 7(1)(e) and (2) SS(US&IB) Regs
8 s57(1)(b) SSCBA 1992
9 Reg 19(3)(e) SS(US&IB) Regs
10 Reg 19(3)(a) SS(US&IB) Regs
11 Reg 19(3)(b) SS(US&IB) Regs
12 s57(1)(b), (c) and (e) SSCBA 1992
13 s57(1)(e) SSCBA 1992; reg 19(2) SS(US&IB) Regs
14 Reg 19(6) SS(US&IB) Regs
15 s122 SSCBA 1992
16 Reg 7(1)(e) SS(US&IB) Regs
17 R(U) 30/53
18 CU/518/1949; *Chief Adjudication Officer v Brunt* [1988] AC 711 (HL) also reported as R(U) 9/88
19 R(U) 14/59; R(U) 14/60
20 Reg 7(1)(e) SS(US&IB) Regs
21 Reg 7(1)(h) SS(US&IB) Regs
22 See for example R(U) 2/87
23 R(U) 7/63

7 Payments from your previous job
(pp27-30)
1 Reg 7(1)(k)(iii)-(v) SS(US&IB) Regs
2 Reg 9 EP(RUB&SB) Regs
3 Reg 7(1)(k) SS(US&IB) Regs
4 R(U) 4/82
5 Reg 7(1)(k) SS(US&IB) Regs
6 R(U) 6/85
7 R(U) 5/74
8 Reg 7(1)(d) SS(US&IB) Regs
9 Reg 7(6) SS(US&IB) Regs
10 Reg 7(5) SS(US&IB) Regs
11 Reg 7(6) SS(US&IB) Regs

12 s99 EP(C)A 1978
13 Reg 7(5)(b) SS(US&IB) Regs
14 EP(VL)O 1992
15 Reg 7(5)(c) and (6) SS(US&IB) Regs
16 s30(4) SSCBA 1992
17 s30(1) SSCBA 1992; reg 24 SS(US&IB) Regs; R(U) 8/83
18 s122(1) SSCBA 1992 'payments by way of occupational or personal pension'
19 CP/7/1987
20 Reg 25 SS(US&IB) Regs

8   Disqualifications
(pp30-38)
1   s28(1)(a) SSCBA 1992
2   s28(1)(e) SSCBA 1992
3   R(U) 2/77, para 1
4   R(U) 8/57, para 6
5   R(U) 10/52
6   R(U) 10/53
7   R(U) 26/56
8   CU/190/1950
9   s26(6) SSCBA 1992
10 s28(1)(a) SSCBA 1992
11 s28(1)(e) SSCBA 1992
12 Reg 22 IS Regs
13 R(U) 2/54; R(U) 7/74
14 s28(4) SSCBA 1992; R(U) 3/91
15 *Crewe v Social Security Commissioner* [1982] 1 WLR 1209 (CA) also reported as an appendix to R(U) 3/81; R(U) 20/64(T); R(U) 4/87
16 R(U) 14/52
17 *Crewe v Social Security Commissioner,* supra
18 R(U) 4/87
19 R(U) 19/52
20 R(U) 6/53
21 R(U) 13/52
22 R(U) 19/52
23 R(U) 2/90
24 R(U) 4/87, para 9
25 R(U) 14/52
26 R(U) 15/53
27 R(U) 18/57
28 R(U) 13/52
29 R(U) 27/59
30 s29 SSCBA 1992; reg 12G SS(US&IB) Regs
31 Reg 12G(2) SS(US&IB) Regs; R(U) 1/92
32 s28(1)(b) and (f) SSCBA 1992
33 s28(6)(a) SSCBA 1992
34 s28(1)(c) and (g) SSCBA 1992
35 s28(1)(d) SSCBA 1992
36 Reg 12E(2)(a) SS(US&IB) Regs

37 Reg 12E(2)(b) SS(US&IB) Regs
38 Reg 12E(2)(c) SS(US&IB) Regs
39 Reg 12E(2)(d) SS(US&IB) Regs
40 Reg 12E(4)(b) SS(US&IB) Regs
41 Reg 12E(2)(e) SS(US&IB) Regs
42 Reg 12E(4)(a) SS(US&IB) Regs
43 Reg 12H SS(US&IB) Regs
44 Reg 12E(5) SS(US&IB) Regs
45 Reg 12E(6) SS(US&IB) Regs
46 Reg 12E(7)(a) SS(US&IB) Regs
47 Reg 12E(7)(b) and (8) SS(US&IB) Regs
48 s27(1)(b) SSCBA 1992
49 s27(1)(a) SSCBA 1992
50 s27(3)(a) SSCBA 1992
51 R(U) 23/64; R(U) 24/57; R(U) 4/62; R(U) 1/70
52 *Presho v Insurance Officer* [1984] AC 310 (also reported as an appendix to R(U) 1/84)
53 s27(2)(a) SSCBA 1992; R(U) 6/74
54 s27(2)(b) SSCBA 1992
55 s27(2)(c) SSCBA 1992

9   Special rules for people over pensionable age
(pp38-39)
1   s25(2)(b) and (c) SSCBA 1992
2   s25(5) SSCBA 1992; reg 6 SS(WB&RP) Regs
3   EC Dir 79/7, Art 7(1)(a)
4   EC Dir 79/7, Art 4; *Secretary of State for Social Security v Thomas, The Times,* 22 August 1990 (CA)

10   Special rules for students
(pp39-40)
1   Reg 7(1)(m) and (3) SS(US&IB) Regs

11   Other benefits
(p40)
1   Reg 22 IS Regs
2   s126 SSCBA 1992

12   Tax
(pp40-41)
1   s617 ICTA 1988
2   Reg 14 IT(E) No 13 Regs

Chapter 3:   Benefits for people incapable of work

1   Incapacity for work
(pp43-49)
1   ss57(1)(a)(ii) and 68(11)(c)(i) SSCBA 1992; reg 7 SS(SDA) Regs

2 Reg 3 SS(US&IB) Regs; reg 7 SS(SDA) Regs
3 R(S) 7/60; R(S) 2/78
4 CS/320/1950
5 s58(1) SSCBA 1992; reg 7A SS(SDA) Regs as amended
6 Reg 3(3) SS(US&IB) Regs; *Hunt and Merriman v Insurance Officer* (CA) reported as R(S) 3/86; CSS/5/1987
7 R(S) 6/86
8 s58(2) SSCBA 1992; reg 8A SS(SDA) Regs as amended
9 Reg 3(4) and (5) SS(US&IB) Regs
10 CS/8/1979; CS/42/1987
11 CS/35/1987
12 CS/42/1987
13 Reg 7(1)(f) SS(US&IB) Regs as amended
14 Reg 2(1) SS(ME) Regs
15 Reg 5 SS(ME) Regs
16 Sch 1 para 31 NHS(GMPS) Regs
17 Reg 17 SS(C&P) Regs
18 R(S) 3/90
19 s53 SSAA 1992; R(S) 3/84
20 R(S) 1/88
21 R(I) 13/75
22 R(S) 7/85
23 R(S) 6/85; R(S) 7/85
24 R(S) 11/51
25 s57(1) SSCBA 1992

2   Statutory sick pay
(pp50-57)
1 ss152-5 and Schs 11 and 12 SSCBA 1992
2 s163(1) SSCBA 1992; reg 16 SSP Regs
3 s151(2) SSCBA 1992
4 Reg 4 SSP Regs
5 Reg 16(2) SSP Regs
6 s153(3) and Sch 11 para 2 SSCBA 1992
7 *Secretary of State for Social Security v Thomas*, The Times, 22 August 1990 (CA); *Barber v Guardian Royal Exchange Assurance Group* [1991] 2 WLR 72 (ECJ)
8 Reg 3 SSP Regs
9 R(SSP) 1/86
10 Reg 10 SSP(MAPA) Regs
11 s152(2) SSCBA 1992
12 s152(5) SSCBA 1992
13 s152(3) SSCBA 1992; reg 2A SSP Regs as amended
14 s153(2) SSCBA 1992; reg 3(3) SSP Regs
15 Art 10 reg 1408/71 EEC
16 Reg 2A SSP Regs as amended
17 Reg 3A SSP Regs as amended
18 s154(3) SSCBA 1992

19 Reg 5(2) and (3) SSP Regs as amended
20 R(SSP) 1/85
21 Reg 7(4)(a) SSP Regs
22 Reg 7(4)(b) SSP Regs
23 Reg 7(5) SSP Regs
24 Reg 7(1)(a) SSP Regs
25 Reg 7(1)(b) SSP Regs
26 Reg 7(3) SSP Regs
27 s156(3) SSCBA 1992
28 s157 SSCBA 1992
29 s163(2) SSCBA 1992; reg 19 SSP Regs
30 CSSP/2/1984; CSSP/3/1984
31 Reg 17(3) SSP Regs
32 s157(3) SSCBA 1992
33 s155(1) SSCBA 1992
34 s155(4) SSCBA 1992
35 Sch 12 para 1 SSCBA 1992
36 Sch 12 para 3 SSCBA 1992
37 s4(1) SSCBA 1992
38 s14(3) SSAA 1992
39 s14(1) SSAA 1992
40 Reg 16(1) SSP Regs
41 Reg 22(1) SS(Adj) Regs
42 ss20(3) and 22(1)(a) SSAA 1992
43 Reg 22(3) SS(Adj) Regs
44 Reg 9A SSP Regs as amended
45 Regs 9 and 22 SSP Regs

3   Sickness benefit
(pp57-60)
1 ss31 and 57 SSCBA 1992; reg 19 SS(C&P) Regs
2 Sch 4 SSCBA 1992
3 Reg 24 SS(C&P) Regs
4 Reg 5 SS(ME) Regs as amended
5 s31(2), (6) and (7) SSCBA 1992
6 Reg 17 SS(US&IB) Regs
7 R(S) 2/53
8 R(S) 9/51

4   Invalidity benefit
(pp60-64)
1 s33 SSCBA 1992
2 ss33(3), (4) and (5), 44(4) and Sch 4 SSCBA 1992
3 s34 SSCBA 1992
4 CS/27/1991
5 s47(1) SSCBA 1992
6 Sch 12 para 1 SSCBA 1992
7 Sch 12 para 1 SSCBA 1992
8 Reg 7A(3) and (4) SS(US&IB) Regs
9 Reg 7A(1)(c)(i) SS(US&IB) Regs
10 Reg 7A(5) SS(US&IB) Regs
11 Reg 8A SS(US&IB) Regs as amended
12 s33(1)(b) SSCBA 1992
13 s33(4) and (5) SSCBA 1992

14 s102 SSCBA 1992; reg 31 SS(US&IB)
    Regs as amended
15 CS/27/1991
16 DSS internal circular SB/213 para 34
17 s40 SSCBA 1992
18 s41 SSCBA 1992
19 ss40(7) and 41(7) SSCBA 1992; reg 3
    SS(W&WIP) Regs

5 Severe disablement allowance
(pp64-69)
1   ss68 and 69 SSCBA 1992
2   Sch 4 SSCBA 1992
3   Sch 2 Part I IS Regs
4   CS/27/1991
5   s68(5) SSCBA 1992
6   reg 7(2) SS(SDA) Regs
7   Regs 4 and 5 SS(SDA) Regs
8   Art 4 Dir 79/7 EEC; *Secretary of State
    for Social Security v Thomas, The
    Times*, 22 August 1990 (CA)
9   Reg 8 SS(SDA) Regs; CS/20/1986
10 R(S) 2/87
11 Reg 7(3) SS(SDA) Regs
12 s68(13) and Sch 6 SSCBA 1992
13 Reg 10 SS(SDA) Regs
14 s36 SSA 1975 as originally enacted
15 *Insurance Officer v McCaffrey* [1984] 1
    WLR 1353 (HL)
16 *Clarke v Chief Adjudication Officer*
    [1987] ECR 2865 (ECJ)
17 Reg 20 SS(SDA) Regs
18 *Johnson v Chief Adjudication Officer*
    (Case C31/90 ECJ ll July 1991);
    CS/111/1989
19 *Johnson v Chief Adjudication Officer
    (No. 2)* (Case C410/92 ECJ)
20 Reg 19(1) and Sch 4 para 2 SS(C&P)
    Regs
21 Reg 6 SS(SDA) Regs
22 Reg 9 SS(SDA) Regs

Chapter 4: Maternity pay and benefits

I Statutory maternity pay
(pp70-75)
1   s164 SSCBA 1992
2   s164(2)(a) SSCBA 1992
3   s171(1) SSCBA 1992
4   s166(1) SSCBA 1992
5   s166(2) and (4) SSCBA 1992
6   s166(8) SSCBA 1992
7   s166(2) SSCBA 1992
8   s166(5) SSCBA 1992
9   Reg 6 SMP Regs as amended

10 s4(1)(a)(ii) SSCBA 1992
11 Sch 13 para 1 SSCBA 1992
12 Sch 13 para 2 SSCBA 1992
13 Reg 27 SMP Regs
14 s165(1) SSCBA 1992
15 s165(2) and (3) SSCBA 1992
16 Reg 2(1) SMP Regs
17 Reg 2(2) SMP Regs
18 s165(6) SSCBA 1992; reg 8(2) SMP
    Regs
19 Reg 8(1) SMP Regs
20 s171(1) SSCBA 1992; reg 17 SMP Regs
21 s171(1) SSCBA 1992
22 s164(6) and (7) SSCBA 1992
23 s164(8) SSCBA 1992; reg 3 SMP Regs
24 Reg 9 SMP Regs
25 s57(2) SSCBA 1992
26 s164(4) SSCBA 1992
27 Reg 22(3) SMP Regs; reg 2 SMP(ME)
    Regs
28 s164(4)(b) SSCBA 1992
29 s15(1)(b) SSAA 1992; reg 24 SMP Regs
30 Regs 25 and 32 SMP Regs
31 Regs 22(4) and 23(3) SMP Regs
32 s15(2) SSAA 1992
33 Reg 7 SMP Regs
34 s164(2)(b) SSCBA 1992
35 Reg 21 SMP Regs
36 Reg 20 SMP Regs
37 s164(2)(a) SSCBA 1992
38 Reg 11(1) SMP Regs
39 Reg 13 SMP Regs
40 Reg 14 SMP Regs
41 Regs 2(3) and 23(2) SMP Regs
42 s171(1) SSCBA 1992; s2 SB(D)A 1992

2 Maternity allowance
(pp75-77)
1   s35 SSCBA 1992
2   Reg 2(1)(a) SS(MA) Regs
3   s35(1) and Sch 4 para 4 SSCBA 1992
4   s35(1)(d) SSCBA 1992
5   s57(2) SSCBA 1992
6   s35(2) SSCBA 1992
7   Reg 2(3) SS(ME) Regs
8   Reg 14 SS(C&P) Regs

Chapter 5: Widows' benefits

I Introduction
(pp78-83)
1   R(G) 1/80
2   R(G) 2/63
3   R(G) 1/73
4   Reg 2(1) SSFA(PM) Regs
5   ss37(3) and 38(2) SSCBA 1992

6 R(G) 1/53
7 R(G) 3/81
8 R(G) 3/71
9 R(G) 2/64
10 *Robson v Supplementary Benefits Commission* [1982] 3 FLR 232 (QBD)
11 CI/142/1949; R(I) 14/51
12 Sch 7 para 20 SSCBA 1992
13 Sch 7 para 21 SSCBA 1992
14 s4(1) FA 1982
15 s5 FA 1982; R(G) 1/90
16 s4(1C) FA 1982 as amended
17 R(G) 2/90
18 s4(1E) FA 1982 as amended
19 Reg 28(2) SSCP Regs
20 s617 ICTA 1988
21 Reg 3 SS(OB) Regs
22 Reg 40 IS Regs
23 Reg 8 and Sch 1 para 13 IS Regs
24 Reg 17(1)(d), Sch 2 paras 8 and 15(1) IS Regs; reg 2(4)(a) and (5)(a)(ii) CB&SS(FAR) Regs
25 Reg 9(2)(d) SFM&FE Regs as amended
26 s3 SSAA 1992

2 Widow's payment
(p84)
1 s36 SSCBA 1992
2 Sch 4 SSCBA 1992
3 s36(2) SSCBA 1992

3 Widowed mother's allowance
(pp84-85)
1 ss37 and 60(2) and (3) SSCBA 1992; reg 16 SS(WB&RP) Regs
2 ss39, 44, 45, 46(2) and Sch 4 SSCBA 1992
3 s37(3) SSCBA 1992
4 s37(2) SSCBA 1992
5 Reg 16(2) SS(WB&RP) Regs

4 Widow's pension
(pp85-86)
1 ss38 and 60(2) and (3) SSCBA 1992
2 ss39, 44, 45, 46(2) and Sch 4 SSCBA 1992
3 s39(4) and (5) SSCBA 1992
4 s39(6) SSCBA 1992
5 s38(2) SSCBA 1992

5 Non-contributory widows' benefits
(pp86-87)
1 Regs 13(2) and 14(1) SS(WB&RP) Regs
2 Reg 14 SS(WB&RP) Regs

3 Reg 13 SS(WB&RP) Regs
4 Reg 4 SS(WB&RP) Amdt Regs 87

6 Industrial death benefit for widows
(pp87-88)
1 s106 and Sch 7 para 15(1) SSCBA 1992; reg 23 SS(GB) Regs
2 Sch 7 para 15(4) SSCBA 1992
3 Sch 4 para 10 and Sch 7 para 16(2) SSCBA 1992; reg 24 SS(GB) Regs
4 Sch 7 para 16(3) SSCBA 1992
5 Sch 7 paras 15(2) and (3) SSCBA 1992

Chapter 6: Retirement pensions

1 Introduction
(pp89-93)
1 s78(1), (2) and (7)-(9) SSCBA 1992; regs 9, 11 and 12 SS(WB&RP) Regs
2 s122(1) SSCBA 1992
3 Reg 19 and Sch 4 SS(C&P) Regs
4 Reg 15 SS(C&P) Regs
5 Sch 5 paras 1 and 2 SSCBA 1992
6 Sch 2 SS(GRB) No 2 Regs
7 Sch 5 para 2(5) SSCBA 1992
8 Sch 5 para 4 SSCBA 1992
9 s28(4) SSA 1975 as originally enacted
10 Reg 4(1)(b) SS(WB&RP) Regs
11 Reg 4(1)(a) SS(WB&RP) Regs
12 *Chief Adjudication Officer v Pearse*, *The Times*, 18 June 1992
13 Reg 2 SS(WB&RP) Amdt Regs 92
14 Reg 2(3) SS(WB&RP) Regs
15 s54 SSCBA 1992; reg 2(3) SS(WB&RP) Regs
16 Reg 2(1) SS(WB&RP) Regs
17 Reg 2(2)(a) SS(WB&RP) Regs
18 s53(4) SSCBA 1992; reg 2(2)(b) SS(WB&RP) Regs
19 s617 ICTA 1988
20 Reg 40 and Sch 2 paras 9 and 10 IS Regs

2 Category A retirement pension
(pp93-95)
1 s44(1) SSCBA 1992
2 ss44(4) and 45 SSCBA 1992
3 ss34(3) and 47(1) SSCBA 1992
4 s47(2) SSCBA 1992
5 Reg 3 SS(C&P) Regs
6 s48 SSCBA 1992; reg 8 SS(WB&RP) Regs
7 Reg 8(2) and (3) SS(WB&RP) Regs
8 Reg 8(2) and (4) SS(WB&RP) Regs

9   Sch 1 SS(WB&RP) Regs
10 s48(3) SSCBA 1992
11 s48(2) SSCBA 1992
12 Sch 7 SSA 1975 as preserved by Sch 1 para 20 SSA 1979
13 s48 SSCBA 1992; reg 8(1)(a) SS(WB&RP) Regs
14 s48 SSCBA 1992; reg 8(1)(c) SS(WB&RP) Regs
15 s48(2) SSCBA 1992
16 s52 SSCBA 1992

3   Category B retirement pension for a married woman
(p96)

1   s49(1), (2) and (3) SSCBA 1992
2   s50(1)(a)(i) and Sch 4 SSCBA 1992

4   Category B retirement pension for a widow
(pp96-97)

1   ss49(4), 60(2) and (3) SSCBA 1992
2   s49(5)(a) SSCBA 1992; reg 7 SS(WB&RP) Regs
3   ss44, 45, 50(1)(a)(ii), (3) and (4) SSCBA 1992
4   ss38, 39(4), 49(5) and 50(1)(c) SSCBA 1992
5   Reg 7 SS(WB&RP) Regs
6   s49(7) SSCBA 1992

5   Category B retirement pension for a widower
(p98)

1   s51 SSCBA 1992
2   ss44, 45 and 51(2) SSCBA 1992
3   s51(4) SSCBA 1992

6   Category D retirement pension
(pp98-99)

1   s78(3) SSCBA 1992; reg 10 SS(WB&RP) Regs
2   s78(6) and Sch 4 para 7 SSCBA 1992
3   Reg 3(b) SS(C&P) Regs

7   Graduated retirement benefit
(p99)

1   s36 NIA 1965 as kept in force by Sch 1 SS(GRB) No 2 Regs; Art 7(1) SSBU(No 2)O 1991
2   s37 NIA 1965 as kept in force by Sch 1 SS(GRB) No 2 Regs
3   s36(4) NIA 1965 as kept in force by Sch 1 SS(GRB) No 2 Regs
4   Dir 79/7 EEC

5   *Clarke v Chief Adjudication Officer* [1987] ECR 2865 (ECJ)

Chapter 7:   Benefits for severely disabled people

2   Disability living allowance mobility component
(pp101-108)

1   s73 SSCBA 1992
2   s73(1)(d) SSCBA 1992
3   Reg 4 SS(DLA) Regs
4   s73(4) SSCBA 1992
5   Reg 3(1)(a) SS(DLA) Regs
6   Reg 12(1)(a) SS(DLA) Regs
7   Reg 12(4) SS(DLA) Regs
8   R(M) 2/89
9   CM/208/1989
10 CM/47/1986
11 R(M) 1/83
12 R(M) 1/81
13 R(M) 3/78
14 CM/23/1985
15 R(M) 3/78
16 Reg 12(1)(b) SS(DLA) Regs
17 Reg 12(2) SS(DLA) Regs
18 Reg 12(3) SS(DLA) Regs
19 Sch 2 SS(GB) Regs
20 Reg 34(2) SS(IIPD) Regs as amended
21 s73(3) SSCBA 1992; reg 12(6) SS(DLA) Regs
22 R(M) 3/86
23 CM/5/1986
24 s73(12) SSCBA 1992
25 Reg 42 SS(C&P) Regs
26 Reg 42(4) SS(C&P) Regs
27 Reg 6 MA(VSB) Regs

3   Disability living allowance care component
(pp108-114)

1   s72 SSCBA 1992
2   Reg 4 SS(DLA) Regs
3   s72(6) SSCBA 1992
4   s75 SSCBA 1992; reg 3 SS(DLA) Regs
5   s72(1)(a)(ii) SSCBA 1992
6   s72(6)(a) SSCBA 1992
7   House of Lords debates, *Hansard*, 7 March 1991, col 1554
8   s72(1) SSCBA 1992
9   *R v National Insurance Commissioner ex parte Secretary of State for Social Services* [1981] 1 WLR 1017 (CA), also reported as an appendix to R(A) 2/80
10 R(A) 1/87

11 *R v Social Security Commissioner ex parte Butler* (unreported), February 1984
12 R(A) 3/86
13 House of Lords debates, *Hansard*, 25 March 1991, col 884
14 R(A) 3/78
15 R(A) 1/83
16 R(A) 2/89
17 CA/15/1979 approved in R(A) 1/83
18 CA/33/1984
19 R(A) 3/89
20 R(A) 1/73
21 R(A) 2/75
22 *Moran v Secretary of State for Social Services reported as an appendix to R(A) 1/88*
23 *R(A) 5/81*
24 *R v National Insurance Commissioner ex parte Secretary of State for Social Services* [1974] 1 WLR 1290 (DC), also reported as an appendix to R(A) 4/74
25 R(A) 1/78
26 R(A) 3/74
27 R(A) 2/75
28 CA/86/1987
29 Reg 7 SS(DLA) Regs
30 s72(5) SSCBA 1992
31 s66(2) SSCBA 1992
32 s66(2)(b) SSCBA 1992

4   Attendance allowance
(pp114-115)
1 s64 SSCBA 1992
2 Sch 4 SSA 1975 as amended
3 Reg 5 SS(AA) Regs
4 s66(1) SSCBA 1992

5   Matters common to disability living allowance and attendance allowance
(pp115-124)
1 s617 ICTA 1988
2 Regs 6, 7 and 8 SS(AA) Regs; regs 8, 9 and 10 SS(DLA) Regs
3 Regs 8 and 9 SS(DLA) Regs; regs 6 and 7 SS(AA) Regs
4 Reg 10 SS(DLA) Regs; reg 8 SS(AA) Regs
5 Regs 9 and 10 DLA Regs (unamended); regs 7 and 8 AA Regs (unamended)
6 Reg 10 SS(DLA) Regs; reg 8 SS(AA) Regs
7 s21(3) SSAA 1992
8 Reg 6(8) SS(C&P) Regs
9 s1(3) SSAA 1992

10 Regs 6 and 11 SS(DLA) Regs; reg 3 SS(AA) Regs
11 Reg 16(1) SS(IDLA) Regs
12 s54(2) SSAA 1992
13 s54(1) SSAA 1992
14 s54(6) SSAA 1992
15 s71(3) SSCBA 1992
16 Reg 11 SS(IDLA) Regs
17 Reg 13 SS(IDLA) Regs
18 Reg 43 SS(C&P) Regs
19 s30(1) SSAA 1992
20 Reg 26A SS(Adj) Regs
21 s30(2) SSAA 1992
22 s31(3)(c) SSAA 1992
23 ss32(2) and 3 SSAA 1992
24 s32(4) SSAA 1992

Chapter 8:   Invalid care allowance

I   Introduction
(pp125-128)
1 s70 SSCBA 1992
2 Reg 19(2) and (6) SS(C&P) Regs
3 Sch 1 SS(C&P) Regs
4 R(A) 3/81
5 Sch 4 SSCBA 1992
6 s617 ICTA 1988
7 Reg 10 SS(OB) Regs
8 Reg 8 and Sch 1 para 4(a) IS Regs
9 Reg 8 and Sch 1 para 4(b) IS Regs
10 Sch 2 para 14ZA IS Regs; Sch 2 para 14ZA HB Regs; Sch 1 para 16 CTB Regs
11 Sch 2 paras 13(2)(a)(iii) and (b) and 14ZA IS Regs and HB Regs; Sch 1 paras 14(2)(a)(iii) and (b) and 16 CTB Regs
12 Reg 40 IS Regs; reg 33 HB Regs; reg 24 CTB Regs
13 Reg 4(1) SS(ICA) Regs
14 CG/6/1990
15 R(G) 3/91
16 Reg 4(2) SS(ICA) Regs
17 Reg 8 SS(ICA) Regs
18 Reg 5 SS(ICA) Regs
19 s70(5) SSCBA 1992; reg 10 SS(ICA) Regs
20 Dir 79/7 EEC; *Secretary of State for Social Security v Thomas, The Times*, 22 August 1990 (CA)
21 Reg 11 SS(ICA) Regs

Chapter 9: Industrial injuries benefits

2 Industrial accidents and diseases
(pp130-139)
1 CI/257/1949; CI/159/1950
2 R(I) 22/59
3 R(I) 1/76
4 R(I) 8/81
5 R(I) 1/82
6 R(I) 7/56
7 s94(1) SSCBA 1992
8 *Fenton v Thorley* [1903] AC 443 (HL)
9 *Jones v Secretary of State for Social Services* [1972] AC 944 (HL), also reported as an appendix to R(I) 3/69
10 *Trim Joint District School Board of Management v Kelly* [1914] AC 667 (HL)
11 *Roberts v Dorothea Slate Quarries Co. Ltd* [1948] 2 All ER 201 (HL)
12 R(I) 24/54; R(I) 43/55
13 R(I) 43/61; R(I) 4/62
14 R(I) 18/54
15 CI/159/1950
16 *Moore v Manchester Liners Ltd* [1910] AC 498 at p500 (HL)
17 *R v National Insurance Commissioner ex parte East* [1976] ICR 206 (DC), also reported as an appendix to R(I) 16/75
18 R(I) 1/59
19 *R v Industrial Injuries Commissioner ex parte AEU* [1966] 2 QB 31 (CA), also reported as an appendix to R(I) 4/66
20 R(I) 10/81
21 *R v National Insurance Commissioner ex parte Reed* (DC), also reported as an appendix to R(I) 7/80
22 s94(3) SSCBA 1992
23 *R v Industrial Injuries Commissioner ex parte AEU* [1966] 2 QB 31 (CA), also reported as an appendix to R(I) 4/66
24 R(I) 46/53
25 R(I) 17/63
26 *R v Industrial Injuries Commissioner ex parte AEU* [1966] 2 QB 31 (CA), also reported as an appendix to R(I) 4/66
27 s98 SSCBA 1992
28 s99 SSCBA 1992
29 R(I) 1/88
30 R(I) 12/75
31 R(I) 4/70
32 *Nancollas v Insurance Officer* [1985] 1 All ER 833 (CA), also reported as an appendix to R(I) 7/85
33 ibid
34 R(I) 6/82
35 R(I) 12/52
36 s101 SSCBA 1992
37 s100 SSCBA 1992
38 R(I) 6/63
39 ss108(1) and 109(1) SSCBA 1992; reg 2 SS(IIPD) Regs
40 Reg 3 SS(IIPD) Regs
41 R(I) 3/90
42 CI/202/1990
43 Reg 2(c) SS(IIPD) Regs
44 Reg 4 SS(IIPD) Regs
45 Reg 6(2)(c) SS(IIPD) Regs
46 Reg 7 SS(IIPD) Regs
47 s45(1)(a) and (b) SSCBA 1992
48 *Jones v Secretary of State for Social Services* [1972] AC 944 at p1009 (HL), also reported as an appendix to R(I) 3/69
49 s60(3) SSAA 1992
50 s103(2) and (3) SSCBA 1992; regs 15A and 15B SS(IIPD) Regs as amended
51 s103(3) SSCBA 1992
52 Sch 2 SS(GB) Regs; Sch 3 SS(IIPD) Regs
53 Reg 11(6) SS(GB) Regs
54 Sch 6 para 1 SSCBA 1992
55 Reg 11(8) SS(GB) Regs
56 Reg 11(3) SS(GB) Regs
57 Reg 11(7) SS(GB) Regs
58 Reg 11(4) SS(GB) Regs
59 Reg 21 SS(IIPD) Regs
60 Reg 22 SS(IIPD) Regs
61 Sch 6 para 6 SSCBA 1992
62 Sch 6 para 7 SSCBA 1992
63 s45(3) SSAA 1992
64 Reg 29(a) SS(IIPD) Regs
65 Regs 29(b) and 34(b) SS(IIPD) Regs
66 ss94(1) and 108(1) SSCBA 1992
67 s2(1) SSCBA 1992
68 Reg 10(6)(c) SSB(PA) Regs as amended
69 Regs 2, 4 and 6 SS(EEEIIP) Regs
70 Reg 3 SS(EEEIIP) Regs

3 Disablement benefit
(pp139-143)
1 Sch 4 SSCBA 1992
2 s103(1) amd Sch 7 para 9(1) SSCBA 1992
3 Reg 20(1) SS(IIPD) Regs
4 Sch 7 para 9(1)(a) SSCBA 1992; regs 12 and 14 SS(II&D)MP Regs
5 Sch 7 para 9(1) and (2) SSCBA 1992; reg 14 SS(GB) Regs
6 Reg 7(5) and (6) SS(II&D)MP Regs
7 s617 ICTA 1988
8 s104 SSCBA 1992
9 Reg 20 SS(GB) Regs
10 Sch 4 SSCBA 1992; reg 19(b) SS(GB) Regs

11 Sch 4 SSCBA 1992; reg 19(a) SS(GB) Regs
12 s105 SSCBA 1992
13 Sch 7 para 1 SSCBA 1992; reg 11 SS(II&D)MP Regs; SSA86(Comm 5)O
14 Sch 7 para 10(1) SSCBA 1992; SSA86(Comm 5)O
15 Reg 19 and Sch 4 SS(C&P) Regs
16 Regs 25(2) and 36 SS(IIPD) Regs
17 *McKiernon v Chief Adjudication Officer, The Times*, 1 November 1989
18 Sch 6 para 4(3) SSA 1990 (not consolidated)
19 CI/532/1989; CI/278/1991
20 s47(1) SSAA 1992; reg 29(1)(a) SS(Adj) Regs
21 s47(4) SSAA 1992; reg 29(1)(a) SS(Adj) Regs
22 s47(6) SSAA 1992
23 s47(7) SSAA 1992; reg 34 SS(Adj) Regs
24 Reg 48 SS(Adj) Regs
25 Reg 68 SS(Adj) Regs
26 s47(9) SSAA 1992
27 Reg 40 SS(GB) Regs

4 Reduced earnings allowance
(pp143-147)
1 Sch 7 paras 11 and 12(1), (2) and (7) SSCBA 1992
2 Reg 23(a) SS(IIPD) Regs
3 Reg 40 SS(GB) Regs; R(I) 2/86
4 Reg 17 SS(GB) Regs as amended
5 Reg 23(b) SS(IIPD) Regs as amended
6 *R v National Insurance Commissioner ex parte Mellors* [1971] 2 QB 401 (CA), also reported as an appendix to R(I) 7/69
7 R(I) 28/51
8 R(I) 65/54
9 CI/80/1949
10 Reg 2 SS(II&D)MP Regs
11 Reg 17 SS(IIPD) Regs
12 *R v Deputy Industrial Injuries Commissioner ex parte Humphreys* [1966] 2 QB 1 (CA), also reported as an appendix to R(I) 2/66
13 R(I) 22/61
14 Sch 7 Part IV para 11(4)-(7) SSCBA 1992
15 R(I) 3/83
16 Reg 2 SS(IIRE) Regs
17 Sch 7 para 11(10) SSCBA 1992
18 Sch 7 para 11(14) SSCBA 1992
19 R(I) 8/67
20 Sch 7 para 11(10) SSCBA 1992
21 Sch 7 para 11(10) SSCBA 1992
22 Sch 7 para 11(11) SSCBA 1992
23 Sch 7 para 12(6) SSCBA 1992
24 R(G) 4/68

5 Retirement allowance
(p148)
1 Sch 7 para 13 SSCBA 1992
2 Sch 7 para 13(4) SSCBA 1992

6 Industrial death benefit
(pp148-149)
1 Sch 7 paras 14(1) and 17 SSCBA 1992
2 Sch 7 para 17 SSCBA 1992

Chapter 10: Benefits for children

I Child benefit
(pp150-155)
1 ss141 and 146 SSCBA 1992
2 Reg 2(1) CB&SS(FAR) Regs as amended
3 s142(1) SSCBA 1992
4 Reg 5 CB Regs as amended
5 Reg 6(1) CB Regs
6 Regs 1(2) and 7A CB Regs as amended
7 Regs 7B and 7C CB Regs
8 Reg 7(4) CB Regs as amended
9 Reg 7D(1) CB Regs as amended
10 Reg 7D(2) CB Regs as amended
11 Reg 7D(1)(e) CB Regs as amended
12 Sch 9 para 1 SSCBA 1992; reg 16(6)(a) CB Regs
13 Reg 16(6)(b) and (7) CB Regs
14 s147(1) SSCBA 1992
15 R(F) 3/85
16 R(F) 1/81
17 Reg 16(8), (9) and (10) CB Regs; reg 8 CB(Amdt) Regs
18 Sch 9 para 3 SSCBA 1992
19 Reg 10 CB Regs
20 Regs 1(2), 7(3) and 7D(1)(b) CB Regs as amended
21 Sch 9 para 5 SSCBA 1992; reg 7C CB Regs as amended
22 Reg 7B CB Regs
23 Sch 9 para 1(1)(a) SSCBA 1992; reg 16 CB Regs
24 R(F) 2/81
25 R(F) 2/79
26 s143(2) SSCBA 1992
27 s143(3)(a) SSCBA 1992
28 s143(3)(b) and (c) SSCBA 1992; reg 4 CB Regs
29 s143(4) SSCBA 1992
30 s143(1)(b) SSCBA 1992
31 R(U) 14/62

32 R(U) 3/66
33 Reg 2(3) CB Regs
34 Reg 2(1) CB Regs
35 s13(1) SSAA 1992
36 Sch 10 para 1(2) SSCBA 1992
37 Sch 10 SSCBA 1992
38 s147(3) SSCBA 1992
39 Reg 14 CB Regs
40 Reg 11(1) and (2) CB Regs as amended
41 *Grove v Insurance Officer* reported as
    an appendix to R(F) 4/85
42 Reg 11(3) CB Regs
43 Reg 19(6)(a) SS(C&P) Regs
44 Sch 10 para 1(2) SSCBA 1992
45 Reg 13 SS(C&P) Regs
46 Reg 7 SS(C&P) Regs
47 Reg 23(1)(b) SS(C&P) Regs
48 Sch 8 para 1(a) SS(C&P) Regs
49 Sch 8 paras 1(b), 3 and 4 SS(C&P) Regs
50 Sch 8 para 2(a) SS(C&P) Regs
51 Sch 8 para 2(b) SS(C&P) Regs
52 Reg 23(3) SS(C&P) Regs
53 s617 ICTA 1988
54 Reg 40 IS Regs

2   One parent benefit
(p156)
1 Reg 2(2) and (2A) CB&SS(FAR) Regs;
   R(F) 4/85
2 Reg 2(2) CB&SS(FAR) Regs as
   amended
3 s617 ICTA 1988
4 Reg 40 IS Regs
5 Reg 2(4)(a) and (5) CB&SS(FAR) Regs
6 Reg 8 SS(OB) Regs

3   Guardian's allowance
(pp156-158)
1 s77 SSCBA 1992
2 Sch 4 SSCBA 1992
3 s617 ICTA 1988
4 Reg 40 IS Regs
5 Reg 7(4) SS(OB) Regs
6 Reg 19(6)(a) SS(C&P) Regs
7 s77(2) SSCBA 1992
8 R(G) 11/52
9 R(G) 6/52
10 Reg 2 SS(GA) Regs
11 CWG/3/1978
12 s77(10) and (11) SSCBA 1992
13 Reg 3 SS(GA) Regs
14 s77(10) SSCBA 1992; reg 4 SS(GA)
    Regs
15 Reg 5 SS(GA) Regs

4   Child's special allowance
(p158)
1 s56(6) SSCBA 1992
2 ss56(1) and (2), 80(6) and 81 SSCBA
   1992
3 Sch 4 SSCBA 1992

5   Industrial death benefit for children
(p159)
1 Sch 7 paras 14(1) and 18 SSCBA 1992;
   reg 32 SS(GB) Regs
2 *Insurance Officer v McCaffrey* [1984] 1
   WLR 1353 (HL); Sch 7 para 15(1)
   SSCBA 1992
3 Reg 33 SS(GB) Regs
4 Sch 4 Part V, para 12 SSCBA 1992

Chapter 11:   Increases for dependants

2   Extra money for your wife
(p161)
1 ss23, 82 and 83 SSCBA 1992; regs 8,
   12 and Sch 2 SSB(Dep) Regs
2 Reg 19(6) SS(C&P) Regs
3 Sch 4 SSCBA 1992; SSBUO 1993

3   Extra money for your husband
(p162)
1 ss23 and 84 SSCBA 1992
2 R(P) 3/88
3 *Secretary of State for Social Security v
   Thomas, The Times*, 22 August 1990
   (CA)

4   Extra money if you are not married
(pp162-163)
1 s82(4) SSCBA 1992; reg 10 and Sch 2
   SSB(Dep) Regs as amended
2 Reg 19(6) SS(C&P) Regs
3 Reg 10(2)(f) SSB(Dep) Regs as amended
4 Sch 4 SSCBA 1992; SSBUO 1993

5   Extra money for your children
(pp163-164)
1 ss80 and 81 SSCBA 1992
2 Reg 19(6) SS(C&P) Regs
3 Sch 4 SSCBA 1992; SSBUO 1993
4 Reg 4A SS(C&P) Regs

6 Residence and maintenance
(pp165-166)
1 Reg 2(4) SSB(PRT) Regs
2 Reg 2(2) SSB(PRT) Regs
3 R(S) 3/74
4 R(U) 3/66
5 Reg 3 SSB(Dep) Regs
6 R(U) 25/58
7 R(S) 3/74
8 R(U) 14/62
9 R(S) 1/59
10 Reg 3 SSB(Dep) Amdt Regs
11 R(I) 20/60; R(S) 12/83
12 R(S) 2/85
13 Reg 2 SSB(Dep) Regs
14 CS/130/1987
15 Reg 2(1) SSB(Dep) Regs
16 Reg 2(2) SSB(Dep) Regs
17 Reg 2(2)(i) and (ii) SSB(Dep) Regs

7 The earnings rules
(pp166-168)
1 Regs 8(2) and 12 SSB(Dep) Regs
2 Regs 8(6) SSB(Dep) Regs; s45(3) SSA
   1975 (as it existed immediately prior to
   its repeal by s29(2) and Sch 6 SSA
   1985)
3 ss82 and 83(2)(b) SSCBA 1992; regs
   8(4) and 12 and Sch 2 para 7 SSB(Dep)
   Regs
4 s92 and Sch 7 para 8 SSCBA 1992
5 *Cottingham and Geary v Secretary of
   State*, (CA), 2 December 1992; *see also*
   CP/7/1987
6 s80(4) SSCBA 1992; Sch 3 para 2B
   SSB(Dep) Regs as amended

8 Trade disputes
(p168)
1 s91 SSCBA 1992

9 Tax
(p168)
1 s617 ICTA 1988

Chapter 12: Contributions and earnings-related pensions

1 Introduction
(pp170-173)
1 s1(1) SSCBA 1992; s162 SSAA 1992
2 s1(2) SSCBA 1992
3 s21(1) and (2) SSCBA 1992
4 s2(1)(a) SSCBA 1992
5 s2(1)(b) SSCBA 1992

6 *Ready Mixed Concrete South East Ltd
   v Ministry of Pensions and National
   Insurance* [1968] 2 QB 497 (QBD);
   *Global Plant v Secretary of State for
   Health and Social Security* [1971] 3All
   ER 385 (QBD)
7 Sch 1 paras 1-5 SS(CatE) Regs
8 Sch 1 para 6 SS(CatE) Regs
9 Sch 1 paras 7-12 SS(CatE) Regs
10 s21(5)(d) SSCBA 1992
11 s5(1) SSCBA 1992
12 Sch 1 SS(EF) Regs as amended
13 s17(1)(b) SSAA 1992; and see generally
   Secretary of State v Scully,
   Independent, 22 June 1992 and
   Casenote *WRB 109* (August 1992), p10

2 Payment of contributions
(pp173-180)
1 ss6(1)(a) and 13(1) SSCBA 1992; reg 60
   SS(Con) Regs
2 s6(2) SSCBA 1992; reg 58 SS(Con)
   Regs
3 s2(1)(a) SSCBA 1992
4 Reg 119(1)(a) SS(Con) Regs
5 Reg 119(2) SS(Con) Regs
6 Reg 119(3) SS(Con) Regs
7 Reg 120 SS(Con) Regs
8 Reg 120(2)(b) SS(Con) Regs
9 s2(1)(b) SSCBA 1992; reg 119(1)(d)
   SS(Con) Regs
10 Reg 119(1)(c) SS(Con) Regs
11 Regs 121 and 122 SS(Con) Regs
12 Reg 123A SS(Con) Regs
13 Regs 119(1)(e), 120(2)(b), 121 and 122
   SS(Con) Regs
14 Reg 58(b) SS(Con) Regs
15 Reg 100 SS(Con) Regs
16 s22(4) SSCBA 1992; regs 5(2), 7(3),
   7A(2)(b), 8(2)(b) and 9(6) SS(Cr) Regs
   as amended
17 Reg 103 SS(Con) Regs
18 Reg 101(1) SS(Con) Regs as
   amended
19 ss6 and 7 SSCBA 1992
20 Regs 8(2) and 8A(2) SS(Con) Regs
21 s8(1) and (2) SSCBA 1992
22 s27 SSPA 1975 as amended (not
   consolidated); para 2(a) SS(C1CCP)O
23 s3 SSA 1986 (not consolidated)
24 s3 SSPA 1975 as amended (not
   consolidated); reg 104 SS(Con) Regs
25 Regs 89 and 115 SS(Con) Regs as
   amended
26 Regs 10, 11, 12, 12A and 17 SS(Con)
   Regs as amended
27 s9(2), (3) and (4) SSCBA 1992

28 s27(2) SSPA 1975 (not consolidated); para 2(b) SS(C1CCP)O
29 Sch 1 para 3 SSCBA 1992
30 s1(2) SSCBA 1992
31 s11 SSCBA 1992
32 s11(5) SSCBA 1992
33 Reg 25 SS(Con) Regs
34 Reg 26 SS(Con) Regs
35 s11(1) SSCBA 1992 as amended
36 Regs 98 and 123A-F SS(Con) Regs; reg 2 SS(Con) Amdt 4 Regs; reg 13B SSB(PA) Regs as amended
37 Reg 17 SS(Con) Regs as amended
38 Reg 26A SS(Con) Regs as amended
39 s13 SSCBA 1992
40 s14 SSCBA 1992
41 Reg 34 SS(Con) Regs
42 s13(1) SSCBA 1992 as amended
43 s15(1) and (3) SSCBA 1992
44 Regs 62-66 SS(Con) Regs as amended
45 Reg 67 SS(Con) Regs as amended
46 s114 SSAA 1992
47 Reg 39 SS(Con) Regs
48 Reg 54(2) SS(Con) Regs
49 Reg 38 SS(Con) Regs
50 Reg 27(3)(b) SS(Con) Regs as amended
51 Reg 38(5) and (6) SS(Con) Regs as amended
52 Reg 43 SS(Con) Regs

3 Credits and home responsibility
(pp180-184)

1 Reg 3 SS(Cr) Regs as amended
2 Regs 5(2), 7(3), 7A(2)(b), 8(2)(b), 9B(3) and 9C(3) SS(Cr) Regs as amended
3 Reg 9(1) SS(Cr) Regs as amended
4 Reg 9(9) SS(Cr) Regs as amended
5 Reg 7A SS(Cr) Regs as amended
6 Reg 4 SS(Cr) Regs
7 Reg 8 SS(Cr) Regs
8 Reg 7 SS(Cr) Regs
9 Reg 9C SS(Cr) Regs as amended
10 Reg 9B SS(Cr) Regs as amended
11 Reg 3(1)(b) SSB(MW&WSP) Regs
12 Reg 3(1)(a) SSB(MW&WSP) Regs
13 Equal Opportunities Commission v Secretary of State for Social Security, ECJ Case No C9/91, reported at [1992] 3 CMLR 233
14 Reg 9A SS(Cr) Regs as amended
15 Reg 2(2) SSP(HR&MA) Regs as amended
16 Reg 2(4) SSP(HR&MA) Regs
17 Sch 3 para 5(7) SSCBA 1992
18 Sch 3 para 5(7)(a) SSCBA 1992

4 Contribution conditions for benefit
(pp185-188)

1 s21 and Sch 3 paras 1 and 2 SSCBA 1992
2 s21(1) and (2) SSCBA 1992
3 s21(6) SSCBA 1992
4 Sch 3 paras 1(6) and 2(6) SSCBA 1992
5 Reg 3(1) SSB(MW&WSP) Regs as amended
6 Reg 15 SS(STB)(T) Regs
7 s21 and Sch 3 paras 1 and 2 SSCBA 1992
8 Reg 7(1)(b) and (c) SS(US&IB) Regs
9 CS/174/1949; R(U) 13/80
10 Sch 3 para 3 SSCBA 1992
11 Sch 3 para 4 SSCBA 1992
12 Sch 3 para 7 SSCBA 1992
13 Reg 13(1) SS(STB)(T) Regs
14 Sch 3 para 5 SSCBA 1992
15 Sch 3 para 5(8) SSCBA 1992
16 Reg 6 SS(WBRP&OB)(T) Regs
17 Sch 3 para 5 SSCBA 1992
18 Sch 3 para 5(8) SSCBA 1992
19 Reg 7(7) SS(WBRP&OB)(T) Regs
20 Sch 3 para 5(5) SSCBA 1992
21 Reg 7(7) SS(WBRP&OB)(T) Regs
22 Reg 6 SS(WB&RP) Regs
23 s60(4)-(6) SSCBA 1992; regs 13 and 14 SSB(Dep) Regs as amended; reg 6(2) SS(WB&RP) Regs

5 The State Earnings Related Pension Scheme (SERPS)
(pp188-191)

1 s54 SSCBA 1992
2 s27 SSPA 1975 as amended
3 s29 SSPA 1975 as amended
4 s15 SSA 1986
5 s7 SSA 1986
6 ss1 and 2 SSA 1986
7 s3(1)(a) SSA 1986
8 s3(1)(aa) SSA 1986 inserted by s1(a) SSA 1993
9 s4 SSA 1986
10 s3(1)(b) SSA 1986
11 ss18 and 19 SSA 1986
12 ss33, 44 and 45 SSCBA 1992
13 ss50 and 51 SSCBA 1992
14 Art 2 SSREFO
15 s45(1) SSCBA 1992
16 Art 4(3) SSBU(No 2)O 1991

Chapter 13:   Residence conditions and going abroad

2   Residence and presence conditions
(pp193-196)

1   Reg 3(1) SS(SDA) Regs; regs 2 and 3 SS(SDA) Amdt Regs
2   Reg 3(3) SS(SDA) Regs
3   Reg 2(1) SS(AA) Regs; reg 2(1) SS(DLA) Regs; reg 9(1) SS(ICA) Regs
4   Reg 2(4) SS(DLA) Regs
5   Reg 2(5) SS(DLA) Regs
6   Reg 2(2)(d) and (e) SS(AA) Regs; reg 2(2)(d) and (e) SS(DLA) Regs
7   Reg 9(2) SS(ICA) Regs
8   Reg 9 SS(WB&RP) Regs
9   Regs 11(1)(d) and (e), 13(1) and 14(1) SS(WB&RP) Regs
10 Reg 10 SS(WB&RP) Regs
11 s146(2)(a) SSCBA 1992
12 Reg 2(2) CB(RPA) Regs
13 Reg 2(3) CB(RPA) Regs
14 s146(3)(a) SSCBA 1992
15 Reg 4 CB(RPA) Regs as amended
16 s146(2)(b) and (3)(b) SSCBA 1992
17 Regs 3 and 5 CB(RPA) Regs
18 Reg 5(2)(b) CB(RPA) Regs
19 Reg 5(2)(d)(i) CB(RPA) Regs
20 Reg 5(2)(d)(ii) CB(RPA) Regs
21 Reg 3(2)(b) CB(RPA) Regs
22 Reg 6(1) SS(GA) Regs as amended
23 R(S) 1/66
24 R(S) 1/66
25 Reg 2(2) SS(AA) Regs; Reg 2(2) SS(DLA) Regs; Reg 6(2) SS(GA) Regs; Reg 9(3) SS(ICA) Regs; Reg 3(2) SS(SDA) Regs
26 Reg 11 SSB(PA) Regs as amended
27 R(P) 1/78
28 R(G) 2/51
29 CG/204/1949
30 R(P) 1/78
31 R(G) 2/51

3   Absence from Great Britain
(pp197-198)

1   ss113(1)(a) and 146 SSCBA 1992
2   Reg 2 SS(AB) Regs; reg 4 SS(MB) Regs; reg 4 SSB(MF) Regs; reg 11 SSB(PA) Regs
3   Reg 2 SSB(PA) Regs as amended
4   *R v Social Security Commissioner ex parte Akbar, The Times,* 6 November 1991 disapproving R(S) 1/85
5   Reg 4 SSB(PA) Regs as amended

6   Reg 6 SSB(PA) Regs
7   Reg 4(2A) SSB(PA) Regs as amended
8   Regs 10, 10A and 10B SSB(PA) Regs as amended; regs 2 and 4 CB(RPA) Regs
9   Reg 9(3) SSB(PA) Regs as amended
10 Reg 9(4) SSB(PA) Regs
11 Reg 9(5) SSB(PA) Regs as amended
12 Reg 10C SSB(PA) Regs as amended
13 Reg 13 SSB(PA) Regs
14 Reg 13A SSB(PA) Regs

4   Northern Ireland, The Isle of Man and the Channel Islands
(pp198-199)

1   Reg 2 and Sch 1 SS(NIRA) Regs; Art 2 and Sch 1 SS(IoM)O
2   Sch 1 SS(J&G)O
3   Reg 12(1) SSB(PA) Regs

5   The European Community
(pp199-201)

1   Art 6 Reg 1408/71 EEC; R(U) 4/84
2   Art 2 Reg 1408/71 EEC; *Walsh v National Insurance Officer* [1980] ECR 1639 (ECJ); R(G) 3/83
3   Reg 1247/92 EEC
4   *Pinna* [1986] ECR 66 (ECJ)
5   *Ten Holder v Nieue Algemene Bedrijfsvereniging* [1986] ECR 1821 (ECJ)
6   *Petroni v Office National des Pensions pour Travailleurs Salaries* [1975] ECR 1149 (ECJ)
7   *Coppola v Insurance Officer* [1983] ECR 43 (ECJ); R(S) 13/83
8   CS/102/1977 reported as *re an Italian claimant* [1978] 2 CMLR 331
9   Art 10 Reg 1408/71 EEC
10 Art 69 Reg 1408/71 EEC
11 R(U) 5/78
12 Dir 79/7 EEC
13 *Secretary of State for Social Security v Thomas, The Times,* 22 August 1990 (CA)

Chapter 14:   Other general provisions

1   Periods of interruption of employment
(pp202-205)

1   s57(1)(d)(i) SSCBA 1992
2   s57(1)(d)(ii) SSCBA 1992
3   Reg 15 SS(US&IB) Regs
4   s57(1)(a)(i) SSCBA 1992; regs 7 and 7B SS(US&IB) Regs

5   Regs 7(1)(f) and 13(2)(a) SS(US&IB)
    Regs
6   Reg 13(2)(b) SS(US&IB) Regs; Sch 1
    para 14 IS Regs
7   Reg 14 SS(US&IB) Regs
8   s57(1)(a)(ii) SSCBA 1992; reg 7(1)(c)
    and (f) SS(US&IB) Regs
9   s57(2) SSCBA 1992
10 Reg 5(1)(a) SS(US&IB) Regs
11 Reg 5(1)(b) SS(US&IB) Regs
12 Reg 5(2) and (3) SS(US&IB) Regs
13 s57(1)(e) SSCBA 1992
14 Reg 4(1) SS(US&IB) Regs
15 Reg 4(3) SS(US&IB) Regs
16 s57(1)(d) SSCBA 1992
17 ss33(7) and 68(10) SSCBA 1992

2   Hospital in-patients
(pp205-207)
1   Reg 17(4) SS(HI) Regs; reg 6(2) SS(AA)
    Regs; reg 10(5) SS(DLA) Regs
2   Reg 2(3) SS(HI) Regs
3   Reg 5 SS(HI) Regs as amended
4   Regs 6 and 7 SS(HI) Regs as amended
5   Reg 16 SS(HI) Regs
6   Regs 8 and 10(1) and (2) SS(DLA) Regs
7   Regs 6 and 8(1) SS(AA) Regs
8   Reg 21 SS(GB) Regs
9   Sch 7 para 10 SSCBA 1992
10 Reg 11 SS(HI) Regs
11 Reg 13 SS(HI) Regs

3   People in legal custody
(pp207-208)
1   s113(1)(b) and Sch 9 para 1(a) SSCBA
    1992
2   Reg 2(2) and (8) SS(GB) Regs
3   R(S) 1/71
4   Reg 2(6) and (7) SS(GB) Regs
5   Reg 2(3) SS(GB) Regs
6   Reg 2(2) and (8) SS(GB) Regs
7   CS/541/1950
8   Reg 10(2)(d) and Sch 2 para 7(b)(ii)
    SSB(Dep) Regs as amended
9   s113(1)(b) SSCBA 1992 – Child benefit
    is not a 'benefit under Parts II to V' of
    that Act and therefore outside the scope
    of the disqualification.
10 Reg 2(5) SS(GB) Regs
11 Sch 9 para 1(a) SSCBA 1992; reg 16(6)
    CB Regs
12 Reg 16(2) CB Regs

4   Overlapping benefits
(pp208-211)
1   Reg 4(5) SS(OB) Regs
2   Reg 6 SS(OB) Regs

3   Reg 6 SS(OB) Regs
4   s43(1) SSCBA 1992
5   ss52(2) and 53(2) SSCBA 1992
6   ss16(1), (2) and (6) SSCBA 1992; reg 2
    SS(MAP) Regs as amended
7   Reg 3(2) SS(OB) Regs
8   Reg 3(3) SS(OB) Regs
9   s34(4) SSCBA 1992
10 s50(2) SSCBA 1992
11 Reg 4(3) SS(OB) Regs
12 Reg 4(4) SS(OB) Regs
13 Reg 6 SS(OB) Regs
14 Reg 9 SS(OB) Regs
15 Reg 10 SS(OB) Regs
16 Reg 8 SS(OB) Regs
17 Reg 2(4)(a) and (5) CB&SS(FAR) Regs
18 Reg 8 SS(OB) Regs
19 Reg 7 SS(OB) Regs

5   Calculating earnings
(pp211-212)
1   Reg 2 SS(CE) Regs
2   Reg 3 SS(CE) Regs
3   Reg 4 SS(CE) Regs

6   Christmas bonus
(p212)
1   ss148, 149 and 150 SSCBA 1992
2   s148(2) SSCBA 1992
3   s149(2) and (3) SSCBA 1992
4   Reg 38 SS(C&P) Regs

7   Recovery of benefits from
compensation payments
(pp213-214)
1   *Nabi v British Leyland (UK) Ltd* [1980]
    1 WLR 529 (CA)
2   Reg 9 EP(RUB&SB) Regs
3   s81 SSAA 1992
4   Reg 2 SS(R) Regs
5   s81(2) SSAA 1992
6   s81(3) SSAA 1992; regs 3 and 4 SS(R)
    Regs
7   s97 SSAA 1992
8   s98 SSAA 1992; reg 11 SS(R) Regs
9   *Hodgson v Trapp* [1989] AC 706 (HL)
10 s2(1) Law Reform (Personal Injuries)
    Act 1948 as amended
11 *Jackman v Corbett* [1988] QB 157 (CA)
12 s6 Fatal Accidents Act 1976

8   Deductions from benefit
(pp214-215)
1   Reg 15 SS(PAOR) Regs
2   Reg 16 SS(PAOR) Regs
3   Regs 15 and 16 SS(PAOR) Regs

4 Reg 105 HB Regs
5 s78(2) SSAA 1992; reg 3 SF(RDB) Regs

9 Criminal offences
(pp215-216)
1 s112 SSAA 1992
2 s116(2)(a) SSAA 1992
3 *Clear v Smith* [1981] 1 WLR 399 (DC)
4 *Barrass v Reeve* [1981] 1 WLR 408 (DC)
5 *Regina v Livingstone Stewart* [1987] 9 Crim App R(S) 135 (CA)
6 s114(4) SSAA 1992
7 s114(1) SSAA 1992
8 s54(1) SSA 1986; reg 132 SS(Con) Regs as amended
9 s111 SSAA 1992
10 s110(7) SSAA 1992

Chapter 15: Administration

1 Claims
(pp218-224)
1 s1 SSAA 1992
2 Reg 3 SS(C&P) Regs as amended
3 Reg 4 SS(C&P) Regs
4 R(SB) 3/89
5 Reg 4(6) SS(C&P) Regs
6 Reg 5 SS(C&P) Regs
7 Reg 4(7) SS(C&P) Regs
8 Reg 33 SS(C&P) Regs
9 Reg 8(1) SS(C&P) Regs
10 R(P) 1/85
11 Reg 8(2) SS(C&P) Regs
12 s180 SSAA 1992
13 s20(1) SSAA 1992
14 R(SB) 29/83
15 Reg 9(1) and Sch 1 SS(C&P) Regs
16 Reg 9(2), (3) and (6) and Sch 1 SS(C&P) Regs
17 Reg 9(4) and (5) SS(C&P) Regs
18 Regs 13-15 and 39 SS(C&P) Regs
19 Reg 17 SS(C&P) Regs
20 Reg 19 and Sch 4 SS(C&P) Regs
21 Sch 5 para 1 SS(C&P) Regs
22 ss65(4), (6) and 76 SSCBA 1992
23 Reg 4 SS(AA) Regs; reg 13(c)(i) SS(C&P) Regs
24 Reg 19(3) SS(C&P) Regs
25 Reg 19(2) SS(C&P) Regs
26 s1(2)(b) SSCBA 1992
27 Sch 3 para 2 SS(C&P) Regs
28 R(S) 10/59; R(S) 3/69; R(SB) 17/83
29 CS/371/1949
30 R(P) 1/79
31 R(I) 28/54

32 R(SB) 6/83
33 CS/50/1950
34 R(U) 9/74
35 R(U) 35/56
36 R(S) 5/56
37 R(S) 14/54; R(G) 4/68; R(U) 9/74
38 R(S) 14/54
39 R(S) 10/59; R(S) 11/59
40 R(S) 11/59; R(G) 1/75
41 R(SB) 6/83
42 R(I) 6/54
43 R(G) 2/74
44 CWG/6/1950
45 R(P) 1/85
46 Reg 19(2) SS(C&P) Regs

2 Decisions
(pp224-228)
1 s20 SSAA 1992
2 s38(1) SSAA 1992
3 s21(1) SSAA 1992
4 s74 SSAA 1992; regs 7-10 SS(PAOR) Regs
5 *Jones v Department of Employment* [1989] QB 1 (CA)
6 s21(2) SSAA 1992
7 s68 SSAA 1992
8 See *Legal Action*, October 1990, p21 for further discussion
9 ss68(4)(a) and 69(4)(a) SSAA 1992
10 CIS/787/1991
11 Regs 42 and 56 SS(Adj) Regs
12 Regs 43 and 57 SS(Adj) Regs
13 Reg 44 SS(Adj) Regs
14 Regs 45(2), 58(2) and Sch 2 SS(Adj) Regs
15 Reg 3(3) SS(Adj) Regs
16 Reg 19(2) SS(Adj) Regs
17 s17(1) SSAA 1992
18 Reg 21(1) SS(Adj) Regs
19 Reg 21(3) SS(Adj) Regs
20 s17(4) SSAA 1992; reg 15 SS(Adj) Regs
21 Reg 16(1) SS(Adj) Regs
22 s18(3) SSAA 1992; reg 16(2) SS(Adj) Regs
23 Regs 27 and 29(2) SS(Adj) Regs
24 s45 SSCBA 1992; reg 29(1) SS(Adj) Regs
25 Regs 29(1)(a), 50(1) and 62(1) SS(Adj) Regs
26 Reg 29(9) SS(Adj) Regs
27 Reg 30 SS(Adj) Regs

3 Reviews
(pp228-234)
1 s25(1), (2) and (3) SSAA 1992; reg 17(4) SS(C&P) Regs

2 R(M) 5/86
3 R(S) 6/78; R(M) 5/86
4 Reg 17(4) SS(C&P) Regs; R(S) 3/89
5 R(S) 3/89
6 s25(2) SSAA 1992
7 s69 SSAA 1992
8 Reg 65(1) SS(Adj) Regs
9 Reg 65(2) SS(Adj) Regs
10 Reg 64A SS(Adj) Regs
11 s28 SSAA 1992
12 Reg 19(2) SS(Adj) Regs
13 s19(1) SSAA 1992
14 s47(1) SSAA 1992; regs 29(1)(a), 50(1)
    and 62(1)(a) SS(Adj) Regs
15 Regs 50(1) and 67 SS(Adj) Regs
16 R(I) 16/57; R(P) 3/73
17 s47(4) SSAA 1992; reg 29(1)(a) SS(Adj)
    Regs
18 s47(7) SSAA 1992
19 s47(2) SSAA 1992; regs 29(1)(a) and
    62(1)(c) SS(Adj) Regs
20 R(M) 5/86
21 Reg 66(1) SS(Adj) Regs
22 Reg 68 SS(Adj) Regs
23 s47(9) SSAA 1992; regs 29(1)(a), 50(3)
    and 62(4) SS(Adj) Regs

4 Payments
(pp234-235)
1 Regs 22 and 23 SS(C&P) Regs
2 Reg 21 SS(C&P) Regs; reg 12
    SS(PAOR) Regs
3 Regs 30 and 33 SS(C&P) Regs
4 Regs 34 and 35 SS(C&P) Regs
5 Reg 2 SS(PAOR) Regs
6 Reg 3 SS(PAOR) Regs
7 Reg 4 SS(PAOR) Regs
8 Reg 37 SS(C&P) Regs
9 Reg 37A SS(C&P) Regs

5 Recovery of overpayments
(pp235-239)
1 s71 SSAA 1992
2 ss71(3) and 155(1) SSAA 1992
3 s22(5) SSAA 1992
4 s71(5) SSAA 1992
5 R(SB) 34/83
6 R(SB) 9/85
7 R(SB) 18/85
8 CSB/790/1988
9 CSB/790/1988
10 CSB/249/1989
11 R(SB) 54/83
12 R(SB) 21/82
13 R(G) 2/72
14 R(U) 6/70
15 R(SB) 21/82

16 s71(1) SSAA 1992
17 R(SB) 40/84
18 R(SB) 15/87
19 R(SB) 15/87
20 Reg 41 SS(PAOR) Regs
21 *Secretary of State for Social Security v
    Tunnicliffe, The Times,* 8 January
    1991 (CA)
22 R(SB) 44/83
23 s71(9) SSAA 1992; regs 16 and 17
    SS(PAOR) Regs
24 s71(10) SSAA 1992
25 R(U) 7/75
26 R(S) 2/80

Chapter 16:   Appeals

1 Social security appeal tribunals
(pp241-245)
1 s51(1) and Sch 2 paras 2 and 5 SSAA
    1992
2 s40 SSAA 1992
3 s41(5) SSAA 1992
4 s40(2) SSAA 1992
5 Sch 2 para 4 SSAA 1992
6 Reg 25(1) SS(Adj) Regs
7 Regs 24(2) and 25(1) SS(Adj) Regs
8 s56 SSAA 1992
9 s22 SSAA 1992
10 s98(7) SSAA 1992
11 Reg 3(3) and Sch 2 para 4 SS(Adj) Regs
12 R(M) 1/87
13 Reg 3(5) and (6) SS(Adj) Regs
14 s22(1), (2) and (5) SSAA 1992
15 Reg 3(7) SS(Adj) Regs as amended
16 s29 SSAA 1992
17 s21(2) SSAA 1992
18 Reg 4(2) SS(Adj) Regs
19 Reg 4(4) SS(Adj) Regs
20 Reg 24(3) SS(Adj) Regs
21 Reg 25(1) SS(Adj) Regs
22 Reg 25(2) SS(Adj) Regs
23 Reg 26(1)(a) SS(Adj) Regs
24 Reg 25(3) SS(Adj) Regs
25 Reg 10 SS(Adj) Regs
26 Reg 11 SS(Adj) Regs; R(S) 3/89; R(U)
    3/89
27 Reg 3(3) and Sch 2 para 8 SS(Adj) Regs
28 R(S) 3/89; R(U) 3/89

2 Medical appeal tribunals
(pp245-247)
1 Reg 31(2) SS(Adj) Regs
2 s46(2) SSAA 1992; regs 46 and 60
    SS(Adj) Regs
3 s98(5) SSAA 1992

4 Reg 3(3) and Sch 2 para 2 SS(Adj) Regs
5 Reg 37(1) SS(C&P) Regs
6 Reg 3(7) SS(Adj) Regs as amended
7 s46(3) SSAA 1992; regs 46(2) and 60(2) SS(Adj) Regs
8 Reg 31(3) SS(Adj) Regs
9 Reg 32 SS(Adj) Regs
10 Reg 31(4) SS(Adj) Regs
11 Reg 31(5) SS(Adj) Regs

3   Disability appeal tribunals
(pp247-249)

1 s42(3) and (4) SSAA 1992
2 Reg 3 SS(US&IB) Regs as amended; reg 9 SS(SDA) Regs as amended
3 Reg 26G SS(Adj) Regs
4 Reg 26E(2) SS(Adj) Regs
5 Reg 26C SS(Adj) Regs
6 s55(1) SSAA 1992; reg 26F SS(Adj) Regs
7 s33 SSAA 1992
8 s55(2) SSAA 1992
9 Regs 26E(5) and (6) SS(Adj) Regs

4   Social security commissioners
(pp249-254)

1 ss23(1), 34(1) and 48(1) SSAA 1992
2 R(A) 1/72
3 R(A) 1/72
4 *Baron v Secretary of State for Social Services* (CA), reported as an appendix to R(M) 6/86
5 R(M) 1/83
6 ss23(9), 34(4) and 48(3) SSAA 1992
7 Reg 26(1) SS(Adj) Regs; reg 3(1) SSCP Regs
8 Regs 3(3), 26 and Sch 2 para 5 SS(Adj) Regs
9 Reg 3(1) and (3) SSCP Regs
10 Regs 3(3), 32 and Sch 2 para 6 SS(Adj) Regs; reg 3(1) and (3) SSCP Regs
11 Reg 3(2) and (5) SSCP Regs
12 Reg 7(1) SSCP Regs
13 Reg 5(2) SSCP Regs
14 ss23(3) and (4), 34(2) and (3) and 48(1)(d) and (2) SSAA 1992

15 s23(2) SSAA 1992
16 s29 SSAA 1992; R(P) 1/82
17 s4 FA 1982
18 Reg 27(3) and (4) SSCP Regs
19 Reg 15 SSCP Regs
20 s57(1) SSAA 1992
21 Reg 17(4) SSCP Regs
22 Reg 22(2) SSCP Regs
23 s23(7)(b) SSAA 1992
24 s23(7)(a) SSAA 1992
25 *Innes v Chief Adjudication Officer*, (unreported) (CA), 19 November 1986
26 Regs 24 and 25 SSCP Regs
27 ss24 and 34(5) SSAA 1992
28 Regs 27(2) and 31(1) SSCP Regs
29 *White v Chief Adjudication Officer* [1986] 2 All ER 905 (CA), also reported as an appendix to R(S) 8/85
30 s24(2)(b) SSAA 1992
31 RSC 0.59 r.21(3)
32 RSC 0.3 r.5 and 0.59 r.14(2)
33 RSC 0.59 r.14(2), (2A) and (2B)
34 RSC 0.59 r.21(2)
35 RSC 0.59 r.4(3)
36 *Bland v Chief Supplementary Benefit Officer* [1983] 1 WLR 262 (CA), also reported as R(SB) 12/83

5   How to prepare an appeal
(pp254-260)

1 R(I) 2/51; R(I) 33/85
2 s53 SSAA 1992
3 R(I) 12/75
4 R(SB) 22/86
5 *Nancollas v Insurance Officer* [1985] 1 All ER 833 (CA), also reported as an appendix to R(I) 7/85
6 R(I) 12/75
7 *Chief Supplementary Benefit Officer v Leary* reported as an appendix to R(SB) 6/85; see generally CS/140/1991
8 R(G) 3/62; R(U) 4/88
9 R(U) 4/88
10 *Pepper v Hart* [1992] 3 WLR 1032
11 ss2(4)(a) and 15(1) LAA 1988

Index

disqualification from benefit (*cont.*)
- leaving job/training voluntarily 33-35
- misconduct 30-33
- trade disputes 37-38
widows' benefits 79, 79-81, 81-82, 84, 88
divorced women
child's special allowance 158
retirement pension 94-95
widows benefits 78
doctor
see: adjudicating medical practitioner, medical certificate, medical examination

E
early retirement
credited contributions 183
treatment of occupational pension 29-30, 168-169
voluntary unemployment 34
earnings
calculation of earnings 211-212
rules
- adult dependant's increase 161, 163, 166-168
- child dependant's increase 164, 168
- invalid care allowance 127
- invalidity benefit 61
- retirement pension 90
- unemployment benefit 23-25
widows' benefits 82
payments from previous job 27-30
reduced earnings allowance 143-148
statutory maternity pay 71, 74
statutory sick pay 54-55
therapeutic earnings 43-45
see also: occupational pension, occupational sick pay
earnings factors 173, 190
earnings limits for contributions 172, 176
earnings related retirement benefit
see: graduated retirement benefit, SERPS
earnings replacement benefits 4-5, 208
EC
see: European Community
education
credited contributions 182
definition for child benefit 150-151
exclusion from claiming invalid care allowance 127
see also: student
employee
contributions 173, 176-177
definition of employed earner 171-172
industrial injuries benefits 139
statutory maternity pay 72-73

statutory sick pay 50-52
employer
liability for contributions 176-177
statutory maternity pay 72-73
two employers 71
employment
continuous employment for statutory maternity pay 74-75
gainful employment for invalid care allowance 127
leaving employment voluntarily 33-35
misconduct 30-33
refusal of offer of employment 36-37
suspension from work 25
working in period of incapacity 44-45
see also: employee, earnings, industrial injuries benefits, period of interruption of employment, work
employment training
see: training course
epilepsy
disability living allowance/attendance allowance 112
error of law
anti-test-case rules 225-226
ground for review or appeal 230-231, 231-232, 246, 249-250
European Community
benefit arrangements 199-201
examination, medical
see: medical examination
exceptionally severe disablement allowance 141
ex gratia payments
late claims 224
extension benefit for child benefit 151

F
failure to attend medical examination 59
failure to attend Restart interview 16-17
failure to disclose a material fact 215, 235-236, 237-238
failure to take up employment/training 35-37
false statement
see: misrepresentation
family credit 155
family fund test 165-166
fares to tribunal 241
fares to work and interviews 266
Finland 201
fitness for work 43-49
forces
see: armed forces
forfeiture rule 81-82, 251
foster child 152, 157
France 199-201

reviews (*cont.*)
  disablement benefit 142-143
  disability living allowance 123-124
  medical board 232-233
  Secretary of State 232

S

school leavers
  child benefit extension period 151
  credited contributions 182
Secretary of State's decision 227
  child benefit 153
  claims 219-220, 221
  contributions 173
  review 232
  statutory sick pay 56-57
self-certification 46, 54, 58
  see also: medical certificates
self-employed
  contributions 174, 177-178, 179-180
  definition 171-172
  industrial injuries exclusion 139
SERPS 188-191
  calculation 189-191
  contracting out 189
  deferral of retirement pension 90-91
  invalidity benefit 61, 188
  overlapping benefits 209, 210
  personal pensions 189
setting aside tribunal decision 245
severe disablement allowance 64-69
  abroad 197
  age addition and married women 65
  amount 64-65
  claims and backdating 68, 221-222
  choosing between retirement pension and
    severe disablement allowance 92-93
  conditions of entitlement 64, 66-68
  day of incapacity 43, 203
  disability conditions 66-68
  disability working allowance 65
  disqualification 69
  increases for dependants
  – adult 160, 161-163
  – child 160, 163-164
  in custody 207-208
  in hospital 205-206
  non-contributory invalidity pension 65,
    67-68
  overlapping benefits 208-209
  people over pensionable age 66
  period of incapacity 43, 202-204
  prisoners 207-208
  residence/presence test 193
  students 66
  taxation 65
  treatment for income support 65

  *see also: incapacity for work, period of
    interruption of employment, sex
    discrimination*
sex discrimination
  EC law 201
  – increases for dependants 162, 163
  – invalid care allowance 127-128
  – invalidity benefit 61, 62-63
  – reduced earnings allowance 146
  – retirement pension 89-90
  – severe disablement benefit 66
  – sickness benefit 59
  – statutory sick pay 50-51
  – unemployment benefit 38-39
share fishermen 174, 178
sheltered employment 266
sheriffs' court 57, 239
short term benefits 5
short time working 26
sickness
  credited contributions 181
  see also: incapacity for work
sick pay
  *see: occupational sick pay, statutory sick
    pay*
sickness benefit 57-60
  abroad 197
  amount 57
  claims and backdating 58, 221-222
  conditions of entitlement 57
  contribution conditions 185-186
  credited contributions 181
  day of incapacity 203
  disqualification 59-60
  in custody 207-208
  in hospital 205-206
  increases for dependants
  – adult 160-161, 161-163
  – child 163-164
  linking rule 59, 204-205
  overlapping benefits 208-209
  payment 58
  people over pensionable age 58-59
  period of incapacity 43, 52, 202-204
  pregnancy 71, 73, 75, 76
  prisoners 207-208
  statutory sick pay 59
  tax 58
  treatment for income support 58
  *see also: incapacity for work, period of
    interruption of employment*
signing on 11-12
  daily signing 12
  invalid care allowance 126
  widows 83
single parent
  see: one parent benefit, widows' benefits